HEBREW REBORN

Hebrew Reborn

SHALOM SPIEGEL

Meridian Books

The World Publishing Company

CLEVELAND AND NEW YORK

The Jewish Publication Society of America

PHILADELPHIA

SHALOM SPIEGEL is William Prager Professor of Medieval Hebrew Literature at The Jewish Theological Seminary of America. Born in Bucovina (then part of
Austria-Hungary), Professor Spiegel received his Ph.D.
from the University of Vienna in 1922. After teaching
in Palestine he came to New York where he taught first
at the Jewish Institute of Religion. He is the author of
a number of studies in biblical and medieval letters,
including *Ezekiel or Pseudo-Ezekiel, A Prophetic At-
testation of The Decalogue,* and *Noah, Daniel and Job.*
His monograph *Me-Agadoth Ha-Akedah* was awarded
the Louis LaMed Prize for 1950. Dr. Spiegel is a vice-
president of the American Academy for Jewish Research, honorary member of the Israel Hebrew Language Academy, as well as Chairman of the Educational
Advisory Committee of Hadassah.

The author has supplied a few supplementary bibliographical entries
and a number of minor revisions for this paperbound edition.

MERIDIAN BOOKS

Published by The World Publishing Company
2231 West 110th Street, Cleveland 2, Ohio
The Jewish Publication Society of America, Philadelphia
First Meridian printing July 1962

To My Fatherly Friend

DR. ARTHUR BIRAM

Principal of the Beth Sefer Reali at Haifa
Whose Self-consecration
to the New Hebrew Education
in Palestine
Has Been an Inspiration to the Author

CONTENTS

CONTENTS

PREFACE

WHILE engaged in research in the field of medieval Hebrew poetry, I was invited by the Society for the Advancement of Judaism in New York to give a series of lectures on modern Hebrew literature under its auspices. Were it not for the friendly encouragement of some of my hearers, the notes for the Monday evening lectures given from November 26, 1928, to March 11, 1929, would have remained long unpublished. The author himself thinks them hardly more than temporary formulations; not settled conclusions, but rather suggestions for further research. In the present state of the science of Hebrew literature—which as yet lacks an exact bibliography and collected, let alone critical editions of its classics, many of which are still scattered in barely accessible periodicals, and while its most significant writers still await their monographs—any review of its general development must inevitably be pre-scientific.

Moreover, a popular approach made it necessary at times to present the *consensus omnium* even where I myself had gone on to other views. This is the case particularly in the first part of the book, where the true development of Hebrew letters seems to me to run aside from that movement for enlightenment which is accepted as the head and front of modern Hebrew literature. This view, itself a survival of the Haskalah, covers up more significant bonds with the older Hebrew literature of the so-called Middle Ages. A popular presentation seemed unsuitable for such a revision of current evaluations, which must necessarily place the center of gravity in other than the recognized personalities of the era in question.

There remains the pleasant task of making acknowledgment for aid received. I wish here to thank the Society for the Advancement of Judaism, and particularly the leader whom it is so fortunate to have, an original thinker and reinterpreter of Judaism, Professor Mordecai M. Kaplan, who has often encouraged and always stimulated me. I also owe thanks to the library of the Jewish Theological Seminary, whose rich collection is placed at the service of all interested by a friendly staff inspired by the example of their ever helpful and widely learned head, Professor Alexander Marx. I am particularly indebted to my English teacher, Miss Lotta Levensohn, who so kindly worked upon these pages with untiring patience, and without whose coöperation the book could not have been published in English. My thanks are also due to Mrs. Sally Neumark-Brainin for her splendid translation of two chapters, and to one of my students, Mr. David Samuel Gruber, who drew the jacket for the book, skilfully adapting a design from a medieval Jewish prayerbook. A few chapters of the book, though mostly in abbreviated form, appeared in *The New Palestine, S. A. J. Review* and *The Jewish Institute Quarterly,* to the editors of which cordial acknowledgment is hereby made. Lastly, I feel it a distinction and a great service that Mr. James Waterman Wise did not shrink from the effort of a careful examina-

PREFACE

tion of the manuscript, which owes a number of improvements to his excellent sense of style.

Of course, this acknowledgment of assistance implies no transfer of responsibility.

SHALOM SPIEGEL.

New York City
October, 1930

INTRODUCTION

AN attempt is here made to introduce to the Western reader unfamiliar with Hebrew the most significant figures and currents of the new Hebrew literature. It is intended to place beside the Jewish literati writing in foreign languages, from whom a notion of the contemporary Jew is commonly derived, those modern Jewish poets and thinkers who have continued, unmoved, to write in their ancestral tongue. The life-stories of these Jews form a vivid pageant of diverse careers—messiahs, philosophers, cynics, saints, apostates, fanatics, heretics—which merit attention if only for their strange variety. Yet, out of all this diversity of Jewish types, there emerges something higher, common to them all, which I have observed reverently, and which I pray I may somehow succeed in conveying: the magic of an ancient language which, beyond all mere outward form, carries within itself a destiny, a predetermination that befalls every one who does creative work in it. Far-off generations and landscapes still live within this language, a heritage of the past which no one can escape, and which may be felt even in the work of Jews writing in alien tongues.

Most clearly, however, does this magic of the language appear in its own writers, for they carry in their blood its creative mystery, the destinies and forces in dead and still unborn generations of Jews. They therefore can tell more truly what Jews are like than their colleagues who write in foreign languages.

This chapter of Jewish literature, moreover, should arouse interest because it has not remained literature merely, but become life: it is being realized through the heroic attempt of an uprooted people to create bases for a new life in its ancient homeland—through a threefold return to Land, Language, Labor—as is now being done by the Jewish pioneers in Palestine.

PRELUDE

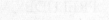

CHAPTER I

THE MIRACLE OF HEBREW REBORN

A quiver full of steel arrows, a cable with strong coils, a trumpet of brass, crashing through the air with two or three sharp notes, such is Hebrew. A language of this kind is not adapted to the expression of scientific results. . . . The letters of its books are not to be many; but they are to be letters of fire. This language is not destined to say much, but what it does is beaten out upon an anvil. It is to pour out floods of anger, and utter cries of rage against the abuses of the world, calling the four winds of heaven to the assault of the citadels of evil. Like the jubilee horn of the sanctuary, it will never be put to profane use. . . .

ERNEST RENAN.

HEBREW reborn—but, was it ever dead? Or, if it was, how can a dead language be born again?

The millions of Jews all over the world who say their daily prayers in Hebrew, not only understanding but fervently feeling their sense, will reject the notion of a rebirth of Hebrew as impudent sacrilege. And the educated Jew, having for hundreds of years without a break used Hebrew for all his cultural needs, reading and writing the language and even at times employing it in purely commercial correspondence, will be able to see no sense in talk about a Hebrew revival. It would make him indignant to be told that Hebrew had ever been dead. Much more so even than the classical philologist who, when it was pointed out to him that Greek and Latin are dead because they are no longer heard in life, replied with feeling: then there are many other dead languages, correct English for example.

Such a jest evades, it does not solve the problem. Taken in all its gravity, the problem reaches down to the very roots of renascent Hebrew. For it questions nothing less than its genuineness, its very existence. It asks: Can a forgotten language actually be revived, made really alive again? Is the rebirth of such a language authentic?

No one doubts that it is possible to learn a language, any language at all, in such a way that its use will convey an impression of life. This can be done not only by single individuals, but by large groups, whole classes of society.

However, expansion in numbers is still no proof that a language is actually alive.

A ready example of this is, of course, the Latin language, despite the annoyance of our philologist. True, it had an important history in antiquity, and was for centuries the medium of expression of all the cultivated classes of western Europe. It had important scientific achievements: not only works like the *Summa theologia* of Aquinas, but tremendous secular creations like the *De revolutionibus orbium cœlestium* of Copernicus, the *Meditationes de prima philosophia* of Descartes, Spinoza's *Ethica more geometrico demonstrata,* and even Newton's work of genius on the mechanics of the universe—to mention only a few titles—were written in Latin. And yet the language was dead; despite all possible scientific precision, it was irresurrectably dead. The living forces that had once impelled it, from Plautus and Ænnius down to Cæsar and Cicero, had spent themselves. No longer was there the ring of verses of such unimpeachable authenticity as those of Propertius, as even the love lyrics of the learned Horace, not to mention the folk-accents, so full of life and vitality, of Ovid: take, for example, his magnificent cry of horror, which could have resounded only in a living language and escaped only from a born poet, that his words unconsciously shape themselves into songs: *Sponte sua carmen numeros veniebat ad aptos.*

In later centuries, despite its wide currency, the Latin language was a subject of scholarly education only. No longer was its unspoken law, its mystery of natural growth, carried in the bloodstream. Its inner life was extinguished, dead.

Is it otherwise the renaissance of Hebrew?

Before attempting a reply to this question, let us make it even more difficult. It seems to me that when a man of our time with some knowledge of history hears of the renaissance of the Hebrew language, he is bound to associate with it the notions he entertains concerning its namesake in general history: the Renaissance and Humanism in Italy of the fifteenth century, which later spread over the whole of western Europe. It must at once be said that Hebrew does not gain by this association of ideas. For, modern historic science seems to have liberated itself from the judgment of the humanists, finding their evaluation of that period warped and exaggerated. The Renaissance was picturesque, alluring—but an illusion. Classical antiquity could not be conjured back to life. It was, as stated, irrevocably dead. The humanistic interest in antiquity was not the driving force of that age, as the classical philologists would like us to believe. This interest was and remained the affair of a small circle of "intelligentsia" (scholars, artists, humanists), but it had no real depths. We may be critical of Oswald Spengler, the poet of history, but he did sum up the yields of the historic science of our day when comparing the Renaissance with the volume and power of a true movement such as the Gothic, which pervaded the remotest recesses of life. From the knightly tournament to village architecture, from the cathedral to the peasant's hut, from language-structure to the bridal ornament of the village maiden, from the oil painting to the song of the minstrel—everything bore the stamp of a unified symbolism. Compared with so true and forceful an outburst of life, it is seen how extrinsic, unsubstantial and unreal was this so-called Renaissance, this conscious reaching-back to the obsolescent forms of antiquity. It was a drawing room affair for world-shunning dreamers; at best, a matter of good taste in the castles of the princes and Mæcenases of those days. It was only because the science of history itself was for long dominated by the humanists that it was not recognized how superficial and immaterial had been the hold of the classical upon that age; how, at most, it had manifested itself in costume and gesture, but had never penetrated down to the roots of existence.

The true power of that age was not galvanized antiquity, but the renaissance, or better, the *naissance* of the Italian folk which had concealed itself behind the external classicizing forms. And even though Petrarch himself was particularly proud of his Latin imitations of the Horatian odes, not only his fame, but his real significance, lie in his work in the language of the vulgus, *volgare,* which he esteemed very lightly, but which to-day is the Italian tongue. The Horatian world lay buried deep, it could never again be roused to life. "The larger part of me will escape Death," wrote Horace. Yes, as a memory in the minds of scholars; never again in the hearts of a living people. No longer did any mother croon to her baby Latin lullabies whose rhythm would later influence the thinking and writing of the grown man. No longer did any peasant drive his plow singing Latin songs of village life and labor, whose folk accents still echo in the courtly, pruned verses of the bucolics and georgics of Virgil. No longer did anyone sing erotic songs of allurement in Latin, roguish and merry as those that delight us even in the consciously creative Horace. No longer did anyone curse so roundly, so powerfully, or so vividly as in the comedies of Plautus. The life of the Latin language was gone, irredeemably gone. One might learn its petrified forms, but no life of its own could be awakened within it.

Now, perhaps, the whole scope and weight of the problem will become clearer: has there really been a rebirth of the Hebrew language? Has Hebrew really awakened to a freely creative life, to a natural, organic growth. At this point it no longer suffices to say that Hebrew lived on in the synagogue, in learned discussion, in correspondence, in books. For medieval Latin also lived on in the same way. And it still lives in the church. Just as with the Latin of the scholars, the whole life of Hebrew grew out of books, its roots were always in the book, in the Holy Book primarily.

That is not so in Palestine to-day.

II

Jabniel, a tranquil nook in Lower Galilee. A flock of geese trail down the hill, two sturdy, sunburnt girls following. They speak enchanting Hebrew. Their father, a farmer devoted to his farming—and a *Maskil,* voices his doubts. "Every morning I face a dilemma: whether to send them to the pasture, or to school. Which is more important, that they do lessons or tend the geese? Who can say?"

The girls lead the geese into the poultry yard. You join them. One of them, evidently assigned to the care of the fledglings, explains how the incubator works. "Our poultry is multiplying," she says, and her eyes flash with pleasure. She turns the eggs twice a day. In order not to interchange them, she marks each egg, before placing it in the incubator, with the word "evening" or "morning." Then she knows when they are due to be turned, and toward which side of the incubator. "And there was evening, and there was morning, one day!" She smiles coquettishly, picks up a booklet which had fallen to the floor and wipes it off on her apron. It is a Hebrew booklet on poultry-raising.

I was reminded of the psychological tests we used to have at the university, when we would give a "stimulus word" to a subject, and he had to respond with the first word that came into his mind through association of ideas. Were this girl to be such a subject she would undoubtedly react to the word 'erebh (evening) with—"incubator." And, if she happened to be of the eye-minded type, she would visualize the top of an egg in an incubator bescrawled with a blunt pencil.

Try to imagine how a *Talmid chakham,* a learned Jew of former generations, would have reacted to such a "stimulus word." He would doubtless have called up words from books, especially from sacred books. And were he, also, of the eye-minded type, he would have visualized an old book such as Bialik somewhere describes, of crude, crumpled parchment, spotted with tallow and wax dripped from candles in lonely midnights, between its pages faded white hairs plucked from beards in meditative speculation, and silk threads from prayer-shawl fringes, now ritually void, and yellowed with age and wear.

What wonder then that the Holy Tongue of the *Talmid chakham* has a totally different ring from the secular

Hebrew, so rustic and dewy fresh, of the goose girl of Jabniel. Hers is not a bookish language, and far less is it a language of sacred books. If there be any traces of books in her speech, it comes from the booklet on poultry-raising which slipped out of the incubator on to the floor.

How important is such a booklet for a language! Here names are given to things, *direct* names, much more difficult than learned palaver or even poetic embellishment, which talk *around* things. This latter cannot be indulged in in a booklet on poultry-raising written for village use: here one must give each thing its correct, living, only name.

Therefore, were I asked to name books which testify to the resurrection of Hebrew, I would refer the inquirer not to belles-lettres, but to a few other booklets similarly concrete in topic, for instance to the recent publications of the agricultural experiment station in Palestine on "Diseases of the Eggplant," "Sterility in Cows," "On Manure," etc. These are the new *Seder Zera'im* in the *Mishnah* of our renewed life.

Moreover, some of these booklets, though written for practical uses, already show certain literary values. Were I asked to name the best book of modern Hebrew prose, I should choose, not a resounding name from among famous contemporaries, but Eliezer Joffe's book on "Vegetable-Growing." And if surprise were expressed at my choice, I should insist: may such works be multiplied in Israel! For its sake I would gladly forego the toy lyrics of our ultra-modernists. The Hebrew language has always been strong in poetry, it is the old domain of the "jubilee horn of the sanctuary." Its conquest of the secular, however, is a new distinction. In the book on vegetable-growing are found the three virtues of all plain prose: precision, brevity, and clearness. These qualities, combined with inimitable rustic simplicity, make its prose classic. Every piece of a farming implement, every part of a plant, every agricultural task, the chemical processes of fermentation—each has a distinct name of its own. A language of this kind is adapted, not only to express "scientific results" with an exactness possible only in languages with a long culture, but—what is far more difficult of achievement—it is fit to be the medium of secular daily life, to convey the spontaneous outcry, to express the crudest and most primitive needs, to afford speech for life in its most contradictory manifestations.

Hebrew in Palestine no longer has the remoteness of a "holy language." It has been forced from the narrow confines of exalted utterance, from the Sabbath limits of choice usage, from the atmosphere of rigid solemnity, from the resounding notes of a "trumpet of brass." No longer is it a cathedral of unearthly height, but a homelike cottage for daily use.

Hebrew in Palestine is no longer a language of abstractions, anæmic, unimpressionable, unresponsive to current needs and experiences. It has recovered its faculties—its sight and its hearing, its senses of touch and smell, its capacity for motion. Again it pulsates, and plays up and down the whole color-scale of life.

In Palestine, the reign of the *Melitzah,* of the stereotyped Biblical manner, is a thing of the past. Formerly, spoken Hebrew used to be a series of quotations. (It still is so in the Galuth.) Anger was expressed in wrathful words from Amos. Distress in the terms of the Psalms. Doubt via Ecclesiastes. The innovators and revolutionaries of those days went to the length of quoting the later Hebrew of the Midrashim, the Talmud, the Prayer-book. The current language was a fixed coinage which might be exchanged, but never melted down and reminted. The Bible verse either tapped the way before them like a blind man's stick, or trailed after them. The thought was born of the form which forced itself into the hand, and not the reverse. Hebrew speech or writing consisted of scattered fragments from the Bible in varying mechanical combinations. Bible verses were simply dismembered and joined together again in new unions. The language was used like inorganic matter; even when knowledge and command of Hebrew were adequate, shells of language were gathered without any feeling that a living mollusc dwelt within.

In Palestine of to-day the mollusc has awakened within the shell, the creative potencies of the language have been renewed. Hebrew is completely freed from its enslavement to the Biblical text. Its metal has been smelted down in the furnace of a revived language-sense, and minted anew. Word origins have been forgotten. Exactly as in other living languages, the paternity of words has ceased to be remembered by those in whose mouths they are current. Conquests and discoveries in which individuals take pride have been absorbed into the language and become the possession of the general public, freely enjoyed by every one. Even the old language forms are known chiefly in their new incarnations. A Palestinian teacher relates that once, as he was explaining to his class some peculiar usages of the Hebrew of the *Mishnah* and its deviation from the Biblical standard, they came upon the phrase *Me'emathai mathchilin* ("When does one begin?"). He asked whether anyone knew the source of the quotation, referring, of course, to the passage in the *Mishnah* which reads, "When does one begin the morning (or the evening) prayer?" A young girl slipped a note to her friend which the teacher indiscreetly captured as usual and read: "I know the source. Isn't it, 'When does one begin to love'" (alluding to the opening sentence in Moshe Smilansky's popular Hebrew novel *Toledoth Ahavah Achath*). The girl was joking, of course, but she had doubtless seen the words for the first time not in the *Mishnah,* but when secretly devouring the captivating love story, hidden from the eyes of her father.

The young Palestinian generation, born and bred in Hebrew, inhale the language from the air, from the street, from their whole environment. The heritage of the entire lingual past is in their speech, yet they are not aware of it. They have not the memory of an epigonus, the oppressive sense of carrying a barren inheritance. Past and present coalesce in their language, one enriching the other. Both elements have fused so thoroughly that they are no longer to be distinguished.

I recall the wonder of some Palestinian children when questioned by a newly arrived young teacher on whose diploma the ink had hardly dried. Like a philological pedant, he asked them how many times the word "already" occurs in the Bible. "Too many to count," replied a pupil, "you can't help using it in almost every sentence." The surprise of the class was intense when they heard

14

that it occurs only in Ecclesiastes. The question itself was alien to them, although (or perhaps because) their understanding of the Bible is far truer than that of the graduate who comes with a headful of wisdom from Marti, Duhm, Ehrlich and the others. For the children of Palestine, no work is more intimate, more vivid or impressive than the Bible. It is for them a contemporary book, while Bialik is one of the elder writers who needs commentaries and tiresome explanations that chill the warmth of immediate impression.

Hebrew in Palestine has to-day the force of an accomplished fact, a fact in the soul and in the blood—the force of nature. The old virtues that Hebrew retained even in books have continued with it in Palestine: unique conciseness, allusiveness, concomitant by-values of meaning possessed only by a language heavy with ancient memories. To all this Palestine has added unexpected resiliency, mercurial adaptiveness, the naturalness and freshness of the instinctive, the pungent simplicity of village talk, of the gossip of women, the chirping of babies. There is in the language an untranslated genuineness of thought and feeling.

Let me prove this with an anecdote. There is often much historic value in anecdotes even when they are fictitious. Novalis was right when he called them historical molecules. Life has a way of symbolizing itself in the form of a simple, unrepeated and yet typical moment, which is to say, in the anecdote.

Though I do not vouch for its authenticity, a story is current in Tel Aviv to the effect that Ahad Ha'am and Bialik once stood together in the street talking Russian, either absent-mindedly or from force of habit. A small boy who happened to be passing reproached them with the slogan of the *Gedud Maginne Hassafah* (Legion of the Defenders of the Language), shouting: "Jew! Speak Hebrew!" They were amused, of course, and decided to find out whether a little Yiddish or Russian had not stuck to the boy in his parents' home, whether Hebrew was really his primary tongue. Bialik began to talk to him, and Ahad Ha'am pinched his ear. The youngster immediately yelled out the Hebrew equivalent of "Leggo!" And, not knowing who his interlocutors were, he called back as he ran away, *"Chamor Zaken!"* ("You Old Donkey!"). We may assume that the old philosopher was less hurt at the boy's insult than overjoyed at the genuineness of his Hebrew reflex.

Hebrew in Palestine possesses even the virtues of illiteracy. We, the people of the subtle *Talmide chakhamim,* have already in Palestine the ignoramus type, the *'Am Ha-Aretz.* The People of the Book have illiterates who speak Hebrew fluently without being able to read or write, having picked it up in the market place. True, there are current mistakes in the spoken Hebrew that grate upon the ears of our grammarians. And the present writer must admit that Hebrew in Palestine seems to him, also, to have liberated itself from books too soon. The modern career of Hebrew is still too short to be able to dispense with its great literary inheritance. Yet it would be foolish to ignore the fact that there is a revolt, both deliberate and intuitive—as in every other prospering language —against the tyranny of books and grammar. One day we shall be compelled, we purists and pedants, to write

the current errors and wrong usages into our dictionaries
and grammars and to teach our pupils that a wrong usage
of a certain word has become current in the spoken
Hebrew of Palestine, and that makes it right. Life breaks
grammar.

Spoken Hebrew in Palestine has new idioms of its own.
"Idiom" (cf. the French *idiotisme*) misleadingly suggests
idiocy, but even the most correct and elegant speech draws
its sap from idiom. For, it is precisely these idiosyncrasies
of speech, its peculiarities and anomalies, that lend to
each language its particular aroma and untranslatable individuality or character. Grammar when not the mere
neutral registration of what speech forms are, but the
regulative ideal of what, according to the laws of logic
and analogy, they ought to be,—grammar in this sense is
the natural enemy of idiom. There is eternal strife
between the two. Grammarians who desire to refine a
language to grammatical purity and logical regularity,
emasculate and cripple it with the monotony of correctness.

More. Hebrew possesses, in addition to idiom—and in
gratitude for this we should really recite the *She-heche-
yanu* blessing—a *slang* of its own, with all the pictorial
vulgarity of slang and all its drastic overemphasis. So far
as slang is translatable at all, I shall try to cite some
examples.

When I came to Dagania for the first time—I was still
new to Palestine then—my first encounter with the oldest
child in the colony, Gideon, the son of Joseph Baratz,
proved to me that I still had to study Hebrew. "You are
not one of us," the rascal welcomed me with malicious

chutzpah, before I had had time to say a single word, and so perhaps reveal through my Hebrew accent that I was a newcomer. "You have a herring!" he went on. Seeing that I was puzzled, he pointed to my collar. When I still failed to understand, he pulled at my four-in-hand tie. "None of our people wears such a . . . herring!" And I was irrevocably done for in his eyes.

As for myself, I prefer this slang word to any of the recent artificial innovations. It has the color of its *milieu,* the truthfulness of a confession. That one word betrays the whole outlook of pioneering Palestine, the elemental simplicity of its life, its contempt for the superfluous, its disgust with the dandies of the Levantine towns.

How much artlessness and pugnacity are there in the slang phrase *Hirbatzti bo!* ("He got his!"). One can almost see the flashing eyes and the tightened muscles. Or, *Akhalta cherbon!* ("You have eaten humble pie!") to tease some one who has been taken in . (It is a pity, though, that at times Arabic influence is seen in the Hebrew slang.)

And then, how coarsely it is possible to curse in Hebrew, how effectively obscene jests can be told! What salvos of laughter greet the jokes of the Palestinian Hebrew cabarets, *"Hakumkum"* ("The Tea Pot") and *"Hamat'ate"* ("The Broom"). There is much force and pithiness in the Hebrew slang drawn from sex life. Slang grows mostly out of sex. These Hebrew terms are uncouth, and yet they breathe a healthy sensuality. They have life, and in them inheres the delicious grossness of the Bible. They bear authentic testimony to the awakened life in the language.

III

If anything be capable of proving the inward genuineness of the Jewish national renaissance, it is the rebirth of the Hebrew language of our day. This event alone has borne witness to the truth of life, to the truth of nature in our national revival. Before the Hebrew language became a folk tongue, spoken with the spontaneous simplicity of a natural phenomenon, one might not have been able wholly to still one's doubts. Perhaps, who knows, one might have said to himself: All this awakening to a national consciousness after decades of self-estrangement and assimilation—is only a matter of wishing, of longing for bygones, of forced effort. Perhaps this attempt is as artificial as some party programs and political movements; perhaps it is something inorganic at bottom which, though it might be established by technical means, can never be infused with the breath of life. Anything can be organized, but no one can make life. In the mechanical world we are clever, we put things together and take them apart, we fill the vacuum of the universe with chatter and bustle. In the biologic world, we are illiterates, puzzled infants yearning to obey and to worship, praying for a miracle.

The revival of Hebrew and its transformation into a colloquial tongue with all the defects and virtues of a living language; the revival of Hebrew literature and its development within the last decades to a high intellectual and emotional level, and such progress in vocabulary as would have filled any civilized people with pride—these things have proven beyond a doubt the physiological genu-

19

ineness of our rejuvenation as a people. These are not phenomena to be achieved by wishing or straining. There is in this process something of the mystery of birth, of the wonder of natural growth, a gift of God. Such phenomena cannot be hastened or retarded, they are not to be made by hands. One must wait humbly for the miracle.

And, indeed, the rebirth of the Hebrew language and literature is a miracle. Always when the genesis of this renaissance is considered, one must become aware of the futility of conscious, willed effort, which thinks to command the course of events, but is itself driven by far stronger and more archaic urges than our conscious volitions.

The fathers of the Berlin *Haskalah* (enlightenment movement) revived the Hebrew language and created the modern Hebrew literature. If they were to start up from their graves and see what has happened to the work of their hands, they would be overcome by the utter uselessness of man's conscious striving, especially when he struggles against his own blood. Inevitably, history has played them a memorable prank.

They intended something else, something fundamentally different. They wanted to bring their people closer to the nations of Europe by means of Hebrew; to introduce them to the world of foreign values, through Hebrew; to spread, through Hebrew, the gospel of the rationalism that discarded nationality, and consequently denied racial individuality to the Jewish people. They wanted, through Hebrew, to make their people hunger for other languages; and finally to pave the way, through Hebrew, for assimilation and absorption.

Hebrew for them was not an end in itself, but a means to an end, an implement that, when it had served the purpose, could be thrown away. At least, this was their mental attitude, though the heart clung to the old language despite the objection of the head. However, the teaching of the head was that Hebrew was only a temporary expedient. The champions of the Berlin Haskalah had no other medium through which to reach their people. Yiddish they despised. The Gentile languages were not understood by the people. Therefore they used Hebrew to decoy the Jews into the foreign world and the foreign languages.

But language has a logic of its own, and a destiny of its own. Once awakened to life, Hebrew would not return to the prison of the tomb, would not be enslaved to aims and purposes set up for it by alienated sons. Hebrew escaped from their hands. This is the marvel of the organic creature: that, on the day it enters the world, it begins to live its own life, beyond the control of its father. It is a living organism, autonomous and self-impelling.

The power of a language can scarcely be gauged. Language is more than language. Within langauge lie concealed magic forces of nature and history, lees of instinct and culture, a heritage of emotions, habits of thought, traditions of taste, inheritances of will,—the Imperative of the Past. It is impossible to measure the power and influence of all this upon the soul, upon its consciousness and upon its subterranean strata.

Just so Hebrew could not be handled with the laws of logic. It had, like all language, its own laws of inner growth, the irrationality of fate. Once called into being, it developed according to its own spirit. It broadened and grew until it demanded all the conditions required for a thoroughgoing revival and sovereignty over life. To use a term of Professor Mordecai M. Kaplan's, it wanted to function as a complete civilization. In the Haskalah generation, Hebrew called upon the young forces to revolt against the yoke of tradition, which hindered young blood from creative utterance. Yet, after the negation and the license of the last champions of the Haskalah, that same Hebrew language brought the prodigal sons back to their people, and awakened national aspirations within them.

Still more. Hebrew revived old, forgotten yearnings for the motherland, and impelled the first pioneers to go up to Palestine to live the Hebrew life. They understood that unless there were a Hebrew Palestine, unless the language took root naturally in a homeland, unless in one corner of the world, at least, Hebrew were the primary and only language of thought and emotion, the language in the Galuth would remain a toy, a pastime, a subject for unworldly pedants to busy themselves with. After its revival in Palestine as a spoken language, Hebrew realized that it had no future unless it were implanted in the earth and stood firmly in the soil; and it tempted its zealots not only to Hebrew thought and speech, but to Hebrew labor. It has created not only the Hebrew University on Mount Scopus, but also the numerous Hebrew villages in Palestine and the new type of Hebrew farmers and laborers, the healthy basis whereon Hebrew scholarship and letters can rest.

It is as though the genius of the language knew that

without contact with the roots of things, without return to the soil, without a regeneration of our existence through the life of labor, all that we may call Hebrew culture will be lifeless and devoid of truth; it will be an aping, a forgery, a theft of foreign values, a parasite. The Hebrew word, the Hebrew thought, the Hebrew culture must tend to ground themselves in the soil, for the soil alone gives content and import to all national values. And so Hebrew became the vehicle of the whole Jewish rebirth, for, with the sureness of instinct, it at once discovered that there is no redemption for the Jewish spirit unless it be rooted once again in the ancient mother earth whose clods are turned up by a Jewish plow.

How significant is the hidden and rarely apprehended inner affinity of all expressions of the life of a people. What we have here laid down as the postulate of the Hebrew language in the cultural domain—that it must become rooted in the soil and in labor—is at the same time the direction toward which our economy and our politics point. All forms of the existence of a people, however independent and even antagonistic they may seem, have something within them that leads them all, some invisible spell that drives them all in the same orbit: they belong as much within a single system as the various types of organic life in a region. Which is another token of the biologic truth of our renaissance.

IV

This book tries to suggest that the prank of fate upon the Maskilim is not yet played out, that Hebrew reborn steers its course, once more, against the knowledge and perhaps intention of its carriers, away from their goal, *homewards*. It seems inevitably to tend to resurrect the innate religious forces locked within the language during its hibernation, as it were, through many centuries.

Hebrew was revived by the fathers of the enlightenment for the sake of a holy war against religion. And behold, this very language, in accordance with a hidden commandment of its nature, leads slowly but surely toward a revival of Jewish religious values. For, within the forms of this language there lies religious content; its spirit and capacity for expression, its figures of speech and modes of thinking, are permeated with the religious contents of generations, ever since the Hebrew language became the vestment of the thought of our people. In the long history of this persistent nation there was no secular Hebrew; olden religious charms are invoked even in its most profane utterances, and break forth just where one thought to have avoided them. This unescapable enthrallment to the pious forces of the Jewish past, to the religious legacy of an ancient civilization, can be readily discerned in the lives and thought of even the most incorrigible heretics in modern Hebrew letters.

Unless all the signs lie, this seems to be the path of Hebrew reborn: From alienation and treason to the heritage of the fathers, through the unhappy inability to escape it, to a joyous affirmation and renewed covenant with the creative forces that live in bygone and future generations of Jews.

In the following chapters, the attempt will be made to trace that path.

BOOK I

IN THE ERA OF ENLIGHTENMENT

CHAPTER II

A MESSIAH

There is in every Jew the stuff of a Messiah; of a mater dolorosa in every Jewess.

MOSES HESS.

FROM the unlovely Corso Cavour in Rome a steep stair-case leads up to a secluded square where the forsaken church of San Pietro in Vincoli is situated. Though it is an early Christian basilica, the Doric columns in its nave suggest that it may be a Roman temple appropriated early in the fifth Christian century, when the pagan divinity of the southland had to make way for the less pictorial Asiatic cult.

Art-lovers come on pilgrimages to this church in whose dusky interior is enshrined Michelangelo's magnificent statue of Moses. This "Moses," like the "Slaves" in the Louvre, is merely a fragment of the gigantic sepulcher planned by the powerful Pope Julius II. Though it is wedged between two female figures usually taken for Rachel and Leah, and imprisoned within a frame which dwarfs and constricts the form of the Jewish Prophet—or, rather, of the giant Italian condottiere—one can under-stand how not only the art-loving compatriots of Michel-angelo, but even the image-less and image-hating Jews swarmed out of their Ghetto like cranes to see it (so Vasari relates) and wore away the great toe of its out-stretched foot with devout kisses.

The rudiments of the sepulcher planned by Julius II are, of course, included in the obligatory rounds one makes to famed works of art in Rome. In the same church, fol-lowing the advice of Baedeker and Burckhardt's guide

book, one observes the badly faded paintings of the enig-
matical Massaccio, and tells himself that many of these
things, when judged from photographs and descriptions,
promise much more: a feeling that every museum visitor
knows. I had viewed all these things and was about to
leave the church when I happened to overhear the assiduous Italian mendicant monk lauding the art of a tomb that
I had found merely conventional, but my attention was
caught by his remark that it harbored the remains of
Nicholas Cusanus. In the dimness of that *composite*
sanctuary, devoted first to the antique Roman divinity and
then to the Christian god, and which was now become a
shrine for art lovers through the genius of Michelangelo,
there rests the remarkable, richly contradictory *composite*
personality which, Janus-headed, faced both the Middle
Ages and modern times. A profound man, whose mind
was still shadowed, like this church wherein he is buried,
by the mystic half-light of scholasticism, though he burned
with the desire for light and knowledge. Rigidly pious
and orthodox—for he was a high dignitary of the church
—and yet drawn to pantheism; modern in his criticism
of the modes of cognition and in his anticipation of Copernicus' revolutionary ideas, but rooted deep in the Middle
Ages by his speculations concerning the attributes of the
angels, his prophecies of the end of the world, and his
call to crusades against the infidels. Giordano Bruno
thought it was the cardinal's robe which impeded Cusanus'
free stride; in truth, however, it was not outward considerations, but an inner bond with the things of old which
restrained the forerunner of the free spirits of modern
times—of Bacon and Descartes. All three strive for the

laurels of the father of modern philosophy. English-written histories of philosophy, of course, make the new day dawn with the Englishman Bacon, the French with Descartes, and the German with Nicholas of Cusa.

I have called up the shade of this remarkable man because he always somehow reminds me of a similar figure in which the pious Middle Ages and the restlessness of modernity stuggle with one another. I am thinking of the poet who is usually characterized as the father of modern Hebrew literature, the pseudo-Messiah Moshe Chaim Luzatto. Pseudo-Messiah and father of modern Hebrew literature—these are contradictions which need not exclude each other; rather, as an Nicholas Cusanus' profound teaching of *coincidentia oppositorum,* they hint at the deeper unity in the man.

The likeness between Cusanus and Luzatto does not lie only in both appearing in periods of transition, there are some resemblances in their philosophic teachings as well, which deserve to be studied. Here the two men are used to prove that divisions into epochs are mere schematic aids to memory, scientific paper-frontiers overflowed by the stream of history. Divisions of time are abstractions for the use of the schools; in life, the old and the new are indissolubly fused.

For, like all other artificial divisions, this designation of Luzzato as the father of modern Hebrew literature is purely arbitrary. His imitation of European—and more particularly—of Italian masters in his dramas (e.g. the *Pastor Fido* of Battista Guarini) was no new thing in the Hebrew literature of Italy. Already, at the end of the thirteenth century, that delightful rogue and most frivolous Jew of the Middle Ages, Immanuel ha-Romi (c. 1270-c. 1330) whom many Jews, obedient to the prohibitions of the *Shulchan 'Arukh,* still avoid because of his droll perversions of biblical passages into the most obscene ambiguities—that same Immanuel ha-Romi betrayed an excellent knowledge of contemporary non-Jewish literature and often took Christian poetry as the theme for imitations that surpassed the originals, or for purposes merely of literary persiflage. It was in Italy, too, that, a century later, Mose di Rieti (1388 c. 1460), following in the traces of Dante, wrote a Jewish "Divina Commedia" —his *Mikdash Me'at* (A Little Sanctuary)—in terzetti of which a Christian scholar said, "They are as pure, as melodic, as forceful and profound—and therefore often as difficult to understand—as those of Dante himself." By 1574 there had appeared the *Meor 'Enayim* (The Light of the Eyes) of Azariah de Rossi of Mantua (1514-1578), which showed evidence of the author's wide reading in classic and patristic literature. Then there was Leo da Modena (1571-1648) who may be compared with de Rossi in scope and erudition, for he translated from Ariosto in his youth, had an excellent knowledge of the classics, and—among other works—wrote pastoral poems in the Italian manner. Even dramas had been written in Hebrew before Luzatto's time; for example, by Mose ben Mordecai Zacuto (died in 1697) who, in his youth, wrote an early Hebrew drama, *Yesod 'Olam* (An Everlasting Foundation) portraying the martyrdom of Abraham the iconoclast, in order to comfort his fellow Jews who were being tortured by the Inquisition. Another work of his, a long poem, *Tofteh 'Arukh* (Tophet Preordained) is also dramatic in form, as may be seen from the recent edition by D. A. Friedman.

It is thus clear that Italian Jewry was familiar with the spiritual currents in its environment long before the time of Luzatto. That Luzatto has been characterized as a path-breaker is due only to the proximity of his age to that of Mendelssohn, and to the misinterpretation of his drama *Layesharim Tehillah* (Praise to the Righteous) which the later "enlighteners" thought presented a problem of "enlightenment," the struggle between "Reason" and the "Mob"; for they misunderstood his more philosophic, let alone pious and Kabbalistic, spirit.

Before describing the beginnings of the new Hebrew literature in Germany, it will therefore be well to examine somewhat closely the almost contemporary personality of Luzatto in Italy, since his life and struggle are instructive as the transition to and background for what comes later.

In the history of Hebrew literature, Luzatto is usually praised as the author of three dramas. His other work, simply because it is not in accord with the secular tendencies of the new Hebrew literature, receives only passing mention; and that but rarely. In addition to the drama above referred to, neo-Hebrew circles know his *Migdal 'Oz* (Tower of Strength), also a drama, to which may now be added a youthful little work published by Dr. S. Ginsburg of New York in 1927, the *Ma'ase Shimshon* (The Story of Samson).

I should like to show, through a brief sketch of the poet's career, how incidental and unimportant these dramatic works seemed to Luzatto himself, and how they in part originated merely as writings for particular occasions. They were not necessary expression for their author, they reveal no fundamental currents of his soul. Had Luzatto known that the three dramas so casually written for the entertainment of his friends would one day be put forward as the sum total of his life's work, he would have felt it a profound insult.

Luzatto was born in 1707 in the city of Padua of wealthy parents belonging to one of the most illustrious of Italian-Jewish families. His father, a large silk merchant, spared no expense to give him a thorough education. Thus in early youth Luzatto secured a wide knowledge of Hebrew and also of Latin, which in Italy was still the medium of educated men. He appears also to have known Greek and French. When only in his sixteenth year, he wrote a lovely elegy upon the death of the poet, physician and preacher Isaac Vita Cantarini. In his seventeenth year he composed a Hebrew rhetoric, *Leshon Limmudim* (The Tongue of the Learned), dedicated to his teacher Isaiah Bassan, wherein he revealed an astounding knowledge of the theories of art, and tried independently to grasp the peculiarities of Hebrew composition, occasionally quoting poetic efforts of his own in order to explain some of the theories he is dealing with. Finding a lack of suitable examples among his Hebrew predecessors when writing his chapter on the drama, he resolved to write a drama himself. His *Ma'ase Shimshon* was the result. It is the immature work of a seventeen-year-old, and yet it is irreproachable in its handling of the Hebrew language; interesting, too, for the misogynistic tendencies so early revealed in its interpretation of the Samson legend. Who knows but that his Delilah already carried a supplementary Kabbalistic meaning to betoken those dark, seductive forces with which our young Samson himself was struggling? For he had already included the secret doctrine in his rhetoric, when treating of poetry. Early inducted into the Jewish occult lore by his teacher Isaiah Bassan, the fiery, highly gifted youngster was enthralled by Kabbalistic fantasies. So, too, his second drama, *Migdal 'Oz* which, also, was written for an occasion—the wedding of his teacher's son—may not have been merely an imitation of Guarini's *Pastor Fido,* but a work subconsciously permeated by Kabbalistic thought. Its content easily admits of allegoric interpretation: a king locks up his only daughter in a high tower, promising to give her as wife to the man who will find the secret path leading to it. Of course a venturesome knight without reproach appears, and of course there is a villain who tries to prevent him from reaching the princess. The drama having been written in honor of marriage festivities winds up with a happy wedding and the bliss of the virtuous. This simple love legend is, however, permeated with Kabbalistic symbolism: the high tower is the true teaching of God, to which there is but one secret path, the Kabbala, found, our poet thinks, by himself. Like the villain in the story, his opponents remain standing outside the gates, and are not admitted into the true mysteries.

Biographies of Luzatto, written by "enlightened" spirits, often describe, with regret and displeasure, how Kabbalistic extravagance benighted the clear mind of the poet until, in the end, he believed himself to be receiving revelations from a mentor-angel, like Mose Zacuto, whose dramatic and Kabbalistic tendencies remind us of Luzatto in other ways as well; or like Isaac Lurya, or even so sober a mind as Joseph Karo. Under the spell of a higher inspiration, as he thought, Luzatto wrote a second *Zohar,* and came to look upon himself as the predestined messiah, appointed to redeem Israel.

This much must not be disputed. M. S. Ghirondi, who admired Luzatto to excess, tried to clear him from the slanders of his fanatical opponents, but in attempting to deny the alleged sin of messiahship, the very thing that he adduced as proof showed up the more clearly how genuinely and enthusiastically Luzatto believed in the possibility of a messianic redemption. And since Joseph Almanzi's affectionate yet objective biography, it is no longer possible to doubt that Luzatto imagined himself a messiah. He lets the Prophet Elijah say clearly, "When the *Shekhinah* leaves the Galuth, you will lead it back."

Yet all earlier descriptions of this phase of Luzatto's life lack a sympathetic understanding of both the forces of his soul and the contemporary conditions which let so promising a talent run to seed in messianism.

The age of assimilatory enlightenment did not believe in the possibility, or the genuineness, of a return to Zion: all attempts at messianism were branded as quackery and phantasy. We who to-day are engaged in a similar enterprise—the upbuilding of Zion—have a different conception of messianism. Perhaps it, too, like Zionism in our day, though built up on enthusiasm, was nevertheless a movement based on the real forces of the Galuth-life.

Why should we not believe that before our time also

there were earnest strivings to establish the Jews as a nation in their own land? Perhaps, too, the messianic movements were not merely unfortunate examples of frenzy and delusion, as the *Juedische Wissenschaft,* still a child of the assimilatory and Zion-hating enlightenment, considered them, but rather the manifestations of the same forces that have produced the national renaissance of our time.

Two examples may suffice for illustration. The first, and more striking example is the career of David Reubeni, at the height of the Renaissance period. In his efforts to win the secular and religious powers of the Western world for the creation of a Jewish Palestine, even a Graetz was inclined to see simply another wild pursuit of a chimera. No additional material about the career of Reubeni has become available since Graetz's masterwork, but we would to-day evaluate his career quite differently. For the same historic sources hold other messages for other generations. Every age reads them differently. We would to-day interpret the activity of Reubeni not as a fantastic gesture of despair, but as an honest and serious diplomatic undertaking; an attempt to transform the life and destiny of the Jews through real forces that existed within the people. Perhaps Reubeni and his aids aimed not merely at martyrdom, but at victory.

Quite the same thing is true of the greatest and most romantic of the Jewish messianic movements known to us, which ended most tragically, because so ludicrously. I refer to the profound impression created by Sabbetai Zebi, which, even in so sober and skeptical a mind as that of Spinoza, gave rise to the thought that, given such vigorous enthusiasm among the Jewish people and the mutability of contemporary conditions, it would not be altogether impossible that the Jews should win back their land.

Why, then, should not Moshe Chaim Luzatto, who must have heard much about the deeds of Reubeni and Molcho in Italy, and who could even have felt something of the ebbing tides of Sabbetaism (Sabbetai died in 1676, or barely a generation before Luzatto was born)—why, then, should not Luzatto have believed seriously that the tragic fate of the Jewish people could be turned aside through inner unity and the will to redemption: that through inner consecration the banished Glory of God could be redeemed?

As a matter of fact, such was the actual content of his Kabbalistic philosophy: that an awakening on Earth would give rise to an awakening in Heaven, and that Israel would be redeemed to peace, "speedily and in that generation." From examples furnished by the Jewish history of olden times, Luzatto learned that he who is called to redeem the people must make himself ready for the task and be prepared for action.

However that may be, unless Luzatto is regarded as a man of upright faith and integrity, it is not possible to understand his heroic defiance when persecuted by the rabbis. The anathema was at first proclaimed against him without mention of his name, when the zealot Mose Chages of Altona persuaded a number of German rabbis to pronounce the ban against Luzatto's activities in an indirect way so that it was to apply to all who wrote in the language of the Zohar in the name of angels and saints. Later, six rabbis of Venice openly proclaimed the ban against him, condemning his writings to be burnt (December, 1734), because he was inflexible, and would not permit himself to be swayed from what he thought to be his calling. Steadfastly he declared to those rabbis of Venice:

> Behold, by the God Who has chosen me, I swear this day that even if bound upon the altar of God, I shall not renounce my innocence, and shall not permit the fear of flesh and blood to descend upon me: for I do the commandment of the Lord. And, as our father Abraham did not fear the fire of the Chaldees, nor Hananiah, Mishael, and Azariah the fiery furnace, nor the martyrs of Ludd death itself, so I shall not heed the temptations of Samael and the great Satan who stirs up strife; but, like a fortified city, and an iron pillar, and brazen walls, I shall rise to perform the commandments of the Lord, for He will do that which is good in His eyes. And the fruits of my truth will be that the Glory of God will know that there is a servant unto the God of Israel.

His steadfastness under persecution was a matter of doctrine with him; it drew its support from the Kabbalistic conception that the *Shekhinah* also voluntarily assumed suffering in order to annul the guilt of its sons:

> And this is the praise and the laud of the *Shekhinah* for her inextinguishable love of Israel: And thus also the Messiah takes upon himself the afflictions of Israel, for, otherwise, the people could not stand. Therefore the Messiah and the *Shekhinah* stand together, and shall not be divided from one another.

To the rabbis these ideas seemed dangerous. Or, perhaps, as Jacob Emden declares in his outspoken way, the Venetian rabbis at first spared Luzatto because he was rich and his family influential, but they did not hesitate later when his family fell a prey to misfortune, and he himself was almost impoverished. This inference, unfortunately, has some plausibility.

Luzatto had to leave Italy. He went to Amsterdam (via Frankfort); there, like Spinoza, he supported himself at diamond-cutting and produced works precious as jewels. From Amsterdam he went on a pilgrimage to the Holy Land in order, so Almanzi reports, to realize the dream of his youth by gathering together the dispersed of Israel, so that Jacob might return to his own land and find peace for all time. But together with his wife and son, he died of the plague at Acco in his fortieth year. Beside his alleged grave in Tiberias (next to the tomb of Rabbi Akiba), Oriental Jewesses now bewail their own griefs, as mournfully as if they guessed what great hopes were buried with Luzatto's premature death.

Of his literary remains, the drama *Layesharim Tehillah,* also written for a special occasion—the wedding of one of his followers—is especially well known. It is an allegory where Truth and Reason must battle long with Deceit, which misleads the Mob (all these being dramatis personæ), until finally a storm comes, *deus ex machina,* and helps virtue to conquer. It is a ripe, pain-hardened little work full of delicate poetical and philosophical ideas, interpreted, as said above, by the Maskilim as a call to enlightenment, when, in fact, it was anything you please but that. It was a call to his own Truth and to his own Reason, which was not rationalistic in the least. Rather, it was what the epistomology of Cusanus would call neither *ratio* nor *intellectus,* but that intuitive grasp (*visio sine comprehensione*) to which the true essence of things reveals itself and which has nothing to do with rationalizing.

Luzatto is also said to have left behind him a book of one hundred and fifty psalms, paralleling throughout the Biblical psalms, which breathe the chastest piety and are written in the purest Biblical style, after the heart-beat of the *parallelismus membrorum.* He was charged, during the period of his persecutions, with having boasted that his psalter would oust the Davidic one. Though this was obviously a libel, it caused the poet much grief. His teacher Bassan had to come to his aid by testifying that Luzatto's psalms were not inspired by a mentor-angel, but were poetic creations as could clearly be seen from the manuscript, which was full of "crossed-out lines and erasures such as occur in the natural process of composition, when one writes and crosses out and writes again."

Luzatto also wrote other liturgic poems for synagogue use, such as fifteen eight-part stanzas for Passover arranged not only on the acrostic of Moshe Chaim, but altogether traditional in content and in meter—this by the alleged father of the neo-Hebrew secular poetry. It is a grateful dispensation of fate and a sign of the healthy instincts of our people that it was not misled by the chatter of the litterati, but kept its eye open to the true values of its great men. Thus, by far the most popular of Luzatto's works, going through more editions than any other and becoming a real folk book, was not one of his poetic or dramatic efforts, written for play and pastime, but an ethical treatise, *Mesillath Yesharim* (The Path of the Righteous), which became the favorite pocket and traveling companion for many a pious Jew who could never have inferred from the devout little book that its author had been excommunicated by official Judaism. *Mesillath Yesharim* is a guide to true saintliness which, the author thinks, is not something bestowed upon a few by divine grace, but can be acquired by every pure and humble soul by continuous training and self-education. Following one of the early sages, Rabbi Pinchas ben Yair, it reveals the pilgrims' way to holiness through all its stages of caution, zeal, cleanliness, humility, fear of sin, etc., up to ultimate saintliness. Pious belief here is paired with fine psychological intuition and simplicity of language. The people understood that this booklet contained more of the authentic legacy of Luzatto's life and purpose than his æsthetic efforts.

A large number of his religious, philosophical and Kabbalistic works still await publication. Others exist in unreliable editions, and at that only in rare and scattered copies. These works deal with the most varying problems of Jewish hope and thought, with the secret implications of the *Musaf* prayer of the New Year festival; the transmigration of souls; the mysteries in the arrangement of the Seder; with the soul, the four worlds and the ten spheres (*Maamar Hachokhma*); the character and methods of Talmudic legend (*Maamar al Haagadoth*); the rules of Talmudic logic (*Derekh Tebunoth*); the principles of a mystic's dogma (*Maamar al Ha-'Ikkarim*); a guide to the study of the sciences (*Sefer Derekh Chokhma*). "One Hundred and Thirty Eight Gates of Wisdom" is a systematic presentation of Luzzato's Kabbalistic system, while "The Way of the Lord" is a lucid analysis of the main problems of the Jewish philosophy of religion, distinguished by its orderly arrangement and grace of style. In addition to these, many works are referred to by his biographers such as the "Dispute between Reason and the Soul," or the "Anthology of Intentions," to mention only two, all these showing the wide scope of his literary activities just as they prove how essentially a product of tradition and how typically old-fashioned was the "forerunner of the new Hebrew literature." That had been shown not only by his messiahship; it was demonstrated in the fact that his most serious and significant works were written not for æsthetic enjoyment, but purely for religious edification—after the manner of those medieval Jews who were ashamed to be merely poets, that is to say, artists without other aim: Jewish literature of old wanted to teach, to guide, to remake the scheme of things. Even Moses ben Ezra, the virtuoso of form who engaged in pure, aimless art with more intention and more interest than others, once admitted:

> And I too, in the days of my youth and my young manhood, thought poetry to be a virtue, in which one might take pride, and to my mind, my poems are worthy of keeping my memory alive. But later I abandoned and forsook poetry as the stag leaves the shade of his shelter: because I yearned to devote my life to things more worth while.

The same attitude was even more pronounced in Luzatto, for he places his skill in words wholly at the service of his religious idea. He desired to elevate men's hearts, to purify their natures, to lead souls to a future kingdom of God: "Everything," as he envisaged it, "that has been spoiled and degraded in the Galuth will be restored at the Redemption, and will be improved even beyond its original state, for, in that day, the *Shekhinah* will be improved and adorned more than ever before." Toward this Restoration, art, too, should contribute, willingly assuming as a distinction rather than humiliation the duties of an *ancilla theologiæ,* the service of the religious idea.

The seventeen-year-old writes a book on rhetoric, and then does some incidental dramatic sketches which he would certainly have objected to see esteemed as the most valuable of his literary productions. Such an estimate is, indeed, a false evaluation, even though it is put forward in the histories of modern Hebrew literature. It is a later interpretation in the spirit of the Haskalah, that makes out this authentic example of the Jewish destiny in the Diaspora to be an uprooted imitator of European æstheticism.

Though European culture was not unknown to Luzatto (as it had not been unknown to his predecessors in earlier centuries), it always remained for him alien, the exile, the house of slavery. Like all Jewish poets before him, he disdained to ignore this fact of Being-in-Exile. The world around them was exile, and would remain so. They were wanderers (not, indeed, shipwrecked, or vagabonds, but pilgrims) who sought, at God's command, to reach their home through the purgatory of the Galuth. Yet more. In order not to forget the Being-in-Exile, Luzatto, with all the Jewish poets who had preceded him, disdained to apprehend the world at first hand; because, if once they were to let the world stream in upon them, they would become at home in it, and then it would cease to be exile. Hence all Jewish poetry in the Galuth shows estrangement from Nature. This ban of the contemporary world was continued for centuries in Jewish poetry by means of the constant presence of the written word. So, too, Luzatto created his style by continuously leaning upon the Scriptures. The Bible, another environment, preëmpted that of the outer world, and made the latter a seeming, or, rather, a simile. Thus, the written word is used not to illustrate something out of contemporary life; but, on the contrary, contemporary events are used to illustrate the written word—they become, in fact, an illustration for the Scriptures. When Jewish poets designate—as Luzatto still does—Christianity as Edom and Islam as Ishmael, they are not using the written word as commentary upon the present, but make the present a commentary upon the Scriptures. History and contemporary life hold no surprises for them, because everything has been anticipated in the Bible. "Is there aught in the vain events of everyday life that is not already contained in the Torah of Moses and the Holy Scriptures?" Thus wrote even the great historian, Azariah de Rossi.

The messianic hope and the dismissal of the outer world —motives which still pervade Luzatto's work so strongly —make him an organic link in the long chain of traditional Jewish literature, which rests altogether on these two basic principles of medieval Judaism. It was only the Haskalah that undermined these two fundamental factors in Jewish history, placing Jewry and its separate existence in question, and plunging it into a profound crisis from which only gradually, during recent decades, have we been emerging. Therefore, the epoch of the Haskalah is rightly considered one of the most decisive in Jewish history.

CHAPTER III

A HUNCHBACKED PHILOSOPHER

I call to witness other members of my generation, descendants of cultivated German Jews, as to whether I exaggerate, whether some of them have not, like myself, had hours in which they have been ready to curse the day on which the magnanimous Lessing patted on the crooked shoulder a certain Moses Mendelssohn.

LUDWIG LEWISOHN.

IN the previous lecture, I tried to show the two basic forces in Jewish life and letters which continued unaltered through the ages until the advent of the Haskalah: the rejection of the environment and the messianic hope. That as late as the eighteenth century, in the *age of Voltaire,* Jewish messianism still had the power to capture so richly gifted a personality as Rabbi Moshe Chaim Luzatto, affords striking insight into this misjudged movement, just as it helps us to understand the whole epoch in question.

The sudden desertion from age-long motives of Jewish life for an affirmation of the lands of their exile as home, on the one hand, with the surrender of the ancient dream of the restoration of Zion, on the other, reads like a strange romance. We ourselves are still so much influenced by the after-effects of the Haskalah and so estranged from the authentic Judaism of former centuries that not even through modern Zionism have we been able to learn to grasp the whole range and implications of this break with the deepest impulses and traditions of the folk.

The break appears to have been abrupt and sudden. Luzatto died in 1747, still incorporating Judaism unbroken and in full vigor. Yet only three years later, in 1750, there appeared in Berlin the two small issues of the first Hebrew periodical, *Koheleth Musar,* edited by Mendelssohn and his associates, which are usually taken to mark the beginning of a new era. Moreover, the North of

Europe was much less advanced than free Italy, and Berlin not less, but incomparably more deeply rooted in Jewish medievalism than the progressive Mediterranean cities. In Mendelssohn's day rabbinical Judaism still had the power and the authority to assert itself against all innovations, and this in ways that occasionally seem comic to us. We find, for example, in the annals of the Jews of Prussia of that period that Abraham Posner, a Jew, performed the then unheard-of act of cutting off his beard; and that the Jewish leaders and the father of the offender secured a royal decree ordering Abraham to let his beard grow again.

How, then, did the new movement bring a change in the Jewish view of the world?

Some Jewish historians, still thinking in terms of anecdote, usually answer this question with the oft-repeated story of how the hunchbacked, fourteen-year-old Jewboy knocked at the portals of one of the gates of Berlin in 1743; how at first he was repulsed by the Jewish watchman, a sort of police official whose duty it was to keep out such poor as were likely to burden the community; and how, once the boy had mentioned that he had come to Berlin to study under Rabbi David Fraenkel, he was allowed to enter. It is further related how this misshapen, awkward, outwardly repulsive Jew became one of the most famous writers of Germany, the pride of the German Jews, and later of all Jewry. In some Jewish historical writing the chief share in the so-called Jewish emancipation is still ascribed to Moses Mendelssohn, as though that whole movement came into being merely because he was born in Dessau on September 6, 1729, an estimate which the two hundredth anniversary of his birth recently celebrated proved still to be widespread.

Actually, the Hebrew Haskalah is an offspring and a particular phenomenon in the general European movement for enlightenment, which, like the French Revolution, was fathered by eighteenth-century rationalism. A bold and sober age undertook to make a thorough revision of the values and ideas hallowed by tradition through hundreds of years. It approved only that which reason justified, and denied everything that had become merely historical. The dictatorship of reason in the eighteenth century went much further than Humanism and the Renaissance movement, which, at least, revered classical antiquity. Rationalism, on the contrary, broke entirely with the past as with error and prejudice, and placed all of life, all content and striving, in the bare present. History to the minds of the rationalists showed nothing— save the immature understanding of earlier generations. Even Lessing, in this regard wholly a child of his time, said: "Accidental historic truth can never become a proof of the inevitable truths of reason." It was Rudolf Eucken who rightly remarked that "accidental" in this connection means "real." Human reason is able to achieve and should achieve—self-reliantly, without revelation and independently of all tradition—natural (i.e., rational) right, natural morals, natural religion. Therefore, one of the basic motives of rationalism is criticism of religion, battle with the church and with intolerance, and the postulate of freedom of conscience. In place of the principle *cuius regio eius religio* comes the slogan of the enlightened absolutism, the legitimate child of rationalism, as formulated by Frederick the Great: "In my states everyone may be saved after his own fashion." Freedom for all! Even for the Jews!

Political and social ideas were exposed to still more fundamental criticism. Without comprehending historically developed forms, rationalism urged the idea of the enlightened state founded on a voluntary social contract, which assures to all its individuals favorable and orderly development. No social group is to possess more or greater rights than any other, none shall have its rights abridged—for that involves injury to the state itself. Rationalism demanded the complete abolition of the remains of the feudal system with its clearly defined orders of society, its privileged nobility, its guild bourgeoisie, and its enslaved peasantry, a system in which there was simply no room for other groups, and hence none for the Jews. The hallmark of that century is the legalized leveling of the whole population within the state, the wiping out of historical (at that time thought the equivalent of "senseless") distinctions, so that the state, the product of reason, might dominate. There were to be no distinctions of origin, faith, past, occupation, property—one law for all, equality for all. Even for the Jews!

Still more. From the ideas of universal freedom and equality grew a third—fraternity. These allegedly cool rationalists, the dispassionate champions of pure reason, who seemed to exclude everything emotional and to believe in self-interest as the mainspring of human activity, became enthusiastic and ardent apostles of the fraternization of all mankind. Men, released from all historic bonds, were to fuse into one, so to speak, by virtue of *amor hominis intellectualis.* Freedom, Equality, Fraternity for all—and for the Jews as well!

At this the Ghetto was obliged to prick up its ears. Such a thing was unusual even in the long history of the Jewish people. Former centuries had been distrusted by the Ghetto; there was no belief in their honesty and enthusiasm. The two mighty movements of the Renaissance and the Reformation had passed without any visible or particular influence upon Jewry, while Europe was awaking as if from sleep, gulping the delights of the new life with zest. "It is a joy to live!" sang Ulrich von Hutten. But the Ghetto continued quietly in its old ways, and went on stubbornly, magnificently banning the outside world, holding to its messianic trust.

Quite different, however, was its reaction to the ideas of rationalism which, through the French Revolution, had grown from an affair of the intellectuals into an all-impelling reality. Judaism was enervated by terrible prosecutions; petrified and exhausted by its rigorous adherence to tradition; deeply shaken, disillusioned and betrayed through false messianic movements.

Thus, the ideas of awakened mankind in Europe found us a broken people. We were in no state to attract power from the new currents for the rejuvenation of our own aims as healthy peoples would do, as the Jewish people itself had done in its days of greatness and creativity. Therefore, the new ideas brought it low.

A handful of youthful, venturesome spirits, lured by the calls from the Christian world, left the Ghetto for the great world of Europe, where they met with a friendly reception. Intoxicated with the glitter and freedom of the new culture, they fell a prey to the delusion that the prophetic "end of days" had dawned, when all the peoples would fraternize, and the earth would be "full of the knowledge of the Lord as the waters cover the sea." When they returned to the Ghetto, they were ashamed of its narrowness, of the old faith, of the medieval forms of life, dress, language. How, indeed, could the European nations grant the Jews access, as equals, to the joys of culture, when they were so backward and so alien to culture? But if only the Jews would learn the language of their foreign environment, drop their medieval costume, adapt themselves to secular learning, they would be welcomed to the enjoyment of all rights of citizenship with enthusiasm. Thus, out of shame before the European world and out of the belief that only lack of Western civilization hindered the Jews from achieving full legal equality with the other peoples, there swelled the current of life and letters known as the *Haskalah,* which aimed to enlighten the Jews, to bring them closer to general culture, to secularize, and to Europeanize.

Quite in the spirit of rationalism, the Haskalah preaches a dictatorship of reason (the word Haskalah itself is derived from *Sekhel* or reason) ; and, in the name of reason and progress, the inherited values of rabbinical Judaism are subjected to a criticism which deprecates the two chief factors for the preservation of the Jewish people in the Dispersal as foolishness and superstition.

The center and cradle of the Haskalah was Berlin, where the Jews achieved prosperity sooner than elsewhere (in the reign of Frederick II), and were the first to take part in German culture. It is true, too, that its most distinguished representative (and for the *Maskilim*—adherents of the Haskalah—the highest ideal) was Moses Mendelssohn (1729-1786). He achieved fame not so much through his German writings, though he was a skilled stylist, if not of the usually advertised value; not so much through his philosophical essays, which are pleasant, though of exaggerated fame; not so much through the example of his life which, though correct, was conciliatory, and not free from compromise. Mendelssohn really owes his fame to a work he thought humble and which he did in the declining years of his life. He attached no particular importance to it, and had to be persuaded to have it published. Yet its continuing influence has eclipsed not only all Mendelssohn's other achievements, but even the whole Haskalah epoch in Germany. This work is his translation of a part of the Holy Scriptures into German (1783).

> I found after some investigation [he wrote in a letter] that the remainder of my energies would suffice to render a service to my children and perhaps to a considerable number of my people, if I provided them with a better translation and explanation of the Holy Scriptures than those hitherto available. *This is the first step to civilization,* from which my nation, alas, has held itself so aloof that one might almost despair of the possibility of improvement.

Despite prohibition and anathema, this translation soon achieved wide circulation, and made its way everywhere. Mendelssohn taught the Eastern Jews the German language, which thus became, as it were, the official language of Jewish enlightenment. Since his time, *Deitch* has been the synonym for heretic in Jewry. Through Mendelssohn's translation, his generation acquired a secularized understanding of the Scriptures, which were robbed of their deeper mysteries, of their assumed anticipation of all historic events of the remotest future. The Bible was released from the traditional rabbinical interpretation which, though sometimes a misinterpretation from the viewpoint of grammar and philology, was, nevertheless, historically effective, maintaining the identity of the Jewish people, and therefore pragmatically *true*. Viewed critically in the spirit of rationalism, the Bible, from having been the supporting pillar of Judaism, became an enticing call to the strange, free world of Europe, and a spark of revolt against the traditional heritage. It no longer served to ban the outer world, but was the first book to stimulate people toward sound æsthetic appreciation in the European sense, that is, toward affirmation of the alien environment. The result was that the pious spurned the study of the Bible altogether.

Graetz exaggerates, but is still not far from the truth when he says: "Thousands of Talmud devotees from the great houses of study in Hamburg, Prague, Nicholsburg, Frankfurt-am-Main, Fuerth, and even of Poland, became nothing but young little Mendelssohns . . . the inner liberation of the Jews dates . . . from this translation."

The second lever of the German Haskalah was publicistic writing in Hebrew. Even though the early attempt of 1750 had failed, a handful of Maskilim litterati in Königsberg in 1783 established the first secular periodical in Hebrew, *Hameassef* (The Gatherer), which was to become the organ of their movement. "The language of the periodical was Hebrew," as Abraham Geiger, himself a champion of the aims of the Haskalah, bears witness, "for, had they been written in pure German, the works would have remained incomprehensible; or, if the medium had been the Jewish dialect, the growth of the æsthetic sense would have been still further hindered." In this the *Meassefim* were really little Mendelssohns and believed, as he did, that "Yiddish had contributed to the unmannerliness of the common man": they considered nicety of language a means of uplifting Judaism. Thus was Hebrew used as a means to an end, though it cannot be denied that they loved the language itself. This affection for Hebrew, in many of them, may have been strengthened by the increasing recognition accorded to it in Christian circles at that time: Herder had lately written in enthusiastic praise of the "spirit of Hebrew poetry." That their love of the language was not too profound is obvious from the fact that they had their children taught every language but Hebrew. For, after all, their real goal was general culture, Hebrew being for them merely the means that was to pave the way for a European, or, more precisely, the German language. Therefore, as soon as the Jewish youth had learned the language of the country, and could drink of the general culture from the original source without the mediation of the Hebrew periodicals, the *Meassefim* themselves could be dispensed with (1811); and the voice of Hebrew was soon stilled in Germany. Attempts to revive the Hebrew periodicals failed time and again. In 1794, Joel Loewe summed up the matter in a clever Hebrew pun: "I was asked," he writes, "whether *Hameassef* would cease publication or whether it would continue, and I replied that there will be no lack of writers so long as there are readers." However, there was soon to be a lack not only of readers but of writers of Hebrew in Germany. The older generation was beginning to die off, and the new generation had not learned the Hebrew language.

Estimating the literary value of the German Haskalah, one finds it to be very slight. It consisted of mediocre imitations of mediocre literature. As a rule the alien poets whom they translated were of low rank. Thus, from the German they translated Haller, Rammler, Gellert; from English, Gay, George Henrici, Goldsmith, Young, Ossian, Pope. For the rejuvenated German poetry of Goethe and Schiller they had no understanding. The so-called Moderns usually limp after Yesterday, and have no eye for the genuine forces of their times. Even the works of the most important writer of the German Haskalah, Naphtali Hartwig Wessely (1725-1805), who wrote a Hebrew "Mosaid" after Klopstock's "Messiad" have merely historical and linguistic significance. One scarcely finds poetry here, only enthusiasm for the beauties of the Hebrew language. The others have not even this linguistic importance, and deserve mention only because they unwittingly became the instruments of a Hebraic renaissance despite their own purpose and incapacity.

Before I discuss the wider implications of the German movement for enlightenment I should like to quote the judgment of a Christian scholar, who revealed the root of the evil in this literature better than many a Jewish critic, and who can relieve me of some part of the responsibility for adverse judgment on the epoch in question. He wrote: "As soon as Jewish poetry loses the center of the Jewish faith; the consciousness of the national indestructibility;

the sense of national preference by divine grace; and the hope of regaining its erstwhile glory,—it also loses its soul and its noblest powers. It decays and bears no more natural fruits."

II

Its literary shortcomings notwithstanding, the German movement for enlightenment is an incisive event in Jewish history. Its example led East European Jewry off the straight path for a long while. It bequeathed to later generations the embarrassing question of the Jew in Western civilization. An unheroic generation offered to the problems of a great epoch a warped answer which placed the Jew in a fatally false position among the other peoples. Which in turn hindered the rest of the world from taking a normal attitude toward the Jew—effects that still continue down to our own day.

Up to the very threshold of modern times, the Jew concerned himself little with the judgment of the alien world. The scorn of his enemy hurt, but it did not wound him; it could not degrade him in his own eyes. For it was God's inscrutable will that the redemption should be preceded by exile. Hence His people bore patiently and humbly the arrogance, the persecution, and the contempt of the unjust, trusting in His Name: for all shall pass, but Thou and Thy word shall not pass. The hatred of the world threatened the physical existence of the Jew, but it had no power to corrupt his soul. Against the peril of corruption, he was safeguarded by his trust in God. The love of the Jew for his God enabled him to see even in his enemy the instrument of the divine judgment, and compelled the impossible: love of one's enemy. Read the most humane and moving confession of a love of God that is exalted to the extreme of loving one's enemy, written in the Middle Ages, during the Crusades (which cause one who knows Jewish history to turn away in horror) by one of the most authentic mouthpieces of Israel, Jehuda Halevi:

Since thou hast been the abode of love,
My loves have camped wherever Thou hast camped.
The reproaches of mine enemies have been pleasant to me for
    Thy sake:
Leave them, let them afflict him whom Thou dost afflict!
My foes learned Thy wrath, and I loved them,
For they pursued the victim whom Thou didst smite.
From the day that Thou didst despise me, I despised myself,
For I shall not honor what Thou hast despised.
Until the indignation be overpast, and Thou send redemption,
To this, Thine inheritance that Thou didst once redeem.

The hatred of the world for the Jew thus becomes a part of the divine world-order, and can have no venomous influence upon his soul.

This reading into Jewish history of a divine plan, stubbornly adhered to despite all outward seeming of world and time—which refuted it every day—collapsed in the emancipation period. The alien enemy world presented, promised to present, as if by its own impulse, freedom and equality to the Jews, without merit or sacrifice on their part, without their having been historically prepared for a sudden grace of fate. Freedom was thrown to them as an unmerited favor, like alms. And alms shame the recipient.

The Jews' protective illusion against the contempt of

the world was dissipated. The inimical outer world that they had hitherto banned, whose judgment had never mattered to them was now, for the first time in the history of the Diaspora, looked to with a sense of inferiority; in fact, its opinion, though as adverse as ever, despite all the watchwords of progress, became the criterion of the Jews for their own estimate of themselves. Only now did the Jews feel the whole tragic range of the problem: What was the real reason why the Jews were always and everywhere hated and despised? Was it conceivable that in a two thousand years' struggle one side should show only cruelty, tyranny and greed, and the other only suffering innocence? Why did so many otherwise noble and highly gifted nations pour out the vile, to quote Treitschke, the diabolic forces that slumbered in the depths of their souls upon the Jewish people in particular, and upon the Jewish people only? Was it thinkable that we should always have had the right on our side, and that the others trampled upon it?

That indeed is quite impossible. Once raised, the doubt gnawed ever more stubbornly: Why, then, was it so? Were we not hated because we did not want to surrender our separateness and to resolve ourselves into the community, with which at times we have been bound up through centuries of history? Because we alone refused to submit to the command of history: to give up our peculiar individuality, the surrender of which is the tragic and inescapable destiny of a nation without a home? Because we have woven ourselves into deceptive dreams, misled by vanished memories of former greatness and by fantastic hopes for our future; because we have lost all sense of present reality, its rights and its duties? Because we are Jews so much, and men so little?

A radical change had taken place in the psychology of the Jewish people, for, up to that time, only the enemy had spoken of it in such terms. Ever and again, during our millennial passage through the midst of the nations, charges have been raised against the "certain people scattered abroad and dispersed among the peoples, whose laws are diverse from those of every people"—thus not only in the book of Esther. Juvenal brings the same accusation against the Roman Jews:

> *Romanas autem soliti contemnere leges,*
> *Judaicum ediscunt et servant ac metuunt ius.*

This reproach, hitherto flung at us in manifold forms by the alien environment, was now raised by the Jew himself. Up to that time, humanity and Judaism had been identical in Jewish eyes—indeed, Jews had always believed that Judaism *was* noblest humanity; now, humanity was regarded as the antithesis of Judaism. For this generation, humanity was that other, alien world which the Jew had always denied. And Judaism was no longer divine preference for an ancient civilization, but the contemptuous judgment of the alien world, a shamed admission of inferiority, a badly veiled *mea culpa,* or—to quote the cynical genius of the time—a misfortune. And the whole next century was to bleed over the tragic discord between the two concepts of *Jew* versus *Man.*

"Become a man!" was in fact adopted as the slogan of the Jewish enlightenment, which was put forward in numerous variations, whereof the best known is J. L. Gordon's "Be a Jew in your tent, and a man abroad." Logically, this should have meant, "Cease to be a Jew," since Judaism and Humanity now stood to each other in inverse ratio. However, against this intellectual energy to think —let alone live—a problem through to its logical end, something in the Jewish soul protested: the still-not-uprooted national feeling, the unreasoned bond of blood and history—*imponderabilia* for which the age of enlightenment had little understanding, but which nevertheless were stronger than rationalism. The struggle between the two forces: between the intellect which commanded a break with "prejudice" and the feeling of blood-community which, though sneered at as a superstition, would not permit itself to be put down; between the idolatrous cult of the alien and the unextinguished covenant with Judaism; between the conscious striving toward assimilation and the unconscious loyalty to a fellowship of race and tradition—this is the content and the hallmark of that epoch.

The champions of the German Haskalah did not clearly recognize the contradiction implied in their slogan of "Man-Jew." That whole generation lacked the capacity for historical thinking, as Mendelssohn once very honestly confessed. Overwhelmed and deluded by the cosmopolitan watchwords of those days, it sincerely believed that very soon the national differences would be resolved, just as distinctions of race and creed were about to disappear; and the nations would merge into the sea of All-Humanity. But the nations entertained no thought of such a *salto mortale* in the blue of the international heavens; and the Napoleonic wars were soon to cause nationalist distinctions to flare up violently, leaving to the Jews alone the fiction of a blank and featureless world-citizenship.

"Become a man!" is an abstraction and a residue of the medieval vivification of concepts that exist in the intellect alone. Just as in the reality there is no such thing as fruit in general, but always certain specific varieties such as the apple, pear, or nut, so there is no such thing as man in general. When the enlightenment slogan of "Become a man!" had to be translated into concrete terms, it actually meant (as Ahad Ha'am pointed out): Become a German, a Frenchman, an Englishman, etc. But how can one be a Jew and a German, a member of two peoples, a child, as it were, of two mothers?

A painful perplexity of ideas, emotions, conscience ensued. For fear of losing the emancipation it had won, that generation was deterred from declaring free and open allegiance to the Jewish people; while to declare itself unreservedly part of the people among whom it lived and to abandon Judaism altogether, the incomprehensible something within themselves would not permit.

So they saved themselves by a figment, an artifice. The changed status of the Jews within the state which was ushered in with the emancipation, the stripping of the Jewish community organization of all its autonomous and political privileges and of its representative national capacity, and its degradation to a mere synagogual body, gave the impetus to the unfortunate error (possible only in an age so devoid of all historic understanding) that was to be the source of all later dishonesties and misunderstandings, and was to place the Jews in an exceedingly false position among the peoples for many a decade: I refer to the doctrine that the Jews are not a people, but a religious community. The Jew died in shame, and in his stead was born the German, Frenchman, Pole, etc., of the Mosaic persuasion.

But even this "persuasion" was incompatible with the spirit of the new age. The contemporary world of thought (Voltaire, Holbach, de la Mettrie, Diderot, Wolff, Lessing, Reimarus), with its one-sided cult of the intellect which attempted to prove everything rationalistically, with its sharp criticism of religious ideas which, at times (as in France), went to the lengths of atheism and extreme materialism, was unfavorable toward religion in general, and so much the more so toward the Jewish religion, which had become ossified during hundreds of years, having been severed from the natural soil of its fatherland. Even the moderate Mendelssohn, who was sincerely attached to Judaism, said in the spirit of his time (in his chief philosophic work, *Jerusalem*): "I recognize no eternal verities except those which cannot only be made comprehensible through the human intellect, but can also be demonstrated and confirmed by human forces." He soon shielded himself, indeed, by saying that the "fear of God" has drawn a line between free investigation and that loyal obedience to the laws of God which it behooved no honest man to overstep. But that reservation was rejected by the radical youth as logically indefensible, and indulgently explained as senile habit clinging to old prejudices as people cling to beloved old furniture they cannot bear to part with. Youth always inclines to extremes, and how much more so the youth of a people of extremes. Just as formerly, this people went to all lengths in its obstinate

conservatism, so now it lost itself in revolutionary radical-
ism, up to the very point of self-dissolution.

After certain shy attempts, in the days of the *Meassefim,*
at reforms which were concerned only with peripheral
trifles, they went on to subject to the criticism of the intellect the very core and soul of the Jewish religion, the
cause of its survival: messianism.

The faith in messianism had been unshakable throughout the entire course of Jewish history: the more irrational it was, the more strongly it was believed. *Prorsus
credible quia ineptum est.* But rationalism recognized
only the Present, and only that within the Present which
could be justified by the intellect: the "end of days" was
consigned to the lumber room together with historic memories. Equal rights for the Jews seemed to demand not
only the surrender of the Jewish past, but their aspirations
toward an independent future. The little Corsican and
great realist, who had once dreamed of restoring Palestine
for the Jews, soon changed his mind when he saw the
Jews of his generation. "It would be a sign of impotence," he declared, "if I were to drive out the Jews. I
shall find ways of having them seek their Jerusalem in
France."

What the ghastliest torments had not been able to
accomplish, the petty fear of losing legal emancipation
did. The eighteen centuries of passionate faith and heroic
martyrdom in despite of a whole world were simply
asserted to be a delusion—at best a mere poetic fancy, a
metaphor which could be taken literally only by the ignorant, but which the Jew of the new age could easily

explain in the spirit of rationalism and without forfeiting his new position in the state: Thus, in 1822, Lazarus Bendavid wrote in the *Zeitschrift fuer die Wissenschaft des Judenthums:* "No man will take it amiss if the Jew finds his messiah in this, that good princes have placed him on a level of equality with their other citizens, and graciously allowed him to hope that with complete fulfillment of the duties of the citizen, he would achieve all the rights of citizenship"—a servant-like obsequiousness— how unworthy of all the earlier generations of messianic heroism, of sheer human nobility!

This servility of spirit and fearfulness of being thought disloyal led them to eradicate the name of Zion from the prayer book, to eliminate Hebrew as the language of worship, and, in general, to blot out all traces of nationalism from the Jewish rites and festivals. All recollections of national glory were stricken from the memorial tablets of the people, all strivings for national redemption were denied. They reduced themselves to the rank of a religious confession, and repudiated the peculiar character and content of that religion—all this for the sake of winning the confidence of the European world, of showing themselves worthy of emancipation.

But of course the Christian world became no more favorably disposed. The nobler elements were disgusted, while the others, though keeping the slogans of tolerance on their lips, were not so hasty as the Jews in breaking with the past and with all tradition, including their traditional attitude toward the Jews. Even a Goethe said, in a moment of outspokenness, "We tolerate no Jew among us. For how can we concede him participation in the highest culture when he denies its origin and derivation. . . ."

And for the sake of this culture the Jews gave up their all, broke with old, hallowed things. Yet even that did not suffice: there was still lacking complete dissolution, *baptism*. And Heine merely makes a bitter formulation of the postulate of the times: "The baptismal certificate is the admission ticket into European civilization."

Baptism spread like the plague. Much that was young and hungry for freedom turned its back on Judaism. That period cannot be understood if we charge it with treason or low opportunism, for it was not the worst, but, on the contrary, very often the best elements who put it up to themselves as a duty to dare the leap out of the wearily outlived environment into the new world. The efforts to elevate Judaism according to the prescriptions of the Berlin Haskalah and so win the respect of Europe very soon collapsed, and the uselessness of that method was recognized. Thus, for example, the tumultuous young spirits of the *Verein fuer Kultur und Wissenschaft des Judentums* soon gave up all hope, and made a shamed admission of the superiority of previous Jewish generations.

> The enthusiasm for religion, the genuineness of the old relationships has disappeared, but no new enthusiasm has burst forth, no new relationship has been built up. We have been left with the negative enlightenment which despised and disdained what had existed previously, but which did not trouble to give new content to its own empty abstractions. It is a state of complete dissolution [and therefore], it is not worth while to concern oneself about such a crew.

A HUNCHBACKED PHILOSOPHER

Very few indeed had the fine, sensitive manly honor of Gabriel Riesser (1806-1863). "Honor demands that, even though inwardly you may be inclined toward the dominant church, you do not withdraw from your community until the goal is reached, until the Palladium of freedom is conquered for the Jew as well." But the mob of the baptized did not consider it a duty to remain loyally among their fellow sufferers. They lost faith in their people; in the world; and in the "Palladium of freedom." Graetz may have erred in his statistics when he wrote that "within three decades half of the Berlin community went over to the Church," but the epidemic of desertion from the Jewish community was doubtless one of the largest of mass-baptisms.

But even baptism did not liberate that generation. Somewhere in the cellar of their conscience their sickly, timorous Judaism was lurking. Was it the voice of the blood, was it a gnawing consciousness of hypocrisy, of deceit? Hence their exaggerated zeal in exhibiting religious sentiments, the very thing that betrays the neophyte; hence the obtrusive displays of alien patriotisms, in their loud overemphasis disclosing the disingenuous convert. Hence in that whole generation the inner discord, distortion, dis-ease, the misery and farce of maladjustment, experienced painfully, ridiculed mercilessly, and mirrored most exactly by the unfortunate victim and most gifted mouthpiece of the age—that strange mixture of subtlety, dreaminess, passion, graciousness of feeling, splendor of wit, emptiness of soul, and cynicism of conscience—in short, by Heinrich Heine. Listen, please, to this convert making merry over baptism:

Do you believe that one's inner nature can be wholly changed through baptism? I don't believe it, and to me it is a melancholy as well as ridiculous sight when the old lice who date back to Egypt, to the Pharaonic plagues, suddenly persuade themselves that they are fleas, and begin to hop like Christians. . . .

Hence in that era so many pathological types, so many shipwrecked lives at odds with themselves and out of tune with the whole world, embittered, eaten up with *Weltschmerz* or *Judengram;* so many natures, apparently profound and yet sick at soul, undermined with disbelief in their own selves, critical, disrespectful, denying all values, mistrusting everything because themselves living in dishonesty, and so becoming the playball of the most conflicting emotions. Hence the type of Jewish revolutionary so frequent in the nineteenth century who hated this world of deceit and hypocrisy and injustice, and in desperation flung himself into movements for upheaval which, perhaps, might change the intolerable order of things. Self-hatred looms here rather than a pious yearning for things to come.

This is the curse of the lie: that it always begets new lies, must always carry a new curse. Decades were to pass before a new generation would discover the fundamental dishonesty in the Jewish attitude caused by the epoch of the Jewish enlightenment; until the old, authentic forces in Judaism stirred once more. Moses Hess saw into it clearly: "So long as the Jew denies his nationality, because he has not the self-denial to admit his solidarity with an unfortunate, persecuted and despised people, his false attitude must become more intolerable with every passing day." By surrender of one's national dignity, one gains the contempt rather than the esteem of the peoples.

This was not understood by the age of the German enlightenment, and thus Judaism was plunged into a profound crisis. It is unjust to make the German Maskilim responsible for the later unfortunate consequences, just as one may not make Mendelssohn responsible for the baptism of his children and the apostasy of that whole generation. They were a small generation, which did not realize the implications of their lukewarm compromises and half-measures. And Mendelssohn himself, correct but mediocre, was not adequate to the demands of a great era. How the generation of Lessing, Herder, Goethe, Humboldt, noble spirits sensitive to every authentic sign of creativeness, could have been enlightened on the Jewish problem and on the magnificent pathos of Jewish martyrdom, and how honest would have been their response! The epoch was far more suited to the purpose than many following, and that Jewish generation cannot be spared from such a reproach. Its false notion that open declaration of one's Jewishness conflicted with the duties of citizenship was not only an error, but cowardice, modern Galuth psychology. Until a generation born in freedom realized the unworthiness of this hypocritical attitude, and said: "If it be true that the emancipation of the Jews in exile is incompatible with Jewish nationality, the Jews ought to sacrifice emancipation to nationality." Thus Hess again, who, however, does not believe that such a dilemma exists.

How that whole Jewish century underestimated the Christian world one can realize with shame and grief when reading the judgment on its attempts at national self-estrangement, rendered as early as 1836, again by that great Christian scholar Franz Delitzsch.

Last year the Jewish community of Rome laid a volume of Hebrew poems of praise at the feet of the "Holy Father." The poems were beautifully copied, and splendidly bound in white satin. They were held together by two locks of gold of artistic craftsmanship, and on each cover was the papal heraldic device embroidered in gold. The writing on the inside was different on every page, and was enclosed within pictures and drawings by the Venetian Christian artist Paoletti, among which were the portraits of the Holy Father himself *and* also that of Solomon. The gift cost ten thousand francs. I see therein a symbol of the present situation of Jewish poetry: how, with or without conviction, it has become the bearer of fulsome praise to the Occident which in Rome devoutly kisses the slipper of the Pope, and in Germany the tiara of philosophy. The cowherd's tune of its home-land no longer awakens in it that home-sickness which erstwhile, in the Exile, was an inexhaustible fount of tears and songs. Poetry struggles, like its singers, after emancipation; and the emancipation of national poetry is its self-destruction. Mediæval Jewish poetry is the document of the freedom of the people in slavery; modern Jewish poetry that of the slavery of the people in freedom; may future Jewish poetry be the living portrayal of the people in freedom.

CHAPTER IV

A PHILOLOGIST

Le cœur est corruptible, mais non pas perfectible.

S. D. LUZATTO.

IN the chapters to follow we shall describe the development and destinies of the Haskalah in Eastern Europe; in geographic progress—which in its essentials corresponds to the chronological—we shall trace the impulse sent forth from Berlin as it gradually penetrated Austria, Poland and Lithuania, then the principal centers of Jewry. It is self-evident that the course of the enlightenment movement in those countries would necessarily diverge from its original trend, for the situation there was entirely different from that obtaining in Germany. This was true even of external conditions: The far greater concentration of the Jewish masses in Eastern Europe, combined with the fact that their non-Jewish environment stood at a lower cultural level, at once greatly diminished the possibility of a tendency to rapid disintegration in the Western manner. Yet this tendency was not entirely absent, as one can see from the history of the Russian Haskalah in particular. But in Eastern Europe the Haskalah was confronted by autochthonous Jewish forces which before its appearance, independent of all alien influence, had flared forth from the folk soul—forces which either had anticipated the enlightenment by themselves preparing the transition to modern thought or else, through a deep-going mystic revival, had rendered the masses quite impervious to the Haskalah. Here are meant the Talmudic reform of Rabbi Elijah of Vilna and the outburst of religious folk energies

associated with the name of Israel Ba'al Shem; even without their train of successors these two figures would suffice to demonstrate the fresh vitality of Eastern Jewry as
well as the creative power of both its rabbinic and its
Kabbalistic heritage as late as the eighteenth century.

The Haskalah can boast no personalities of such caliber.
For both of its most important spirits, though they contributed to the Haskalah periodicals and were the objects
of almost idolatrous veneration by the followers of the
movement, had outgrown the aim and ideology of the
Haskalah, each in his own way. In their youth Nachman
Krochmal and Samuel David Luzatto felt some of the
effects of the modern educational reform instituted by
Wessely and the Berlin enlightenment. But the course
of neither was actually determined by this movement;
their development is quite conceivable without its influence and is rather to be associated with older, more
authentic forces springing from the folk soul itself. They
stand—to name one of their predecessors—in close rela-
tionship to men like Azariah de Rossi.

While the work of both Krochmal and Luzatto was
done within the boundaries of the Hapsburg monarchy,
the scenes of their activity were at the uttermost limits
of the realm. Luzatto lived in the southwest, in the—
then Austrian—Italian cities of Trieste and Padua; Krochmal was in the northeast, in the Galician town of Zolkiew.
Grouped about them are the other representatives of the
Austrian Haskalah, whose names will naturally have to be
mentioned subsequently but who are rather eclipsed by
these two personalities. The only true poetic talent
among those others, one who achieved prominence for his

literary and historical research also, was Salomon Löwisohn of Hungary (1789-1822), whose promise, however,
remained unfulfilled: his short life was early blighted by
insanity.

As they were separated in space by all of Austria so
Krochmal and Luzatto stood at two opposite intellectual
poles of Judaism. Both, it is true, attempted, by com-
bating the alien enlightenment, to restore the old affirmations of Judaism; both, filled with an identical love for
traditional values, endeavored to preserve them for posterity. Yet they were absolutely dissimilar mental types,
two contrasting manifestations of Jewish life. Kabbalisti-
cally one might say that the souls of Maimonides and
Jehuda Halevi were reincarnated in them; it is no coincidence that they felt drawn to the two greatest Jews of
the Middle Ages. Krochmal's work was—very properly,
though most likely not by himself—given the name of
Maimonides' philosophic *magnum opus*. And Luzatto
devoted two of his books to the poetry of Halevi, while
he violently attacked Maimonides in several essays. The
vehemence of his attack forced the usually retiring
Krochmal to enter into a public dispute with Luzatto.
The record of this admirably objective quarrel bears
witness to two opposed yet equally justified views of
life.

The two men represent two different reactions to the
universe, two different answers to the eternal problems
and eternal needs of humankind. It is one's spiritual
kinship with one or the other of these modes of thought
which makes one choose either of these philosophies and
recognize it as "truth." Attempts at proof or disproof

are bound to be futile to the opposite mentality. As is the case with most systems of metaphysical faith, each considers his own creed to be scientific cognition. But this is a failing common to all philosophizing, and beside the point withal.

The crisis which confronted the Jewish emancipation period was caused, as has been said, by the feeling of the incompatibility of traditional dogma with the spirit of the times. The historic heritage of Judaism and the demands of contemporary rationalism appeared mutually exclusive. Since the German enlightenment set up reason as the highest tribunal, for whose gracious approval religion must beg, the conflict in German Jewry could not but have the outcome previously described.

Krochmal and Luzatto provided two different philosophic solutions of the conflict without surrendering their historic Judaism. Hence their significance and their influence upon the Hebraic life of recent times. Both reconciled Judaism with modern philosophic thought: Krochmal by regarding the two as identical, Luzatto by presenting them as eternally at variance. Krochmal united faith and knowledge to form a single magnificent cosmic concept, while Luzatto opposed them to each other as two entirely different realms of the spirit—both equally justified, but fundamentally dissimilar. Krochmal's concept was a creed illuminated by the modern scientific spirit. Luzatto, on the other hand, disputed the view that religion is an inferior degree of science; according to him the two are as unlike and unrelated as tone and color. Neither is less "true"; they are simply different.

The difference, of course, was due to the divergence of

their intellectual development. Krochmal had a definite inclination and deep love for philosophic speculation; Luzatto had an equally profound aversion to it. He read the various philosophic systems in order to refute them. That such an attitude does not necessarily hinder one from being a great thinker is proved by Ghazzali, the most brilliant mind of Islam. Luzatto never reveals such philosophic genius. His thoughts frequently fail to go beyond the casual and personal. Although his unusual, striking personality gives them living concreteness, adding to their freshness and charm, it detracts from their objective—i.e., typical—worth. But, once purged of their subjective elements, they may be developed into a philosophic *Weltanschauung* which would be a projection of Luzatto's ideas.

II

Samuel David Luzatto (1800-1865) was a scion of that noble Italian Jewish family which we already know through Moshe Chaim Luzatto. Samuel David, however, spent his youth in straitened circumstances and had to struggle against poverty once more in his last years. His father, Ezechia, was a poor artisan of Trieste, a wood-turner. But he was familiar with the Holy Scriptures and with the occult lore of the Jews and cherished a passionate love for the Hebrew language, in which he sought to write a commentary to the Pentateuch. Fragments of this commentary are known to us through the autobiography of his son. Exodus 17, 13, for example, is interpreted as follows: " 'And in the morning the dew lay round about the host'—behold and learn the greatness of him who lives by his own labor; for lo, even those who ate manna had to work, to carry it several miles to their abode and to bring home a double quantity on the eve of the Sabbath."

This righteous man considered it his duty not only to assure his son of a thorough Jewish and general education but to teach him a trade as well. Samuel David, however, after completing the courses offered by the Trieste school which was conducted according to the reform principles of Wessely, continued to study alone eagerly and with great industry, and refused to choose a trade. The pious wood-turner did not insist; but so great was his religious conscientiousness that he demanded from his son a written testimonial to the effect that he, the father, had made sincere though futile efforts to persuade his son to learn a trade. This document was intended to accompany him into the grave.

The young Luzatto's critical and scientific gifts, which manifested themselves quite early, caused no religious conflict in his soul. When he was still a boy it occurred to him that the vowel and accent symbols of the Bible were of comparatively recent origin and had been unknown in Talmudic times, and that accordingly the *Zohar*, the principal Kabbalistic book, which uses the vowel and accent signs as a basis for its speculations, must date from some later time. As a result the Jewish occult lore to which the father adhered soon lost all meaning for the son. The boy wrote down his views, and a cousin sent the manuscript to the then famous writer Isaac S. Reggio (1784-1854) of Görz. The friendship which ensued between the two later led to Luzatto's appointment to a post in the Collegio Rabbinico established at Padua in 1829, where he remained active until his death.

Luzatto was a man of many talents—a poet, a teacher, a scholar, of wide and varied interests. He published two volumes of verse entitled *Kinnor Na'im* (The Pleasant Harp) which Delitzsch regarded as containing seeds that may flower into an entirely new period of Jewish poetry. And although this view is exaggerated one cannot deny that his synagogal songs—the '*Aboda* of the Day of Atonement, which depicts the divine services as conducted by the high priest, or his elegy on the destruction of Jerusalem—reveal genuine feeling and impeccable style. But all too often his verses remain speculative or philological. Thus his poem *Like Portions,* in which he upholds the curious theory, to which Emerson also subscribes, that God has apportioned equal measures of joy and sorrow to everyone even in this world—an idea to which he adheres in his philosophic deliberations as well. In one of his satirical poems he derides the technical progress of civilization, which merely causes an increase of war, murder, theft, poverty, disease and premature death. This sort of civilization, which is built up on superficial courtesy rather than true kindness of heart, he names "Atticism." From his autobiography we know that the reading of de Jaucourt's article on Paris in d'Alemberts' *Encyclopedia* early connected "all vices with the Athenian character" in his mind. Later he endeavored to develop this prejudice into a philosophic outlook on life.

Animated by a fervent love for Hebrew, Luzatto was drawn irresistibly to grammatical and philological research; in these fields he probably is still the ranking

Hebrew scholar. None has had a more thorough understanding of the structure of the Hebrew language in even its most intricate detail. Very few have penetrated so deeply into the meaning of medieval literature, particularly the writings of the great Spaniards. With tireless zeal he sought lost Hebrew documents of the Middle Ages and despite his poverty disregarded cost where the acquisition of rare manuscripts was concerned. His researches in the synagogal poetry of the Jews are classic; and in his unselfish devotion to Hebrew lore he distributed his finds among other scholars—Rapoport, Steinschneider, Dukes, Sachs, Geiger and, most particularly, Zunz. When the last-named reproached him with being too generous and with sharing the fruits of his labors with some who were unworthy, Luzatto replied: "You have judged me correctly. If Satan himself were to come to me with a request for a manuscript to publish in Hell I would kiss his hands and fulfill his every wish. For the aim of my work is not personal profit or glory."

The fact that the "science of Judaism," a child of the German enlightenment, was not cultivated in the Hebrew language and the Jewish spirit, met with his sharp disapprobation. It appeared to him, as he complained in his letter to Rapoport, that this science explored the antiquities of Israel as one might pursue archæological investigations into the Egyptian or Babylonian past—merely out of scientific curiosity or personal ambition; and that it was manifestly its purpose to raise the prestige of Israel in the eyes of the Gentiles and thereby to hasten the emancipation longed for so ardently. Once that emancipation should have been achieved, a science of this sort would necessarily vanish. He, on the other hand, wanted a science which, in addition to studying the remarkable qualities peculiar to the Jewish people, would be helpful in their preservation and cultivation. Jewish history, he believed, should guide contemporary Jewish life back to the road of historic Judaism.

Luzatto pursued Biblical studies with especial fervor, and in curious and unique fashion wedded liberal criticism with unshaken faith in the Bible. In one of his youthful works he declared the book of Ecclesiastes to be the product of a later age and to have been fraudulently ascribed to Solomon by another author. As we have mentioned, he also regarded the Masoretic accents and vowels as of rather recent origin—a view which was, incidentally, expressed as early as the sixteenth century, by Elijah Levita; and in his interpretation of a number of passages he showed himself independent of the traditional version and made some unquestionably felicitous suggestions for critical corrections. It is told, however, that when Luzatto saw the many alterations which others began, in constantly increasing numbers, to make on the basis of his criticism of the Masoretic tradition, when he saw the sacred Scriptures fall prey to clumsy rummaging, he was frightened by his own audacity. Fearing an abuse of his methods, he retraced his own course and himself began to reaffirm the authenticity of the Masorah which he previously had undermined. He wanted definite assurance, for example, that there would be no emendations in the text of the Pentateuch, which had been guarded so carefully by the Jews; and he disputed with especial vehemence that the book of Isaiah after chapter 40 is to be ascribed to a later prophet of the Babylonian Exile. Indeed, he quarreled with his best friends when they dared question the unity of the book of Isaiah—although he himself considered a small portion of it to be of separate origin.

A characteristic letter to Jost tells us the reason for his agitation:

> If ever passion and vehemence break forth in my writings it is never in defense of any of my private opinions, but only where there is a question of *certare pro aris et focis*. . . . The point involved is not to ascertain whether a definite chapter is to be ascribed to this or that prophet, but to know whether the principal prophecies of Judaism precede or follow the events. We must know whether the God of truth or the spirit of falsehood and deceit dictated the words: "Who hath declared this from ancient time? Who hath told it from that time?" (Is. 45, 21). He who maintains that this is untrue undermines Judaism and combats all revealed religion. And can one who views with sorrow the open decline of religious faith ever repress all passion and vehemence?

This letter throws much light not only on the dogmatic and conservative viewpoint of Luzatto, but on his instinctive aversion to all deceit as well. To his mind, much weightier scientific grounds for regarding the Second Isaiah as of later origin would have to be brought forward, arguments much more conclusive than the mere dubious hypotheses of modern Biblical criticism, ere so grave a falsification in the religious tradition of Israel can be assumed. Similarly, Luzatto censures not so much the liberal views of Abraham Ibn Ezra (d. 1167), the Spanish Bible commentator, as his hypocrisy, the manner in which he at one moment exalts tradition to the skies and declares it to be infallible, only to contest it in ambiguous fashion a little later. "I do not reproach Ibn Ezra because he departs from Talmudic tradition, but because he does not openly acknowledge truth." On the other hand, Luzatto eulogizes that supreme master of Biblical exegesis, Salomon Ben Isaac, known as Rashi (d. 1105); for although this sage made much use of legend as a means for the edification of the people, he saw simple and natural elucidation as his true task. He was free of false and alien philosophies—unlike the supposedly emancipated Ibn Ezra, who despite his knowledge adhered to various astrological superstitions and other current follies of his day. Rashi had a genuine "Jewish soul," while Ibn Ezra had become innerly confused by Islamic philosophy.

Even more severe is Luzatto's criticism of the great Jewish philosopher Maimonides, whom he accuses of having adulterated Judaism with Aristotelian elements and thus having done far more harm than good to his people. Maimonides had reduced Judaism to a mere system of dogmatic concepts, although its essential aim is but to indicate the proper course of action and not to provide knowledge. Following Aristotle and his Arabic interpreters, he taught that only men who attain philosophic cognition of God achieve immortality of the soul, while the others vanish completely at death, like animals. The teaching of Judaism, however, is that he who strives only to acquire knowledge of the Torah, and not to realize its precepts in actual life, is godless.

Ere we proceed to Luzatto's philosophic ideas let us note that he never elaborated them into an actually systematic book, not even in his *Yesode ha-Torah* (Fundaments of the Law) which he considered his best work. He incorporated them repeatedly in his various scientific writings as his artistic inclination prompted, frequently with a striking lack of appropriateness. His first attack on Maimonides, for example, was launched quite suddenly in the course of a perfectly innocent discussion of the disposition and plan of the Mishnah. This procedure brought about exactly what he had endeavored to avoid: After withholding his opinion for years in order not to arouse misunderstanding or a public scandal he finally permitted that with which his heart was overflowing to pour forth through his pen in an entirely unsuitable place.

For Luzatto Judaism is more than revealed legislation. It is an eternal constituent of the human soul, an unquenchable need deeply inherent in human nature to transform the existing world in the image of what ought to be. It is an ethical and cultural force which is to guide the conflict of all against all into channels of mercy and justice. The Law revealed to the Jews is intended not to teach knowledge but to determine action, to ennoble volition and through rule and precept to form character. Its goal is not truth, as in the case of philosophy, but the good and the moral. Hence it is not essential that its every word be strictly true; and for the same reason one may not as yet deny its divinity. Perhaps the preservation of human society requires certain educational illusions analogous to the illusions nature frequently employs. And his voice has almost a Nietzschean sound: Perhaps knowledge at any price is but a beautiful instrument for the destruction of man?

Judaism, therefore, is not a system of rational truths, as Maimonides proclaimed; instead, it teaches the practical virtues, a moral mode of life, aspiration to the ideal ethical state of man and the world, however far and even unattainable this state may be. Luzatto believes that the fundamental doctrines of Judaism were known to the Patriarch Abraham long before the revelation through Moses. For the godly course which the former prescribed to his children and his house was the practice of justice and neighborly love. Accordingly Luzatto prefers to give to the spiritual content of Judaism the name "Abrahamism."

In Luzatto's eyes the first seed from which all virtues spring is pity, which provides the impulse for every noble deed and which, expecting no recompense in either this world or the next, bears its reward within itself—the peace which follows upon the healing or alleviation of another's pain. He deeply resents the Spinozistic expression *muliebris misericordia*—womanish mercy; indeed, he believes that the saintly life of the thinker of Amsterdam was possible, despite his teachings, only because of the still effective ethical heritage he owed to his Jewish ancestors.

"He who feels no pity is not of the seed of Abraham," declares a Talmudic saying. "Mercy is no Hellenic virtue," says the classic philologist Böckh. Luzatto soon constructed his concept of Abrahamism in contrast to Hellenism—or Atticism, as he designates it. Finding his ideas misinterpreted—through lack of understanding rather than malice—he formulated them in French; the following is an unabridged translation of his exposition:

> The civilization of the world to-day is a product of two dissimilar elements: Atticism and Judaism. To Athens we owe philosophy, the arts, the sciences, the development of the intellect, order, love of beauty and grandeur, intellectual

and studied morality. To Judaism we owe religion, the morality which springs from the heart and from selflessness, and love of good. Atticism is progressive, for the intellect is capable of continuous development and of ever new discoveries. Judaism is stationary, its teachings are immutable. The heart is capable of corruption, but not of further perfection: goodness is inborn, while wickedness is acquired. Judaism may rid itself of some addition which is foreign to it; it may restore itself to its primordial condition; but it cannot be perfected. Atticism, being progressive, takes on ever new forms, through which it pleases, charms and attracts. Judaism, ever immutable, appears older and uglier every day; consequently it bores, displeases, repels. Hence the apparent dominance and triumph of the former over the latter.

Yet there is in human nature an inextinguishable need for the good. Beauty and grandeur cannot take the place of good. Society needs emotion; but intellect and Atticism, far from inspiring emotion, weaken it and snuff it out. This is why human nature reacts—and always will react—in favor of the heart, of good, of Judaism.

If ever Atticism should suffer defeat human nature would likewise rally to its defense, for intellectual development is included among its needs. Then Atticism may conquer anew; but never shall it enjoy a lasting preponderance unclouded by opposition and reaction.

As a result the course of civilization is necessarily periodic, and not steadily progressive. There is no point at which it may halt. A state of repose is inconceivable without a perfect conciliation of the two elements; and this could not take place without great sacrifice on the part of the progressive element, which would have to subject its onward march to very considerable and useless restraint. The stationary element is, by virtue of its essential immutability, incapable of sacrifice.

It might, of course, shake off those of its components which are distinct from morality. That is to say, it might renounce its quality as supernatural revelation and dispense with all its theological and historical portions; or it might, while preserving its divinity, divest itself of all or some of the ceremonies unconnected with morality. But in either case it would lose if not all, at least a large part of its influence over the human heart—an influence which it owes entirely to faith in its divine origin and its changelessness. All such sacrifices nothwithstanding, moreover, the conflict between Judaism and Atticism would never cease, because of the essentially progressive nature of the latter as opposed to the antiprogressive character of the other.

We have already remarked upon the pointed disapproval contained in the word "Atticism" as employed by Luzatto. It was not easy for him to find the philosophic viewpoint "beyond good and evil," which would enable him to do full justice to the legacy of Greece as it has affected Western civilization. The statement just quoted is his most commendable attempt at neutrality; in his other utterances we hear the Jewish prejudice even more clearly and recognize the unaccompanied voice of his Abrahamistic heritage, the ethical fervor of the race. Luzatto is roused to wrath because, although Judaism has been overwhelmed, human nature has not reacted in its favor, has not displayed in sufficient measure its need for the good. He is even more indignant that the descendants of Abraham, who are the historic carriers of the immutable element of civilization, have bartered away so cheaply their Judaism, which is incapable of sacrifice, for the illusion of the emancipation. For thereby have they mutilated the best that lies within themselves and deprived humanity of an original and essential contribution.

As the guardian of an eternal doctrine Israel is endowed with eternal life. Its vocation is not that of preserving its teachings in immortal books and then, this duty done, being reabsorbed into the great family of Adam. It has, rather, been chosen to practice the teachings of Abraham actively and steadfastly to the end of all time, to assure their abiding realization in a living community. True, this doctrine has been proclaimed for all men and all peoples, and the ideal to which it looks forward is that of the entire civilized world—the Kingdom of God and the sanctification of His Name, for which the Jews pray daily in the *Kaddish* and the Christians in the Lord's Prayer. Yet it is not the mission of the Jews to be the *capsarii* of the nations (to use St. Augustine's analogy with the slaves who in Roman antiquity carried the children's schoolbooks; intrinsically the same thought is contained in the mission concept of Reform Judaism, which, however, adds a touch of self-complacency: *We* have been chosen to be the teachers of mankind). According to Luzatto the practicing of that doctrine in our daily lives constitutes our sole duty. Keeping the doctrine eternally in the foreground is the Jewish contribution to civilization.

The philosophy of Luzatto found no successors. Despite the antirationalist reaction which dawned in the West with the nineteenth century, despite Chateaubriand and Lammenais, Schleiermacher and Fichte—of whose age we find echoes in Luzatto, though he does not reflect their views directly—the Haskalah continued for decades to follow in the trail of the shallow enlightenment of the past century. While it acknowledged Luzatto in his more limited scientific field, it rejected his general views as those of a bigoted reactionary, thus approaching the attitude of the apostate Kovner. To the Maskilim progress was paramount. And here was a man who dared brand Judaism as eternally antiprogressive—a statement which may have been exaggerated for the sake of antithesis and which probably signifies nothing more than what that illustrious Christian teacher of Vienna, Adolf Stöhr, meant when he said that progress is possible not in ethics but only toward ethics. The concept of ethics has remained unchanged since the earliest times; only the number of the ethical-minded varies.

Another factor which hindered the spread of Luzatto's doctrines was his rejection of all philosophic thought as Atticism, which would forever remain alien and hostile to Judaism. Like Ghazzali and Jehuda Halevi he taught that even though one means to help religion with philosophy, the former would merely suffer harm, all good intentions notwithstanding. But the Jewish spirit of that period refused to be thwarted in the demand that its religious heritage be permeated with modern science and philosophy, and therefore felt Luzatto's solution to be an evasion. The need for rationalization as ineradicably Jewish as the mystic tendency was not satisfied until a little later, by Nachman Krochmal.

But Luzatto's point of view, freed from the incidental prejudices of its temperamental author, expresses a typically and eternally Jewish trend. Through introspection or, as more frequently happens in modern times, through the contrast presented by others the Jew rediscovers again and again that despite his masterly mimicry, despite even sincere admiration for "all gifts, all graces, all genius" of an alien world, he is unalterably of another mold. He may call it Abrahamism, Mosaism, Nazarenism or Hebraism; sometimes he may be unable to define it at all. But always, though it may not conform exactly to Luzatto's definition or views, it will be somehow tinged with a like religious thought and aim. The Jew may suppress or denounce it, reject or conceal it, attempt to escape it or yield to its power—but he will find no peace until he accepts it as a fact or even affirms it as a distinction.

CHAPTER V

A GALICIAN SOCRATES

It is not conceivable that honest investigation could have been forbidden us.

SAADIAH GAON.

I

IN his essay on Nachman Krochmal, Schechter says:

> I am probably expected to give some account of the state
> of society in which Nachman grew up. I regret that I must
> ask to be excused from doing so. I cannot consent to take
> the reader to Krochmal's land. And if I might venture to
> give him my humble advice, I should only say: By all means
> stop at home.

Yet you, I hope, will not take it amiss if I lead you to
this man's home which, despite its ill-repute (in America
his countrymen are called *die gestrofte*) produced during
the middle of the nineteenth century by far the most notable spirits of the Haskalah. Even Graetz, though he was
not too favorably disposed toward the "Poles," admits that
Galicia was the birthplace of Jewish Science.

When Galicia was severed from Poland in 1772 and
annexed to Austria, it was thereby brought into direct
contact with the spiritual life of Germany, becoming one
of the first lands of East European Jewry to be washed by
the stream of the German enlightenment. Even before
its separation from Poland, Galicia had had economic and
—consequently—spiritual intercourse with the western
Germanic countries. But it was only after its annexation
to the Hapsburg crownlands that it really came within the
orbit of German culture. Wholly in the spirit of enlightened absolutism, Joseph II of Austria (1765-1790) undertook to Europeanize the Jews through compulsory education, and to make them, if not free, at least free-thinking.

Hartwig Wessely in Germany so eloquently approved the emperor's purpose that he almost came under the ban of the ultra-pious. The Galician Jews struggled desperately against the obligatory schooling, and withdrew their children both in lawful ways and otherwise.

Nachman's father, a merchant of Brody (a commercial border town in northeastern Galicia), often went to Berlin on business, and is said to have had meetings there with Mendelssohn. Yet even he readily permitted his wife to pay six golden ducats a year to the school authorities so that his son might be exempted from the blessings of the imposed education.

Though fairly well-to-do, Solomon Krochmal was obliged by the strict Jewish custom of his day to have his son Nachman (born February 17, 1785) reared in the tradition-hallowed manner, namely, through education in the Talmudic and rabbinic literature only. However, by that time the Western Haskalah had penetrated even into Brody, which had its little group of Maskilim including, among others, D. B. Ginsburg, some of whose verses appeared in *Hameassef,* and who reprinted the rhetoric of Moshe Chaim Luzzato; Mendel Lefin, who recast a part of Maimonides into lucid Mishnaic Hebrew, and translated a popular work on medicine by Tissot and a treatise on morals by Franklin; and, for a time, J. L. Ben Ze'eb, the grammarian. Under such influences, the talented youngster must have been permitted to seek out some of the less approved books. It sounds like a personal confession when, in later years, Krochmal defends Maimonides and Ibn Ezra against the charges of S. D. Luzzatto, saying: "What man of all those whom the spirit of the

Lord moved to mediate on the spirit of Israel did not first quench his thirst at these two good springs?"

Having been married before he was fifteen (some say, even before he was fourteen), Krochmal went, after the custom of those days, to live at the home of his father-in-law, a wealthy Jew of Zolkiew, where, carefree and undisturbed, he pursued his studies for many years. By "undisturbed," I mean merely freedom from economic handicaps, since the path to a European education in the rigidly Orthodox community of the East Galician townlet was not smooth. In 1841, a few decades later, when the Haskalah movement had already made few breaches in the walls of the Galician Ghetto, S. J. Rapoport wrote bitterly, recalling his own struggles.

> It is easy for you [i.e., the Jews of the Germanic countries] to avoid onesidedness and to study various sciences, for you possess many schools and teachers in every branch of learning. This is not the case in the countries of the north [i.e., Poland and Russia] even at present,—much less was it so thirty or forty years ago. There is no teacher, no guide, no helper, for the Jew who desires to improve himself in any way, or even wishes to learn something more than he has been brought up on. He who wishes to enter upon a new path of learning must prepare the way for himself. And if he find the way, how many the "rocks of offense" that will beset his path, how many impediments will threatening friends and relatives put in his way. His friends will come to take all the scientific books out of his house and will say [paraphrasing the prophet Amos, vi 10], Is there any yet with thee, and he shall say, No. Then they shall say, hold thy peace, lest thou and thy house be burnt with fire. And if we, your friends, do not do this, know you not that there are bigots in the town, who persecute every Maskil and his household, as we have so often heard to our grief and shame? Indeed, though he have a lion's

heart, it shall melt within him. Therefore the number of Maskilim there is small to this day.

In such an environment and under such conditions, depending upon himself alone, without teachers or instruction, Nachmal Krochmal gained not only a most exact knowledge of medieval Jewish philosophy, but also made his way into the foreign world of the German philosophy of Lessing, Mendelssohn, Kant, and (later) Schelling, Fichte, and Hegel. In addition to Hebrew, he acquired German, French, Latin and—it would seem—Arabic and Syriac. His wide range of knowledge and scientific interests made the home of this Jewish sage probably the most advanced outpost of culture in the whole Slavic East. During the age of Emancipation in the German West, the Jews looked up with a sense of shame to the superior German civilization; but here we find a Jew bestowing upon an otherwise obscure East Galician town the claim to mention in the annals of human thought. Zunz, to whom Krochmal in his will bequeathed the task of editing his works, immortalized the town on the title page: *Scripsit Nachman Krochmal incola Zolkiewiensis.* So, in general, if some day a history of civilization should be written, not by national divisions, but on purely geographical lines—by countries—many localities, in Eastern Europe in particular, will strive for honorable mention less because of their dominant majority populations than by virtue of the spiritual achievements of their Jewish minorities.

In the Galicia of that time there was no danger that the Jews would assimilate with their neighbors as they had done in the Germanic countries. This fact explains why the course of the Haskalah was bound to be different in Galicia: The stimulation from abroad stirred the living forces within its people to independent cultural achievements that rank with the best in Jewish history.

What Berlin had been for the free-thinking Maskilim, Zolkiew became as the domicile of Nachman Krochmal— a place of pilgrimage for all the aspiring young spirits of those regions. Zolkiew was a small, typically East Galician town with perhaps no more than eighteen hundred Polish-Ruthenian inhabitants and about four hundred Jewish families. It lay within a pleasant mountain landscape with the romantic ruins of old castles; but its houses were poor and shabby, and it is not likely that the streets then were less filthy than now. In the Jewish quarter of the town, there was one house which, though outwardly not very different from the others, harbored a scholar's study which was exceptional indeed in those days. On the study table there lay the most conflicting spiritual products of widely varied epochs and peoples: beside Spinoza's *Ethics* lay a collection of Midrashim; beside the *More Nebukhim* of Maimonides lay Kant's *Critique of Pure Reason;* beside Azariah's *Meor 'Enayim, L'histoire des Juifs* by the French Protestant cleric Basnage; beside the *Zohar,* the standard-work of the Kabbala, the Roman Odes of Horace; beside tractates of the Babylonian or the Jerusalem Talmud, the writings of the dissolute Lucian. As a contemporary reports in pious Hebrew, "All these books, remote from one another in their content as East from West, lie together in peace and love and friendship. No Satan is there to disturb them. No one sets them against each other, and none puts any of them to shame."

As upon Krochmal's table, so in his mind the most conflicting forces of the day lay peaceful and reconciled beside one another. From his outward appearance, it could hardly have been guessed what revolutionary thoughts were locked up in the inconspicuous and wholly traditional figure of the typical *Talmid chakham,* which was so common in Galicia at the time. Krochmal's loyalty to tradition was carried even into his manner of dress, which deviated in no wise from that of his brethren who, knowing him to be a godly man and of unimpeachable piety, once called him to head his community for a time.

Now and again it was noised about that he read heretical books, and once he was openly censured for not keeping aloof from heretics who had forsaken Judaism. This was when he had had communication with the Chakham of the Karaite sect in the neighboring town of Kokusow. But the wise, pious scholar knew how to appease even narrow-souled fanatics: his irreproachable ways with God and man compelled their respect.

So did his economic independence, which enabled him to pursue his studies for their own sake, so that he did not need to use the Torah as a spade to dig with. In later years he became impoverished, chiefly owing to the death of his wife who, in the old Jewish way, had managed all their business affairs, so as to leave him leisure for the study of the Law. Yet, even then, when he was offered a public post in the community, he refused flatly.

The character of our communities is such [he wrote in the purest German] that nothing is too important and nothing too trivial to offer the occasion or pretext for partisan quarrels or controversies. Were I to become the occasion, though unwittingly, of factional strife, it would be more painful for me than the death by starvation that I seek to flee from.

Even when his reputation had penetrated into the West, and he was invited to become chief rabbi of Berlin, he pleaded:

> I beg that you will promptly and earnestly announce my unconditional refusal, and in the most decisive terms. . . . It has never entered my mind to fill the post of a keeper of conscience, or to occupy myself with the conduct of the religious affairs of a community; such a purpose would have been in harmony neither with my theological researches nor with my whole personality.

He chose the modest and almost humiliating occupation of bookkeeper in Brody, his birthplace, until the spiritual compulsion to write down his teachings, rather than the persuasions of his daughter, led him to spend his last years in her home at Tarnopol, where he died on July 31, 1840.

In his unconquerable dislike of selling his knowledge, Krochmal reminds us of Socrates who, though not always able, like his Galician counterpart, to refrain from the practice, stoutly opposed it in theory. In other ways, too, Krochmal reminds us of the Greek sage—chiefly by his amazing gifts of teaching. Quite in the spirit of Socrates' "art of midwifery," he at once recognized the spiritual forces latent in a pupil and divined to what particular uses they might be put. Fostering the pupil's self-confidence, Krochmal helped him to independent achievement. Thus the teacher might say, with Socratic irony and yet

not without truth, that he had merely assisted at the birth
of his pupil's spiritual offspring. Krochmal's friends and
pupils speak with eloquent gratitude of the joys of his
instruction even after many years, for he knew how to
find the corresponding field of activity for each man's
talent. So, Samson Bloch's intercourse with Krochmal
led him to the geographical studies which resulted in his
book, *The Paths of the World*. He encouraged Meir
Halevi Letteris and Dr. Isaac Erter, the gifted satirist, in
their literary inclinations, at the same time refining their
tastes through Hebrew and German literature. I. B. Levinsohn, the father of the Russian Haskalah, admits unen-
viously that the leavings of Krochmal's table sufficed him,
like other writers, for the filling of large volumes. Even
S. J. Rapoport, who was then still wandering restlessly
in the fields of poetry and philosophy, and also trying
his hand at natural science and astronomy, was helped
by Krochmal to self-discovery and realization of his abili-
ties as a historian.

In this, too, Krochmal resembles his Greek predecessor:
it is just as difficult with him to decide how much of the
master has been incorporated into the writings of the
pupils. If this be so with a Plato who towers above his
master, how much truer is it of the Galician Socrates who
poured forth his thoughts generously, and who, despite
the large number of his pupils, always remained the most
significant talent among them. He did not care to put
his ownership on record. For many decades he could not
be moved to publish anything, for, again like Socrates, he
preferred to unburden himself in conversation and oral
teaching. He hated the idea of being a literary man,

despised publicity. He confided in initiated pupils only,
warning them against overmuch scribbling. He used to
quote the delightful Talmudical saying of Rab Huna who,
speaking in the name of Rab Acha, says: "Regard not the
Law as one looks upon a grown-up daughter, whom one
would gladly hand into another man's keeping. Accept
it rather in the spirit of the Scriptures: My son, *keep* my
words and lay up my commandments with thee." Nothing was less to his taste than hastily written literature that
aims at hurried instruction, the sort of writing that tries
to market lately snapped-up and half-digested opinions,
just as a weary father is ready to throw his aging daughter
into the arms of the first man who comes along. Depth
of insight can be acquired only in quietude with the slow
passage of time. Nimble-fingered productivity is suspect.
He does not love his thoughts who is ready to throw
them off at all times and to all men. He therefore
demanded even more than the precept of Horace: *nonum
prematur in annum.* He would be content with no less
than ten years.

He himself never felt fully prepared, continually educating himself further. He once jestingly called himself
the perpetual student, and could say with Solon: "As I
grow old, I gain ever more knowledge." Often he heard
his friends complain that he kept the result of his
researches to himself, while so many lesser men flooded
the market. Mendel Lefin once charged him with ego-
tism, saying: "What does the splendor of the sun avail
us unless it send forth its beams? . . . You who could
so readily enlighten your people by grasping the author's
pen, will you withhold your hand? Will you hide in the

recesses of your house, and say, I am become wise?
Behold, you have become wise. You have gained insight.
But have you become wise for yourself alone? Was it
not to nurture souls that the Lord has sent you hither, to
open sealed eyes, and to let the oppressed go free? Lift
up your eyes, I pray you, and behold high mountains cleft
so that springs may flow forth from their midst to restore
the soul. Here the earth opens many mouths, to bring
forth bread in abundance. There the lily sprouts and
blossoms in all her beauty to gladden the eye of the
beholder, and to offer fragrance to his nostrils. And a
man, shall he profit himself alone? By my faith, this man
seems very strange to me. I do not understand him!"

Besides his inner aversion from publishing half-finished
work, there was also the outer consideration that he might
be misunderstood or slandered. Thus, he confesses in a
letter to S. D. Luzzato:

> Fearing the Lord, I hesitate to teach things that are as
> coals of fire, for even unwitting error weighs, in truth, like
> wickedness. And, on the other hand, I tremble before the
> wrath of the zealots who are poor in knowledge, entangled
> in the bonds of custom, and sometimes in the chains of
> malicious stupidity. And who knows how to go against all
> these groups?

This was not cowardice on his part, nor was it con-
ciliatoriness. He taught his pupils to stand up courage-
ously for what they thought right, regardless of public
opinion:

> Great fear and submission before the unworthy who exalt
> themselves [he wrote] show and betoken a servile spirit
> and a depraved soul which was destined from birth for
> slavery and serfdom. One who desires to rise above the

mob with its confused notions and its corrupt morality must be valiant and energetic, strong as a lion to fight the battles of the Lord against those who hinder, terrorize and persecute. And if every moment he must be asking himself, What will the people say, What slander will the bigots spread, What evil will the enemies devise,—such questions will darken his reason and confuse his judgment. Had the great sages of our people been fearful, we should not have had many a treasure, and their most precious works would not have been published. For all of them knew well what grief and sorrow would come upon them by reason of their writings. The prototype of them all is the *Rab* [Maimonides], the Teacher, the Light of Israel, who confessed in his preface that he would help one and enrage thousands, and intended to hide his book so that it might not become a target for the arrows of every fool. And if you should search out the matter, you will find that so it was with the last of the sages and with the early ones, and with the early among the early ones, back to the prophets, peace be upon them! The mob goes bound in the chains of every rascally priest, every pretender to holiness, every bigot, every wizard and conjuror, every miracle-worker and quack. Against one who opposes them they incite the wild beast of many mouths and no eyes, as the wise Frederick of Prussia pictured the mob.

It was not fear of the mob that held Krochmal back, but rather his high and subtle sense of responsibility, his awe of truth, his deep love of the teachings of Judaism which, as the frightful example of the German enlightenment had taught, ought not to be exposed to arbitrary interpretation. Until, in the end, he realized that his silence was a sin against the very values that he cherished, and that it was his duty to write in order to strengthen the vacillating minds and "the perplexed of the time."

To tell the full truth, were I not assured of the mercies of Heaven, and did I not know that the testimony of His

Name is true, and that the vessel [Judaism] is strong enough
to contain both the old and the new, and that it can triumph
over the passage of time and changes of place, I had now
turned back out of great fear lest I cause loss and injury
where I intended to strengthen and to improve. . . . It is
becoming for us to say: "It is time to do the work of the
Lord: they have made void thy law" (Psalm 119, 126).

That Krochmal was still bound by many inhibitions
even when he at last engaged in the writing he had so
long postponed is evident from numerous passages wherein
he persuades himself over and over again that it is his
duty to publish what he has attained to in a lifetime of
strenuous intellectual labor. Judaism had been so shaken
by contemporary events and by pseudo-science that he felt
himself bound for truth's sake to keep silent no longer:

> We shall declare and repeat, again and again, that just
> as in former generations there was danger of revealing much
> that was covered, so, in our time, there is as much and even
> more danger of covering that which was revealed by others,
> —a vain and injurious procedure that is of no help what-
> ever. To help, in truth, is to continue to search out and
> to investigate, lifting up our eyes to the God of Truth,
> Who will not forsake them that seek Him. Happy are we,
> whose goodly portion is the Word of God and the Law of
> Truth that need not fear research and testing from any side
> and in any manner.

One is at a loss here which to admire most—Krochmal's
outspoken, scientific courage, or his pious, unshakable trust
in God: this union being, in general, a trait of the Jewish
philosophy of religion. Thus Saadiah, too, wrote a thousand years ago: "It is not conceivable that honest investigation could have been forbidden us."

Krochmal died over his book. He had asked in his

will that his writings be handed to Zunz (whom he had never met) for editing. Zunz undertook the task, aided by Steinschneider, and the book appeared in Lemberg in 1851, eleven years after Krochmal's death. The editors called it *The Guide to the Perplexed of the Time,* but Krochmal himself may have intended to give it the title of *The Gates of Pure Belief.* The work is a gigantic fragment, of a design and aim so bold that it must necessarily have remained incomplete, like the torsos of the never-ready, because supergifted, Leonardo, who could never declare his work finished. Yet, for all its incompleteness, *The Guide to the Perplexed of the Time* contains a world of ideas: it is the profoundest book of Hebrew genius written in modern times.

II

It would be stupid to dare a summary. The more so in view of Krochmal's known aversion for any abridged conclusions in science, which to him were worthless and unenlightening. He once even asserted that "he who knows, for example, that the world is round and inhabited on all sides is no more intelligent than one who thinks it flat and inhabited only on its flat surface. Only he will achieve true intelligence who understands the logical process by which the truth is arrived at."

It would be particularly unfair to this man to adopt the very procedure he disapproved by giving merely the final conclusions, when to him the *way* of thinking and research was the important thing. Moreover, it would be absurd to devitalize this colossus of ideas by a brief presentation of its contents. Even a bare listing of the subjects treated in it would exceed the limits of our space. I can merely attempt to give an approximate notion of Krochmal's *method of approach* when dealing with the great problems of Judaism. For that in particular seems to be his legacy to later generations.

The age of enlightenment based all phenomena on reason, resolved all reality into reason, and allowed only what was reasonable to stand. The Berlin Haskalah, including Mendelssohn, wanted to base Judaism on naked reason altogether, to admit as real within Judaism only that which harmonized with the demands of reason, or rather with the rationalism of their time. Their attitude cost Judaism a surrender or, rather, a denial of its paramount forces and tendencies, and led to the unhappy consequences to be observed in the German Jewry of those days. The significance of Krochmal's book rests on this, that he tried to build it, not upon rationalistic abstractions, not upon theoretical speculation, but upon life, truth, actual experience: the *historic reality* of the Jewish people. To paraphrase a saying of Hegel's: while Jewish enlightenment admitted as real only what was reasonable (in the rationalist sense) Krochmal declared everything real in Judaism to be reasonable, meaning that those actual, impelling forces which had grown into traits of folk-character in the course of a history of thousands of years, are truth in Judaism.

Krochmal introduced into the philosophy of Jewish religion the historic concept of Time. The concept formulated in the preface of his book, "To search out, to reveal, and to establish all the phenomena of Judaism in and through the actual period of their origin" forms the basic idea and chief philosophic merit of his book. Alluding to its title, some have said that with the sure grasp of genius he at once discovered that the real perplexity of his time was Time. He saw that the dissonance within Judaism from which his contemporaries suffered, sprang from inadequate insight into the character and the effects of time in history, without which no historic manifestation, hence Judaism, too, can be understood.

Both the naïve, rigidly Orthodox champions of the old, for whom there is "no early and no late" in the Torah, and who jumble all periods of Jewish life into one another, keeping late intellectual acquisitions and ancient beginnings indiscriminately side by side in a timeless ideality, and the precipitate moderns who, just as indiscriminately, fling aside all the past, all the traditions of long generations in their blind zeal for the abstract notion of a reason above and outside of time—"they take the limited opinions of their own age, and think them eternal truths"; both these camps (the "fools among the believers" and the "light-minded among the scorners," as Krochmal calls them) suffer from a lack of understanding of the Time category both in general and in Jewish affairs. Neither camp distinguishes between the accidental and the essential, between what is conditioned by time and transitory, and what is unconditioned and permanent; and so both fail to understand Judaism.

"At both extremes," wrote Krochmal, "there is a lack of true faith in our time. Both extremes are alike in believing that religion is what they used to believe in childhood; and the difference between them is only this: that some rejoice when they can find opportunity to cast suspicion and doubt upon that faith, while the others—and they are the majority—endeavor to strengthen and sustain faith with fantasies and various exaggerations—futile measures in an age when knowledge is widespread." Against these extremes of naïve faith and equally childish unconditional skepticism, Krochmal wishes to set up a lucid faith, an interpretation of Judaism matured in the light of modern philosophical criticism.

Approaching Judaism as an historic manifestation, he attempted to explain it by the historic method, and never troubled about the shallow question—religion or people—posed by the enlighteners. Everywhere, he takes for granted the undeniable fact of the existence of the Jewish people and civilization. He is much more interested in the far profounder question of the essence of Judaism. He wants to explore and define it, not speculatively, not in the manner of rationalistic dogmatism, but empirically, on the basis of the reality of Jewish history. By study of custom and ritual, of the principles of faith and spiritual peculiarities that have revealed themselves in our people during its long history; by study of its cultural relations with other peoples and other civilizations—of the influences in them which we have accepted and even more of those that we have rejected; by study of all these, he attempts to "fix definite impressions and finally to achieve a clear knowledge of ourselves, of our individuality and character, of the Jewish soul in its totality as it has exhibited itself in history, so that we may learn a lesson for the future."

In his opinion, research was to be pursued in Judaism not in order to gain emancipation and equality of rights for the Jews, as was done in Germany by a Zunz—and how much more by others!—a type of research that narrowed Judaism apologetically. Nor was it to be a pure and disinterested research for the sake of science, which makes a virtue of the vice of aloofness from life. Rather, research in Judaism should aim at self-knowledge in order that "the perplexities of the time" might be surmounted, and that "we make ourselves wise for the future." It should teach us how to build for that future. This thought, which was later persistently championed by Ahad Ha'am, was in fact formulated long before by Krochmal.

Self-knowledge for the sake of the present and the future was to be derived from Jewish historical science, which received its most decisive stimulus from Krochmal. He was the first to think out the basic ideas of Jewish history, at a time when Jewish history did not even exist. Nevertheless, he succeeded in establishing both the facts of Jewish history and the philosophic generalizations that he built upon them. For Krochmal possessed what the age of enlightenment lacked—an historic sense that in him amounted to genius. He had a delicate faculty of detecting the heartbeat of the age in every record, and could at once assign it to its proper time and place. This capacity of discerning the peculiarities of various epochs was with him no analytic process that could be taught, but an intuitive art, refined and guided, however, by his highly scientific critical sense. Mated with this unusual historic gift were an equally unique philosophic depth and ability to synthesize.

Borrowing Hegel's outward form rather than his actual

dialectic procedure, Krochmal saw three stages in every historic process: sprouting and growth, vigor and maturity, decline and extinction. Every people passes through three stages until the idea, the spirit which it represents, is realized; and then that people disappears from history. Nevertheless, the idea for which it once lived, usually continues effective in history, being taken over by other peoples. So, when the ideas peculiar to the civilizations of antiquity—the Greek, Roman, etc.—were realized, they themselves disappeared. Outwardly observed, the Jewish people, too, passes through the three stages of growth, maturity, and decline; but, because the idea for which it was created and by which it lives, is the "absolute Spirit," the source and sum of all spiritual existence, or, as Krochmal sometimes puts it more definitely, the Eternal God— this people can never perish, its ideal being imperishable. In this sense, Krochmal wrote the words of Micah, "Let all peoples walk each one in the name of its god, but we will walk in the name of the Lord our God forever and ever," over "Gate VII" of his work, entitled "Nations and their Gods." He meant by this to indicate that, seen in the light of philosophy, the problem of Jew versus Man, which his whole generation and even Berditchewski, at the threshold of our own day, bled over, did not exist at all. Every nation has its own spirit, or—in the language of Krochmal—its own god. One nation has the spirit of beauty, others have law, physical courage, science, knowledge and fear of the Lord. But there need be no quarrel or strife among all these gods.

It is just the existence of so many differing worlds of thought that confers spiritual wealth upon mankind, even

as the variety of colors in the rainbow does not cause them
to conflict with one another, but to harmonize in a higher
beauty. There is no antithesis between Judaism and humanity. On the contrary, in a certain sense humanity is
Judaism. All the forces prevailing in the world, by which
the different nations live, are contained within the "universal soul" of the Jewish people in the measure that it
is the bearer of the faith in the one God, the "absolute
Spirit," the source of all spiritual being.

Krochmal makes an outline of Jewish history from the
beginning, showing it to have passed three times through
the natural cycle of the three-stage process of history. And
it is not difficult to read into the intimations which
Krochmal left behind that he saw his age as the spring-
tide of the fourth cycle of Jewish history, as a new significant epoch of renewal for the Jewish people. In the
signs of his time, in the awakened love for the Hebrew
language, in the birth of Jewish Science, he saw a rejuvenation of the "absolute Spirit," which lives immortally
in his people. Indeed, some even claim that he recognized
the idea of the new renaissance (which was hardly understood in his day, and which, if understood, would have
been strenuously fought) : the national consciousness as
the inner force and aim of the new epoch.

This bald outline of Krochmal's train of thought cannot
possibly convey an idea of the winged beauty of his his-
toric-philosophic concept: his pages must be read. Here
is a powerful effort to establish the idea of messianism,
of divine preference for the Jewish people, with the
weapons of critical idealism which had been forged from
Kant down to Hegel.

This effort, as S. Rawidowicz justly complains, has been unjustly deprecated as Jewish Hegelianism, though Krochmal drew upon many other sources, both Jewish and general. It is perhaps to be described as Hegelianism only because of its effects, namely, in the spirit of the Hegelian "cunning of the idea," he clothed the old and authentic content of Judaism in the terminology fashionable in his day, and so saved it for his generation.

It is from Krochmal that Reform Judaism borrowed the idea of the Jewish mission. Though he did indeed declare that we have been the "teachers of humanity," he did not accept our expatriation and dispersion as advantages and perquisites for that mission, but as transitory evils. There is a purpose in exile, if, as in Egypt and Babylonia, it be a preparation and initiation for ingathering in Zion. He lauded those forces of national solidarity which, despite the influences of alien culture and the perils of the foreign environment, kept us an ethnical unit. He held that the Jews had kept their memories of their fatherland, and the customs and traditions of their ancestors while in Egypt in order to be prepared, once they were freed from foreign domination, to establish a lofty order of society, and to conduct their own national affairs. Conversely, with a broad hint at his Western coreligionists who wrote on Jewish Science in foreign languages, he spoke of the Hellenized Jews of Alexandria, who "grew and prospered for more than four hundred years, but their wisdom and most of their writings vanished without a trace, and the little that remained is but as a brand plucked from the fires of destruction. Doubtless this was because they forsook the holy tongue of their inheritance. Let posterity look and take this lesson to heart."

It is Krochmal's merit, in the philosophic sense, that he demonstrated that Western philosophy did not cause, but was able rather to relieve the crisis in Judaism created by the German enlightenment; and that he saved and justified the ancient fundamentals of Judaism by the very use of philosophy, with which it was usually challenged in his age. Out of his philosophy there clearly speaks a refusal to barter the imperishable and eternal idea of Judaism for the more fashionable but transitory ideals of other peoples—a refusal the more weighty because few honored, enjoyed and understood their thought-worlds in their farthest reaches better or more gratefully than he. And yet, it was just study and understanding of foreign civilizations that gave him the power to seek a new and proud affirmation of Jewish preference by divine grace. Once again, he taught that Judaism was to be looked upon as a distinction, and so became a guide to the perplexed of his own time. And of many times to come.

Though to-day, after the collapse of the classical philosophy of the West, the outer metaphysical vesture of Krochmal's work may not convey what it did on his lips and in his time, and though some of his conclusions cannot be upheld to-day, much in him remains imperishable for future ages. There remains his method of approach to the problems of the Jewish people, his masterly use of the *historic method,* which alone affords insight into the four-thousand-year-old phenomenon of the Jewish people. We of to-day, who have still come no nearer to the actual aim of Krochmal's researches, namely, the recognition of the Jewish self in its historic totality, are far from having a right to the luxury of civilizations sicklied o'er with too much archival thinking, the right to revolt against historicism. There remains, too, the aim which Krochmal set up for Jewish Science, and which can guide many coming generations: self-knowledge for the sake of a wiser molding of the future.

Krochmal might also serve as a guide to our generation in that he overcame the fashionable folly of his century, originated by the German Haskalah, of basing Judaism upon the Bible alone: a kind of modern Karaitism, which is still continued in certain neo-Hebraic circles. He provided a foundation for Judaism in the empirical reality of all the spiritual creations of the Jewish genius—chiefly, therefore, in the Talmud. So, the whole Galician Haskalah is favorably distinguished from the German and the later Russian Haskalah by Talmudism.

The especial scientific merit of Krochmal's work, the importance of his researches in various special fields, can hardly be exaggerated. We have only to read the abundant praises showered upon him, which, however, deserve to be taken quite literally. Jost, despite his blind admiration for Mendelssohn, ranked Krochmal far above him as the outstanding thinker and scholar in Jewry. Graetz gladly admitted that it was Krochmal who knew how to exploit the rich mines of the Talmud, and who threw so much light upon one of the obscurest epochs in Jewish history that all who followed, himself included, could easily find their way by his luminous footprints. I. H. Weiss, the great investigator of the Halakha, spoke of Krochmal as the "pure fount of the wisdom of Israel, which feeds and will continue to feed all other springs," gratefully admitting his own indebtedness. And Schechter, to mention but one more, testified: "I may assert with the utmost confidence that there is scarcely a single page in Krochmal's book that did not afterwards give birth to some essay or monograph or elaborate treatise, though their authors were not always very careful about mentioning the source of their inspiration."

Still more important, even, than his dominating influence upon individuals, examples of which could be multiplied, and upon the general fields of Hebrew science and Hebrew letters (Abraham Mapu, Ahad Ha'am, Berditchewski, and others), was his influence upon the Jewish anonym, the common man, in his own and later generations.

By a kind of peaceful penetration, Krochmal's flood of ideas, though unmentioned and at times even combated, poured itself over the whole of Jewish life, making its way even into circles which defy all modern influences. His *Guide to the Perplexed of the Time* was not the Melitzah booklet of a Maskil that could be contemptuously ignored, for even his opponents felt obliged to bestow upon it the title of *Sefer*, "book," the hallmark of honor stamped upon Jewish achievement.

For one who knows how to read history, it is both uplifting and instructive to note how this seemingly traditional, pious Jew, who never left his nook in Eastern Galicia, and never gave the pious cause for anger—for he lived a holy life that was yet free from all taint of hypocrisy—was one of the greatest and most influential revolutionaries of the spirit in Judaism.

There is said to have been a clause in his will—in this, too, he followed an old Jewish custom—providing that the table at which he had studied all his life was to be used as his coffin. But that table, on which the great inheritance of Judaism and the best of the European world of thought had lain peaceful and reconciled together, could no longer be buried. Through the example of his life, it had become a new *Shulchan 'Arukh,* a "table prepared," for the young generation. Surveying his life story, a critical spirit like Zunz, who, in his reverence for Krochmal went so far as to call him a man of God, did not hesitate to comment upon it in the manner of the old Jewish *Derash,* surmising a something higher in an unimportant coincidence: "He was born on the birthday of Moses, the seventh of Adar, and died on the same day as Aaron, the first of Ab."

CHAPTER VI

A WONDER-WORKER

It may sometimes happen that thine own hand inadvertently strike thee. Wouldst thou take a stick and chastise thy hand for its heedlessness, and thus add to thy pain? It is the same when thy neighbor, whose soul is one with thine, because of insufficient understanding does thee harm; shouldst thou retaliate, it would be thou who wouldst suffer.

RABBI SHMELKE OF NIKOLSBURG.

A. B. GOTTLOBER was an indefatigable champion of the enlightenment in the land of Russia even when that ideal was already on the wane; in one of his satires he recounts how the *Chasidim*—"the pious"—persecuted a youth who ardently yearned for culture. In the eyes of a Maskil the adherents of this mystic-religious movement, which emanated from Podolia and Volhynia about the middle of the eighteenth century, were even more retrograde and obscurantist than the Talmudic-Rabbinic zealots. Gottlober relates that some fanatic Chasidim of the little town Kazib—the name means "fraud"—caught the son of one of their deceased fellows reading the *Sepher Hamiddoth*, an ethical treatise of N. H. Wessely; and since the author was well known as an exponent of the enlightenment in Berlin and as a friend of Mendelssohn it was clear that the book could contain naught but wanton heresy. Vain were the protestations of the boy that the book was pious in spirit and in excellent agreement with Jewish tradition. His tormentors resolved to burn the book publicly, with ceremonies presided over by their Zaddik and so impressive that the youth would be cured of his evil inclinations once and for all.

With considerable complacency and little wit Gottlober continues to describe how haste and, of course, also the Chasidic love for strong drink—a trait which no Maskilic presentation of this movement fails to mention—caused

Wessely's work to be confused with a book of the same name by the Chasidic Rabbi Nachman of Bratzlav, so that the latter volume was burned while the other was saved. Darkness was vanquished by light; and our author is visibly elated that unreasoning popular superstition claimed as its victim a worthless screed rather than the book of a sage of the German enlightenment.

To-day we would not quite agree with this view. Burning of books, of course, is always vandalism. But were we confronted with the necessity of selecting only one of these works for preservation for posterity we should give preference to the mystic of Bratzlav, beside whose intellectual and literary forcefulness—not to mention the power of his religious genius—even the best which Wessely offers seems second-rate. Gottlober's tale is particularly significant because it has chosen the most important representative of the Western Haskalah and his most Jewish book— a circumstance which reveals all the more clearly how questionable this literature is in comparison with a genuine movement of the Jewish spirit, as exemplified by Chasidism.

Yet one would find no account of the Chasidic contribution in the extant manuals of Hebrew literature. A fact strange and striking for two reasons: first, because Chasidism has attracted a number of notable scholars and men of letters in the course of the past few decades and even has aroused more than purely literary interest. Secondly, because, though one accept the narrow point of view—particularly erroneous in the case of Jewish writing —that *belles-lettres* constitute the sole subject-matter of literary history, one cannot gainsay that in this field also

Chasidism has made some highly original contributions. Rabbi Nachman of Bratzlav, to retain our example, is unquestionably the greatest fabulist among the Jews. No Jewish movement has given rise to a richer or more colorful store of folk-tales, myths and legends. Not only the sacred volumes of the Chasidic doctrine but well-nigh all the popular Chasidic books have been written in Hebrew; the Yiddish publications are mostly very much abridged and diluted translations. Nor should we underestimate the rôle of Chasidism in the development of Hebrew lexicography. For it created, though without conscious intent, a comprehensive terminology of its own for its new religious concepts; and the growth and spread of that terminology among the folk bears weighty testimony to the flexibility and vitality of the Hebrew language.

This neglect of the literary contribution of Chasidism is—to perhaps an even greater extent than the equally unscientific manner in which the totality of latter-day Jewish religious and scholarly writing has been ignored— eloquent proof that our official histories of Hebrew literature still retain the imprint of the Haskalah heritage. They regard the whole of Hebrew letters as equivalent to the literary movement of the enlightenment and to the secular Hebrew writings that followed in its wake. Nowhere have Maskilic evaluations, long outgrown in other intellectual domains, persisted more stubbornly than in the field of literary criticism.

II

We should consider the attitude of the Haskalah toward Chasidism as grounds for grave reproach had not history taught us how often the so-called intellectuals have sinned against humanity—how often they, far more than the unperverted masses, have opposed epoch-making spiritual revolutions with dull hostility. The Haskalah felt itself obliged to seek literary stimulus abroad, quenching its thirst with the stale water of broken cisterns, though sparkling fountains gushed forth near at hand. The new Hebrew literature might have gained incalculably much from the store of Chasidic legends had these had a background of artistic tradition, of a well-developed narrative form. It is the tragedy of these legends that they found no support in artistic forms already completely molded or at least coeval with them—such support as the Buddhist legends received from the Hindu art-fable, or the Franciscan legend from the early Italian *novella*. Hence the priceless ore in the mine of Chasidic legend remained in a crude state.

The adherents of the enlightenment, however, saw only dross and waste rubble there. They could not sense or understand the awkward simplicity, the crude depth of the folk, the uncontrollable vehemence of religious experience, the clumsy attempts to stammer the ineffable. They saw merely the repellent exterior; and because they rejected the irrational and unæsthetic they viewed the entire Chasidic movement as an aberration and a snare, as quackery or, at best, self-delusion. Thus was it judged even by Graetz, who—true to his rational interpretation of Judaism—considered all mysticism the original intellectual sin. Ahron Marcus, that keen-minded automath, was unable to refrain from commenting that it would have been better if Graetz had ignored the last phase of Jewish history as well as the first; having commenced with the crossing of the Jordan he should have stopped before the crossing of the Vistula.

We must realize that apparently every age has but a definite capacity of insight before we can understand the Maskilim, who saw in Chasidism only the uncouth frenzy and ridiculous superstition inevitable in every religious mass movement. We become humbler and more sparing with our reproaches when we know what even a genius of the caliber of Nachman Krochmal—whose mind had grown far beyond the scale of values accepted by the Haskalah—thought of Chasidism. He maintained this attitude despite the fact that he himself, according to the statement of his son, appears to have come of the family of Israel Ba'al Shem, the founder of the Chasidic movement. Krochmal pointed out repeatedly that in its beginnings Chasidism developed only in backward regions:

> in that den of robbers Wallachia, in the waste steppes of the Ukraine and in the villages on the Hungarian frontier. All these are new settlements devoid of tradition, composed of fugitives and exiles from neighboring countries. In the old communities famed for their learning, on the other hand, the Chassidim are a very insignificant factor, cowering like mute dogs unable to bark. . . .

That the first adherents of a doctrine provide no basis for arguments against it—a fact which may be gleaned from the history of all religions—escaped even this born philosophic historian. He regarded the leaders of the Chasidim as low-grade charlatans, and despite his usual aversion to sarcasm satirized their doings. Thus he told, to cite an example, of the wonder-rabbi who had the higher and nether spheres at his command but who none the less was helpless and livid with fear before an ordinary policeman who had mistreated him. Though habitually careful in his choice of words Krochmal described the rabbi as the "rogue and sinner of Berditchev." We hesitate to think that he might have meant the author of the *Kedushath Levi*, the blameless Rabbi Levi Isaac of Berditchev, who was so frequently abused by his antagonists and who even experienced the brutality of the police—though not to such an extent as that great thinker and martyr of Chasidism, Rabbi Shneur Zalman of Ladi, whom his Jewish denouncers twice caused to be incarcerated.

Small wonder, therefore, that the minor lights of the Haskalah revealed even less understanding of Chasidism and with even greater vehemence and malevolence combated its "superstition" in the name of science and civilization. The activities of the Chasidim seem to have inspired but a single form of writing among the Maskilic literati: *difficile est saturam non scribere.* Opposition to Chasidism gave birth to modern Hebrew satire.

Megalle Temirin (The Divulger of Secrets), a satire by Josef Perl (1773-1839), the Galician author and herald of the enlightenment, enjoyed great popularity in its day. This volume, which appeared in 1819, imitates the pious manner of the Chasidic miracle books. It was considered a very successful counterpart to the *epistolæ obscurorum virorum,* to which it claimed to be an addition. A number of Maskilim, indeed, declared that the writer had so accurately struck the tone of folk origin that his satire was accepted by some faithful Chasidim as one of their own books. What is more, the historian Jost used it as his principal source for his account of Chasidism.

The result was much inferior to, say, a historic portrait of Socrates based on Aristophanes alone; for that matter, Perl is not to be mentioned in the same breath with the great Greek satirist. His parody relates the adventures of the Chassid Obadya ben Petachya, presumably the author of the volume. Having in his possession the sacred tomes of the miracle-working Rabbi Adam, the teacher of Rabbi Israel Ba'al Shem, our writer was enabled to render himself invisible and thus to witness undisturbed the secret procedures of the Chasidic conventicles and of the wonder-rabbis, and to unveil their mysteries. Another book by Perl, *Bochen Zaddik* (*The Test of the Righteous*, 1838), parodies the story of the Ba'al Shem's voyage to Palestine and lauds the agricultural efforts of the Jews in Southern Russia. This work is related to and probably influenced by the endeavors of Isaac Baer Levinsohn in the cause of the enlightenment in Russia.

While the work of Levinsohn will be discussed in the next chapter, we may here briefly mention his satiric polemic writings against the Chasidim. This meek and pious man had no capacity for invective and even less poetic fancy; as a result the effect of his satire is one of labored sophistry. But it is highly typical of the feud of the Maskilim against Chasidism. In *'Emek Repha'im* (*The Valley of the Dead*), which like other satires was published under a pseudonym, a somnambulist describes what he has seen in the infernal regions and shocks his listeners with the amazing news that the rabbis who had been known as miracle men and saints are not in heaven, as had been expected, but in hell. One of these wonder-rabbis, seeking to justify himself before his tormentors in

the next world, had told how the naïve need of the masses
for an object of veneration had suggested to him the
assumption of leadership; and he had explained that, pos-
sessing neither Talmudic nor secular learning, he had been
unable to enter any career except that of a Chasidic rabbi,
who had only to pray publicly with wild and frenzied
gesticulations in order to be considered a man of God.
The reproach that the Chasidim were uneducated igno-
ramuses has, indeed, always been hurled at the movement;
this even by the Orthodox foes of the Haskalah, those who
represented the Talmudic and rabbinic traditions and who
have since been styled the *Mithnaggedim,* i.e., "opponents" (of Chasidism).

True literary merit is found only in the satires of Isaac
Erter (1792-1851), a contemporary and compatriot of
Perl who has already been mentioned among the disciples
of Krochmal and from whom Levinsohn took, among
other things, the form of the dream vision—Erter's favorite. That Erter wrote excellently is beyond dispute; his
Hebrew prose writings are some of the finest of the Haskalah period. Yet it is an exaggeration—of which Graetz
and after him others have been guilty—to compare him
with either Heine or Isaiah. For he did not have Heine's
demoniacal wit or felicitous whimsicality, not to mention
his poetic qualities. As for the comparison of merely
clever and correct prose with prophetic utterances—this
does not even merit refutation.

In his satires, which were collected under the title
Hatzofeh Lebeth Israel (*A Watchman unto the House of
Israel*) Erter lashed the absurdities of East European
Jewry, its confused tangle of superstition and scholastic

learning; he spared neither the Mithnagdim nor the Chasidim. When a Lemberg rabbi issued a writ of excommunication against a number of innovators, including Erter, the latter retaliated with a furious satire which, attacking a voluminous tome of the rabbi's, conceded only the title page as his own work and branded the entire book as an example of intellectual thievery. Particularly did he deride the Chasidic angelology and the doctrine of the transmigration of souls, which had been taken over from the Kabbala. In one of his visions the innumerable angels whom, according to Kabbalistic and Chasidic teachings, the prayers of the righteous call into being every hour complain that the reckless creation of new angels by pious Jews is causing heaven to become overcrowded, and voice a demand for birth control. Here Erter very skillfully describes the disputes of the angels in the celestial spheres with unmistakable allusions to the petty quarrels between the various Chasidic sects—quarrels which became more and more prevalent with the progressive degeneration of Chasidism. In his longest and best-known satire Erter uses the doctrine of metempsychosis—which occurs so frequently in popular Chasidic writings—to decry with searing scorn a number of types and abuses characteristic of community life among the East European Jews. A brief extract, from the account of a soul of its experiences in the body of Chasid, will suffice as an example:

> I became a Chasid—a man who drinks brandy like water, who abandons his father and mother, his wife and children to go to his rabbi and imbibe his obscure teachings, to seize the crumbs from his plate with lightning agility. As I

prayed I would leap and run, clap my hands and demean myself like a madman. When I sang the Sabbath and festival hymns all who heard me vowed that both the cormorant and the bittern dwelt in my throat. My cry rose to the heavens—I skipped like a ram on the tables and benches. And when my throat grew dry and my tongue failed for thirst brandy poured into me like water, into my entrails like a rushing stream . . . until, inflamed by the liquor, I myself was consumed by fire, rising as an unsavory burnt offering unto the Lord.

In its next incarnation this soul was a frog, as this animal leaps about and croaks like a Chasid—although it drinks no brandy, only water. . . .

The remaining polemic writings of the Haskalah against Chasidism may be passed over, for they are all inferior to Erter, who himself, indeed, frequently becomes coarse and oversteps the limits of good taste. In the Haskalah novels, including those of Smolenkin, the Chasid is portrayed as stupidity or baseness incarnate; the contemporary feud with the Chasidim is woven even into historical novels of ages long past. When A. Mapu, for example—in his Biblical novel *The Sin of Samaria*—describes the idolatry of northern Israel, the false prophets, and "the drunkards of Ephraim" it is clear that he means the Chasidim also. We know that he intended to attack Chasidism more directly in another novel, of which, however, only fragments have been preserved. This, although in his youth his mother had to resort to force to tear him away from that movement, under whose spell he had fallen, and although his poetic, romantic imagination should have enabled him to perceive more than the ugly surface.

The first to adopt a language other than the official speech of the enlightenment were Hess (1862) in the

West and, a few years later, Zweifel in the East. Moses
Hess, it is true, made only a cursory remark—but one
revealing deep understanding—in his classic of the Jewish
renaissance, *Rom und Jerusalem*. He believed that the
current criticism of his day, while justified in its opposition to some aberrations of Chasidism, failed entirely to
comprehend its true nature and historic significance. As
a socialist he was naturally attracted by the community
spirit of the Chasidim, whose rich and poor help one
another and are equal in the sight of God and of their
Zaddik. And he was convinced that the basic qualities
of a sect capable of such self-denial and fervor must be
something more than coarseness and ignorance. With his
clear vision he saw Chasidism—in contrast to the sancti-
moniousness of a literal faith frozen into superficial forms
—as an instrument for the intensification of the Jewish
spirit whose effect would be incalculable if the Jewish
national movement were to take advantage of it. For he
realized that, unlike the Western reform movement, Chasidism was still instinctive and fed by the living forces of
the Jewish religious spirit, and therefore much more genuine and of far greater portent.

Despite an occasional display of insufficient knowledge
his subtle intuition gives proof that only awakening
national consciousness was able to discover something of
worth in the derided and discredited Chasidic movement.
Too much credit cannot be given Eliezer Z. Zweifel (1815-
1888) for having had the courage to subject the origins
of the Chasidim and of their opponents to a rigid and
unprejudiced examination and in a scholarly book to plead
for a revision of the distorted opinion of Chasidism then

prevalent. How much courage was required for the shaking off of the accepted Haskalah views can be seen from the violence with which the Maskilim attacked Zweifel: at times the priests of unbelief are the most intolerant. He was accused of treason to the cause of the enlightenment. Ch. S. Slonimsky, his colleague at the Rabbinical Seminary of Zitomyr, publicly protested against him, declaring that Zweifel's views were by no means shared by the other members of the faculty and would hardly be able to lead the student body astray. Others interpreted the very name of the dissenter (the German word *Zweifel* means "doubt") as an indication of mental wavering and lack of balance. J. L. Gordon, the poet laureate of the period, refused to believe that Zweifel was serious. Still others made the downright assertion that he had been bribed by the Chasidim.

When he wrote his book, whose first volume appeared in 1868, Zweifel seems to have been fully aware that his new valuations would arouse wrathful objection. The very title reveals his caution and his consideration of prevailing beliefs: *Shalom al Israel* (*Peace unto Israel*). We may see this also from his well-chosen scriptural motto: "I will hear what God the Lord will speak: for He will speak peace unto His people and to His saints (*Chasidim*), that they do not turn again to folly." The book itself speaks with equal reverence of Moses Mendelssohn, the idol of the Haskalah, of the Gaon of Vilna, the genius of Talmudic lore and of Israel Ba'al Shem, the founder of Chasidism. To Zweifel, all three are manifestations of God's will to renew Jewish life. Indeed, the conflicts which they inspired unshackled spiritual life and awakened the latent forces of the popular soul. Only petty minds blinded by partisan hatreds are unable to see that these three are alike heralds of the Lord, that they all serve his commands.

On the whole Zweifel's thought is imbued with a curious mixture of the religious and scientific spirit. It is, indeed, very interesting to trace how his piousness and scientific objectivity combined to bring Zweifel to his recognition of Chasidism and its founder. One destined to exert as fundamental and far-reaching an influence as the Ba'al Shem, he reasoned, must necessarily have been granted the help of God. Or, to use a more scientific mode of expression, so powerful a movement—a movement which, emanating from Podolia and Volhynia at the middle of the eighteenth century, had attracted the Jewry of all Poland as well as of northeastern Hungary and Moldavia by the beginning of the nineteenth and after another fifty years embraced almost half of the Jewish masses— cannot be devoid of positive values, does not permit of a purely negative explanation.

Zweifel's greatest merit lies in his having been the first to state this question rather than in his contribution to the answering of it. The excerpts he so assiduously collected from the writings of both the Chasidim and their opponents are still instructive and highly to be recommended to the student, although the rationalistic approach inevitable, because of the course of the author's evolution, prevented him from gaining insight into the true significance and ultimate mysteries of the movement. This fine scholar, whose style alone is sufficient to assure him of a place of honor in Hebrew letters, also has some other very excellent works to his credit; the recognition that has been accorded him is far less than he deserves.

The subsequent changes in the evaluation of Chasidism will not be discussed here. At the end of the century poets and serious scholars suddenly discovered in it unsuspected beauties and glimpses of fathomless spiritual depths —this at a time when the movement had already reached formal rigidity and was approaching degeneration. It is true, however, that Chasidism embraces a large number of adherents even to-day and in its decline still reveals traces of past grandeur which indicate that it may yet become rejuvenated.

Chasidism found its historian in Simon Dubnow, the enthusiastic biographer of its leaders in S. A. Horodezky. Among the belletrists it inspired several writers of fiction, such as J. L. Peretz, M. J. Berditchewski, Yehuda Steinberg and that greatest of living Hebrew narrators, S. J. Agnon. But its principal champion is Martin Buber, who—with the faithfulness of the poet, thinker and spiritually kindred mystic—has revealed and transfigured the soul of Chasidism.

III

At the present time Chasidism constitutes the last link in the long chain of Jewish mysticism, the most recent historic manifestation of an uninterrupted tradition whose beginnings probably extend to the dawn of Jewish life, to the apocalyptic portions of the Old Testament. Official Jewish religion and philosophy have systematically combated Jewish mysticism through nearly all the centuries; but they have not succeeded in forcing the popular yearning for God to yield an inch of its ground. As Chasidism found its antagonists in both the Maskilim and the Mithnagdim, so the Kabbala—the mystical tradition of Judaism—was almost constantly confronted with two other forces of the Jewish spirit: religious orthodoxy, whose primary concern was the Law, and rationalism, representing the viewpoint of philosophy—a term long synonymous with Aristotle. Both rejected the mystic lore of the people with equal vehemence, though for different reasons. The heritage of these two hostilities is to be found among modern Jewish scholars, who still, as their personal inclinations may dictate, retain the one or the other motive for objection. They have long attempted to disavow the Jewish tendency toward mysticism and to discount its manifestations as a lamentable reaction, temporary at best, against the rule of lucid reason. When the unbroken historical continuity of this "aberration" of the Jewish spirit could no longer be doubted, they made efforts to prove it a strange plant in the vineyard of Israel, of Iranian, Hellenic or Albigensian origin. Some, indeed, went so far as to trace Chasidism not only to pietism—of which its adherents doubtless had never heard—but even to the doctrines of the Mongolian Buddhists. All this, however, has cast no more doubt upon the originality of Jewish mysticism than Assyriology has cast upon the Bible or—to take a more familiar example—than modern students of literature with their search for plagiarisms have cast upon the genius of Shakespeare.

Although it presented a fundamental revolution of Jewish life Chasidism took over the entire tradition of Judaism without ever questioning its validity in the slightest, but illuminating it from within and stimulating it anew. The language of the Chasidim was that of the guardians of the Law and of the masters of the Kabbala, but imbued with new meaning, and with subjective force. As the new movement felt no impulse toward making even the slightest change in the cyclopean array of Jewish ritual— the introduction of the Sephardic mode of prayer being the most radical innovation of which it may be accused— so it was also based entirely upon the cosmological theory of the esoteric doctrines previously prevailing. Yet in its elaboration of both the Law and the Kabbala its procedure was not eclectic, but highly individual and independent. Particularly important for an understanding of Chasidism is its modification of the traditional cosmology of the Kabbala.

If one discounts historical development and changes one may give an approximate and fairly suggestive outline of that fundamental content of the Kabbala which determined Chasidism. The root of all Kabbalistic speculation is the question: How can one conceive of finite creatures beside that highest Infinite Being Who sums up the total of existence? How can one conceive the temporal and imperfect beside the Eternal and Perfect One Who alone exists truly? How can the world exist beside God? The primary answer to this question is given by the Kabbalistic doctrine of the *emanation* of the spheres—or the world—from God. (Some Kabbalistic ideas suggest rather the term *effulguration*—a distinction that need not detain us at present.) As water pours from a vessel so the world flowed forth from God. It was God's wish to become less inscrutable, to be known and loved. He desired the free subsistence of something unlike Him that would be able to recognize and love Him in freedom. And He released the world. Once it had emanated from the divine oneness its development was limited only by its own endurance. Set free, it flowed over, wave rising upon wave, sphere rushing out of sphere, world towering over world. This the Kabbala calls "the breaking of the vessels." Unable to contain divine abundance the world burst from its bounds and flowed forth to the ultimate limit of all transformation, the objects of sensual perception in time and space. At this uttermost limit the divine billow broke at last: Nothing flows forth from matter—it no longer has the power of emanation.

Thus God and the world are essentially identical, "like the snail whose garment is part of its body." Evil as such does not exist, but only diminishing degrees of good. The imperfect merely cloaks and confines the perfect. Hence the Kabbala calls the powers of evil *kelipoth*—casings that enclose the divine. As creation receded farther and farther from its original source it became more and more turbid and confused, fell more and more into lower and less spiritual regions separated from God by ever thicker coverings. Its outermost and densest shell is the physical world we inhabit, which is therefore also called the "world of casings."

This overflowing of the world has, so to speak, caused God to be split into two parts, which, however, are still one: the Divine Being—*Elohuth*—which has withdrawn beyond the ken of its creatures, and the Glory of God— *Shekhinah*, literally "indwelling," the divine splendor that permeates the world—which is a prisoner in material

objects. Entangled in the physical world, the glory of
God is forced to wander about in what the Kabbala terms
the "exile of the *Shekhinah*." Not until the age of deliverance, in the "world of perfection"—'*olam hatikkun*—shall
God be reunited with His Glory that inhabits the world;
for then shall the world return to its fountainhead.

The Kabbala teaches nothing less than that this deliverance of God can be brought about by man and by man
alone. Only he is capable of causing to flow back the
divine stream that has been sent forth, of making "the
Jordan well upward." For man occupies the central position, constitutes the connecting link between the worlds;
he is composed of both spirit and matter, of both nucleus
and casing, and can decide for either. In him alone the
struggle between good and evil is no aimless interaction
but conscious activity. Only he is free to choose between
the higher and the lower, between strengthening the power
of light and increasing the power of darkness, between
bringing the *Shekhinah* nearer to its source and banishing
it farther. It was for his freedom that God released and
created the world; from him alone did God desire free
recognition and love. The purpose and meaning of all
creation is comprehended in man.

Man alone is able to do that of which none of even the
higher worlds is capable—to give the impulse for the
transfiguration into the '*olam hatikkun*. It is true that he
can only begin it; but that is his task—to provide the
impulse, nothing more. This is the meaning of the first
word of the Bible. "At the beginning" is construed:
"For the sake of its beginning" God created the world.
When the motion arises "below," when the impulse ema-

nates from there and the reflux commences, divine grace will respond.

That this did not occur long ago is due to the course of human history, which repeats the history of the world—a biogenetic principle, as it were, of the Kabbala. To the "breaking of the vessels" there corresponds the fall of man. The first, original soul contained within itself all future souls and was as stainless as its Creator. But when man was found wanting, the souls were dimmed and burdened with "casings." Since then sparks of baseness have flown into holy souls and sparks of holiness into evil souls. The soul of the messiah, however, cannot descend from the realm of the unborn into life until all the souls and all the fragments that sprang from the first soul and that now are scattered in the world of casings are purified of their turbidness and come back to their source. This purification of errant souls can take place in two ways: through *gilgul,* or rotation, and through *'ibbur,* or impregnation. *Gilgul* means the entry of a wandering soul into a body at the moment of its birth to remain there until its death. The abode of such a soul may be the body of a man, but not necessarily; it may also be a stone or a lower animal, a stream or a plant. The souls inhabiting such bodies may rise through self-purification or fall into ever lower spheres through new sins.

Because this course might take too long we have the other, *'ibbur.* Even though he already possess a soul a man may at any moment of his life receive another or several others which form a union with him because they are akin to him—i.e., because they sprang from the same emanation of primeval man. This may occur for the benefit of the advenient soul, which in one of its earlier incarnations may have left uncompleted some task that it now desires to finish; after the accomplishment of its task it leaves the body it had entered. Or else the impregnation may take place that the man may be fortified at moments of weakness, that the new soul may help him in his rise and purification. Rotation and impregnation, therefore, cleanse the souls clouded by trespasses and exiled to the world of casings; after their period of wandering is over they are enabled to return to their sacred fountainhead. Then shall the Kingdom of God commence. Here the Chasidim use the simile of the prince who does not allow the banquet to be served until the last guest has arrived.

As the course of the cosmos is repeated in the history of man so it finds another counterpart in the history of Israel. When the overflowing vessels burst the *Shekhinah* was forced into exile; after the fall of man it accompanied him in his expatriation from Paradise. After every defection on the part of Israel the *Shekhinah* also goes into banishment, into the *Galuth,* and together with Israel awaits the hour of redemption. The dispersal of Israel over the entire earth and among the seventy nations which inhabit it has a definite purpose, however; that the holy souls and fragments of souls which have strayed to those regions and among those peoples may be delivered and purified. Once this "mission" is completed the messianic kingdom shall commence and the *Shekhinah* return home from the triple exile into which it was cast by the sins of the world, of man and of Israel. The distress of the world, of mankind and of the Jewish people shall come to an end when the universe shall have regained its divinity.

A WONDER-WORKER

To Isaac Lurya of Safed (1534-1572), who despite the influence of the older Kabbalistic doctrine upon him contributed much to the evolution of this cosmology, we owe the endeavor to make the cosmic process here outlined dependent upon the actions of a few individuals. According to him the unconditional devotion of men who dedicate themselves to the cause of salvation, who practice the utmost asceticism—fasting, immersion in water, remaining awake through the night, ecstatic concentration and absolute love for everything and everyone—can cause what an old ordinance prohibits, the "hastening of the end." All souls would then be cleansed at a single stroke, and the soul of the messiah be drawn down by force from the realm of the unborn into life.

This doctrine demanded austere self-denial, torturous penance and mortification. The apostle of the Luryan Kabbala, Chaim Vital Calabrese, prescribed, for example, that every week one must fast two days and nights, without interruption except for one exceedingly frugal meal after which one's head must be sprinkled with ashes; there must be ashes on the bread that is eaten and tears in the water that is drunk, as it is written: "I have eaten ashes like bread, and mingled my drink with weeping." He who sins must make appropriate atonement. Thus for example one who is guilty of anger must expiate with a course of one hundred and fifty-one fasts, an amount corresponding to the numerical value of the letters which make up the Hebrew of "anger."

Ever greater numbers of despairing zealots were drawn toward the ascetic Kabbala; this because of the cruel massacres of Ukrainian Jewry, because of the tragic mock-

ery of the great messianic movement which bore the name
of Sabbetai Zebi—and which would never have reached
such grave proportions had it not been for the enormous
influence of the Luryan Kabbala—and because of the hopeless misery of the Jews caught in the anarchy of the declining Polish kingdom.   Moreover, the Luryan mysticism
incorporated all the religious regulations of Talmudic
Judaism in its fanatic asceticism and, indeed, made these
commands more drastic wherever possible, so that it was
not involved in the otherwise continuous strife between
the Law and mystic lore.

One is astounded at what the philosopher Salomon
Maimon (1752-1800) writes in his autobiography of
the ascetic excesses of his Polish compatriots even in his
own day. He describes how some, after having practiced every sort of self-flagellation, emulate the errant
Glory of God by "going into exile"; clad in sackcloth they
wander from place to place, refusing food and drink even
when they are faint with hunger, until their strength is
exhausted and—alone and unseen, far from home—they
collapse in death.

An asceticism so powerful and so chaotically meaningless could not but be accompanied by spiritual frenzy and
derangement, from which the most fantastic sects derived
sinister gain. In Poland followers of Sabbetai Zebi continued longer and more persistently than elsewhere to
cherish their belief, convinced that he would soon be resurrected and that his conversion to Islam had a hidden
significance. Some even taught that a pretense of conversion to Catholicism, corresponding to Sabbetai's embrac-
ing of the Moslem faith, was a prerequisite of salvation.

In 1759 Jacob Frank and his adherents actually took this course. The debauched orgies of this sect—which furnish another proof that asceticism and lasciviousness go hand in hand in certain periods—reflect the spiritual decadence and the wretchedness of the age.

The life and work of the founder of Chasidism fall into this period shaken by utter contrasts. Israel of Miedzyborz (*circa* 1700-1760) was called by the traditional name of the miracle-worker: *Ba'al Shem,* the master of the Name, of the magic Name of God; by adding the adjective *tov* —good—to this appellation he gave it a new significance, that of a man of good repute, of one who enjoyed the confidence of the people. A simple villager, held in but slight esteem by the rabbis because of his lack of Talmudic learning and his thaumaturgic practices, he is none the less one of the pivotal figures in the religious history of the eighteenth century.

The Ba'al Shem took over the magnificent Kabbalistic cosmology according to which man is responsible for the fate of God in the world. But he changed the sign of this cosmology, so to speak, giving it the form of joyful affirmation of life. For he taught not retirement from the world but the principle of loving the world in God, not mortification but the hallowing of all passions, not asceticism but delight in God. We might almost say that this very proclamation of joy as the sole true form of worship—following upon the excessive tension of asceticism and the centuries of rigidly austere adherence to the Law —must have generated a feeling of relief from an oppressive burden.

Our relics of the Ba'al Shem, who never wrote down his

doctrine, consist of only a few letters. Two of them very severely condemn fasting and self-castigation as iniquitous sins invented by Satan, whose intention it is to afflict man and alienate him from God. To his disciple and literary heir, Jacob Josef of Polennoye, who had ventured into the dark regions of extreme asceticism, the Ba'al Shem wrote:

> I received the letter indited by your unsullied hand and saw from its first lines that Your Highness believes mortification necessary. This shocked me to my innermost soul. By the counsel of God and His *Shekhinah* I order you to abandon such dangerous practices, which are but the outcome of melancholia and depression. The Glory of God reposes not where there is mourning but only where joy in His dictates prevails. For it has been explicitly commanded: "Thou shalt not hide thyself from thine own flesh."

The story of how this man and Rabbi Dov Bär—an even greater disciple, who continued the teachings of the Ba'al Shem—were converted to a more cheerful worship of God constitutes one of the finest portions of Chasidic tradition.

Flagellation, taught the Ba'al Shem, is incapable of tearing up evil by the root, but can merely suppress it for the time being. Joy, on the other hand, finds a divine spark, be it ever so small, even at the root of evil; and with the aid of this spark evil can be permanently abolished. This process the Ba'al Shem styled *hamtakath hadinim:* The commandments are "sweetened" at their source—they lose their iron severity, doff their austere mask, poise for flight to heaven on wings of joy. For evil is but the lowest degree of good, veiling and obstructing it. Good is held captive in the material casings; but if it endures and asserts itself these casings open and are merged in it.

The knowledge of the power of good and the unreality of evil should cause man to rejoice; for he is able to dissolve evil in good, to liberate the fallen divine sparks from their imprisonment in matter. No need for the unusual or unexpected obtains here. Every action, however ordinary or profane, can express worship of God if its spirit is one of consecration and reverence. One can best serve God by performing the simplest duties of everyday life with utter truthfulness and purity of mind. The Ba'al Shem liked to recall Enoch, the son of Jared, who was only a cobbler but who, with every thrust of his awl as he sewed together top-leather and sole, united God with His Glory that inhabits the world. For this he was raised up to the powerful demiurge Metatron, the "Prince of the Countenance."

Not the action as such, but the purity and hallowedness of its intent are decisive. He who communes with God as he prays and sings, as he eats and speaks, as he conducts his business and takes the prescribed plunge-bath, raises the fallen divine sparks and brings the errant *Shekhinah* nearer its fountainhead. For in itself no action, however mean and meaningless it may appear, is profane or petty. If it is accompanied by sanctification of the soul every deed is holy, every act leads to God.

> Let there be no sadness in him who is traveling and therefore unable to pray and study as he has been accustomed. God wishes us to serve Him in all ways. Perhaps He has sent thee abroad to enable thee to serve Him in another

manner—by speaking to men or listening to their utterances—which thy devotion may exalt to worship of God.

Similarly man should suppress none of his impulses but use them in the service of God. When a pious man desires an article of food it is because the divine sparks imprisoned in that food—the sparks which give it fragrance and flavor—want him to release them. Thus Rabbi Sussya of Annopol (d. 1800) explained the Scripture which says of Abraham that he stood *above* the angels who were his guests; this because he was familiar with the sanctification of the partaking of food, which was unknown to them. Sparks of divine splendor dwell even in sin, else it would be unable to subsist or to move even the smallest member. "And what are the sparks that dwell in sin? Repentance. At the hour of thy repentance and of thy turning away from sin the sparks that were in it are raised to the upper regions." To employ the metaphor of Rabbi Dov Bär, sin contains repentance as the olive contains oil. One of the later Zaddikim, Moshe Leb of Sassow (d. 1807), of whose altruism stirring reports have come to us, liked to say that even atheism contained an element of good: "For when a man comes to thee and asks thy help thou shalt not give him trifling aid and piously say: 'Have faith and pray to God in thy need.' Instead thou shalt deal as if none but thou alone were there to help him."

Even the opponents of the movement admitted, indeed, that the Chasidim succeeded in bringing rich and poor together in a community characterized by a mutual readiness to help and in which the preëminence of property, while not actually abrogated, had lost much of its privilege and prestige. As the commandment to love one's fellow men received a deeper significance in the cosmology of the Chasidim so it gained more intense reality in their life. When a father complained to the Ba'al Shem that his son had forsaken God, and asked what he should do, he was told: "Love him more than ever." It is as if the deficiencies in the world's economy of forces could be counterbalanced only by an increased amount of love. Rabbi Shmelke of Nikolsburg (d. 1778) was once asked by a pupil: "How can I fulfill the commandment to love my fellow man if he does me harm?" The rabbi replied:

> Thou must understand the command aright: Love thy neighbor as one who is like thyself. For all souls are one. Each is a spark of the first soul, which permeates them all as thine own soul permeates every part of thy body. It may sometimes happen that thine own hand inadvertently strike thee. But wouldst thou take a stick and chastise thy hand for its heedlessness, and thus add to thy pain? It is the same when thy neighbor, whose soul is one with thine, because of insufficient understanding does thee harm; shouldst thou retaliate it would be thou who wouldst suffer.

For Shmelke's pupil Moshe Leb, who has been mentioned above, this doctrine became the instinct which guided his life. He sat at the bedside of all the sick boys of his city, nursing and tending them. Once he said: "He who cannot suck the matter from the boils of a child sick with the plague has not yet gone halfway up the height of love for his fellow men."

Particularly fervent is the Ba'al Shem in his doctrine of the value of prayer. Though all everyday acts lead to the fountainhead of the world, he taught, no road can exceed that of prayer in purity and perfection. He who

prays with ardor—*hithlahabuth*—not in penance or torment but joyfully and with exaltation, brings closer
together the spheres that have drifted apart and unites
God with His creation. The most beautiful miracles of
Chasidic legend illustrate the power of hallowed prayer.
Thus when the Ba'al Shem prayed in an open field one
Sabbath the cattle grazing there raised their front legs and
stood on their two hind legs, in the posture of man. So
powerfully beatific was his prayer that even the beasts were
filled with passionate longing to return to God.

As the merit of the actions of men is determined not
by the deed itself but by the consecration of the spirit
behind it, so the worth of prayer depends not upon the
words employed nor on the erudition of him who prays
but solely upon the accumulated force of devotion. Frequent use has been made in our literature of the Chasidic
tale of the ignorant peasant boy who on the Day of Atonement—seized by a powerful urge to worship, yet unable
to pray—committed the sin of blowing his shepherd's
pipe, to the violent dismay of his father and of the congregation. The Ba'al Shem, however, cut short his own
prayer, saying: "On the wings of his prayer this boy has
borne all our lame prayers to the palace of God." Then
there is the even more beautiful legend of the little farmer
boy who, having been left an orphan at an early age, was
unable to read, but who had inherited a large, heavy
prayer book from his parents. On the Day of Atonement
he brought it into the synagogue, laid it on the stand and,
weeping, cried out: "Lord of creation! I do not know
how to pray, I do not know what to say—I give Thee the
entire prayer book!"

God loves not so much the man of learning and intelligence as the man of simple mind who artlessly and confidently puts all his faith in heaven. Rabbi Nachman of Bratzlav used this simile: "As a father rejoices when his son makes his first halting steps and finds delight in him although he cannot walk, so the Holy One, blessed be He, finds delight in every one in Israel who endeavors to fulfil a commandment." Just as Chasidism deprived wealth of its preëminence it also removed learning from the even higher position it had held among the Jews for so many centuries. The worth of a man is determined not by his knowledge—whether of the Talmud or of the Kabbala—but by the purity and sincerity of his prayer, by his nearness to God. The untutored masses, which heretofore had felt worthless and abashed before the unquestioned intellectual aristocracy of the scholars, were now suddenly liberated of that humiliating contrast and thrown upon their own merit and dignity. The gospel of joy, of the consecration of everyday life and of the nearness of the simple common man to God made Chasidism a popular movement which neither the disdain of the enlightenment nor the excommunications of orthodoxy could stay. Its doctrine spread with the fiery, liberating forcefulness of divine revelation.

Into the life of the least of men it brought echoes and glimpses of another world, of another causality of events, which helped him bear the humiliations of his daily life. For this life is but an illusion; in truth the poorest man of Israel is intrinsically a helper of God. The aspect which determined the success of Chasidism was not the new element in its teaching; this it had, essentially, taken over from the Kabbala. But it penetrated the masses, which its predecessor had failed to do. Of the exalted Kabbalistic cosmology that had been limited to a few chosen spirits it made a religious folk-movement, a reality of community life.

Chasidism did not evade the messianic impulse. But it relieved the yearning for messianic redemption of the fierce impatience and hysterical frenzy which, in passionate expectation of the ultimate goal, regarded the present time and place as empty and meaningless. Chasidism taught that man may approach God at every point of his existence and in all the events of his ordinary life; thus it cast the splendor of future salvation over the period of earthly life and illuminated the soul with confidence and serenity. In the earlier Kabbala the worship of God was but a means to an end. In Chasidism joy in God almost became the purpose and goal in itself.

The position of the Holy Land as the central point of the Chasidic doctrine of redemption is perhaps even more personal than in earlier Jewish mysticism. Tradition tells us how the Ba'al Shem felt a powerful urge to go to *Erez Israel* and how at the threshold of the Holy Land mysterious forces compelled him to turn back. His work was waiting for him—his new congregation and doctrine could not spare him so soon. But even in the lifetime of the Ba'al Shem his disciple and brother-in-law, Rabbi Gerson of Kutov, migrated to Palestine; to the correspondence of this Rabbi Gerson, incidentally, we owe the most detailed and valuable of the Ba'al Shem's letters. After the master's death two of the disciples who had been closest to him went to Palestine, and in 1777 they were followed by a group of three hundred Chasidim under the leadership of Rabbi Menachem Mendel of Vitebsk; these settled in the ancient Kabbalistic city of Safed, and later in Tiberias. The great-grandson of the Ba'al Shem, Rabbi Nachman of Bratzlav—who felt it to be his vocation to counteract the incipient decay of Chasidism and who therefore had less right than anyone else to abandon his followers—desired at least to receive the blessing of that holy soil which he believed to be the source of faith and the gate to heaven. Refusing to be held back by any consideration whatsoever, he was almost heartless in his behavior to his own family, whom he gave into the care of charitable strangers; in order to obtain the money required for the journey he sold all the furnishings of his home. Upon his return he forbade the writing down of any of his former teachings: for his true life and his true doctrine had begun only in *Erez Israel.* The liturgy of the Bratzlav Chasidim includes a moving prayer which petitions for that genuine yearning for the Holy Land which overcomes all obstacles and leaves one no rest until one has trod on consecrated ground. To the other Chasidim also Palestine meant more than a mere pious wish; probably Horodezky is right when he says that the majority of Jewish pilgrims to Zion in the last century came from the ranks of the Chasidim.

Mention must also be made of the decline of Chasidism, which eventually degenerated into narrow sectarianism and brought it into close correspondence to the picture its Maskilic opponents drew of it. It has been rightly pointed out that the germs of the degeneration to which it would soon fall prey lurked in the fundamental tenets of Chasidism. The aim of Chasidism was to become a movement of the masses; but the sublime *ethos* which it taught and the force of unalloyed spiritual concentration which it demanded were beyond the powers of the majority. According to a principle resembling that of Ph. J. Spener—with whose name the Ba'al Shem most probably was unfamiliar and whose aim it was to preserve the spirit of Pietism by means of an *ecclesiola in ecclesia*—the life of the Chasidic Zaddik was to present to his congregation an example of absolute holiness. While Chasidism was guided by men of deepest fervor and forceful leadership the masses still echoed something of the richness and purity of their spirit. But when, as happens in every successful movement, the reward of the leader changed from martyrdom to material comfort, his position began to be abused and Chasidism suffered a sharp decline.

But in the brief period of its purity—less than half a century—it fathered succeeding generations of disciples and their pupils which impelled Buber to say that no other religious movement has to its credit so great a number of independent personalities arising in such rapid succession.

IV

Chasidic literature falls into two principal categories: the writings which record Chasidic doctrine, and popular books. The latter are regarded as of small importance, while the former are considered sacred. It is the tragedy of Chasidism that either its greatest spirits felt no impulse to write—perhaps because they were born leaders

and teachers—or else the many duties with which the
new movement burdened them left them no time for literary pursuits. The doctrines currently ascribed to the
founder of Chasidism are largely derived from very incomplete notations made by his pupils. Only one who
knows of the inevitable discrepancy between what a teacher
says and what his students understand him to have said,
can fully comprehend the inadequacy of such sources.
The story goes that at the sight of a written record of his
oral teaching the Ba'al Shem once exclaimed: "I have not
spoken a single word of this!"

The first Chasidic author was the master Talmudist
Rabbi Jacob Joseph of Polennoye (d. 1782), a disciple of
the Ba'al Shem. Rabbi Jacob Joseph wrote his books—
the first of which, *Toledoth Jacob Joseph* (1780), is regarded as especially authoritative—as commentaries on
the Bible; and this determined the type of almost the
entire literature of Chasidic lore. His record of the Ba'al
Shem's utterances, introduced by the formula *shama'ti mi
mori,* "I heard from my teacher," is still revered with
worshipful awe by the masses and generally recognized as
the most authentic source of the Ba'al Shem's doctrine.
One wonders, however, whether the rabbi may not have
been too erudite to preserve with simple faithfulness the
master's voice. In the history of Chasidim, the significance of Rabbi Jacob Joseph's books is more polemic than
constructive: they are defiant in nature, endeavoring to
confute the rabbinic authorities with argument and satire
in order to clear the way for the young and persecuted
movement.

The fine work of developing Chasidic thought and

training great leaders to succeed him was done by the most important of the Ba'al Shem's disciples, Rabbi Dov Bär of Miedzyrzecze (Mesritch) called the "Great *Maggid*," or itinerant preacher (d. 1772). Even Rabbi Jacob Joseph was forced to admit, though unwillingly at first, that the *charisma* of the Master lived on in him, and to concede to him the leadership of the movement. He, it is true, was too gifted a teacher to be able to write, although he yearned acutely for the permanence of the written word. Besides, he found sufficient occupation in the storms and worries and incipient expansion of the movement which was the center of such violent contention. As a result his own formulations have been brought down to us only in unreliable records by his pupils. But his philosophic legacy was taken over by independent disciples through whom his doctrines reached further development and depth.

I shall mention but two of these: Rabbi Menachem Mendel of Vitebsk (d. 1788), who emigrated to Palestine and whose posthumous collection of lectures and letters, *Peri Ha-aretz* (The Fruit of the Land) continued the Maggid's fundamental concept of the omnipresence of God, Who is to be found in the soul of all things; and the even more independent Rabbi Shneur Zalman of Ladi (d. 1813), the founder of the Lithuanian branch of Chasidism whose name, *ChaBaD*, was derived from the initials of the three highest of the ten *sephiroth*, or spheres, which according to the Kabbala emanate from God: *chokhma, bina* and *da'ath*—wisdom, reason and knowledge. The name itself clearly indicates the fundamental tendency of this school: its aim was to restore to rabbinic study its authority as the way to God. The school was both a product of the rationalistic strain of Lithuanian Jewry and a conscious adaptation to it. Yet—surely not because of this—Rabbi Shneur Zalman's book *Tanya* is perhaps the most felicitous and concise of all presentations of Chasidism.

As for popular Chasidic books—the most famous is the first of them, which determined the essential character of all the rest. It is a volume of miraculous tales and legends about the Ba'al Shem, entitled *Shivche Ha-Besht;* (*The Praises of the Ba'al Shem*); its first edition, which appeared in 1815, has been followed by innumerable reprints. The book was published anonymously. It was compiled by a son-in-law of the Ba'al Shem's disciple and scribe. The book is poorly composed—an ancient failing of the Semites—indiscriminate in choice and vulgar in style to boot, it is a miscellany of the legends about the Ba'al Shem which sprang up so luxuriously in the half century after his death. The fervent response engendered to this book, coupled with the hero worship with which the Ba'al Shem's successors were regarded, gave rise to a vast number of similar stories concerning the lives and works of his disciples and their followers. These tales were conceived not in the brain of a conscious artist but in the rude, inarticulate mass mind. They are quite primitive and devoid of form; yet in all their clumsiness and crudity they bear witness to the rebirth of mythical lore among the Jews.

That Chassidim should provide fertile ground for artistic mythopœic faculties was manifestly inevitable. Its cosmology, which ascribed to man influence upon things eternal, caused every event to be invested with mythic quality: to be a part of the symbolic cosmic process and to affect the destiny of God. As a result Chasidism has given birth to an abundance of myths, legends, folk tales as well as stories and anecdotes, all of which tell of man as the adjutant of God. They rank among the most individual and powerful creations of the Diaspora. Unfortunately their lack of polished literary form has deprived them of the prestige of works of art. Moreover, the religious sincerity of the Chasidim was accompanied by an undisguised dislike of art, an aversion to careful, conscious, elegant writing.

A learned man who partook of the Sabbath meal at the home of Rabbi Baruch, the grandson of the Ba'al Shem, said to his host: "Let us now hear you talk of your doctrine—you speak so beautifully!" "May I be struck dumb ere I speak beautifully!" was Rabbi Baruch's reply; and he said nothing more. Such resentment at æsthetic classification is a thoroughly Jewish reaction. This heritage of distaste for art is perceptible even in Rabbi Israel of Ruzyn (d. 1850), whose life and speech were no longer naïve, whose similes and aphorisms betoken conscious polish. He cited this passage from the Bible: "An altar of earth thou shalt make unto me . . . and if thou wilt make me an altar of stone, thou shalt not build it of hewn stone: for if thou lift up thy tool upon it, thou hast polluted it." The altar of earth Rabbi Israel interpreted as the altar of silence, which is more pleasing to God than aught else; but if the altar be constructed of words these must be unhewn.

Accordingly the literary historian must, in his consideration of Chasidism, keep in mind that these people were concerned with something quite other than art and literature even when they entered those domains. We are told not only that the Ba'al Shem spoke in sublime similes —like all primary religious figures—but also that he was able to fascinate the masses with his tales. Tradition adds that these tales were such that everyone heard in them a personal message which was to shape his entire life, although they addressed themselves to all. The tales which have come down in his name are, indeed, charming in their simplicity and marvelous in their fantasy. Their purpose, however, is almost invariably other than artistic. This may be illustrated by an example:

A woman who had long yearned in vain for motherhood at last gave birth to a son; but after two years of happiness she lost the child. Thereupon the Ba'al Shem told the weeping mother the story of a childless king in a distant land who had vainly consulted all his magicians on how he might secure an heir to his throne. Finally one of them advised him to forbid the Jews of his realm to exercise their faith; for only the prayers born of their despair would be able to move God to give him a son. The king issued the prohibition. The pious community was shaken with grief and terror—the dreadful cries of the Jews rose to heaven. Then one of the transfigured souls in Paradise was seized with compassion and came before God, offering to return to the nether spheres as the son of the king. The prince was born; but because his soul was supernal he stood so high above all men that his father could find no teachers who would be able to do him justice—until a stranger instructed him in the

Jewish faith and he, burning with holy fervor, abandoned the palace and became a Jew. All this is told in colorful and imaginative detail; but in a version that has manifestly been mutilated and vulgarized. When, after the prince's death, the soul whose compassion had moved it to sacrifice itself for Israel stood before the divine tribunal only a trifling charge was brought against it: that it had spent the first years of its life on earth amid the pomp and worldly vanity of the royal court. In order to atone it would have to descend to earth once more, to be nursed for two years by a pious Jewess. The story closes with the Ba'al Shem's words to the sorrowing mother: "Dost thou, pious woman, regret having nourished a sainted soul for two years?"

Such is the atmosphere in which Chasidic tales were woven. They are not intentionally narrative fiction but a pious, ecstatic utterance of personal miraculous experience. This is the case even with the most gifted maker of Chasidic tales, Rabbi Nachman of Bratzlav (d. 1810), who is the greatest story-teller the Jews have produced so far. Unlike his great-grandfather this quaint thinker and visionary conceived his fables not to relieve the distress of the people but as a vestment for his doctrines. Although his motive was to teach, his stories grew beyond their purpose, losing themselves in an overflowing abundance of vivid invention and fanciful detail that causes both author and hearer to forget the didactic aim. I cite as an example his two most famous tales, *The Master of Prayer,* and *The Seven Beggars.* These are complex stories in which fable is born from fable, imagery is framed in imagery; convincing in their concreteness, most audacious in their fantasy and ennobled by a profound symbolism.

Unfortunately these stories also have come down to us in an exceedingly distorted, incomplete and inartistic version—a fate shared by all the finest productions of Chasidism. As in its cosmology the vessels of the universe —unable to contain the divine abundance—burst, so our records of Chasidic doctrine and legend are but mutilated fragments, "sparks" of the divine, debased by "casings" born of chaotic confusion. Yet even in their mean garb they tell of the beauty and fire which once animated them and which still are latent in them, awaiting artistic "deliverance." They are the raw material for a new legendary epic, a Jewish *Gilgamesh* that is waiting for its poet.

CHAPTER VII

A SAINT AND A SATIRIST

Vilna, my famed grandmother, city and mother in
   Israel,
Jerusalem of the Exile, thou hast comforted an eastern
   people in the north. . . .
Even thy drawers of water were drawn from the source
   of the great in Torah.
Every wall is soaked in tradition, in the odor of Sabbath
   cooking. . . .

                                          Z. SHNËUR.

IT is related of Napoleon that when he beheld the predominantly Jewish city of Vilna, he was the first to call it the "Jerusalem of Lithuania." And truly, Vilna is an old, venerable "city and mother in Israel," saturated with Jewish traditions and memories of Jewish deeds of the spirit. The life-stories of her most eminent sons have been assembled in a book by S. J. Fuenn, and the genius of the place sung by Z. Schnëur in a magnificent poem whose introductory lines I have set at the head of this chapter.

Geographic conditions in Lithuania bred a very distinct type of Jew differing sharply from the types of other lands, one not without consciousness of its own superiority: the man of intellect, sober, scholarly, austerely logical, rejecting with disgust all vague emotions. The Lithuanian Jew is known and feared for his "guter Kopf," which the Latin would render *felicis cerebri*. He loves plain, direct, keen thoughts, and even in poetry prefers curbed, ordered utterance. So that it was not only the ban imposed by the Gaon, but an innate, rational-skeptical attitude of mind which made the Lithuanian Jew the outspoken opponent of Chasidism, the *Mithnagged,* as if by predetermination. He could not become enthusiastic over the illusion and wonder-filled world of Zaddikism like the credulous Jew of the Ukraine, whose belief in the miraculous powers of the rabbi could not be shaken by any inconvenient reality: when, as the story goes, the great fire which his Zaddik had envisaged in a distant city did not materialize, the Chasid was in no wise daunted; even though there were no conflagration, just think how wide was the *rebbe's* range of vision! So easy of belief the Lithuanian Jew is not. He is hard-headed, shrewd, a scorner; as the folk-jest has epitomized him, the born *epikores.*

This native clarity of mind should have predisposed the Lithuanian Jews in particular toward the Haskalah which, having sprung from rationalism, claimed that it could base everything upon the intellect. And yet no achievements or personalities of real greatness accrued to the movement in this numerically superior Jewry. No figure arose of the rank of a Mendelssohn or an S. D. Luzatto, not to mention a Krochmal. That this circumstance does not tell against Lithuanian Jewry, but rather against the Haskalah movement itself, is proven through the Gaon of Vilna, Rabbi Elijah, the last great genius of classical rabbinism, before whose greatness and power of personality the whole of the Russian Haskalah fades into vapid insignificance.

Though standing on the threshold of the new day and a contemporary of Mendelssohn's, Rabbi Elijah (1720-1797) was still a wholly autochthonous and authentic product of the Jewish folk-spirit. Untouched by foreign influences—he commanded no language but Hebrew—and thus much more the legitimate representative of Rabbinical Judaism than even the great theologians of the Middle Ages, who were not uninfluenced by the Greek-Arabic civilization, in the eighteenth century this giant of

the spirit bears witness to the still inexhaustible abundance
of traditional Judaism, as well as to the profuse vitality
of Lithuanian Jewry. All alone and quite independently,
relying solely upon inner Jewish sources, he developed
principles of critical-scientific cognition of such severity
and discipline that, compared with them, the intellectual
level, the thought and the writing of the Maskilim seem
nothing but clumsy trifling.

Wholly uninfluenced by the German Haskalah, in fact
before its appearance, this great steward of the rabbinical
heritage demanded the widest possible secular education
out of the needs of rabbinic Judaism itself and independently of the Western enlightenment. Just as the Gaon
himself commanded an amazingly wide range of knowledge and scientific interests, so his conception of Jewish
education was broad-minded and surprisingly modern. He
left behind seventy works covering various fields of both
Jewish and general knowledge: commentaries on nearly
all the books of the Bible; treatises on Biblical geography,
chronology and archæology; commentaries on the Mishna
and the Jerusalem Talmud; critical annotations to all the
Tannaitic Midrashim as well as to the Babylonian Talmud; a commentary on the *Shulchan 'Arukh,* which is perhaps his most important work; notes and commentaries
on the classics of the mystic literature like the *Sepher
Yezirah* and the *Zohar*—in brief on the whole of the
Jewish spiritual heritage; and, at the same time, works on
astronomy, trigonometry, algebra, and grammar. In his
modesty he believed that everyone could become a *Vilnor
Gaon*—*vill nor* "if only one wants to"—(a Yiddish pun
on the name of the city). Everything depended upon a

reasonable system of instruction, and such a system he developed out of his own experience and disagreement with the prevailing Jewish educational methods of the time.

He insisted that everyone ought to secure a knowledge of the Bible at first hand, and not through accidental quotations from its text in the rabbinic literature. For a correct understanding of the Scriptures, the study of Hebrew grammar is essential, since otherwise their text cannot be properly explained. Only after this should the Mishna and then the Talmud be studied; education should not, after the warped habit of the Ghetto, begin with the Talmud. But, in turn, for a proper understanding of Jewish knowledge, he required a general education. So it was the Gaon who counseled the study of the secular sciences because, "if a man be ignorant of the secular sciences, he is tenfold more ignorant of the Torah," which embraces them all. In this spirit the Gaon everywhere encouraged the pursuit of the sciences, especially of mathematics; and it was at his suggestion that Baruch of Sklov translated Euclid into Hebrew.

The Gaon's educational methods gained practical application through the Yeshiba of Volozhin, founded by Rabbi Chaim Volozhin, a gifted pupil of his. There the most outstanding talents in Russian Jewry received their basic education and lifelong inspiration. I shall have occasion in the following pages, to refer to that great institution in connection with the careers of Hebrew writers of rank. To be a graduate of Volozhin meant not only having a thorough knowledge of Jewish sources, that is to say, an original Jewish education, but also a certain unmistakable stamp and character that contributed to the reputation of the Yeshiba no less than the profound knowledge of its graduates. It would be well worth while to devote to this unique institution of learning a monograph in which its whole influence upon Jewish life, within Russia and without, should be described.

When it is considered that the influences of the Gaon long continued to operate in the Yeshiba of Volozhin, it must be agreed that the inner liberation and cultural growth of East European Jewry were not dependent solely upon influence from Germany. Smolenskin even thought that the horrible example of Germany prejudiced the effectiveness which would in other more favorable circumstances have accrued to the bold plans of the Gaon, whom the people revered as a saint. I. H. Weiss called him outright the "first sower of enlightenment upon the soil of Russia." His whole aim was to base Jewish learning upon reason and not upon authority, upon exact philological meaning and not upon traditional interpretation. If emancipation from blind submission to authority be a sign of modernity, then the Gaon rather than the Haskalah is the initiator of the modern Jewish era in Russia.

II

As the "father of the Russian Haskalah," or the "Russian Mendelssohn," Isaac Baer Levinsohn (1788-1860), called *RIBaL* after his initials, won a wide reputation. Even the most radical spirits in the new Hebrew letters mentioned his name with respect—not excluding the apostate Kovner and the heretic Berditchewski. And it is noteworthy that Levinsohn enjoyed almost equal esteem among the champions of the old, to whom he sagely never gave the least offense. That this kindly, friendly man wrote biting satires under a pen name, full of sneers at the Kabbala and Chasidism, could barely have occurred to them. His pious mode of life was the best proof that enlightenment and Jewish religion were not irreconcilable. This was the most effective propaganda for the slogans of the Haskalah in the pious countries of Eastern Europe.

Levinsohn probably owed his circumspection and his forbearance toward traditional usages to his Chasidic mother country—he came from Kremenetz in Volhynia—and perhaps also to Krochmal, with whom he had the privilege of coming into contact for a time in Zolkiew. However that may be, he always tried to find sanctions for the Haskalah in the older literature, tracing out the new ideas in the Talmud and other accepted sources—an old device of all innovators. He realized that time was required for historic changes, and therefore preached patience to those who agitated for the new ideas:

> Concerning the Haskalah [he wrote] I have already declared that it should not be brought about all at once, but only by degrees, and that so we shall have good results; but that if it be forced through quickly, it will be a stumbling-block in our path, as the Scripture has it: "By little and little will I drive them out before thee . . . lest the beasts of the field increase upon thee."

Without a certain measure of indulgence, Levinsohn's books will to-day be found unreadable both for their content and their form. His style is long-winded, wearisome, stiff, and his ideas purest platitudes; even in those days, if it be remembered that this was the period of the Gaon or of Krochmal. To mention him in the same breath with them is unfair: the good man is put to unmerited shame.

But possibly commonplaces are useful in the education of the masses. The rare atmosphere on the heights of a Gaon or a Krochmal does not agree with everyone. Levinsohn's books were of the popular sort, written with the shows and semblances of scholarship, filled with quotations from Jewish and occasionally even from foreign sources. So he gained many followers, a circumstance aided by the fact of a Russian government subsidy.

In his best-known book, *Te'udah be-Israel* (the title apparently intended to mean learning in Israel), he discusses the five "main problems" of enlightenment: Should a pious Jew study the Hebrew language and grammar? May he study foreign languages? May he pursue secular sciences? If so, what are the uses of such sciences? Granting them to be useful, do they injure the faith?

In these questions and certainly in his answers, we recognize an appealing simpleton, with a kind heart and stale common sense. Yet his idea of education, though, or perhaps because, it is commonplace philosophy, was useful beyond a doubt. He urged that the children be taught Torah, religion and ethics, their "duties toward their fellow men, to the government, and to the people among whom they live. Boys and girls should be taught trades, for idleness and lack of bread is the beginning of all sin." The teachers must be pious and learned men, and especially trained for their calling, which not everyone can follow even if he be educated.

It is not necessary that all the people become rabbis, sages, philologists, physicians and poets. For the common man it is enough to know the usual commentaries, and have a little notion of grammar. He should also know a little about the necessary laws of the *Shulchan 'Arukh,* have the ability to read and write the language of the country a little, and know a little arithmetic. He should be able to read the Hebrew books of exhortation, and also to write a little in the holy language.

"A little" too simple altogether. But who could say that these were not useful proposals? Some may say that their value lies just in their making things easy, in demanding *little.*

Levinsohn concludes his *Te'udah be-Israel* with a plea for the duty of manual labor, particularly of work on the soil, proving the dignity of manual labor from ancient literature and by the examples of great Jewish personalities:

> From this day forth, I shall not refrain from reminding my people and my brethren of the disease that we have inherited, namely: Why do we all set our faces toward commerce, both men and women, large and small, rich and poor? Why do we not follow in the footsteps of our forefathers of old, to engage in agricultural labor? Why have we despised and held aloof from it, so that to-day not a man among us is a farmer, a vine dresser, a husbandman? Such work is condemned, but not justly so; it is looked down upon, but not rightly. Never was labor of this sort thought shameful and low. The contrary, rather. It was held an honorable occupation, a glory, and was given first preference, for it produces the means of life. Not only the poor engaged in it, but also the prominent and the noble. The princes, too, and the kings walked behind the plough together with the common man. God called Gideon the son of Joash the Abiezrite to judge his people when he was beating out wheat in the winepress. Saul the son of Kish, the first king in Israel, even after he was anointed ruler over his people, followed the oxen in the field. Elisha

the son of Shaphat was ploughing with twelve yoke of oxen when he was taken to be a prophet to the house of Jacob. King Uzziah had husbandmen and vinedressers in the mountains and in the fruitful fields, for he loved husbandry.

And so he cites proofs from the Talmud and from the history of other peoples, the Egyptians, for instance, "who in their esteem for agriculture, deified the animals required therefore"; he quotes from Pliny's natural history and from Aristotle's *Politics*—verbosely pleading the worth and dignity of labor on the soil. Levinsohn was quite overcome by the benevolence of the Russian government which, under Alexander I and Nicholas I, fostered agriculture among the Jews. In his enthusiasm he imagined a restoration of economic health to Jewry in Russia a very simple matter. At least one-third of the Jews would be given land to cultivate, and they would also raise cattle and sheep like their forefathers.

The good man did not guess that when the sparsely populated steppes of South Russia no longer needed stimulated colonization, and it was desired to give land to "Russian" peasants, the movement would collapse. He foresaw neither the ukase of 1866 halting the further settlement of Jews on the soil nor the expropriation some time thereafter of a large part of the land in the Jewish colonies which was divided among the Christian peasants.

However that may have been, it is Levinsohn's merit that he and others after him preached the postulate of manual labor, which is perhaps the most useful achievement of the Russian Haskalah. Though itself influenced by the West, the Russian Haskalah in this respect reacted upon its mother-countries. The praises of agricultural work by Joseph Perl and even by Z. H. Chayes seem, for example, to have been inspired by Levinson and the Jewish agricultural settlements in Russia. So that it may be said, with the usual risk of generalization and simplification, that the contribution of the German Haskalah was the revival of the study of the Bible; of the Galician Haskalah, the Science of Judaism; and of the Russian Haskalah, the idea of agricultural labor for the Jews.

III

The enlightenment in Vilna was not so moderate as in Volhynia, Levinsohn's native district. It was influenced by Germany, as the popular name for its adherents, "Berlintchik," testifies. On the whole, we may assume the same tendencies there as in Germany, allowing for such differences as would be due to the differences in environment. Here one finds the same enthusiasm for the beauties of the Bible, the same passion for grammatical correctness, the same fervor for the secular sciences. And though the Russian Haskalah, also, is lacking in greatness, one finds there what could not be found in the circles of the *Meassefim* literati: a certain artistry, which, if not present in the pedantic verses of Adam Hacohen Lebensohn, certainly is manifest in the genuine poetry of his son Micha Joseph (whose name was abridged into *Michal*) who, had he not died all too early, would have fulfilled his promise of becoming the greatest lyric poet of the Russian Haskalah.

As in the German Haskalah so in the Russian, similar disintegrating and negative tendencies can be observed.

Only that in Russia, the great masses—in matters of the spiritual life of a people, quantity is itself sometimes quality—and the lower cultural level of their surroundings did not permit of such consequences as we have lamented in the West. But, as a tendency not to be underestimated, the same forces that made for national dissolution were at work here also: which is obvious from the baptism of the sons of prominent Maskilim. It would be instructive, though it would exceed the limits of this book, to observe, for instance, the destinies of two Jewish boy prodigies of Vilna, both of them masters of Hebrew, and not of that language alone. One of them was Judah Klaczko (1825-1906), who wrote a small youthful book of poems in which he swore to restore the ruins of Zion, and ended up as a Catholic glorifier of the Polish folk-traditions; and the other was J. E. Salkinson (died 1883), a son of a Hebrew poet and teacher in the rabbinical seminary at Vilna, who ended as a missionary and minister of the Presbyterian Church at Glasgow, and translated the Gospels, Milton and Shakespeare into magnificent Hebrew. Indeed this Salkinson's correspondence is most instructive in showing how incredibly deep and genuine a love for Hebrew the baptized minister still had in his heart. In the next chapter, we shall speak of a third apostate, also born in Vilna, A. U. Kovner.

Even when it did not go to the lengths of apostasy, the Lithuanian Haskalah left behind it a hatred against Jewish forms of living, Jewish education, and the rabbis. It was the rabbinical seminary of Vilna which distinguished itself particularly in this hatred of the rabbis, and continued, after it had become a seminary for teachers, to be a nest of alienating tendencies. Even Moses Kleinman, who has written the most friendly estimate of the Haskalah, says of the Vilna movement that it lowered Hebrew to a mere tool, openly demanding that everyone adopt the language of the country, so that wherever enlightenment made inroads, the Hebrew culture had to give ground.

Even in the life and works of the most significant talent of the Russian Haskalah, its annihilating effects can be shown; in fact, through this great example, the whole questionableness of the movement becomes terrifyingly clear.

IV

Jehuda Leb Gordon was born in 1830 of well-to-do parents in Vilna. Up to his death in St. Petersburg in 1892, he remained the poet laureate of the Haskalah, and there are to this day readers who still gratefully treasure their youthful impressions of him as one of the greatest singers in the Hebrew tongue. As in the adage about Maimonides which the Haskalah zealots later stretched to include Mendelssohn, it was currently said of Gordon that after Rabbi Jehuda Halevi and up to his time there had been no second Rabbi Jehuda Leb—an estimate just as exaggerated, of course, as that which denies him any poetic gifts whatsoever: "Gordon likens his pen to a hammer, and he is so fond of the simile that he uses it very often. Indeed, one hears in most of his poems not the heartbeat of the singer, but the stroke of the hammer with which he made his songs." Thus did Reuben Brainin, in

174

one of his most effective essays, criticize Gordon in behalf
of the new poetry which had originated in conscious protest against both the contents and the forms of Gordon's
poetry. This criticism was just toward the new current in
Hebrew poetry, but insensitive to the poetic values of the
period immediately preceding. A poet of high rank like
Tchernichovski had paid tribute to the poetic qualities of
Gordon, especially as displayed in his parables. His satires have a rare power of invective. Gordon's language,
too, even to-day is considered to have classical force; and
we know that to praise his language is to praise the poet.

In his first creative period Gordon was altogether under
the influence of the Lebensohns, father and son, as he
himself acknowledges. He always revered the elder Lebensohn: "I love him with a strong love, for in nothing he
ever wrote did even a tiny error slip from his pen," a characteristic confession for the Haskalah, which esteemed
as an unusual virtue the self-evident need for grammatical
correctness. It was also from the Lebensohns that young
Gordon caught his enthusiasm for biblical themes.

His first great venture was "The Love of David and
Michal," a Biblical poem (1857) where, instead of portraying love, he theorizes about it tiresomely (as Adam
Lebensohn had done about mercy, knowledge and
death), and tries to explain King David's desertion of the
king's daughter whom the shepherd boy had so idolized,
with an improbable philosophy of duty: the shepherd boy
could live and love as he chose, but the king belonged to
his people. More skillfully and closely constructed is his
"Osnath, the Daughter of Potiphar," based upon a Talmudic legend that the chaste Joseph married his mistress's

daughter; the poem contains a few passages of sure artistic design.

Most famous of the poems of his first period, and justly so, is the pretty idyll of "David and Barzillai," in which the octogenarian, when invited by the king to come to live in his palace in the royal city, courteously but decisively refuses: he prefers the tranquillity of his village, the charm of agricultural labor, to the "voice of singing men and women," who, in the restless metropolis, must sing joy with heavy hearts. The watchword of those days, "Back to the Land," rings throughout the poem, echoing the contemporary efforts in Russia in behalf of Jewish agricultural settlement.

One interested in the views of the young poet on other questions of his day, can find them in his two typical, propagandistic Haskalah poems, "The Way of the Daughter of My People," and "Awake, My People." The latter was composed in 1863 after the liberation of the serfs by the liberal Czar Alexander II (1856-1881), the former probably somewhat earlier. The belief in the dawn of a new day, even among the German Maskilim, was never more naïvely expressed:

> Now hath the dawn come forth;
> The sun hath risen, darkness hath fled;
> Bright light shineth over all men;
> It hath touched us also.

Wherefore all this? Because, according to the ukase of the Czar, "to all wise-hearted and enlightened men there will be given appointments and posts in the government." Therefore, "Awake, my people!" "Be a man abroad and a Jew in thy tent, a brother to thy countrymen, and a servant to thy king."

> This land of Eden [sc. Russia] will be opened to you,
> Her sons will now call you brethren,
> From their hearts they will blot out vain and idle hate,
> And will give you their hands in greeting.

It lay with ourselves alone to change our unfavorable destiny.

> Every reasonable man should try to win knowledge;
> Let others learn all sorts of arts and crafts;
> Those who are brave should serve in the army;
> Farmers should buy fields and ploughs.

In his unbounded enthusiasm for the blessings of the enlightenment, Gordon held rabbinical Judaism responsible for the wretched plight of Jewry. In "Between the Lion's Jaws," one of his most finished poems, which describes the decline of Judæa and the death of the heroic zealots in the Roman circus arena, Gordon charges even ancient Judaism with always having been disloyal to the soil—wherefore it was doomed to fall. The teachers of old did quite the same thing as their descendants in the Ghetto; they "taught thee, alas, to go against life, to keep thyself behind fences and walls, to be dead on earth, and alive in Heaven, to dream while awake, and to be sunk in fancies. . . . The dust of thy scribes and the sere leaves of pious talk have covered thee over and kept thee a living mummy for generations."

A similar protest against the hypertrophy of the spirit, which has made for our political awkwardness and estrangement from reality, and also against pious idleness,

which must make way for constructive work and the
duties of civilization, vibrates throughout Gordon's last
historical poem, "King Zedekiah in Prison," written in
1879, while he himself was in prison.   (That the poet,
who was at that time the secretary of the Jewish community of St. Petersburg, landed in jail was probably due
less to the vengeful intrigues of the fanatical opponents of
enlightenment, as he himself believed, than to some official error—mistaken identity perhaps—such as was very
likely to occur in Russia.)   Into the mouth of the cruelly
blinded last king of Jerusalem, Gordon put his famous
accusation against the unworldly fantasts who opposed
the heroic war for the freedom of an enslaved people,
and preached to it lessons of obedience, shame, and servi-
tude.   Why was I, cried Zedekiah, so cruelly punished?
Because I resisted Jeremiah, who wanted nothing but to
bring a sound, laboring folk so low that

> In that day they shall seek with candles in Judah,
> And find no farmer, not one energetic man of deeds.
> Craftsmen shall be despised and humble.
> In the place of the shepherd, of him who sets the goads,
> There will be a prophet or a priest offering sacrifice.
> Every man shall say: I will not plough, I will not thresh,
> For I am a son of a kingdom of priests, of a holy nation.
> Then no sound of labor will be heard,
> But only the voice of them that pray: Praise ye, blessed
>   be . . .
> The earth will be filled with companies of prophets . . .

In the notes with which Gordon supplemented "King
Zedekiah in Prison," "in order to ease a little the bitterness of what has been said," he expressly pointed out the
contemporaneous hints in this historical poem.   The con-

flict between Jeremiah and Zedekiah, he declared, was ancient and eternal: it is the irreconcilable feud between church and state, which is not peculiar to Judaism alone, for even in Gordon's time, as he pointed out, it had broken out in Germany between the monarchy and the papacy in what was known as the *Kulturkampf*. But it was particularly ancient and characteristic in Judaism: the same strife had divided Saul and Samuel; later, in the time of the second commonwealth, the Sadducees and the Pharisees; and, in Gordon's own day, the champions of enlightenment and the orthodox. Gordon considered Jeremiah, because of his prohibitions (xvii. 21) a forerunner of Talmudism, and took Jeremiah's "new covenant" (xxxi. 31) to be nothing other than the Talmud: like Jochanan ben Zaccai at the time of the Second Destruction, he thought, Jeremiah held the religious institutions dearer than political independence.

Against this interpretation of Jeremiah, it would be out of place to cite the results of modern Bible criticism which, for example, holds the Sabbath prohibition (Jeremiah xvii) to be a later interpolation in the spirit of Nehemiah (xiii. 19). Though Gordon armed himself with learned citations from books on Biblical criticism, it was his good right as a poet to interpret the sources in creative freedom, which he rightly claimed for himself later (1883) when commenting on his youthful poem of "The Love of David and Michal."

It was of course contemporary life that sharpened Gordon's eye for the interpretation and criticism of the Jewish past. From his own battle with the fanatics of the Ghetto, he drew the conclusion: "Thus hath it been from the day this people came into being and thenceforth: A struggle between the bearers of the Torah and the Government." A formulation that reminds us very much of Theodor Mommsen's penetrating remark that the Jewish commonwealth necessarily had to bleed away in the irreconcilable quarrel between the state hating religion and the religion hating state, between the necessities of a government and the supernatural interests of a faith. However, Mommsen's fifth volume, in which this subject is treated, did not appear until 1885.

If Gordon at first imposed certain limits upon himself, with the year 1868, when his economic circumstances permitted him a certain independence, he began systematically to brand the abuses of rabbinic Judaism with corrosive satire, even at times with unjustifiable hatred. As distinct from his early, *romantic* period, which hovered in an idealized past, these poems are usually called *realistic,* because they deal entirely with contemporary issues, and seek both to describe and to influence actual life. Here the Russian Haskalah stepped out from the frame of Levinsohn's good-natured peacefulness, and made a sharp and overt attack upon rabbinic Judaism. These were not Gordon's own ideas: M. L. Lilienblum, himself influenced by Galicia, was then publishing his "Paths in the Talmud" in *Hameliz,* a Hebrew periodical, wherein he advocated proposals—though still in a shy and pleading manner—for the reform of the *Shulchan 'Arukh* in the spirit of the new age; one year later, in his "Additions," he became much more vehement. Gordon's impetuous temperament seized upon this invective against Talmudic Judaism: he resolved to bid farewell to fiction.

A SAINT AND A SATIRIST

I shall sing no more, make no more poetry,
I shall but cry violence, make only lament,
And with a great trumpet that not even Satan can seal,
Out of my pity for my people, out of mercy,
I shall tell their shepherds their transgressions,
Their teachers their sins.

In a series of satires he airs his hate against the rabbis
who did not hesitate to destroy the happiness of whole
families for the sake of "The Shaft of the Wagon" or
the "Point of the Yod" (idiomatic titles of two of his
poems meaning "for a trifle").   In the first-named satire,
a narrow-minded rabbi ruined the Passover festival of a
simple but righteous coach-driver because a grain of barley was found in the food cooked by his wife.   In the
second satire—it is one of his most famous poems—he
scores the wrongs growing out of the legal status of the
Jewish woman.   Upon the basis of the *Shulchan 'Arukh,*
Rabbi Wofsi renders a decision that the name of Hillel
which, by the rules of Hebrew grammar, is spelled without a Yod, ought to appear in the *Get,* the bill of divorce-
ment, *scriptione plena,* with a Yod; he will therefore not
permit Bath Shu'a to make a second marriage with the
wealthy Maskil Fabi.

The poem has been much discussed in Hebrew literature.   Ahad Ha'am thought that in Zangwill's novel, *The
Children of the Ghetto,* the problem was more correctly
put, because there the destroyer of a Jewish woman's
happiness is not a narrow-minded rabbi, but her own loving father, who bows before the immutable power of
the law.   Brainin has not unjustly pointed out how phil-
istine and superficial is the tragedy of the Jewish woman
as described by Gordon.   The loss of a financially favor-

able chance of matrimony makes the poet adjure heaven
and earth, and to draw hate-distorted pictures of rabbinic
cruelty. While, as M. Kleinman has rightly reproached
him, he betrayed in another poem strange understanding
for the harsh necessities of the non-Jewish, Russian law:
law must take its course whatever the fate of the individual. It never occurred to him that perhaps Rabbi
Wofsi, whom he accuses of having the soul of a Tartar,
obeyed a not wholly inhumane law which, in order to
avoid fraud, prescribed certain formalities. Nevertheless,
this poem has the undoubted distinction of having introduced the problem of emancipation of the Jewish woman
into Hebrew poetry. A whole generation was reared
upon the famous verses:

> Jewish woman, thy life who knows? . . .
> Unnoticed thou dost enter the world, unnoticed depart
> from it.
> Thy heartaches and thy joys, thy sorrows and thy desires
> spring up in thee and die within thee.
> Thou dost conceive, bear, give suck, wean thy babes; thou
> dost bake, cook and wither before thy time.

In spite of such good passages, all Gordon's satires
against the Talmudic despotism and the alleged baseness
of the rabbis are artistic failures: to-day they seem gross
caricatures and exaggerations. The Maskil's hatred has
spoiled even poetic versimilitude. We do not believe that,
except in the heated imagination of the poet, there were
at any time or place—and certainly not in Gordon's time
—rabbis who gave such stupid and merciless interpreta-
tions to the law.

Gordon's contemporary, Smolenskin, though in his
novels he, too, attacked the obscurantists of the Ghetto

violently, altogether too violently, presents in quite another light not imaginary rabbis, but actual characters in his native environment. He relates that when he was studying in Lithuania, the greatness of a rabbi was popularly adjudged by his leniency in interpreting the law, and that harsh decisions were held to indicate a lack of scholarship in a rabbi. He gives many instances, of which one shall be quoted here, because it opposes Gordon's satirical exaggeration with the exact contrary of the common practice. A woman once came to the famous Rabbi Zalman of Sklov on the eve of the Passover to ask his decision on the ritual purity of food in which a grain of barley had been found. The rabbi ruled that the food was not thereby rendered impure, not knowing that she had already asked the same question of Rabbi David of the same town, and that the latter had adjudged it unfit. The next morning the leading men of the community came to ask him why he had reversed the decision of the first rabbi: for was it not written that when one sage had rendered a decision a second might not overrule it. To this he replied that he had not known of the earlier decision since the woman had not mentioned it. The community leaders angrily called out, "Then she ought to be punished!" But the rabbi replied quietly that one who would make such a ruling in the case of a poor woman on the eve of a festival could not be called a sage, and that therefore he would have had the right to assume that there had been no decision even had the woman been frank Smolenskin adds that similar instances of leniency occur every day.

Gordon's accusations were biased distortions never

less well founded than at a time when, after the Gaon's bold liberation from the authority of the *Shulchan 'Arukh,* religious practices were so much affected by the new currents of thought. How superior to the hate-blinded satirist is a distinguished representative of the old rabbinism and one of the most cultured Jews of the century: Rabbi Zevi Hirsch Chayes, who, discussing the need for certain religious reforms, remarked with lofty open-mindedness: See how various religious customs in these countries gradually disappear, and yet there is no objection.

> The reason is because they are not abolished with shouting and protests and public rabbinical assemblies. We have always known that customs which are incongruous with a given time and place cannot maintain themselves, and are swept away by the currents of the age. Therefore our sages of the Talmud commanded us neither to approve nor to disapprove, to teach neither prohibition nor permission, letting each man do as his heart inclines him. Shouting and protests and public assemblies can bring only harm . . .

for they make the people uncertain about unalterable commandments, which, in turn, must lead to heightened rigor on the part of the rabbinical leaders.

In the face of such humane and modern views on religious development, Gordon's slanders fell flat. The very continuance of the Jewish law through the long centuries is proof of its humaneness. Without continuous adaptation of the written law to the unwritten because ever-changing and self-perfecting inner sense of justice, the Jewish law would have been incapable of maintaining itself against all the storms to which it was exposed unprotected by the power of law-enforcement.

The Maskilim thought the matter much simpler when

they promised themselves complete salvation through a mechanical alteration of the law. Religion grows, it is not made. The people look upon law as hallowed because they believe it divine, and not a handmade statute. When consciously changed, its very roots are threatened; whereas pious interpretation is able to read into it the most heretical meanings and the most radical changes.

In French, the idea would be rendered as expressed somewhere by Ernest Renan: "Religions are like women, who readily grant all to those who know how to take them, but who cannot possibly be forced to the least concession by open violence."

Gordon soon realized the vacuity of the reform proposals of the Maskilim, and himself poked fun at them. In his poem "The Two Josephs ben Simon," the adept in the sciences dreams of the reforms he will introduce:

> I shall make the use of beans and lentils lawful on Passover, and the community beadle will sell all the leaven to one *Goy*. I shall allow card-playing, salt-herring and sausage. Spittle I shall declare *kosher* . . . and permit the sacrificial fowl to be whirled three days before the Day of Atonement, so that the slaughter-house may not be overcrowded.

Such outspoken irony is scattered through many otherwise serious proposals for reform, as if to hint that the poet is laughing in his sleeve at himself and his fellow fighters for hoping even for a moment to effect a betterment in the Jewish destiny through such outward trifles.

For meanwhile life in Russia had taken quite other courses than he had hoped for in his naïve dream of "Awake, My People!" I shall have occasion later to advert to the conditions in Russia, but meanwhile it will suffice to say that a reaction set in after 1870: social reforms were forgotten, Jewish rights curtailed, the masses incited against the Jews until, finally, the 1881 pogroms demonstrated to the full the unreality and fictitiousness of the Haskalah dreams.

The last decade of Gordon's life may be designated as one of utter *nihilism*. His ideals failed in his soul even before they failed in life. He saw that the new generation had alienated itself from religion and from the Hebrew language, from all that nevertheless remained dear and sacred to him. The enlightenment that he preached was an idea; but that generation made a business of it, material advantages, careers. In the old Judaism there still inhered ideal values, but the new Jews were simply—seekers for gain. So he grieved over the Jewish future, shrinking from the consequences of his own ideals. "And our sons? From their youth they have estranged themselves from us; my heart aches and bleeds for them. Ever faster they drift away—who knows how far and for how long? Perhaps to the place whence there is no returning." Embittered and broken, disappointed and deceived in the endeavors to which he had dedicated his whole life, he sings with overwhelming pessimism:

> Alas, who can foreknow the future? Who will tell me,
> Am I to be the last of the singers of Zion,
> And you the last of the readers?

His want of faith and outright nihilism dry up the springs of his poetic inspiration also, and the broken poet laments in a bitter letter: "Of what shall I speak and give warning, whereof shall I sing? All my dreams are void, all my ideals have proven vain and misleading. God has turned away from me, and no longer visits me with new dreams."

He did not believe that it was possible for the Jews to achieve self-emancipation, and wrote in reference to Pinsker's brochure: "Not a people, not a community are we, but a flock . . ."

With Gordon, the Russian Haskalah movement ended, like its mother movement in Germany, in utter despair and self-dissolution. It had undermined all the old affirmations, but could create nothing new for the craving spirit. Its disappointing failure may be summed up in the words which Turgeniev put into the mouth of Samuel Abraham, a Lithuanian Jew: "Our children no longer have our beliefs; they do not say our prayers, nor have they your beliefs; they believe in nothing."

CHAPTER VIII

AN APOSTLE AND AN APOSTATE

A capable cobbler out-weighs a thousand poets.

D. I. PISSAREV.

THERE was once a conflict in Russian literature between Slavophiles and Westernizers which remains fundamentally unresolved to this day: the former argued that salvation lay in holding fast to the simon-pure Russian national ways without the least taint of foreignness, and preached isolation from the Occident, while the latter believed in a spiritual connection with Western Europe as a prerequisite for Russian culture. Both sides had their historians who, as usual, were able to interpret the past either in the Slavophile or the Western sense according to the party paper they took with their morning coffee, —each of course attributing to his own side all that was significant and to the other all that was corrupt in Russian history. As in similar disputes neither party was altogether wrong.

Jewish life in Russia, or, to return to our sheep, the Russian Haskalah, should also be regarded from two viewpoints if we are to avoid one-sidedness. Stress should be laid not, as usually happens, only upon the influence of the German movement for enlightenment, but also upon the autochthonous forces in Jewish Russia itself.

Referring in the previous chapter to the stimulus that came from Germany, I mentioned also some of the indigenous factors of the Russian movement, as for instance the significance of the Gaon of Vilna and of the Yeshiba at Volozhin which was imbued with his spirit. Even in the Yeshiba, the two forces, the foreign and the native,

191

united to create the new type of the Russian Maskil: officially, they studied the Talmud there with genuine enthusiasm and industry, applying the creative methods of the Gaon; but, secretly, they read the works of the German and the German-influenced Haskalah, which roused in them longings for freedom, for foreign lands. In a wider scale, Jewish life of Russia reflected the developments at Volozhin.

In the sixties and seventies of the last century, a new element appears in the play of forces within the Russian Haskalah which, though it originated in Russia, was not uninfluenced by the West. I refer to the positivist tendencies of Russian literature, which exerted great influence at that time. In the then prevailing reaction, Russian positivism provided the radical and revolutionary elements—first among the Russian and shortly among the Jewish intelligentsia—with spiritual weapons. Tchernishevski and Pissarev became a hardly to be overlooked station in the progress of every Russian Maskil: coming to grips with them formed a chapter in the career of almost every Hebrew writer in the Russia of the seventies, even in that of an Ahad Ha'am.

I

Russian positivism has a number of peculiarities, especially that of Russian exaggeration; but it is, as its name implies, a current of the general stream of the positivist philosophy originated by August Comte. The basic ideas of the Russian movement can therefore best be studied in the chief work of its French father, entitled "Course in Positive Philosophy" (published 1830-42). It is a broadly conceived social-philosophic system which intentionally breaks away from all previous philosophizing. The old questions about the essence of things, their first causes or ultimate aims, are discarded as a thousand years' error. Those questions transcend the limits of the human intellect, and are as insoluble as they are idle and without practical import. Positivism desires knowledge that is both possible and useful. It seeks to understand available facts, their sequence and the constant interrelations whose uniformities we call laws. Such knowledge lends us practical power over the affairs of life, which should be the only aim of science: to foreknow in order to be able to influence the course of events. *Savoir pour prevoir.*

Positivism thought of itself as the stage of ripe manhood in the sciences, and of earlier philosophies as more primitive stages of development, comparable with the childhood and adolescence of the human mind. This is the meaning of the positivist doctrine or law of the three states. Philosophy and all the sciences pass through three phases or states of development: the *theological* state, which holds that the events of the world are caused by acts of volition on the part of supernatural powers; the *metaphysical* stage which imputes phenomena to abstract nature-forces, concepts thought to be realities; and the *positive* state, which tries to clear away those arbitrary and always half-personified abstractions by confining itself to the sphere of observation and to the exact data of experience.

Some sciences have already reached this last state of development, while others are still fast encaged either in the theological or the metaphysical transition stage. According to the degree of positivism that they have attained to in the course of history, Comte outlines a hierarchy of the sciences, with mathematics and the natural sciences at the top, and, on the lowest rung, the humanities, the social sciences, or, as he himself was the first to call them, sociology. Theology and metaphysics still struggle within the last-named science, and he thought it the task of his age to make sociology positive. The life of human society ought to be studied by the exact methods of the natural sciences in order to guide the large affairs of the state and of society, not with the passions, but in an intelligent, scientific manner. Knowledge should at last become useful to society and a lever for progress. Comte therefore demands not only the universal education of the youth, but even the establishment of a board of intellectuals which is to have supreme authority in the social sphere such as the natural science experts enjoy in their fields. These expert social authorities are to have the duty and the power to direct the activities of all classes and occupational groups along the line of the common interests and to supervise all educational work—a kind of dictatorship of the intellect or of the positivist philosophy, which is to foster and guide all the forces of society for the benefit and happiness of the whole.

As is well known, the father of positivism ended with a (humanly agreeable) backsliding into the theological stage when, in his *Catechism of Positivism* (1852), he tried to set up a new religion with rites, a cult, and sacraments: the positivist religion of humanity, of which love is the principle, order the basis, and progress the aim; whose dogmas are scientific maxims; whose gods are mankind, space, the universe; whose guardian angels are women, living and dead, and whose saints are great men of olden times, to each of whom a day, a week, or a month is dedicated in the positivist calendar. A curious and instructive end to a matter-of-fact philosophy, which shows that under cover of sober investigation, mystic and religious buds were germinating, perhaps from the very beginning.

Russian positivism did not, indeed, take over this religious aspect, but it did with much ardor adopt the social ethics of positivism which, in the final analysis, may be regarded as religious in character. The Russians borrowed from the system in particular the ideas of social reform, which Comte may have owed to Saint-Simon. That the true aim of philosophy is social, that the affairs of society should be studied by the methods of natural science with the positivist purpose of influencing them—such ideas were watchwords to enkindle men in the Russia of those days. Knowledge as a lever for social reform had here a clear political implication. It meant revolt against the reactionary government and against the official ecclesiastical and intellectual powers which supported it, and which out of reactionary political motives, did not permit science to emancipate itself from the theological and metaphysical transition stages. The old order made science as well as art and religion a sedative for the disinherited, whereas positivism wanted to use them as stimulants for progress. Education of the masses in Russia had not merely a theoretical, but a definitely political aim. Students left their colleges, dressed themselves in the peasant costume, went to the people (*narodnitchestvo*), to the villages, into the peasant huts, to enlighten, that is, to prepare the masses politically. True to the Russian propensity for going to extremes, Russian positivism went so far as to demand from every spiritual utterance, in art or in science, an immediate bearing upon society—in fact, concrete social uses.

It was literary criticism particularly which in Russia carried the teaching of positivism to immoderate lengths. N. G. Tchernishevski (1828-89) declared in a youthful dissertation that the æsthetic theories held up to that time were as false as they were harmful, that art was nothing but a luxury for the rich. But he achieved far-reaching influence only through his novel, *What's To Be Done?* written in prison in 1862. The novel is without artistic merit, but it has a wrathful eloquence that condemns as useless all art without a purpose, demanding that it serve life. N. A. Dobroljubow (1836-61) who himself wrote verses, did not hesitate bluntly to judge all art by its propaganda value. All of them were surpassed, both in fanaticism and in artistry of style and of dialectics, by D. I. Pissarev (1841-1868), who started a crusade against all metaphysical and æsthetic flippancy, berated Pushkin mercilessly, and in all seriousness advised the lyricists to engage in something useful, as, for instance, in the popularization of the natural sciences. A capable cobbler, who can produce a good pair of shoes, outweighs a thousand poets! The last echoes of these art-hating demands can still be heard in Tolstoi's late books.

AN APOSTLE AND AN APOSTATE

II

I really could have spoken of these influences of Russian positivism when discussing Gordon's second period, which is usually termed realistic, except that they are there too vague to serve for illustration. These influences can best be studied in Moses Leb Lilienblum, a fellow fighter with Gordon against Talmudism, whose writings everywhere, apart from his own reiterated testimony, reveal the Russian influence. But this author and communal leader later overcame his positivism, and may even have secured from it the weapons for his subsequent change of mind, when he became the repentant apostle of Jewish nationalism. I wish first, however, to indicate the far more frequent and typical tendency of positivism in the Jewish life of Russia, that of the dissolution of Jewish values. I have chosen as an example of this tendency a man who really does not deserve any mention in a review that ignores many more important names. And if he be adduced here, it is only for the sake of furnishing a crass illustration, of exhibiting a typical line of development in the Hebrew letters of those days.

Here again we have one of the jests of history. Abraham Uri Kovner (1837-1909) always grieved over the writers who devoted themselves to Hebrew literature, which he dubbed a mere "heap of vanities," instead of employing the official language of the country, whereby they could have made themselves more useful and gained more fame. And yet, if he himself to-day receives mention, though not always honorable mention, it is due not to his articles which, from early manhood onward, he wrote in Russian, but to two small compositions of his youth, which in his later years, when he had become estranged from his people, he could no longer even read. In his *Searching Out a Matter* (1865) and *A Bouquet of Flowers* (1868), written wholly in the spirit of the Russian positivists, he criticizes very severely all the aims of the Russian Haskalah, and makes an impudent though stylistically not ineffective attack upon the then most revered names. As he saw it, S. D. Luzzato caused much harm to the Jewish people because, instead of taking up useful knowledge, he occupied himself with idle questions of archæology and theology, thus inclining the Jewish youth toward useless occupations. The happiness of the human race would be fostered not by philologists, but by natural scientists:

> We need useful literature. We have gone far enough in encouraging the youth to write stupid poems and articles full of vanity and a striving after emptiness. Every man who loves his people ought to arouse this generation from their sleep, make them useful to themselves and to others. Upon the writers rests the duty of inclining youth toward work by which they can sustain themselves, and not become a burden upon the community, as happens when they are idle.

Kovner fought against holding the Hebrew language in too high regard, for, like other languages, it is composed merely of a dead alphabet and in itself possesses nothing sacred, since only holy thoughts can confer holiness upon a language. Moreover, it is a vain and hopeless undertaking to try to keep the Hebrew language alive, since the Hebrews long ago lost their political independence. "How can they desire to plant a pleasant vineyard upon a barren rock? Their plants will wither suddenly, and their memory be lost to the world." The great country of Russia needs young talent. Why, then, stick in the Ghetto, if out in the wide world one can be of so much use to others, win so much honor and happiness for oneself?

What wonder that, holding such views, Kovner turned his back upon the Hebrew language, and then upon Judaism itself? Out of passion, or—as he pleaded in court —out of pity for a woman, he became involved in a bank defalcation, and was banished to Siberia. He soon was able to win not only amnesty, but also a job in the government's custom office, which he secured through the recommendation of his prosecuting attorney, and baptism.

Both these booklets of Kovner's, which display much temperament, but also a repellent vanity, are instructive beyond their personal application. They prove that positivism, upon the basis of the Haskalah, was bound to be destructive. That was one of its typical effects upon the Jewish youth of Russia. But it also, though in a lesser degree, made a constructive contribution, in that it stimulated both Jewish socialism and Jewish nationalism.

III

Moses Leb Lilienblum (1843-1910) ran the course of both these tendencies. His life, which he has described for us in detail, as if he realized its typical, more than personal value, illustrates distinctly the ways of that generation. As has been said, Lilienblum began with a *reforming* period, with a fight against the Talmud which was certainly inspired by Galician influence, his model being Joshua H. Schor, a violent but keen-witted critic of the Talmud, called the Galician Voltaire. Lilienblum underwent bitter persecution at the hands of the rigidly Orthodox—in fact, he was almost in peril of his life.

He had to move to Odessa where, instead of the enlightened Jewry he had hoped for, he found all bonds slackened and flaunting desertion from the national and religious values of Judaism that still were so dear to him: indeed, it was his love for those values that made the earnest, pious man propose discreet reforms in the hope of saving what was permanent and valuable in Judaism by drawing the lines against the anachronistic and outlived. But in Odessa he saw that prosperity and the slogans of the Haskalah merely undermined all Jewish idealism; with sorrow he observed the petty careerism of the Maskilim who solved the problems of their people through their personal successes, and hardly troubled about Hebrew and the other watchwords of the Haskalah. He had combated both, the severities of the Talmud and the idle dreams of the Haskalah; but here, in Odessa, was a Jewry that cared for neither, that was concerned for the new literature as little as for the old. And it was this sort of Judaism that he found most objectionable.

In Odessa, also, he became acquainted with Abraham Krochmal, a son of the Galician sage Nachman Krochmal, a free-thinker who was critical not only of the Talmudic but of the Biblical tradition as well, and who bewildered the deeply religious and at bottom very conservative Lilienblum. Abraham Krochmal's teachings that the Holy Scriptures, as they have come down to us, are the work of priests of the age of Jeremiah who wished to conserve the sacrificial cult, ravished the scientifically untrained, credulous mind of Lilienblum of all belief; and he sank into utter *nihilism*.

A picture of those days is preserved in the most poignant psychological document of the neo-Hebrew literature, Lilienblum's autobiography, *The Sins of Youth* (1876), a book filled with dramatic confessions, rare truth and honesty of expression. It is a work of profoundest despair. He longs for the time when he was persecuted by the fanatics, longs for the curses and anathemas that broke forth from pious hearts; because the free-thinking environment, though it pays him compliments now and then, is devoid of all emotion, all faith, all uprightness. Everywhere he sees charlatanism, indifference, cynicism, yawning emptiness. Now he knows that Jewish religion and life cannot be reconciled. They seem to exclude one another: he who becomes free hates religion, he who remains religious rejects freedom. Why have a Hebrew literature when nothing can avert the inevitable doom? He draws up the balance sheet of his life: it is a ghastly failure. "My heart is empty, I am barren as an ice-waste, like an oak hewn down."

While in this frame of mind, Lilienblum became more familiar with the positivist Russian authors. He read Pissarev and Tchernishevski's *What's To Be Done?* which gave him a new affirmation in life. In fact, the positivist philosophy determined the trend of his ideas to the end, even after he had outwardly broken with it and already set his feet in the "Path of the Returning."

The ideas of the third, *positivist* period of his life are stated best in his "Treatise of Elisha ben Abuya," which is full of utilitarian and socialist slogans. It is related in the Talmud of the heretic of antiquity whom Lilienblum makes the ostensible author of this book that he went into the Jewish schools and drove the children away from their studies, asking why they idled there: Let this one become a builder, this a carpenter, this a tailor! Similarly, Lilienblum attacked the sin of idleness and the exploitation of others' labors in this tractate, which appeared in "The Assembly of the Wise" (Königsberg, 1878), a monthly edited by M. Wintchewski. (This magazine was a second unsuccessful attempt to spread socialism in the Hebrew language, the first having been *Ha'emeth,* published in Vienna in 1877 by A. Lieberman, a gentle fantast.)

Wholly in the positivist spirit, Lilienblum preached during this phase of his development against the useless slogans of the Haskalah, its wasteful concern with poetry and philology: true culture consisted of the sciences which would bring personal benefits; and the only noble purpose was to help the poor. Quite like Kovner, he sneered at theology and archæology, at the science of Judaism, at S. D. Luzzato, and went over, in part, to literary work in Russian. He admitted that if he and his friends still wrote in Hebrew, it was because there were many Jews who did not yet understand the language of the country and therefore could not gain an education through that medium. Hence he also admitted that he was not concerned about purity and cultivation of style, and took no pains to guard against Aramaic and even Russian influences in his writing, since in any case Hebrew was soon to be discarded.

In his *Sins of Youth,* he wrote that in the far-off

future all the peoples, including his own, would return
to their common mother, humanity, and that there would
then be no more nationalities, but only human beings. At
a later date he wrote still more positively of cosmopolitan-
ism in the present, no longer postponing it to the future.

> I hold natural sciences above all the other sciences, because
> it is the only kind of knowledge that does not depend upon
> accident or convention, but upon immutable reality. Toward
> Nature I have a natural bent which will not change even
> after my death; but to my people my relation is accidental
> or conventional, because all nationality is only accidental and
> conventional. Therefore, as I even now see it, I am first a
> man and then a Hebrew.

After he had returned, entering then upon his fourth
and last phase, *Jewish nationalism,* he wrote of his socialist period:

> As I thought then, so I think now: that all are obligated
> to work, that it is forbidden a man to enjoy this world
> without contributing something to the sum of existing things.
> But I have never sunk myself in the doctrines of socialism,
> nor investigated their details, because it appeared to me a
> millennial idea. I thoroughly detest coercion and violence.
> All betterment in the life of the race ought to come, it seems
> to me, through historic evolution. And thus the socialist
> ideal also is an ideal of the remote future, to which I do not
> desire to dedicate my labors when more urgent matters
> claim me. . . . My people are persecuted and tormented
> continually. I cannot forsake them and concern myself with
> the workingmen of the whole world.

It was Lilienblum's practical turn of mind that saved
him from the perils of assimilation. Indeed, it may be
that positivism taught him to reject the idea of the assimilation of a people of many millions, as unrealizable.

So that it was not only the pogroms of 1881 that led

him in his *Way Out of Exile* to the Palestine ideal, even
though he himself ascribed this to the shattering effects
of those days. Then he realized the utter fruitlessness of
the emancipation dreams. Like a sudden illumination it
came to him: we are aliens here, our only salvation lies
in having a home in some corner of God's world. In that
hour of insight, he blessed the very terrors of the pogrom
days: "When the terror had ceased, my spirit was content
and my heart rejoiced that fate had caused me to experience several times within one *week* something of that
which our unhappy ancestors had to endure almost their
whole lives through." He was grateful for the storm
that shook down the fruits of understanding for him.

The analogy happens to be correct, since the fruit must
have ripened before the storm came. As a matter of fact,
the later turn in Lilienblum's life was prepared for slowly:
his austere, earnest spirit, his conservative bent, his deeply
religious disposition, his great love for all the traditions
of Judaism, shouted for affirmation even in his extreme
despair. Nor was he at peace until it was found.

Lilienblum's activity in the "Lovers of Zion" movement,
both of organization and of theory, belongs to the chapter
of the Jewish renaissance, and goes beyond the era of
enlightenment. But it certainly bears traces of the positivist influence which, with his utilitarian habit of mind,
were ineradicable. In the upbuilding of Zion, also, he
demanded a practical attitude, and fought the spirituality
of Ahad Ha'am. Not for the sake of Hebrew culture, but
in order to lift the Jewish people out of its political degradation, was Erez Israel to be restored. And when political
difficulties arose in connection with the conquest of Pal-

estine, it was Lilienblum's practical-positivist Zionism
again which made him realize that not political independence, "not government, but historic citizenship is the
chief thing; that the people should be domiciled upon the
soil of the homeland." Every least bit of progress, every
practical success in Palestine gave him infinite pleasure,
so that there is some truth in the jeers of his opponents
that for Lilienblum one more Jew, even one more goat,
in Palestine constituted a whole Zionist program. It
meant for him one step more toward historic citizenship,
toward the recovery from foreignness which to him sig-
nified the redemption of Israel.

RETROSPECT

Before passing on to the following era of the national
renaissance of the Jews, it would seem well at this point
briefly to retrace the path along which we have come.

A review has here been made of a century of Jewish
history which, though it went astray, is not wholly lacking
in greatness. Its vivid pageant of Jewish types alone testifies in its variety to the still unabated vitality of the race
and foreshadows the rich vistas of its future.

I have tried to point out that the Jewish Middle Ages
which (as Zunz so aptly remarked) lasted to the beginning of the eighteenth century, show *two basic forces* that
remained unshaken down into the eighteenth century, until
the advent of the Haskalah, namely: the banning of the
outward environment and the messianic hope. And I have
tried also to outline the abrupt *volte-face* of the Jews away
from these two basic forces that had been cherished in
Jewish life for centuries—toward an affirmation of the

lands of their exile as home, and the surrender of their ancient dream of the restoration of Zion. This sudden break with the bases of Jewish life in the Galuth without original new values to replace them was bound to endanger the very existence of the people. It gave birth to the unfortunate conception of "Germans of the Mosaic persuasion," to mass-baptisms, to the whole tragicomedy of lies in the life of the assimilated Jew in Western civilization. Even in Eastern Europe, then the reservoir of the Jewish folk, we could observe similar disintegrating tendencies, and we recall that the most able author of the Russian Haskalah, J. L. Gordon, ended in utter nihilism. Himself he believed to be the last of the singers of Zion, and the Jews not a people nor a religious fellowship, but a hopeless, aimless flock. Even a character like Lilienblum's, which was happy only when it affirmed, was in danger of ending up in despair and apostasy. The Haskalah had the power, both in the West and in the East, to impair the old affirmations, but could create nothing new and lasting in their stead.

But let us not be unfair to the merits of the movement, even though they were very often unwittingly achieved. The Haskalah used Hebrew as a secular medium—and it does not matter that at first it used it only for aims that the next era, that of the Jewish national renaissance, was to disavow. The Haskalah secularized our whole conception of Judaism, and therefore our messianic conception as well. It brought the messianic ideal down from heaven to earth—if only in order to reject it. But modern Zionism would have been unrealizable without this secularization of Jewish life. The Haskalah created a new understanding of the Bible, a new revival of interest in the study of Biblical times. It created the Science of Judaism. It gave impetus to agricultural settlement and handicrafts among the Jews, so anticipating and preparing for the "religion of labor" of present Jewish Palestine. This contribution of the Haskalah must not be minimized because it was made sometimes *against* the conscious intents of its protagonists.

It would be an error, also, to see in the emancipation the more or less arbitrary dealings of individual Jewish leaders. The struggle for human rights and the approach toward modern civilization meant a great historic change. Unfortunately, however, because of our Galuth degeneration we did not come nearer to modern civilization in general, but copied instead the peculiarities of the various peoples. The result was that, instead of enhancing and rejuvenating our own values, this approach brought a deadening assimilation, generations of undignified self-obliteration, of distorted and crippled lives.

The Haskalah has been reproached because it did nothing to stem the national disintegration, but it is only fair to remember that these destructive tendencies were at work independently of and without the Hebrew literature. Moses Kleinman is right, when he says that the Hebrew writers often tried to curb and to offset those tendencies. To be sure, even he must admit that this often happened without their knowing it, and in spite of the ideals they preached. It was altogether in this sense that I have spoken of the "prank of history."

But when healthy national self-realization began in Europe to take the place of anæmic cosmopolitan ideals, when the view gained acceptance that every people, like every individual, serves best when it uses its own gifts to the best advantage, it was Hebrew literature, the heir of the Haskalah, that paved the way for the Jewish renaissance.

The delicate, odd beauty of the integral folk-life we led in Europe up to the eighteenth century must not blind us to the fact that, without the fusion with modern Western civilization that was then begun, the age-old urge to national restoration would have run to seed later on as well. Without statesmanlike knowledge of the present-day universe of discourse, this urge would have spent itself as in earlier centuries, in impotent yearnings, in fantastic pursuits, in messianic ecstasies, and could not have burst forth in the modern form known as Zionism.

BOOK TWO

UNDER THE SPELL OF THE NATIONAL
RENAISSANCE

CHAPTER IX

THE HOMECOMING TO ZION

We have, so to say, gone home: Zionism is a return to the Jewish people even before it is a return to the Jewish homeland.

THEODOR HERZL.

POLITICAL Zionism was born late in 1894, at the time of the Dreyfus affair. This fact was openly admitted by Theodor Herzl, founder of the movement, time and again; moreover, obviously unable to free himself from the trauma of those days, he never tired of relating it, as if in it inhered some definitive doctrine of Zionism. Herman Bahr, a friend of Herzl's, and a leading Austrian author, recounts very clearly the version Herzl often gave him of the cruel ceremony he witnessed as the Paris correspondent of the *Neue Freie Presse* of Vienna, when, on the Champs de Mars, Captain Alfred Dreyfus was stripped of his insignia and deprived of his military rank prior to deportation to Devil's Island. Herzl, like most people, was convinced of Dreyfus's guilt, but he was deeply affected by the brutality of the proceedings.

> Born actors, the French lose no opportunity to dramatize a public incident: and here was material for a brilliant effort. It was a magnificently impressive spectacle. An officer breaks the traitor's sword; one by one a sergeant, a corporal and a private strip his insignia from him, and cast them at his feet. Herzl, believing Dreyfus to be guilty, saw the man treated according to his deserts. What he could not understand was the overt delight which showed upon the faces of the spectators. It seemed like a national holiday. Why are these people so delighted? . . . How can they find such intense joy in the suffering of a human being? Granted he is a traitor, but a traitor is still a man.

A colleague of the press, to whom Herzl turned with this question, replied:

No, the French do not feel that he is a man. They see him not as a human being, but as a Jew. Christian compassion ends before it reaches the Jew. It is unjust, but we cannot change it. It has always been so, and will be so forever.

Bahr the Catholic, retelling the story, realizes that in this fateful moment Herzl's Zionism was, had to be, born.

As is known, not only the political Zionism of Herzl, but the *Choveve Zion* movement which preceded him, grew out of a reaction against anti-Semitism. The cosmopolitan dreams of the Jewish youth of Russia and their enthusiastic and honest attempts at assimilation were drowned in the blood-torrents of the pogroms of 1881. In the realm of the Czar, not altogether unlike the Western countries, a period of darkest reaction set in. With the murder of Alexander II and the accession of the intolerant zealot Alexander III, all liberal tendencies vanished, and the reactionary party of the "grand inquisitor" Pobyedonoszev and the absolutist régime triumphed. The ferment of the Russian masses over the curtailment of their rights was systematically diverted, as so often, against the Jews with pogrom propaganda inspired from above until, in 1881, the storm discharged itself in a mass-crime in many south Russian localities. The pogroms were followed by the "Provisional Ordinance" of May 3, 1882, which was to be kept in force with inexorable severity for thirty-five years. Through this ordinance the system of legal persecution of the Jews as an "economically harmful element" was sanctioned: millions of Jews were penned up in the stifling Pale of Settlement which they were not allowed to overstep by a single mile; denied all rights to own or lease land, or even to buy houses; and exposed to the rudest administrative arbitrariness. An authorized, systematic, legal pogrom took the place of the pogroms in the streets.

To understand the bitter disillusionment of the Jewish masses in Russia, we have only to remember the enthusiastic call of the Haskalah barely twenty years earlier: "Awake, My People!" Like J. L. Gordon, all the sanguine Haskalah devotees believed that "darkness hath fled, light shineth over all men." It lay with the Jews alone to give a new turn to their destiny; all enlightened Jews could easily obtain government posts, every Jew could become a farmer unhindered; they need only learn to read Russian and give up their national obstinacy. Even the "practical" plans of Russian positivism, which had captured so many of the Jewish youth, were seen to be utterly futile. This youth was attracted to the *narodnitchestvo* movement less by the lack of rights for the Jews than by the general ideas of political and social liberation. In a spirit of noblest enthusiasm, Jewish students went to the Russian people to arouse its peasants and workers, hoping salvation would come to the Jewish people as well with the dawn of the new morrow. The sons of the Ghetto displayed much self-sacrifice and courage in this revolutionary movement, and many a one paid for this in Siberian prison mines. So much the bitterer was their disappointment during those spring days of 1881, when the incited masses at times attacked even their Jewish benefactors and enlighteners.

The answer of the Russian reality to all the dreams of emancipation came like a most horrible mockery. The ludicrous ineptitude and political naïveté of the Haskalah,

which so tragically overlooked realities, became all too
obvious. And the reader knows, from the career of Lilienblum, that the courageous elements in Jewry resolved to
return to their own people.

Dr. Leo Pinsker (1822-1891), himself for many years
a champion of the russification of the Jews, in place of the
shattered old ideal of emancipation, found the word for
the new ideal of the next generation: *auto-emancipation*.
Such was the title of his brochure, published in 1882, which
became one of the classics of the Jewish renaissance. A
keen-witted physician, he made a penetrating and simple
diagnosis, from which the remedy emerged of itself: the
disease—lack of political unity and national self-esteem;
the remedy—the restoration of the Jewish people upon
its own soil. In Jew-hatred he saw a sort of fear of ghosts,
a horror of the homeless Jewish specter that for thousands
of years had refused to die, a psychosis, which he called
Judeophobia, which, because it was an old inherited disease, could not be cured. Summing up his argument,
Pinsker says that "for the living the Jew is dead; for the
native-born a stranger; for the long-settled a vagabond;
for the wealthy a beggar; for the poor a millionaire and
an exploiter; for citizens a man without a country; for all
classes a hated competitor." Once and for all we must
renounce the idea of converting the Jew-haters; we can
expect the end of our misery to come neither through
"progress" nor through "emancipation." We must again
become what once we were, not a homeless specter wandering over the whole earth and frightening all the living
peoples, but—like other peoples—a people in its own
homeland. The book is pervaded by eloquent grief over

the present condition of the Jewish people, which is in such lamentable contrast to its glorious past: "Our father-land, foreign countries; our unity, dispersion; our solidarity, universal enmity; our weapon, meekness; our defense, flight; our originality, adapting our future to the next day. What a despicable rôle for a people that once had its Maccabees!"

Auto-emancipation, written in German because it contained a "call to his fellow Jews in the West," created no lasting impression there. Within Russia, however, it rang in the birth-hour of the *Choveve Zion* movement, which Pinsker headed up to his death. While his brochure was still on the press in Berlin in the spring of 1882, a group of Jewish youth—students for the most part—was organized in Charkov under the name of *Bilu* (formed from the initial letters of the Hebrew *Beth Jacob, Lechu Wenelcha,* "O house of Jacob, come let us go up"). The *Bilu* set itself the aim of becoming the prototype for pioneer colonization of the ancient homeland. Setting an heroic example while engaged in unaccustomed work in the strange Asiatic milieu, in a neglected, malaria-infested wilderness, subjected to the lawlessness and the political handicaps of the Turkish régime, this handful of intellectual pioneers pointed the way for the solution of Jewish misery by personal abode in the old homeland of the race, becoming the fathers of the new Jewish settlement in Palestine. When in 1896, Herzl appeared on the scene with his *Judenstaat* in the belief that he was offering a wholly new plan, twenty-two colonies were already established in Galilee and Judæa. The enthusiasm for the resettlement of Palestine which enabled these pathfinders to surmount unbelievable obstacles and hardships, was in itself evidence that the idea was no Utopia. For they more than anyone else proved that "if you will it, it is no fable"—words that Herzl wrote as a motto upon his vision of the *Old-New Land*.

The world organization created by Herzl and the further efforts at colonizing Jews in Palestine changed the dream into a fact of world-politics. The World War brought sanction from the Powers for the establishment of a Jewish homeland in Palestine. The mandate to carry out this purpose was granted to Great Britain under the supervision of the League of Nations.

II

In the above brief sketch of the history of national self-discovery, which seemed necessary for an understanding of what follows, I have purposely dealt with the outward, negative circumstances of the birth of the new idea. For Jewish nationalism is often reproached with having originated as a reaction against anti-Semitism—which is taken to be proved by the conversion of both Pinsker and Herzl. This is true, but yet not quite true. It was merely that the pogroms of 1881, as later the Dreyfus affair in the West, shattered the illusions of emancipation which had superseded the old national affirmations, the messianic hope in particular, of the Jewish people. The powerful and sustained movement which Sabbetai Zebi was able to create revealed that the Jews, sixteen centuries after the downfall of their state, could still think of the return to Palestine as imminent, as something that might actually happen any moment. And I have tried to show that even in the age of Voltaire, a man of the eminence and culture of Moshe Chaim Luzatto could in all seriousness think himself a messiah, and envisage the liberation of the Jews through the old Jewish messianism. It remained for the Jews of the emancipation era consciously to surrender the hope of national restoration for the sake of equal rights in the lands of the Diaspora. Jewish enlightenment imagined that the Jew could win full citizenship if only he would consent to obliterate all his national peculiarities. It lay with ourselves alone to find the approach to all the blessings of equality. This dream was dispelled in blood and woe, chiefly through the pogroms of 1881. Now the old, native folk-forces, which had been inhibited and repressed by the illusion of emancipation, again burst forth. Viewed in this light, the Palestine movement becomes not reactive, but spontaneous.

That this is so is proven by nationalist manifestations coming even before the collapse of the emancipation dreams, during their very heyday, in fact: they simply could not be suppressed. Ever and again the thought was expressed, both by Jews and by Christians—and attempts were made to carry it into effect—that only life on its own soil can assure the Jewish people a dignified and satisfying future. Chasidism tried hard to tighten the old bonds with Palestine, to make them more personal; and early stimulated attempts to colonize the homeland. At the beginning of the nineteenth century (1818), the journalist and playwright Mordecai Emanuel Noah called to the whole world to found a Jewish commonwealth—at Grand Island, near Niagara Falls. The corner stone was actually laid in Buffalo in 1825, but the scheme of the Jewish commonwealth of Ararat (so to have been called in allusion to the founder's namesake of the Deluge) collapsed. But both then and later Christian friends of the Jews advocated similar settlements in other parts of the United States. Most of the proposals for the territorial restoration of the Jews, however, remained true to their old home. Beginning in 1840, Moses Montefiore, the great Jewish philanthropist, made repeated attempts to rehabilitate Palestine through Jewish colonization; and, like others with similar aims, he did not permit himself to be discouraged by serious obstacles. From among further voices raised in behalf of reconstituting the Jews as a nation, we shall mention only the Frenchman, Ernest Laharanne, who, in his *La nouvelle Question d'Orient,* advocated an independent Jewish state in Palestine. For this book, like the literary and organizing activities of Rabbi Hirsch Kalischer of Thorn, founder in 1861 of the first colonizing association, fortified the train of ideas independently arrived at by Moses Hess in his *Rom und Jerusalem* (1862), one of the most profound books of the Jewish renaissance.

A disciple of the German romantic philosophy, Hess borrowed from it the scientific refutation of the ideal of cosmopolitan sameness championed by the enlightenment, upon which the whole philosophy of the Jewish emancipation based itself. And, as a friend and comrade-in-arms of Marx and Engels, he knew how to infuse his national ideas with winged social aspirations. In his enthusiasm over the national resurrection of Italy, he believed that the hour had struck for the repatriation of the Jews, for the solution of the "last of the nationality problems." The title of his book is meant to indicate that with the liberation of the eternal city on the Tiber begins also that of the eternal city on Moriah; with the rebirth of Italy, the resurrection of Judæa. Jerusalem's orphaned sons will also be permitted to participate in the great palingenesis of the nations, in the awakening from the deathlike hibernation of the Middle Ages with its evil dreams.

In this sense, Hess dedicates his book to the "lofty champions of all historic peoples striving for national rebirth."

He sees clearly through the whole web of lies of the Jewish emancipation efforts. "Not the old Jew who would sooner let his tongue be torn out than misuse it to deny his nationality, but the modern Jew, is contemptible; he who, like the German scamp abroad, denies his nationality because the hand of destiny rests heavily upon his nation." He realizes how false and untenable is the position of the German of the Mosaic persuasion. "The Jews are something more than 'adherents of a religion,' they are a racial fellowship, a *people,* a nation *all too often* forsaken by its own sons, which every street urchin feels free to jeer at without fear of punishment because it strays about homelessly in the world." He also sees the deplorableness of Jewish reform, with its invented ceremonies, its trite, flowery oratory, and the new hymns whose only merit, as Heine saw it, lay in their correct spelling. Not from without, through outward changes, not in foreign lands; but, in their own homeland,

> only from the national rebirth, will the religious genius of the Jews, like the giant who touched his mother-earth, draw new forces, and again be inspired by the holy spirit of the prophets. It has never yet been given to any man, not even to the master-hand of Mendelssohn, to break through the hard crust wherein Judaism was encased by rabbinism, and to let the light penetrate into it without destroying the

inner core, its national-historic cult, and taking its sacred life.

In like words he speaks most reverently of the orthodox Jewry of eastern Europe, which the Western enlighteners looked upon so condescendingly. In the fervent Hebrew prayers which they daily speed heavenward, he hears echoes from a thousand generations. These east European Jews have "preserved the living kernel of Judaism, I mean the Jewish nationality, more faithfully than our occidental brothers, who have wished to revivify everything in the faith of the fathers save the hope which created that faith and kept it alive through the storms of the ages,—the hope of the restoration of our nationality." To these millions of faithful brethren in the East he looks for a mighty impetus toward the Jewish rebirth on the home soil, whence the Jewish people, erstwhile the spiritual instrument for the social regeneration of the world, will once more help to prepare the historical sabbath of mankind.

With penetrating insight, Hess also recognizes the limits of the Palestinian solution of the Jewish problem. Not all the Jews should, or would want to emigrate. But to all Jews should be restored the feeling of having a home of their own. This would make for inner soundness, whereby they would become the more capable of useful citizenship in foreign lands. From the history of the Jews in the Diaspora and more especially of the Judeo-Spanish period, he drew the lesson that "one could at the same time be a national, patriotic Jew in the strictest and fullest sense of the word, and yet take so loyal a part in the cultural and political life of the country of which he is a citizen that it becomes a second fatherland for him."

THE HOMECOMING TO ZION

Hess's admirable work of modern Jewish nationalism was an all too early cock's crow. Enmeshed in the phantasmagoria of the emancipation era, his fellow Jews of the West saw in the book nothing but "reactionary romanticism," which could only imperil the progress and the equality of the Jews. Abraham Geiger replied to him in this spirit with incredible harshness.

However, from among the millions of faithful brethren in the East to whom Hess felt himself drawn, to whom he wished to go and cry out, "Hold thy banner high, O my people," there arose a man who paved the way for Hess's ideas into their life and letters, and who, with his ardor and glowing eloquence, helped them to victory: a combative, unwearying banner-bearer and herald of the Jewish national awakening who, more than any other writer, was able to sweep the illusions of the emancipation era from Hebrew literature, and thus prepared for the change of heart and the homecoming to Zion. This man was Perez Smolenskin.

III

Born in 1842 in the small town of Monastirshtchina in the province of Mohilev, Russia, Smolenskin as a boy prodigy had the typical destiny of the Hebrew writers of his day: early poverty, early cares, early farewell to youth. Moreover, various peculiarly unfortunate events cast their shadows over his boyhood. Because of a priest's baseless slander, the father of the family had to keep in hiding for a long time, and the brave wife was thrown on her own resources for the support of the six children. A vagabond who desired to marry her worried the family for a time with false reports of the death of its head. And when at last the father was free to return, he found the home robbed of its eldest son. After the harsh custom of those days, the boy was stolen for military service and never again heard from. The occurrence etched itself into our author's youthful memory, and he brands this crime time and again in his novels. *

At the age of ten he was bereft of his father, and at eleven we find him tramping to the Yeshiba at Sklov, where his older brother was already studying. There he found a hospitable reception as the gifted youngest pupil, and, as was the custom in those days, received a scholarship in the form of *"Taeg,"* meals at well-to-do homes on fixed days; and on the Sabbath he was even honored with a seat at the rabbi's table. All went well until it was discovered that he read forbidden books and had secret talks with an old Maskil of the town, who was suspected of laxity. In his thirst for knowledge, the youngster borrowed from him many books which in those days, or rather nights, he greedily devoured in the women's gallery (to escape detection) by the light of a candle stolen from the beadle. When the sin became known, he lost his "days," and was even mishandled. Then he went away to Lubawitch, where he soon won the favor of the Chasidic rabbi because he knew both the Talmud and the Russian language (the latter by government decree had to be taught in Sklov). Smolenskin's "enlightened" eyes could, of course, see only the crude outward shell of his Chasidic environment, which soon disgusted him; but he was not insensitive to the simple nobility of the rabbi.

Soon thereafter he was in Vitebsk, then in Mohilev,

always driven by his *Wanderlust* until he finally reached Odessa, the longed-for haven of the enlightened of that day. Previously he had supported himself as a cantor's assistant or preacher, early betraying a flaming eloquence which vibrates even in his late writings; but in Odessa he became a teacher of Hebrew, soon winning enthusiastic commendations from his pupils. He now studied languages and, of course, following the positivist formula, natural history, to his knowledge of which his writings on cedar trees and elephants testify.

In 1867, he published in the supplement to *Hameliz* a fierce review of the Hebrew translation of *Faust* by Letteris, betraying throughout the influence of the current positivist literary criticism. At the same time he worked on novels, at first merely adapting and translating, since this was the preference of the editor of *Hameliz* (A. Zederbaum); but soon, feeling that it was the true function of the new Hebrew literature to produce original works, he flatly defied his editor. Too independent by nature to be content to work under an editor in any case, he decided to found a periodical of his own, to gather original talents around him, and to create a free Hebrew tribune from which translations should be excluded on principle.

It was no easy matter in Russia to secure a permit to publish a Hebrew monthly; and so Smolenskin, urged on also by his craving for travel, made his way westward, roaming through Germany and Bohemia, and finally settling down in Vienna.

Only after infinite effort was he able to get out the first issue (1868) of *Hashachar* (*The Dawn*) which, by dint of superhuman sacrifice, he kept going to the day of his death. He is telling the literal truth when he offers the engrossing duties and cares of the magazine as an excuse for the hasty composition of his publicistic writings and even of his novels. Not only was his literary work affected by these trying labors, but they undermined his health, so that he died when he was barely forty-three (1885).

> Like a tender mother who does not shrink from any labor or hardship for the sake of her offspring, so I tended and fostered it. I robbed myself of sleep, for years permitted myself no rest, only so that it might be kept up. I was author, proofreader and bookkeeper. I mailed out the issues on time, wrote letters, read letters, read articles. All these things were done by myself alone, not a soul was by to help me. . . . In such circumstances, it will be understood that my minutes were counted, and only in the nights— usually from ten to one or even two o'clock—was I able to do my own writing for *Hashachar*.

This magazine is usually looked upon as the dawn of a new phase in Hebrew literature, that of the national awakening, just as the beginning of the "enlightenment" is usually taken to date from the appearance of *Hameassef* in Königsberg eighty-five years before. This is correct, but we must not look for any sudden break with the earlier trends. For years both Smolenskin and the magazine stood firmly upon the ideological bases of the Haskalah, though from the very beginning there peep forth new ideas of national self-realization, which is only natural in a "twilight of the gods," during a stage of historic transition.

Smolenskin had the extraordinary faculty, still unsur- passed by Hebrew editors, of discovering and encouraging contributors, and grouping them around himself. He won a whole array of talent among both belletristic and scientific writers, so that *Hashachar* became the leading literary organ, and to this day remains the best source for a knowledge of the spiritual problems and forces of the time.

From the very first, however, Smolenskin himself gave the tone to the magazine, chiefly by means of his publicistic articles which, written with contagious enthusiasm and turbulent persuasiveness, always called out numbers both of friends and of enemies, passionate approval and passionate condemnation. He had the capacity of the born journalist to interest the reader; to excite, to compel attention.

In the leading editorial of the first issue of *Hashachar*, defining the policy of the magazine, Smolenskin showed how little he was edified by occidental emancipated Jewry, to which the Maskilim of the West looked up with such envy and reverence. Their undignified aping of everything foreign, even to the forms of religious worship, their indifference to the Hebrew language, which they excluded from the prayer book itself, their cowardly denial of all messianic hopes, seemed to him high treason to the national sanctities. In white-hot anger he promised to wage war against such alienating tendencies:

> All peoples set up monuments of stone, build towers, pour out their blood like water so that their name and their language may not be blotted out. They longingly await the day of salvation when they will again have their own government, and even though that day be remote, they do not cease to hope. We, however, have neither monument nor land, neither name nor memorials save the one

relic that has remained to us from the ruins of our sanctuary, our Hebrew language; yet they regard it with shame and contempt. Those who despise the Hebrew language thereby reject our nation, and have neither name nor memorial in the house of Israel; they are traitors to their people and their faith.

They say to us: Let us be like all other nations! And I agree with all my heart: Let us indeed be like other nations in the pursuit of knowledge, . . . in being loyal citizens of the lands of our dispersion; but let us, also, like them, be unashamed of the rock whence we were hewn. Let us be like them in honouring our own language, our own nationhood! It is not a shame and a reproach to us to believe that there will be an end to our exile, and that the day will come when the sceptre will return to the house of Israel, just as other nations are not ashamed to hope for deliverance from the hands of strangers.

Smolenskin set *Hashachar* a twofold aim where up to that time Hebrew periodicals had had but one.

Hitherto the war has been waged only within, but now it is carried on both within and without. At a time when the eyes of the blind begin little by little to open from the sluggish slumber of years, those who are already wise of heart deliberately turn their eyes away from the language, which is the only thing left to us, and which alone can win the hearts of all Israel to remain one people.

Smolenskin wants to fight both camps—the obscurantism that is alien to culture and the assimilation that is alien to the people, both alike harmful to the furtherance of Judaism that he was fighting for.

On the whole, it can be said of Smolenskin that while in his publicistic writings he attacked the deserters in the West, in his novels he was concerned mostly with the fanatics of the East. To be sure, this division was neither intended nor without its important exceptions. But it is

very obvious that his belletristic writing is almost throughout underlain by Maskilic evaluations: opposition to
enlightenment is almost always identical with the basest
wickedness, is indeed the chief cause thereof. Though
Smolenskin himself seems to have surmounted the Haskalah, he is more one-sided in his fiction than the earlier
Hebrew novelists, who were sometimes able to find a
few human traits in the enemies of enlightenment. An
instance in point is Smolenskin's best-known novel
Hatto'ëh bedarkhe hachayim (Astray in the Paths of Life)
which ran serially in *Hashachar* beginning with the first
number, went through several editions, and became one
of the most influential books of the epoch. Smolenskin
here makes hatred of enlightenment responsible for all the
sins which he heaps upon the characters to the point of
caricaturing.

Uniting truth and fiction, the book portrays Smolenskin's own strayings in life: his youthful struggles at home
(first part); his experiences in the Lithuanian Yeshiba
(second part); and his ramblings among the Chasidim
and afterwards in Western Europe (third part). A fourth
part, added to the second edition in 1876, is almost wholly
publicistic, having been written after Smolenskin was
sobered of all Haskalah delusions.

Despite all its defects, its incoherence and inorganic
composition, the innumerable fantastic accidents in the
plot, its naïve psychology and propagandistic aims, *Hatto'ëh bedarkhe hachayim* won unbelievable influence. It
dealt with no imaginary or bookish problems, but with
actual issues, with the gropings of the youth who were
"astray in the paths of life." What seems to us a literary

defect—that it is a novel with a purpose—was just what Smolenskin's readers welcomed. They could not understand that literature could be an end in itself, for them it had to be useful, readily applicable to their own lives. Smolenskin was effective just because he presented contemporary life, not the Biblical or some other remote and romantic past. Moreover, he never merely presented life, but wrote of it as it ought to be; his books were criticisms and incitements to change. While his artistry may have suffered, his enkindling effect upon his readers was due to just that. Still, here and there the artist in him breaks through in many passages that attest his considerable talent for realistic description.

In the latter respect, *Keburath Chamor* (*The Burial of a Donkey*) is perhaps the best of his novels, being written with much humor and a fresh delight in the telling of a tale. A venturesome wag (Jacob Chaim) plays practical jokes in his ignorant environment, not out of malice, but from sheer exuberance of spirits. However, owing to a spiteful enemy of enlightenment, a local notable named Zebadiah, one misfortune after another befalls him, and finally he is murdered. In revenge and despair his wife Esther has herself baptized. Like the base community leader (Menasse) in "Astray in the Paths of Life," Zebadiah is caricatured as vice incarnate, the essence of all vileness, Smolenskin still following the naïve psychology of the Haskalah literature that saw in its foes nothing but abomination. However, the frivolous, talkative, goodhearted hero is drawn with sure humor and fidelity to life.

Of Smolenskin's other novels, which to this day have their devoted readers, we shall mention here only the

last *Nekam Brith* (*The Vengeance of the Covenant*),
wherein, breaking with the Haskalah ideals forever, he
describes the return of Jewish youth to Jewry after the
pogroms of 1881. The father is pious and wealthy; the
mother an extreme assimilationist; the son, Ben Hagri,
though he was taught Hebrew by his father's wish, goes
the way of his mother. During his university years he
dreams of the time when the last barriers will fall between
Jew and Gentile. Even the pogroms, which did not spare
his own father's home, could not change his views, since
he saw in them only a deplorable accident that ought not
to cause loss of faith in the idea itself. Until a terrible
personal affront stung him to his inmost soul, and he
reverted to his own people. The details of that painful
incident are irrelevant. The delineation, the emotional
experience, the philosophy to which it gives rise, show no
more subtlety than is usual in Smolenskin. But he did
grasp the problem itself with a sure intuition. He created
herein the first literary prototype which assimilation, particularly in its later stages, produced everywhere and with
recurring faithfulness to type. Ben Hagri's way back to
his own people is by no means the way of the worst among
us. They must taste in their very own persons of the fate
that has been ours for centuries; only through personal
humiliation can they become aware of the sublime pathos
of Jewish martyrdom; but then they respond from their
innermost depths. The Talmud rightly says, out of its
experience with such Jews, that "in the place where peni-
tents stand, not even great saints may stand."

However, it is not to his novels that Smolenskin owes
the honorable place which he holds in Hebrew literature.

There is no doubt that in this field he was surpassed by several of his contemporaries whom, for all that, we should hardly care to place on a level with him. It was Smolenskin the publicist, yes, Smolenskin the journalist who, with his ardor and enthusiasm won even reluctant spirits by storm. Despite his occasional loquacity and his hammer-stroke repetition, an irresistible magnetism radiated from his style, from the vital temperament revealed within it. Furthermore, his earnestness and integrity were sensed between the lines, and won him immediate trust. He may not always have been right in his opinions, the sentiment behind them was always right. His penetrating influence confirms the rightness of Goethe's remark that it is the "personal character of the author that wins him recognition from the public, not the artifices of his talent."

Two lengthy treatises in particular, which are still his most popular works, display Smolenskin in his full stature as an apostle of the national renascence. These are *'Am 'Olam* (*The Eternal People*) and *'Eth lata'ath* (*Time to Plant*), both of which ran in serial form in *Hashachar* for several years. It seems preferable to deal with the latter work first, since it is a sort of *pars destruens* for the positive thesis of the former.

Time to Plant is one of the best polemic writings in the Hebrew tongue, an annihilating criticism of Mendelssohn and of the endeavors which, rightly or not, Mendelssohn initiated for Jewish enlightenment. Despite all show of respect, most disparaging criticisms of Mendelssohn the man escape him; yet, on the whole, the idea and the man, the cause and the personality—in so far as so passionate a spirit is capable of this—are kept apart. Smolenskin cannot help showing that Mendelssohn's conciliatory, uncombative temperament is deeply repugnant to him:

> He was a coward by nature and wanted only to be left in peace. He trembled at the sound of a falling leaf, and hated all strife and controversy. Even when surrounded by enemies and opponents, if he could find a place where he might hide silently, he would gladly do so. Such a man cannot be a leader. He did not lead the people, but was pushed onward by them . . . even to a place to which otherwise he would have refused to go.

Centuries after Luther, Mendelssohn rendered the Bible into German, which was no great achievement in itself, nor a service to the Torah. The old Bible translations into Aramaic and Greek were done in times when these were the vernacular tongues of the Jews. But in Mendelssohn's day, "the children of Israel knew Hebrew and not German; they could not understand the source of their faith through a medium still foreign to them." Smolenskin even went so far as to say that Mendelssohn's Bible translation impeded rather than promoted the spread of a knowledge of Judaism, for "when it became known that the children of Mendelssohn and most of his friends and disciples had forsaken the religion of their fathers, how could the pious permit their children to study the Bible and the Hebrew language, seeing that the holy scriptures had become the first step to treason towards Israel?"

But the sharpest shafts of Smolenskin's eloquence are directed against Mendelssohn when he makes him responsible for the notion which since his time has become a creed of the Jewish enlightenment, that we are a religious persuasion and not a people. "I do not say that he was its father, just as I do not say that he was the father of any new idea in Israel. Only his disciples and those who boasted of being his disciples attributed their own thoughts to him, so as to find willing ears; but his passiveness did help to give it much currency."

For Smolenskin the whole future of the Jewish people depended upon a refutation of this theory. For, if we be merely a religious fellowship, we no longer have a common national future, but different destinies for the Jews domiciled in each land of the dispersion. If we be no longer a national unit, Hebrew can at best become the calling of a few scholars; and it would be our duty as, in fact, the Jewish enlightenment has argued since Mendelssohn's time, to lead the Jews to the languages and literatures of their host-nations. But both the hope for national rehabilitation and the most passionate attachment to the Hebrew language could not be extinguished —he felt that he might judge others by himself—in the Jewish soul without destroying that soul itself. Since life refused to give way, he concluded that the theory must be false; and that whoever originated it, whether wittingly or unwittingly, was a false prophet in Jewry. Smolenskin could not but see it as perversity when one, like Mendelssohn, holds the religious commandments and the ritual practices of Judaism obligatory and looks upon those who disregard them as apostates, and yet does not see that it is a far worse betrayal when someone denies its very essence—its most sacred hope, messianism, and the unity of the people. He sees a lack of integrity in the whole conception, which suffers from the same fault as Mendelssohn himself, cowardice.

> To have houses of prayer and choristers and preachers just like the Gentiles, to leave off everything that may not be to their liking, to abandon every opinion that may be unwelcome to them; and since they mistakenly thought the other peoples might take it amiss if we feel ourselves a people, he and they raised their hand to pluck it up by the root.

And in an oft-reiterated, eloquent *quousque tandem,* Smolenskin concludes: how long before we open our eyes and see that it is their cowardice that makes them take a wrong view of things? How long shall we live under the curse of vain fears? "How long until we realize that only the opinions of Mendelssohn and not the spirit of the time is against us?" Opposition to our nationhood comes not from the peoples, but from our wrong estimate of them.

This essay fulfilled a great historic mission. Its occasional personal invective did not impair its purging and educative effect. Its vehemence seemed to say, like Luther, that "he who is in the right may be outspoken." Breathlessly, the Ghetto listened to Smolenskin's refutation. For with Mendelssohn's downfall, the lesser idols lost their hold as a matter of course. Even the half-alienated youth of Russia, whom positivism had robbed of faith in their people, pricked up their ears. "His severe words against Mendelssohn," wrote one of them, "and his smashing of the god of the Maskilim seemed to me an heroic deed equal to that of Pissarev when he annihilated Pushkin." Jewry too evidently offered potentialities of combat, a chance for great ventures, scope for youthful energies!

One must realize what enormous prestige Mendelssohn enjoyed among the Maskilim in order to understand the whole force of Smolenskin's counterblast. Smolenskin knew that his words would give offense, for

> Moses Mendelssohn was to the Maskilim what Moses the Lawgiver was to the Orthodox, the word of God. To him they looked up, on him they modeled themselves, every syllable that issued from his mouth or did not issue, but was said by others in his name, was considered holy. . . . How many thousands of devout Maskilim are there among us who reject and sneer at the thirteen fundamentals, but who declare: I fervently believe that Moses Mendelssohn was chief of the sages and father of the Maskilim; his law is the unalterable law of truth, his way is without fault or blemish.

Smolenskin considered it his duty to free his generation from submission to the new authority, the infallibility of Mendelssohn. The postulate of freedom to criticize and the quest for truth should apply to one's own party as well.

> The Maskilim applaud and shout with joy when Moses and the prophets and the sages of the Talmud are brought before the bar of judgment; then it is said, let us criticize and examine and test. But let one lay hands upon a *Maskil* who has been set up as a teacher, and they will become just as excited as the Chasidim when their rabbis and saints are attacked. Moreover, there be many among us who will say: You may be right, we are unable to deny the correctness of your words, but such things should only be whispered; why give the obscurantists a chance to raise their heads? Why should the hypocrites say, Behold now, here is a man who is not of our camp, and he too lowers the dignity of their teacher, and admits that he did not serve his people well. All this I knew beforehand, yet did I not hold back, for this is the *time to plant,* and it is our duty to weed out our vineyard.

With these words, Smolenskin overstepped the Maskilic limits of his novels, and paid no heed to the risk of being identified with the orthodox foes of enlightenment. All of Hebrew letters were soon to follow suit.

Smolenskin's affirmation behind the "nay-saying" of *Time to Plant* has been, as said above, formulated in his essay *'Am 'Olam* (*The Eternal People*) and he assumed it as an accepted premise; although, in characteristic manner, and like the born leader that he was, he hammered the definitive principles into the memory of his readers through frequent iteration. Basically, the larger part of *'Am 'Olam* also is polemic and negative and aimed against the religious reforms of Western Jewry—something we need not enter into here. His rejection of reform sprang from his underlying thesis that we are not a religious community, but a people. Israel has not ceased and never will cease to be a people. And just because his religion is not only a profession of faith, but also takes the place of land, government, language, and all those natural institutions which make for national unity, this single, unifying bond must be cherished with the utmost care. Thoughtless changes might impair our unity as a people.

Smolenskin is at pains to show that love for one's own people is not incompatible with universal human ideals, but really fortifies and places these upon their natural basis. For love of one's nation is merely an extension of family feeling and affection; and, just as the former is not conceivable without the latter, so it is not possible to think of a universal brotherhood of mankind without the smaller units of the individual peoples. "If we were suddenly to appear and to proclaim to the multitude: Cast out from your hearts love for all you have loved up to this moment, let not your children and your family be dearer to you than the rest of mankind, would not every man who heard such words ignore and laugh at them?" The aim is identical, only "those who favor love of one's nation set a ladder on the ground whose top reaches the heavens, and go up rung by rung until they reach the top, while those who advocate love of all-humanity wish to leap up to heaven at one bound; therefore those who follow them will necessarily fall and fail. . . ."

I quote these crude formulations in order to obviate any impression that he understood the problem of Jewish (and of general) nationalism in its full implications. He had neither the philosophic nor the poetic finesse of Hess, who in one page could say what Smolenskin's whole essays said, or rather did not say.

Even more. Smolenskin lacked the sheer intellectual energy for overcoming his Haskalah past entirely. His idea of nationhood is still vague and indefinite. We are a people; yet, unlike other peoples, we do not need the outer tokens of nationality (land, government). We are a people of the *spirit*. Such we were even in the days of our national independence, when we still lived in our own land. "We were a people whose life did not depend solely upon a government and a land and laws, one which, when deprived of its land, would lose the foundations of nationality; but since the days of antiquity we have been a people of the spirit, whose Torah was to it as a land and a government and laws. . . ." Israel was born on foreign soil; even before it conquered Canaan it knew itself a people, one people. Hence the idea has never taken root in Israel that it would cease to be a people if, like others, it were to lose its homeland and be dispersed throughout the world. Smolenskin believed that even the results of Bible criticism, which assign a later date to the Torah, to a time when the Jewish people already lived upon its own soil, did not vitiate his theory. For him, not the historic events are important, but the causes which made the children of Israel think their nationhood independent of their land. For centuries the Jews believed the tradition that the Torah was given and the people born before the conquest of the land, a belief to which they cling to this day. Therefore, unlike other peoples, they early learned to think and feel themselves a people of the spirit, whose entity is not destroyed with the loss of their land.

The practical outcome of Smolenskin's conception of spiritual nationhood was that for many years he did not advocate territorial repatriation for the Jews, and even rejected the idea. Though only because it seemed to him impracticable and even dangerous to make a premature attempt whose failure would discredit the idea itself. Nor did he always understand that a Jewish national home could well be reconciled with equality of citizenship for the Jews in the lands of their dispersion—in this respect, also, falling considerably short of Hess. In the few years still granted him after the rise of the *Chibbath Zion,* he threw himself whole-heartedly into the Palestine movement.

However, even in his very first articles in *Hashachar,* and also in *The Eternal People,* his theoretical formulation that a land is not essential for Jewish nationality is opposed by his territorial sentiment, his deep grasp of all the implications of Jewish messianism. When once the satirist M. D. Brandstaetter sent him a parody on the messianic belief, he refused to print it, saying: "I too am one of those who believe in the Messiah and in the day of redemption. And not only do I await the redemption, but I would gladly shed my blood were valiant men to rise among us to save the honor of our people. I shall cling to my faith in the coming of the day of redemption, even though it be far off. . . ." Probably the finest passages in *The Eternal People* are those on the messianic hope, which reveal very clearly the inner conflict where the Maskilic head, which would like to remain sober, yet tries to help the turbulent heart by finding arguments for the seemingly impossible.

Even though it be pointed out that this hope will never be realized, we ought not to abandon it. For there are many fine ideals which are not realizable, and yet we do not refrain from teaching them to the public and urging youth to hold fast to them. A good thought is good even when it is not translated into action. Just as we do not say to a poor man that he think the less of charitable deeds because it is not within his power to perform them, so we cannot say to a distressed people, Give up your hope of becoming a people with a land and a government of your own because you are unable to give effect to your desire. Even if it be true, as they say, that it is impossible for Israel to return to its land and to restore its state as aforetime. But there is no such thing as impossible. Things which are impossible now may be actualities a few years hence. Had anyone come a hundred years ago to say that the small Greek nation, the remnant of the ancient Greeks, who also are scattered all over the world, would again set up their kingdom, all the people would have laughed at him, saying, What a fool is this prophet! Yet it came to pass because the people willed it with all their hearts. Had Israel wished to find his land, he would long ago have found it. For he could easily have bought it for a price and brought back to it the persecuted Jews from the many lands of their dispersion. Oppression would cease when it became known that they had a land, a land and a government that would take their part in time of need. . . . Then they would be respected like other peoples. . . .

"If Israel willed it" . . . it were no fable. There, once more, is Herzl's teaching, and the concern of those who followed and will for a still undetermined span follow him. To arouse this national will Smolenskin worked with the unparalleled devotion of the apostle who has no fear of the thorny path of propaganda. A grateful people, remembering the sincerity even more than the achievements of his mission, has allotted him a place of honor in the memory of posterity.

CHAPTER X

THE NEW NOVEL

The Holy One, blessed be He, rehearsed all the good qualities He could give to Israel, and found only poverty.

TALMUD.

THE father of the modern Hebrew novel is generally taken to be the unworldly dreamer of Kovno, Abraham Mapu (1808-1867). Fondness for Biblical Hebrew inspired his two widely read and much praised novels, *Ahabath Ziyyon* (*The Love of Zion*) and *Ashmath Shomeron* (*The Guilt of Samaria*), in which he restored the heroic-idyllic past of the Holy Scriptures. *The Love of Zion* (1853) in particular influenced whole generations, and remained for every Maskil the most delightful of his youthful recollections. Even to-day Hebrew-reading children derive much pleasure from it. (Professor Joseph Klausner wrote only recently of this novel that it is "the most romantic and the most permanent for its immutable value in the entire new literature.") But when, in the sixties of the last century, Mapu turned—under the influence of the times—toward actual life and away from the poetic remoteness of the epoch of Isaiah, his creative faculty failed him altogether. He was no delineator of the lowlands, and his *'Ayit Zabu'a* (*Speckled Bird of Prey*), (which in Hebrew implies a Tartuffe), despite occasional pleasing passages, is an irretrievable failure.

The ability to depict the lowlands of Jewish reality with a plastic power of visualization that opened new vistas in Jewish literature and raised it to artistic worth by the standards of general literature, was the gift of that great epic poet of East European Jewish life, who holds one of the most honored places in both Hebrew and Yiddish letters, Shalom Jacob Abramowitz (1835-1917), famous under his pseudonym of *Mendele Mokher Sefarim,* Mendele the Bookseller. It was the artistic and authentically Jewish form of Mendele's narratives that first established the *modern* novel in Hebrew, and thus proved that the Jews still have the capacity for creating epic art.

I

Epic writing demands calm, the proverbial calm of contemplation, a cheerfulness of disposition that takes joy in beholding, that is eager to embrace the abundance of the visible world. The epic mind revels in the delights of vision, with no aim other than reverent curiosity and astonishment. This art of observation was lost to the Jew. In the Diaspora, where he dwelt for long centuries upon tottering, volcanic ground, living in continual disaster or fear of disaster, his soul became all unrepose and discord, agitated by a feverish uneasiness, able, indeed, on the spur of the moment, to conceive keen concepts, hasty flashes of the spirit, but incapable of that lasting equilibrium and long continuity of mood which are the prerequisite for genuine achievement. The Jew was able to create only fragments, most amazing fragments at times, but no whole image, because he had no unity of will and of spirit; because his idea was a fragment, his emotion a fragment, his soul a multitude of fragments. Hence the short breath of his creations. He could write lyric poems, the children of momentary enthusiasms; but he had not the staying power, the sustained will, the tranquillity of the unsplit soul that epic creation requires. Then, again, the ascetic trend of Jewish history in the

Galuth forbade joy in gazing upon the beauty of the world, that joy without which epic writing is unimaginable. As I have said, the Jew was never to forget that he was in an alien environment, that his heart was not to lust after alien delights. Hence the eye was blasphemed as "a mediator for sin." For gazing was a sin.

These two factors—the outward adverseness of the Jewish destiny and the inward voluntary ban upon all the joys of the alien environment—bred in the course of time a systematic hostility to the eye, to art; bred a proneness toward imageless abstractness which estranged the Jew from nature and from art. Galuth degeneration changed the self-imposed iconoclastic interdict ("Thou shalt not make unto thee a graven image") into an involuntary incapacity for image-making.

That that Jewish obliviousness to art is a product of circumstances and not an inherent peculiarity of the Jewish soul has been proven in modern times by many eminent pictorial artists of Jewish blood. In the art of Hebrew narrative this has been proven chiefly by Mendele, and then by his successors.

In a work of his old age, a veiled autobiography, Mendele portrays "self-taught artists" of the Ghetto in whom the urge to artistic creation worked unknown to themselves, unburdening itself in inadequate pursuits because favorable conditions were lacking. One of them is Herzel the Carpenter, to whom handicrafts afforded not only a source of livelihood, but a purposeless joy of creation, and who was at pains to decorate even the simplest furniture with ornaments and embellishments, following a deeply rooted play impulse which in other surroundings

247

would have made him an artist. Or an even better example is that born wood-carver, Lipa Hareubeni, whom the narrow confines of the Ghetto afforded no other outlet than the occupation of Melamed, and who, as we know from an earlier autobiography of Mendele's, was modeled after his own teacher:

> He was one of those men of the spirit, of the chosen few, who from birth are blessed with fine gifts: with understanding and skill and a kind heart, and who lack nothing at all except good luck. His refined character and habits, his pleasant domicile, the clean furnishings of his home, proclaimed in him the skilled craftsman. He knew how to draw and how to do all manner of artistic work and carving in wood and stone and brass, and had an innate urge to do such work. His fellow townsmen used to honor him with requests to make ornaments for the holy ark; to draw the *Mizrach* picture with all sorts of buds and blossoms and creatures that the fancy of the artist conceived, but that never yet existed in this world; to engrave tombstones; to draw designs for embroideries. . . . He was a teacher of babes; and, while he was teaching them, his hands were busy with pleasing occupations such as drawing and metal-work. This work exalted his spirit, soothed his mind, infused into his heart a strong love for God and His creatures, and sweetened his conversation. His mouth was a bubbling spring casting up pearls, and his eyes flamed with the light of the Torah. . . .

Mendele himself narrowly escaped a similar ignominious fate. He too was of that breed of born artists who transformed whatever they touched into images and pictures. When, in his very early youth, he was introduced to the Talmud which, in his witty manner, he characterizes as the "antique giant and Og, king of Bashan, in world literature," he at once endowed whatever he read with visual form:

When I came there [into the Talmud], I was like a man
for the first time visiting a great fair where many sorts of
merchandise and all manner of curious and desirable things
are displayed, and who is bewildered by the noise and
tumult on every side. Buyers and sellers, brokers and mer-
chants run about in great commotion, seized with the desire
for trading. They babble to each other, wink their eyes,
scrape their feet, quarrel, bargain, barter, with a terrific
hubbub. With my innate power of imagination I gave form
and shape to all who come within the portals of the Talmud.

In a late work he refers similarly to this gift, speaking
of Shlomele, his *alter ego:* "He was beloved for his sense
of humor, and even more for his quickness in noting with
one flash of the eye every odd gesture and trick of speech
of a person, and imitating him marvellously in every detail
like an artist,—until the bystanders would almost burst
with laughter."

Mendele's mimetic gift and powers of plastic represen-
tation were fortunately stronger than the unpropitious
circumstances. Like almost all the poets of the Ghetto,
he had had Sorrow beside his cradle; and like them, he
had no need of seeking out Dame Poverty, having known
her all his life. It was only in his ripe manhood, after he
had richly enjoyed her blessings, that he was able to
divorce her. Irony aside, though poverty endangered his
health and threatened to ruin him as an artist, it was
for all that a source of poetic inspiration which he gratefully celebrated in song. The praise of poverty is quite
in the spirit of the ancient, melancholy Midrash: "The
Holy One, blessed be He, rehearsed all the good qualities
He could give to Israel, and found only poverty. As the
proverb hath it, poverty becomes the Jew as a red saddle-
cloth a white steed." Similarly, the sorrow-calloused

Mendele finds many advantages in poverty. "Nothing is more poetical than poverty. Poverty makes one wise. Poverty promotes household peace, brings the hearts of parents closer to their children and the hearts of children closer to their parents. Poverty refines the soul for noble emotions and good deeds."

And yet all Mendele's efforts at social reform were directed against poverty, against need in every form, which he considered not only a misfortune, but quite like G. B. Shaw, a crime. A contradiction? Perhaps. But a very human one, which conjures up a similar inconsistency from the Italian *trecento*.

In the lower church at Assisi, Giotto di Bondone painted, beside other allegories of the Franciscan vows, one of poverty in which he revealed probably the finest traits of his soul. But the same Giotto wrote against this particular Franciscan virtue one of the most cynical poems of the epoch, *La canzone intorno alla poverta,* which brands poverty as the cause of all sin:

> It driveth judges to injustice,
> It taketh honour from women and maidens,
> And men it seduceth to steal and to rape.

Artists, it seems, need at times to recover from themselves, and to see the converse side of their accustomed opinions. However that may be, personal experiences of poverty taught Mendele to find in the lowlands of life, among the poor and the disinherited, beside filth and decay noble human emotions and delicate poetic beauty.

It is as if the invisible hand of destiny had ordered Mendele's life so that he was to know all aspects of Jewish existence and test every rung in the ladder of Jewish misery, placing him in a period that was a kind of twilight of the gods and allowing him, in the course of a long life, to experience both the traditional authenticity of Jewish forms of life and the new currents of the Haskalah, Positivism and Zionism.

Born in the typical Lithuanian Jewish townlet of Kapyl, in the province of Minsk, Mendele was brought up in the strict old way which he so severely belabored and so affectionately yearned for in later years. Though he did not know the environment of his native land, its history or its customs, his inborn gift of imagination and his studies carried him to distant foreign lands, into the kingdoms of Sichon, King of the Amorites, of the Queen of Sheba; to Assyria, Babylonia, Egypt, in general, to the remote magnificence of the East. He did not know the local Russian vernacular, but he did understand not only Hebrew, but Aramaic in its various dialects. Vivid and enchanting to his imagination was the Oriental plant-world: nothing but vineyards, date-palms, figs, pomegranates, myrtle, acacia, mandrakes, lilies of Sharon. He was barely acquainted with the fauna of his own district, but knew all about the fantastic animals of the Orient: the ostrich, the asp, the viper, the flying serpent, the Leviathan, the Rahab, the behemoth, the legendary dragon as large as Mount Tabor, whose nose alone could be taken into the ark of the Deluge, and the huge bird Bar Yochna, whose egg, when it fell, sank sixty great cities and broke three hundred cedars. . . .

Notwithstanding this curious, one-sided education, and the asceticism of his youth, Mendele fondly recalls childhood memories of being summoned by his father while it was still night to go to the house of study and "learn" in the heavy folios of the Babylonian Talmud. For examples of Mendele's masterly descriptive powers and of the homely guise which nature took on in the alien countryside for the Jewish child reared in pious traditions, the reader is referred to Mendele's ripest and last work *In Those Days*.

Not for long did his childhood idyll endure. The father died when the boy was thirteen, leaving the family in dire poverty. Our orphan had to leave the home nest for the hard world outside. He made for the Yeshiba, going first to Slutzk, and then to other centers of Jewish learning. He went also to Vilna, where for a while in the Gaon's house of study, he could still savor the traditions and the legend that was weaving around this last marvel of rabbinic Judaism. It was then that Mendele tried out the hard bench of the Beth Hamidrash, which usually served him for a bed. Later he was to write that only on that hard bench, as on the hard stone where of old Jacob laid his head, did heavenly visions reveal themselves.

When his mother married again, Mendele returned to his beloved native surroundings where at the mill rented by his stepfather (like Rembrandt at his father's windmill in Leyden) he steeped himself in the mysteries of nature, as if preparing himself to depict its charms with a mastery up to then unknown in modern Jewish literature.

A grotesque accident drove him far away once more. An uncle of his went into bankruptcy and ran away, leaving his wife and children unprovided for. Thereupon the deserted wife was advised by a crippled beggar, whom

Mendele later portrayed as "Fishke the Lame," to travel through the "rich" southern provinces of Russia, ostensibly to seek her husband, but actually to trade upon her own misfortune by *schnorring* (begging). Young Mendele was taken along, because the lame beggar saw in him a fine source of prospective profit: with his unusual equipment of Jewish scholarship, he could be *shadchened* (married off) to a rich girl. Despite all the vexations of the trying journey (of course they traveled in a cart drawn by a weary, bony old mare), it had an unwonted charm for a young poet thirsty for life and eager to observe. It was on this journey that he became acquainted with the habits and customs of the vagabond beggars whom he later described with such historic fidelity. And it was here that the literary character of the bookseller riding about the country in a cart was originated.

When the adventures grew somewhat too lively for Mendele, and the lame rascal annoyed him too much with his beggar's tricks and suggestions of marriage, he decided to steal off secretly. The attempt failed because the lame wretch had taken away his passport which in Russia was more important than its possessor himself. But he managed finally to free himself in Kamenetz-Podolsk with the aid of a young friend of his Yeshiba years.

He left the *schnorrer's* cart, and began, under the influence of A. B. Gottlober, a Haskalah writer who enjoyed much local authority, to devour worldly knowledge and Maskilic literature. After passing the necessary examinations in 1857, he became a licensed teacher in one of the state elementary schools. That same year, his first article, which was devoted to educational questions, appeared in

Hamaggid. The article has been composed incidentally as a private letter in behalf of a teacher who complained of his professional hardships and miseries, but Gottlober sent it on to the magazine.

Therewith began Mendel's literary career, which shoved his personal history into the background. It shall merely be set down here that at times he had to change his domicile, for some piece of literary outspokenness. At last, in 1881, he was called to become director of the Talmud Torah in Odessa, a post which he filled until his death at a ripe old age.

II

Mendele's literary career clearly falls into three periods, which may be designated as the Maskilic, the period of social reform, and the purely artistic. During the first, as will be readily understood, he was imbued altogether with the strivings of his age. He wrote a novel in which even zealots for the old dogma were forced to admit the virtuousness of the champions of the Haskalah (*Study Well*, 1863, revised under the title of *Fathers and Sons* in 1868). Then, following the positivist current, he translated a work on zoölogy into Hebrew (1867). But even after he had gone over to Yiddish in 1865 and embarked simultaneously upon social reform propaganda, he still at times reverted to the ideas of his youth. In 1867 he composed a history of the Russian people in Hebrew; in 1869, collaborating with J. L. Bienenstock, he wrote the *Air Balloon*, and in 1870 *The Fish That Swallowed Jonah*, both in Yiddish. In a sense it is as if he never freed himself from the influences of Maskilism—which is proved, among other things, by the fact that he has never taken a more cordial attitude toward the newer currents of the national self-realization of the Jewish people.

In his autobiography he attempts to explain why he turned his back upon Hebrew and adopted the Yiddish folk-tongue, which he actually raised to the level of a literary language, himself becoming its first classic. Its motive was quite in the spirit of positivism, it sprang from utilitarian considerations. (It is truly interesting to note what varied influences the positivist philosophy exercised: some were impelled by it toward baptism, some toward assimilation, others again toward nationalism and Palestine; and here is one whom it moved toward Yiddish. That the Haskalah, which, at first, made the Yiddish folk-idiom responsible for the unmannerliness of the common man, should finally have led to a conscious fostering of its literature, this is another prank of history.)

"I observed the ways of our people," wrote Mendele, "and desired to give them tales in the holy tongue from the sources of Israel; but most of them do not know Hebrew, and speak the Jewish-German idiom. And what has the author for all his labor and thought if he do not profit his people?" Here we have a clear echo of Gordon's pessimistic outcry, "For whom do I toil?" Mendele knew that Yiddish was merely the dialect of servant girls and tailors' apprentices, that the intellectuals avoided it with scorn and disdain, that up to his time, its literature had been nothing but sheer twaddle and idle talk, and that he had little prospect of winning honors by devoting himself to it. However, "the desire to be useful overcame my concern with imaginary honors, and I said, Come what may, I shall take pity upon Yiddish, the unbeloved daughter; it is my duty to labor for my people!"

It has been suggested that the uncultured environment in which Mendele worked as a teacher must have made him think that writing in Hebrew was ineffective. But surely his going over to Yiddish was no accident, and also something more than a mere "love of utility." It was an artistic instinct that drove the master of realistic description away from the artificialities of translation: the contemporary Jewish life which he described was Yiddish-speaking, and translations into Hebrew sounded unreal and lifeless.

At that time he had not yet created that realistic language-form in Hebrew which forsook the solemn style of the Bible, and absorbed the sappy, flexible, colloquial qualities of the Mishna, the Midrash, the prayer book, the folk-story and folk-legend, and which, when smelted down by his skilled hand, constituted a new phase in Hebrew language-development. This creative achievement in the Hebrew language was not due to Mendele alone of course, for he had his predecessors; but it found in him a most consummate artist. And through this achievement it became possible to absorb all the sparkling folk-life of the Yiddish, and yet to lend to it the artistic distinction of a language of ancient civilization. So Mendele himself, as if driven by a protective instinct, translated the best of his works into Hebrew, and so rescued them for the whole of Jewry and for later generations.

It is not easy to define the limits of Mendele's social-reform period, for actually, like his first, Maskilic period,

it remained a constant tendency in his work all his life
long. Pure art and the reformer's urge to deeds made up
a closely intertwined pair of wrestlers in Mendele's soul,
even when in his very last years, old and weary of struggle, he apparently allowed himself to write for pleasure.
He sneers delicately, in his last work, at his own ever-
indecisive conflict:

> For a long time my pen has been placed between two con-
> flicting opinions in my breast, suspended like Mohammed's
> coffin—as the tradition has it—between two magnets. While
> one tendency draws me toward the past, the other pulls me
> toward what is being done in our own day; and these two
> struggle within me, like two shopkeepers who pounce upon
> a single customer and abuse each other's goods to him.

Only that in his youth, whence his blood and the urge
to action surged up more strongly, the reformer got the
upper hand: "A man is not free to refrain from the labor
of improving reality as far as possible, and must, *nolens
volens,* participate in the work of his own day." In his
riper years he realized that the present did not possess
a "type complete in itself, with a character of its own";
that the Maskilic type was vacuuous and bloodless, a
mere creature of passing alien influences, incapable of
artistic exploitation, while the authentic old forms of
Ghetto life, despite their dark sides, were nevertheless
"delightful vessels of antique impress, all of them the
work of our ancestors, whose spirit they still preserve."

In his first Yiddish works on social reform, Mendele
fought not against the legislative severities of the *Schul-
chan 'Arukh,* which he thought fictitious and to which the
uneducated Yiddish reader was simply indifferent, but

rather against the social evils of the Ghetto, against the communal leaders who robbed the people of their rights (*The Petty Little Man,* 1865), and against the fleecing of the poverty-stricken masses through unjust taxation (*The Meat Tax,* 1869). For characterization here, we shall be content with the motto of *The Meat Tax*—"For the oppression of the poor, for the sighing of the needy, now will I arise"—and the crusade of Weker, the first socialistic preacher in Yiddish literature, who condemned all pure poetry and all polite silence in the face of burning social wrongs: "I cannot keep silent, I must utter the truth. A curse upon him who sees such evils and out of fear stands aloof!"

In 1873, Mendele wrote his famous allegorical work, *The Mare,* a novel with a purpose which will continue to be read for its artistic worth long after its purpose has become immaterial and obsolete. The crack-brained Israel, an extra-mural student, who is studying feverishly in a frenzy of anxiety over his approaching examinations, frees a harassed mare from her tormentors (of course he is a member of the S. P. C. A.). He is overwhelmed when she suddenly addresses him in human speech, asserting she is no scurvy beast, but a prince under a spell. Israel is bewildered and helpless, especially when he observes her closely in the moonlight, and sees her

> eating hay very contentedly and with a keen appetite, like a born animal. Peculiar emotions began to struggle with each other in his heart. At one moment his pity for the forsaken and humiliated mare would get the upper hand, and the next he was filled with anger that she seemed not to mind wallowing in mud. How could she enjoy hay after the terrible blows and all that had happened to her

> during the day! Then it occurred to him that all he had
> seen was nothing but a dream, and that there stood before
> him nothing but a simple, boorish mare!

This contrast between the princely soul and the animal-
like ugliness of a people degenerated in the Ghetto suggested to Mendele the grotesque idea of depicting the Jew
as transformed from a prince into an abject mare. At
first the idea seems æsthetically repulsive; but, as one
continues to read, he is struck by Mendele's skill in min-
ing such a wealth of analogies and so much truth out of
the caricature.

The Haskalah delusion is thrown overboard. When
the mad Israel advises the mare to educate herself in
order to improve her lot, she rebukes him bluntly:

> Fool! To this poor, disgraced creature, they say: "edu-
> cate yourself!" To begin with, why is this decree imposed
> upon me in particular? Behold, there are many animals in
> the world, ignorant horses and donkeys that have never
> been educated in a stable, and yet they earn their living
> without pain. Would that I might grow fat like them!
> What has enlightenment to do with earning a living? Sec-
> ondly, I am like all other creatures, and do not want my
> needs to be supplied merely because I am of some use to
> others. Like all that lives, I am for myself, and live for my
> own sake.

In the year 1869, before composing *The Mare*, Mendele wrote a novel entitled *Fishke the Lame* (revised into
Hebrew in 1888 under the title of *The Book of the Beggars*) which, despite the bias that no book of his is free
from, betokens the triumph of purely artistic elements.
The book grew out of the years when Mendele had become acquainted with the life of the wandering Jewish
beggars, his faithful description of whom makes the book

an authentic historical document. The plot is quite simple. Fishke the Lame is a servant in the bathhouse of his
native Duncetown. He waits vainly for the epidemic
when, in accord with the Jewish custom in such emergen-
cies, he will have to be married off by the community;
waits until, through a happy accident—the disappearance
of a beggar whose wedding was about to take place—he
is united with a blind orphan girl who begs at the ceme-
tery. The crippled pair travel with a caravan of other
beggars from town to town, while the author gives us an
affecting insight into the doings of the ragged crew.
Fishke is unlucky in his marriage. His wife becomes too
intimate with another beggar, the "red-headed bastard",
and he himself finds in the beggar community a hunchbacked maiden whom he learns to love with a chaste and
touching love. He tries several times to divorce his wife,
but is always thwarted, until, finally, the beloved hunch-
back disappears through the cunning of his red-headed
rival, who does not wish to lose her: she is both a good
source of income for the pity she arouses, and the object
of his lust. Fishke goes off into the wide world to
seek her, and is on his way to Duncetown in the hope
of finding her there, when the novel breaks off
abruptly.

The hero is not, however, Fishke the Lame. His love
tale takes up a scant few pages, and he tells the story of
his life to two wandering booksellers, Mendele and Alter,
the latter of whom turns out to be the father of the unhappy hunchbacked maiden. How delicately Mendele
frames the love confessions of the cripple! He succeeds
by his art in banishing our almost unavoidable physical

revulsion, disclosing tender human beauty and ideal love among the rejected of mankind.

> Why should I deny it? I first began to love her out of great pity, later for herself. Something drew me to her: I took pleasure in merely sitting and chatting with her. . . . What? Nothing, just so! Either chat or be silent, and gaze at one another. Goodness shone in her face. She looked at me like a devoted sister upon an unfortunate brother at a time when he feels ill, very ill; and sorrow for me brought tears to her eyes. Then I felt as if a warm wave of delight were flowing through my body. I thought something, I thought. . . . I myself don't know what. Something glowed within me, caressed my soul: Fishke, you are no longer alone in this great world,—and my eyes were wet with scalding tears.

However, the actual theme of *Fishke the Lame* is not the individual, but the colorful life of the beggar-mob in general. This *Book of the Beggars* is a true epic of Jewish beggardom in the sixties and seventies of the last century.

Because of its delicious comedy, great popularity accrued to *The Travels of Benjamin the Third* (1875) a novel in which Mendele, though inspired by Cervantes, ridiculed in a thoroughly Jewish manner, if at times too mercilessly, the Quixotism of the Ghetto. This time the hero's domicile is called Idlerstown. These three—Idlerstown, Duncetown and Beggarstown—constitute to Mendele's mind, the typical sins of the Ghetto: Hatred of manual labor, ignorance, and pauperism, the outcome of the first two. A citizen of Idlerstown was once asked, "*Reb* Jew, what do you do, and how do you support yourself?" At first he scratched himself in embarrassment, and when at last forced to reply, said:

His Name be praised, I have as you see a gift from His beloved Name, an instrument—a voice to sing; so I am often called to pray in the synagogue. I am one of the best *Mohel's* (circumcisers) and *matzah*-bakers in the world. I am also a marriage-broker, and sometimes succeed in that. And I have a permanent seat in the synagogue. I have, between ourselves and the lamp post, a blind still which brings in a little. Nor do I lack a goat which, forfend the evil eye!—gives me a little milk. And not far from here I have a distant relative who helps me out in time of need. But beyond all these things, I tell you that the Lord is a good Father, and the Jews merciful sons of the merciful. And why should a man complain?

Now it once happened that dates from Palestine somehow reached Idlerstown. They created an unusual commotion among the Jews, and everyone rushed to look at them. The Pentateuch was consulted, and the places pointed out where dates were actually mentioned. The event had a much profounder effect than this upon one of the inhabitants, because for years he had read the adventurous travels of Eldad Hadani and Benjamin of Tudela and the miracle tales of *Praises of Jerusalem,* and he intended one day to seek the independent Jewish tribes beyond the Sambatyon, the river that flows turbulently all week long and rests only on the Sabbath. The dates from the Eastern land increased this desire still more, and he decided to make a pilgrimage to Palestine and to the red-haired Jews of the Sambatyon. Being very timid by nature and unused to travel, he began to train for the journey by sleeping all alone in a room, going out alone at night, taking walks beyond the town limits, and similar heroic acts. For a traveling companion he enlisted "Sendril the Woman," so called because he was henpecked and did all manner of women's work. Before Passover his wife would set him to whitewashing with his head wrapped in a large cloth which was tied under his beard. He also peeled potatoes, rolled and cut noodles, and prepared stuffed fish. This Sendril was an admirable companion because he consented to everything and agreed with everybody. Preparations for the journey required little time, for they were already equipped with the essentials: first, they had a knowledge of the Aramaic language of the Targumim spoken by the free Jews of the Sambatyon; and, second, provisions could be begged on the way. Therefore they took with them only what was absolutely necessary for the long journey: praying shawls, phylacteries, and a beggar's wallet. Thus equipped, they started out one cloudless morning, stealing away from their wives in the dim dawn. "And the skirts of their garments flapped and waved in the wind, the travelers resembling a ship at sea with all its sails spread."

I can hardly describe the innumerable adventures, full of delightful humor, which the heroes were permitted to enjoy in various Ghetto towns: how they roused both faith and doubt, becoming the topic of conversation and even of heated controversy; how they were enthusiastically led into town by two ancient and pious virgins who were wont to go out beyond its bounds every evening to await the messiah; how they were almost caught on a narrow bridge by their own wives, who had followed them; how they landed in army barracks, where they were conscripted; how they were there robbed of the glories of hair and beard; how they were made to go through military exercises (childish folly to their Jewish minds); how, when army life became too much for them, they tried to run away; and how, of course, they were recaptured, and then released on the report of a psychiatrist. . . . One laughs to the point of tears over this novel, even though it scoffs so bitterly at all Jewish idealism. Not only is Zionism sneered at; rather, does this book show up the tragicomedy of an uprooted people which, lacking the normal conditions of growth in a homeland, under alien heavens bursts forth into eccentricities.

Aside from any particular tendency, however, we have here an abundance of humor and a telling descriptive art, as a short specimen may indicate:

> Without, the day began to dawn; and inside the house, all was quiet. There was not a sound but the snoring of a houseful of sleepers, each according to his habit: One snored like a banjo, another like a trumpet. One was brief and quiet about it, another went higher and higher on three notes, like one embarrassing his friend with a very difficult question, winding up angrily with puffed-out cheeks. Together they composed a snoring symphony, the noses playing all instruments, in honor of the famous local bedbugs that feasted upon the flesh of the sleepers and drank their blood—Jewish blood.

His most finished and artistically most valuable works Mendele wrote only toward the end of his life, as, for example, his *Vale of Tears* (1888), and his beautiful, mature last work *In Those Days* (1894), from which I have already given some extracts when quoting Mendele's biography. The limits of this book forbid a more detailed account of their contents. In any event, this would serve no purpose, since the plot is wholly a side issue, and the milieu, the *genre,* everything:

THE NEW NOVEL

Truly, what can I tell about our life? Things great and unheard-of? Neither I nor my father's house have amazed the world with our deeds. Dukes, knights, strategists, army leaders, warriors, we have never been; nor have we made love to fair maidens; nor have we tilted at each other like goats; nor have we tried standing by as seconds when blood was shed by others in duels. How to dance with brides and virgins at feasts we have not known; nor have we gone out hunting quarry in field and forest; to the ends of the earth and on remote seas we have not traveled; and new islands we have not discovered; in the assembly of merry men and merry women we have not sat; upon female singers and pleasures we have not wasted our substance; in brief, we have none of the ingredients for a charming tale to please the reader. . . .

But, instead, we have a Cheder, a Melamed, a Melamed's assistant, marriage-brokers, bridegrooms and brides, feeble old folk and tots, infants and women, forsaken wives, widows and orphans, people whose all has been destroyed by fire, and others who have come down in the world, beggars who go from house to house on Sabbath eves, festivals, New Moons, and on any day at all. We have all kinds of calamities, all shades of poverty, all sorts of queer occupations. This, alas, is our life; it is an ugly life, without pleasure or satisfaction, without splendor, without light, a life that tastes like lukewarm soup, without salt or spice.

And yet, with no artificial idealization and even at times with sharp satire, Mendele knew how to portray the radiant beauty of the old Ghetto forms of life, institutions, and figures. He raised up in poetry what in life seemed already irrevocably lost—the authentic medieval Jewry which still existed in Eastern Europe in the nineteenth century. Mendele's writings contain, for the knowledge and edification of later generations, an exact description of this world, with its house of study, synagogue courtyard, old folk's asylum, poorhouse, community home,

burial society, ritual baths; with the figures that populated them, the rabbis, dayanim, cantors, gabbaim, marriage-brokers, melamdim, kabbalists, authors, magnates
and beggars, busybodies, bootlickers and idlers, quacks,
leeches, wonder-workers—there is even an informer. In
Mendele's world nature itself keeps time to the tempo of
the Jewish calendar.

This world has its shadows, its dread curse, but—perhaps because it is already extinct—we are the more inclined to se its brighter sides, its values of Jewish community life and Jewish solidarity. That is why in Mendele's last works, when he himself saw the decline of the
life he described, its forms are so poetically transfigured.
It is as if he wanted to hold fast a little longer to a world
of beauty in the last phase of its twilight. "Stay, O Moment, thou art so beautiful!" But in vain. Time pushes
on, and the distinctive life of the Ghetto irretrievably
crumbles away.

David Frischman, one of Mendele's "grandsons," the
literary generation influenced by him, once said that if a
catastrophe were to destroy Jewish life altogether (as, in
the meantime, has almost happened in Russia), it would
be possible to reconstitute the small-town life of East
European Jewry in the nineteenth century on the basis of
Mendele's writings. For Mendele was the great epic
poet of that Jewry; and his works, in which artistic skill
is mated with historic truth, are of that high, almost antique art that reminds us of the ancient Hellenic epos.
And it is to be hoped that, like the latter, they are to be
the dawn of a new art—in Hebrew.

CHAPTER XI

THE THINKER OF THE JEWISH RENAISSANCE

I have no need to exalt my people to heaven, to trumpet its superiority above all other nations, in order to find a justification for its existence. I know "why I remain a Jew"—or rather, I can find no meaning in such a question, any more than if I were asked why I remain my father's son. I can speak my mind concerning the beliefs and the opinions I have inherited from my ancestors, without fearing to snap the bond that unites me to my people.

AHAD HA'AM.

I RECALL the last time I saw Ahad Ha'am. It was in Haifa, during the summer of 1926. Modestly secluded on Mount Carmel, within the intimacy of his family circle, far from the rejoicing masses of his people in Palestine and the Diaspora, the venerable thinker and leader of modern Hebraism was celebrating his seventieth birthday. Though old age gnawed at his frame and had already seriously impaired it, his still unclouded spirit quietly and proudly watched Time as it passed by, knowing the most precious fruits of his life would remain unscathed. We who reverently surrounded him felt that the aged philosopher had distilled his better self into works that constitute one of the most significant achievements of the Jewish spirit in modern times. He could therefore (to use a simile of Nietzsche's) look on with almost malicious joy while age slowly disintegrated body and mind, as though watching a thief at a treasure-chest, all the while knowing it to be empty and the treasures safely stored away.

Only a few months later he was escorted to his last resting place by a great funeral cortège such as Tel Aviv had never yet seen. A shudder of grief passed through the whole Jewish people, *ke-ebhel yachid,* "as a people mourneth for its only son." For many a year the modest "One of the People" (*Ahad Ha'am*) has been "The Only One of His People" in the public mind. And again we felt: That the death of a Jew, of even a great Jew, could be felt throughout the scattered sections of Jewry as a national loss to the whole Jewish people—this was not the least of Ahad Ha'am's achievements.

I

Outwardly viewed, the simple, modest life-course of Asher Ginzberg (Ahad Ha'am's proper name) was anything but exceptional. Most touching is it to read in his *Recollections* how timid and shy, how lacking in confidence in himself and his talent was the most eminent man of modern Hebrew letters not only in his youth but even in late age. His biography is simple, typical of the nineteenth century Jewish middle-class in Russia. He was born in 1856 of well-to-do Chasidic parents who reared him in strict piety. But the spirit of the times was already stirring, and at eight he secretly learned to read Russian. However, the lasting influences of his education he owed to Jewish tradition, the Talmud, and medieval Jewish philosophy. It was only after his marriage— but before he was seventeen—that the influence of foreign cultures came into his life: first was the Russian culture, chiefly through Pissarev and his positivist comrades-in-arms; and then, much later, came the West European thinkers, especially Spencer. On the threshold of his thirties, after an unsuccessful attempt at study in Vienna, he moved to Germany, and there vainly tried to become a regular university student.

Returning to Odessa, he was attracted to the "Lovers of Zion" movement, headed at that time by Dr. Leo Pinsker. At first he kept humbly silent, but it was not long before he became one of the most influential personalities in that movement, which he censured for spreading itself out too thin in philanthropy. Instead he emphasized the national and spiritual function of the Hebrew renaissance, soon formulating his theory that Zionism answers the spiritual and national necessities of Judaism, but not the economic distress of the Jews. This train of thought was outlined in his first article, which appeared in *Hamelitz* in 1889; and it led him, though at first he resisted, to yield finally to the growing army of his adherents who wished to organize a secret association to carry his ideas into effect. This group was called the *Bene Moshe,* after Moses, the liberator of the Jewish people from Egypt, the name of the organization being intended to remind the members of the example of the deliverance in antiquity and to teach them to sacrifice themselves to the duties of the hour. (Later Ahad Ha'am devoted an essay to Moses which, from the viewpoint of both thought and form, was one of his most finished pieces of writing). In its six years of existence the *Bene Moshe* initiated a number of enterprises, establishing a Hebrew publishing firm in Warsaw, a Hebrew school in Jaffa, and helping to found the village of Rechoboth in Palestine. But, as Ahad Ha'am's cautious minuteness did not fit him for leadership, it is not to be wondered at that Herzl's fascinating call quickly inflamed all hearts, so that the *Bene Moshe* faded out of existence:

Ahad Ha'am fought political Zionism with a vehemence and an austerity which embittered that whole period. He had the unflinching courage to fight alone, and to tell the unpalatable truth in the most solemn hour (just as earlier he had done in the "Lovers of Zion" movement when, unafraid of imperiling the flow of funds which in any case was very slow, he wrote his very compromising *Truth about Erez Israel* in 1891 and again in 1893). In the monthly *Hashiloach* which he edited for years and brought up to a level previously unknown in Hebrew literature and rare in periodical literature generally, Ahad Ha'am reviewed all contemporary events in Jewry from a philosophic watchtower, educating that whole generation through his penetrating gravity of thought and his perfection of form. After leaving *Hashiloach* he rarely appeared in print; but, when he did, it was in some of his ripest and profoundest utterances.

In London (where he was associated with a tea firm) he participated in the Zionist counsels and advised Dr. Chaim Weizmann in his diplomatic endeavors, which led to the Balfour Declaration and to the Mandate of Great Britain over Palestine. However, except for some moving passages in his diary about the horrors of the world war and an extensive correspondence now available in six volumes, he wrote nothing in his later years of the quality for which his name stands. As the first honorary citizen of Tel Aviv, the first Hebrew city, he lived out his last years in Palestine, enjoying the utmost veneration, happy in his own days to have seen the beginnings of the realization of his life work, but even more of the life work of his great opponent, Theodor Herzl.

II

For the Hebrew reader, Ahad Ha'am will always remain the sober and rigorous thinker whose whole bearing proclaimed him illusion-free. His very first appearance in Hebrew life and letters was already characterized by poise and composure. From the outset his whole individuality showed maturity, balance. This distinguished reserve of his was exasperating. His logical equanimity in the face of the life and death problems of a declining people rankled.

Jewish periodical literature had always glowed hot with temperament, agitation, ardor, unrestraint, outpourings of emotion. Such seems to be the national mode of speaking and writing. We have always been accustomed to it from the volcanic admonitions of the prophets down to the storm-tossed works of a Berditchewski or a Brenner. Even in the centers of world civilization, in the repressed countries of the North, through the veil of strange tongues, the Hebrew remained faithful to his temperament in the discussion of public affairs. Compare the most important Jewish publicists in all languages: they all seem to join in Ludwig Boerne's rage against Olympian calm: "A thousand times rather Kotzebue's warmish soup of tears than Goethe's frozen wine!"

Besides, human beings in general are inclined to exaggerate. There exists in all of us a strong inclination, very ancient and inborn, to enhance actual experience, to exaggerate contrasts, to heighten colors, to transform the original facts with a view to more vivid excitement and the more active participation of our emotions. Ecstasy is easier than composure; temperateness more difficult than exaggeration. Straightforward reporting of facts and their objective evaluation constitute the most difficult and the ultimate spiritual conquest.

What wonder, then, that Ahad Ha'am's steady deliberation was not well understood. How insulting was his aristocratic skepticism, his "it seems to me" in matters which to the whole "Youth" were emotional certainties and most sacred yearnings.

There was hardly another Hebrew writer of the new time able to express his thoughts so clearly and precisely. But despite Ahad Ha'am's lucidity of style and rare clarity in the presentation of his thought, there is barely an essay of his upon which he had not to comment with "explanations," "supplements," etc., because he was not understood. We are apt not to understand that which runs contrary to all our habits and opinions. The Hebrew reader was not accustomed to this aloof distinction in style and thought, to this consummate objectivity free from all personal failings (lacking which there is no *human* charm!). He was habituated to immediacy, intimacy, familiarity in his authors, which led him to pardon their occasional lack of the austerities and the exactions of logic.

But here came one who did not consider himself a writer, but only a "guest" in Hebrew literature—one who was all purpose and self-mastery to his finger tips. He was cautious to exasperation, moderate—beyond all the bounds of moderation (as was said of Aristotle: *metrios eis hyperbolen*). He was always demanding the postulate of reason, the "supremacy of reason." He seemed immune to delusions, incurably sober. . . .

It took us long, very long, to learn to listen to the beating of the heart under the mask of seeming logical poise and detachment—to listen to its unrest, its yearning, and its faith. Until we realized that the heart which so ruthlessly weighed idea and reality against each other, was secretly bleeding. . . . Most of us, however, were deceived by Ahad Ha'am's outward calm. We were like the sight-seer who gapes at a work of art and touches the cold marble of a statue without ever guessing at its hidden fire. . . .

In one of the "sins of his youth" entitled *The Dry Leaves,* which, unlike the rest of his youthful writings, he did not condemn to the *Genizah* or limbo of non-publication, Ahad Ha'am relates:

> I recollect a story which I heard or read as a school boy about Abraham the Fool, a village simpleton, who was once seen running excitedly, carrying a club in his hand. As he was running, a calm person met him, who asked, "Whither and whence, Abraham?" "I'm off to beat N. till he bleeds —he's been speaking ill of me," replied Abraham and began to run again. "But," continued the questioner, "you are sure N. will let you beat him? He's larger and stronger than you are. Aren't you afraid he might take a club too and split your skull open?" Abraham halted in surprise, thought a moment, and then remarked, "That's so. You're right." Then he turned to go home.

This early incident seems to have etched itself into Ahad Ha'am's memory. In Abraham the Fool he saw the symbol of his light-minded people which acted before it thought, whose enthusiasm was untempered by reflection. He took upon himself the rôle of the quiet questioner in the story, and came ever and again to instruct his people: But first of all you must have knowledge, first of all you must. . . .

And, indeed, many minds have formed a picture of Ahad Ha'am as a clear-headed thinker, come to sober up the perfervid, to instruct them in the differences between idea and reality, theory and practice. Ahad Ha'am himself loved to coquet with this image of the sober thinker. More than once he emphasized that he was not like "one of the people" (a word-play upon the Hebrew meaning of his pen name) which knows only ecstasy and enthusiasm, but is without knowledge and understanding. Nevertheless, this characterization, be it ever so current and however fully it may have been accepted by Ahad Ha'am himself, is a depreciation of his true personality.

The superiority of the sober-minded is really problematical. If he delude himself in the realm of the abstract as to his superiority—yet, living in a world not of shadows, but of flesh and blood beings—he lacks the highest life-value, he is under the ban of the worst of all defects, sterility.

Once he had begun to think of man and the world, Ahad Ha'am realized this defect in sober-mindedness. Not only his experience and observation, but the will-to-creativeness in spirit and in life, taught him to see both the grotesqueness and the limitations of Abraham the Fool, which are obvious, and those of the sober-minded as well. So long as the fool was a fool, he went safely through life in his naïveté. Had not the sober man come along to disturb and so to weaken him in the midst of his activity, had he been left to run on, as he had begun, in confidence and faith, without too much questioning, he might have succeeded. His simple-mindedness might have been his salvation, and he would have achieved his aim, if only through sheer force of faith alone.

The wise carefully weigh pros and cons in the scale, consider every advantage and disadvantage, and do not stir until they have reasoned out the last detail of the thing to be done. And, behold, while they sit inquiring, those who have faith "come, see, and conquer."

Did Ahad Ha'am, then, know how to sober himself from sobriety?

He who had always preached the supremacy of reason, whose whole personality expressed reason and self-governance, was able, in his most important works and his most inspired hours (by which a man's thinking should be judged), to free himself from the *last delusion* of civilization, from the belief in the sole "supremacy of reason." And so he who, for all his rare talents, could have remained only a doctrinaire, a gifted grumbler and questioner perhaps, became a true creator in the realm of his people's life values, a father of the marvels of its regeneration.

This treason to sober-mindedness did not come upon the thinker unconsciously, stealthily, or unnoted, as he once keenly remarked of Maimonides in words that apply even more aptly to himself:

> Many phenomena show that "emotion" lived in him also, and worked actively but unbeknown in his heart to such a degree that at times it led him off the path of logic; and he let himself become entangled—something unusual with him—in contradictions that have no place in his system. Thus, from this angle, he gives us proof that the most logical person, trying to the utmost to let only reason dominate all his thoughts and acts, still has a hidden corner in his heart to which the supremacy of reason does not penetrate and which is defenseless against "rebels" that rise up to disturb the prevailing "order." . . .

But more than this. He had disdained the judgment of reason in *ultimate questions* not only in the hidden places and in the unconscious, as he described it in Maimonides, but with full intention and awareness. In basic decisions, he knew how to save himself from the intoxication of an exaggerated estimate of the creative value of reason. In his *Way of Life,* we find him writing:

> On the farther side of the limits of reason and demonstration, there is a great and powerful realm whose name is Faith. And there runs through all the controversies between the nationalist Jews and their opponents the distinction: "Those have Faith, and those have it not." In cases of doubt, the convictions and the acts spring from the *heart.*

"In cases of doubt" . . . but there were times when Ahad Ha'am knew that life even oftener than that rebelled against the certainties of reason. But the limitation to cases of doubt is very characteristic of him, and typifies his permanent—not transitory—teaching.

No life-teaching can be built upon the vagueness of the irrational, not for the individual and certainly not for a people. Miracles and accidents provide no base for a program of activity, or for the conduct of state and national affairs. The method of Abraham the Fool in national matters, the salvation of simple-mindedness, means yielding to the mercy of the most dangerous of all tyrannies, that of *Batlanuth* (*laissez faire*). Thence derives his postulate of the supremacy of reason, which is no mere intellectual *credo,* but a testimony to his devotion and sense of responsibility for the people's most vital concerns.

Whenever he fulfilled his burdensome mission of temperateness and came to "extinguish fires" that had flared up without cause, he had the right to give assurance that he had come not to paralyze the hands of the workers, but on the contrary, to guard them against discouragement. Though his somewhat controversial manner preferred negative forms, from "This is *not* the way," to "The Attempt which did *not* succeed," he never really denied any genuine value of his people. Therefore, when this man of deliberation and responsibility said Yes, a marvelous feeling of faith and confidence came over the whole movement, which in itself *alone* made for success.

When he saw men storming the great and powerful realm beyond the limits of reason, he did not refute them with the cheap moderation that conceives the world only in what is manifest and tangible. Though he quietly gave them his blessing, his sense of responsibility and his fatherly anxiety caused him to set up the command of caution and of reason! "Go softly and slowly, be prudent and deliberate—without haste or precipitancy, patiently and cautiously, taking *small* but *sure* steps. . . ."

The impatient and the short-sighted who had not his feeling of responsibility and strong devotion, and who were therefore ready—unlike him—to risk most precious treasures—believed him a dry fanatic of reason. In truth, however, he had experienced both: the achievements of reason and the wonders of faith. He recognized the advantages and the limitations of both, so raising himself above both. Freed from all illusions, from those about reason as well and yet without letting go of what certainties it has, he also, when his people was in distress, knocked at the secret gates "beyond the limits of reason and demonstration. . . ."

III

When he entered Hebrew literature, Ahad Ha'am was
a mature man of thirty-three. His first article, *Lo ze
hadderekh* ("This Is Not the Way"), which appeared in
Hamelitz, was so finished, compact and thoroughly thought
out that it was evident that years of travail had gone to
the achievement of clarity and of a consistent scheme of
thought. The style too, unusually precise and balanced,
which, in this maiden article, shows remarkable finish,
indicates years of training and exercise of the writer's craft.

In other cases, the reader grows along with the author,
follows his spiritual development; but in Ahad Ha'am
the factor of time seems to be excluded. He was uniform
and almost unchangeable from the beginning. The
Hebrew reader saw him only after he had fought his way
through to inner wholeness. He could not even imagine
that Ahad Ha'am too had wrestled, searched, erred,
doubted—until he had found himself. Since he had the
rare restraint in withholding his early works, the "sins of
his youth," from publication, his very first article shows his
whole intellectual scheme entire. Which explains his
ability to write for twenty-five years on end upon the most
varied questions and on the most dissimilar occasions
without ever involving himself in noticeable contradictions, or stepping outside the framework of his philosophy. His articles were almost always written for a particular occasion—and yet they coalesce into a system.
Everything hangs together. His first article contains his
whole spiritual content *in nuce,* the later writings merely
reveal it span by span. Something organic and inevitable

underlies whatever he says. One is reminded of the German thinker who said that "a man builds his philosophy like a beaver—and does not know that he is doing so." There is no more authentic sign of intellectual integrity, for what else, in a philosophic system, means truth?

Ahad Ha'am remained through the years what he had been from the first, writing only under the stress of an inner compulsion. He who had so much to say and a ready answer to almost every question in Jewish life, spoke only when it seemed to him sinful to hold his peace. He never wanted to be thought a writer. There was modesty in this, but also pride. Utterance for him was not merely a literary affair, but a living deed, a penetration of reality, an arbitrament in Jewish life. He saved his word for truly decisive moments so that, being seldom uttered, it might weigh the more.

Ahad Ha'am put the seal of sanctity upon the profession of the Hebrew writer. His own writing, being the matured fruit of an inner cumulation, insight and inability to refrain from speech, enforced respect. People felt that writing for him had the import of worship. They paused to listen to him in respect and obedience.

This same distinguished reticence, which testifies not to poverty but to abundance, marks his style, which became the school for modern Hebrew prose. Never, by so much as a hair's breadth, has he sacrificed thought to form in a language that is fascinatingly euphonic, and over-rich in ready-coined figures of speech. He meticulously avoided every shadow of exaggeration, preferring to incur the reproach of tediousness rather than to risk interesting, but inexact expression. His ascetic aloofness from all manner of word-jingling, which is so unhappily frequent in Hebrew, has made him an authentic renovator of Hebrew style. Buber has rightly said of Ahad Ha'am that, like the Apter Rabbi, he carried a golden scale in his mouth.

This is not only a literary, but a philosophic value. He who improves the word deepens the thought. If the thought be not thereby deepened, the word will not have been improved. Never yet was a man truly creative in speech who was not great in thought. Ahad Ha'am has some marvelous pages on this theme in his essay on *Hallashon vesifrutha* (The Language and Its Literature). In discussing the reproach of poverty which is made against the modern Hebrew language, he adduces a deeper reason in the poverty of thought which prevails in modern Hebrew writing. When truly great thoughts existed in Jewry, they found adequate expression, even in periods when the Hebrew language was on the decline. Ahad Ha'am admonishes the Hebrew writers quite in the spirit of Cato's *"Rem tene, verba sequentur"*: Have original thoughts, and you will not lack for words!

He himself is the surest example of the truth of this dictum. Though he did not outwardly break with tradition, his mode of employing the Hebrew language is epoch-making and revolutionary. He expanded the limits of expressibility in Hebrew to an incredible degree, and endowed the Orientally exaggerated language with the most priceless of the Western conquests—precision.

All who speak and write Hebrew to-day, though they may never have read him, are influenced in their speech and writing by Ahad Ha'am. He trained the Hebrew language into new paths. And though he himself went into a long silence, it went forward by the momentum which he gave it.

Yet he was only a publicist, one who wrote for the day. He wrote only when the occasion called forth his word, on quite specific questions just then on the *tapis*. Each of his articles was directed to a certain moment, and seems to have sprung forth by accident. It seems almost that had there been no outer stimuli, Ahad Ha'am would have written no line. And therein lies his peculiar greatness—that he wrote always for the Here and Now, ever rooting himself in the moment. But, just because he had something to say for his own day, he could say it for all time. Once more he has shown that true greatness never flees the reality, but always joyously affirms the commandment of the hour.

Every question he treats is elevated to philosophic heights, expanded in all its aspects, conveyed from the range of the temporary and accidental to the sphere of absolute meditation. On his fleeting articles we may well inscribe Spinoza's *"sub specie æternitatis."*

Therein he was like the old Jewish scholars and writers who wrote only "Questions and Answers" (*She'eloth Utheshuboth*) for definite occasions in their own time, in answer to daily needs, and yet became timeless. What they wrote in time-conditioned form became somehow a consistent theological or philosophical system. Even in Jewish antiquity, in the prophets, accident created the thing needed: the people's errors led to an ever purer God-idea. Organic mating of publicistic and philosophic elements is typical of the Jew—perhaps that is why the good inherent in each by itself could never quite ripen in

Judaism. Never has it been granted us, either in practical life or in the sphere of pure intellect, to achieve the ultimate and—for us—immanent values. In politics, the Jewish state remained theocratic. In thought, Jewish philosophy remained without science.

So, also, Ahad Ha'am is a Jewish thinker in his mode, but unconsciously rather than by conscious cognition. His manner of thought, which so strangely weds philosophy with public affairs, links him in spirit with Jewish tradition, leaving what is apparently peculiar to the individual rooted in ethnic characteristics. Thence Ahad Ha'am's popularity, in the finest sense of that word, among the Jewish people. The Jews have never really ranked the products of modern Hebrew literature with their ancient classics, but still—with all due esteem—view them as *Melitze-bichelech* (which freely rendered would be "clever journalism"). Among the moderns, only the works of Nachman Krochmal, and later of Ahad Ha'am, have been endowed with the title of nobility that attaches to the word *sefer*. Even if their content was not always approved, it was admitted that they had *weight,* and deserved to be ranged alongside the time-tested works of former generations.

Yet, popular as they are, there is in Ahad Ha'am's works an aristocratic renunciation of ephemeral fame. Something high and commanding in them, deriving from his sincerity, disdained to woo the crowd, but aimed to educate the best individuals. Nothing is to be found there of the *litterateur,* nothing of jealousy, envy, or ambition. Therefore he had not that continuous desire to create, which somehow becomes vulgar. The born aristocrats of the spirit do not seem too keen about creativeness. One quiet autumn evening they fall from the tree, without having been anxiously coveted, claimed, or shaken loose. Though, or perhaps because Ahad Ha'am had no literary ambitions, he became the most important of modern Hebrew writers. Apparently meditating only on his content, he became a finished master of modern Hebrew. He despised poetry, because it works with mere form. In this respect he resembles Plato, great writer and enemy of poetry. And he is like Plato in another respect also: that after his thoughts have long been current coin, he will still be read for the sake of his form alone.

IV

Ahad Ha'am's philosophy is one of the most thorough and original attempts to think the problem of the Jewish renaissance through. This philosophy so satisfied the intellectual needs of its time that it soon ceased to be the private property of its author and became the anonymous possession of the people. Therefore many of his ideas are found incorporated in contemporary Jewish life without people's knowing that they derive from him. Many a person may marvel at finding familiar ideas in Ahad Ha'am's teachings. But it needed his life work to make them so familiar.

Ahad Ha'am's teaching is not, as has been said, manifested in a rounded system even outwardly, since, after all, it was presented merely in the form of newspaper articles. Yet the basic features of his teaching can be readily discerned in the sporadic utterances made for particular occasions.

At the core of Ahad Ha'amism is set the problem of the meaning and import of the Jewish people. What is it that lends to a handful of individuals a seeming that betokens the inner, organic unity of a people? Ahad Ha'am, interpreting history through its heroes, holds that the living-together of numerous individuals gradually evolves, through the decisive influence of "central personalities," a certain group spirit: a common ego. This ego is a social, psychic, all-encompassing phenomenon which, ranging beyond all single individuals, lends to a loosely constituted group the inner character and unity of a people.

The nature of the folk-ego can be readily understood by comparing it with the individual ego. The latter may be loosely defined as the sum of memory plus will, the inner union of impressions in the past with wishes for the future—an organic, spiritual form which grows and develops simultaneously with the body. So, also, the folk-ego is a spiritual structure, an amalgam of past and future, pervading the individual units of the group with a common heritage of memories and aspirations. Hence, to Ahad Ha'am, the Jewish people means the Jewish folk-ego which has grown out of collective impressions gathered in the past and collective hopes for the future. He sees the future of the Jewish people in the destinies of this peculiar, historically shaped, national ego of the Jews.

The kernel of the Jewish problem lies in the dangers to which this Jewish folk-ego is exposed—not in the economic distress of the Jewish masses, dangerous as that may be to the national group, and urgently as relief is required; not even in the moral distress of the people, however seriously sections of it might be imperiled by anti-Semitism. The canker at the roots of the Jewish people is the menace to the integrity of its spiritual life, the progressive dissolution of the Jewish ego.

This menace derives necessarily from the fact of Jewish dispersal. In the varied form-worlds and spiritual atmospheres of alien national civilizations, forces are at work which, though the Jewish folk-ego still asserts itself stubbornly, must influence it significantly and—still worse—variously, in different places. It might happen, in the course of time, that the Jewish people will no longer be *one* people, but, as at the beginning of its national existence, be split up into many single tribes. There would then be not one, but many Jewries, each with a different character and different tendencies according to the land of its domicile. In the inner and outer estrangement of the unrelated communities, the oneness of the people would gradually be lost.

How can Jewish national unity be prevented from crumbling away in this wise? Political Zionism pointed out one method of offsetting disintegration and of assuring a national future for the Jewish people—that of concentration in its own land. But Ahad Ha'am held that an ingathering of most (not to say all) Jews in Palestine within a measurable time was not to be reckoned with. *Kibbutz galuyoth* was a messianic, not a contemporary ideal. Concentration must therefore take another form; a common bond must be created for the shattered parts of Jewry, or—to use an almost universally misunderstood term of Ahad Ha'am's—a "spiritual center" must be created for the Jewish people.

Just as, at the birth of a people, a "central personality" molds an aggregation of individuals into an organic community, so also a people may be reborn—though it be already in the throes of dissolution—if a unifying focus can be found for all its parts. If the group be in a late stage of civilization, this focus will be found not so much in a "central personality" as in dim antiquity, when heroes were worshiped, but in a *central domicile,* where all the dismembered limbs of the nation may become reunited. This central domicile must be chosen not for temporary or accidental reasons. Rather must it be possessed of attractive powers so strong that in a certain measure all the scattered parts of the people will find in it a compensating and directive element to offset the effects of the alien and different influences to which they are exposed.

For the Jewish people, *Erez Israel* offers such a central domicile. The land must again be set in the center of Jewish life, so that it may serve as a "model for imitation" for the people of Jewish stock in all the lands of exile, which, having a common focus, will be transformed from an amorphous dispersion into a circumference for the homeland center.

Ahad Ha'am envisioned a large, compact Jewish settlement in Palestine which would embrace all aspects of life, and live not for itself alone; its significance, as he saw it, would lie in its influence upon the Diaspora. Once the "central domicile" had become the unifying force in the life of the Jews of all lands, it would deserve the title of "Jewish spiritual center." In a word, only through Zion can the integrity of the Jewish folk-ego, the oneness of the

Jewish people and its normal development, be assured for times to come.

The above is but a sketchy outline of Ahad Ha'am's subtle, thoroughly worked out scheme of thought, a crude summary of the bases of spiritual Zionism. The scanty conclusions, which are so fragmentarily formulated here, barely leave room for apprehension of the terse logic of his ideas. As usual, the conclusions of a philosophy are not the best of it. In Ahad Ha'am, we find something a mere system of thought cannot give, namely, the source of many systems of thought: the great man.

Nevertheless, the outcome of Ahad Ha'am's thinking will never lose constructive meaning for the upbuilding of Palestine, or the power to attract intellectual Jews in the Diaspora to Zion. Though his teaching lack the bold grandeur of Herzl's concept of a Jewish *state* (rather than a mere settlement of Jews), it embraces within its scope the Jews of the whole world who, having a common center of interest in the land of their nationhood, will cease to be a pariah-people, and regain their original worth, dignity, and creativeness. Upon the influence which an ordered Jewish community in Palestine will radiate to the collectivity of Jews throughout the world, rather than upon its local value, Ahad Ha'am bases his system of thought. For that reason, his most convinced adherents will always be found in the Diaspora. At the same time, his teaching is of enduring value for Palestine as well. If it lacks the elemental force and magnificent scale of Herzl's solution of the Jewish question, it gains by the lofty inner pathos which demands *qualitative* achievement in Palestine. Ahad Ha'am does not want a Golus-like majority in Palestine at any price, but demands a model community developed by Jewish labor and Jewish genius, whose creative primacy the Jews of all the world will recognize with pride. Ahad Ha'am has repeated time and again, in various connections, that an ancient and cultured people which was once a "light to the Gentiles" cannot accept a minimum reward for all its sufferings, such as younger and uncultured peoples achieve within a short time. Not for nothing did prophets arise in Israel.

This insistence upon the prophetic postulate endows his seemingly modest and circumspect aim with almost visionary splendor.

It is extraordinarily significant that, despite this prophetic ideal for which Ahad Ha'am fought—or perhaps because of it—he showed his sense of responsibility by welcoming every beginning in the practical restoration of Palestine, were it the very least. He did not look down upon small beginnings. He has not "despised the day of small things." And if for others their political extremism was a pretext for avoiding work at the moment, for Ahad Ha'am the ultimate ideal was a goad and a spur to endure patiently the hardships of daily duties and labors.

That the peaceful conquerors of the Emek Jezreel regard themselves as the disciples and legitimate heirs of Ahad Ha'am is no accident. A. D. Gordon expressly proclaimed it so. They alone conceive his perhaps too intellectualized conception of Hebrew culture in a broader and more fundamental sense, for it is they who are trying to draw it forth from the Palestinian soil. The idea that all authentic culture grows out of the soil was implicit in

Ahad Ha'am's own writings. We must not be misled by his surface language, nor by the polemics of disciples who later became his opponents. As with all great thinkers, so with Ahad Ha'am: to understand is to transcend him.

CHAPTER XII

THE MOUTHPIECE OF THE FOLK

When we have found the word for the thing, we are done with it. In all speech there is a grain of contempt.

NIETZSCHE.

WHEN the grateful admirers of J. L. Gordon at his jubilee in 1883 presented him with a gold pen, the pessimist who spoke of himself as the "last of Zion's bards," asked in bitter jest, "My gold pen to my heirs; and my Hebrew pen—to whom?"

In 1892, the year of his death, he called to M. M. Dolitzky, his "companion in the temple of song and neighbor in the courts of the Lord," who by that time had settled in America: "Take thou my pen, go up, inherit my place!"

Did not Gordon feel that Dolitzky with his commendable but slight verses, which enjoyed much popularity at the time for their sentimental love of Zion, could not be heir to the earnest burden of his message? Or was this, too, a pang of renunciation, a choice of despair—since he thought Hebrew in any event doomed?

Gordon hardly suspected that his heir was to be the quite unknown poet who in that same year made his début with a song entitled "To the Bird" in the *Pardes* anthology. He must have seen that publication, for it contained two of his own poems, one of which, by the way, bristled with bad puns.

Nor did the beginner himself seem to apprehend what a high office and heritage he was to enter upon. Or, who knows? Perhaps bold thoughts were stirring within him, the more probably just because he was a beginner. For, in the second volume of *Pardes,* he laments Gordon in a poem called "The Dead Lion," which concludes with this passage:

> A jackal hast thou been to weep our woe,
> Who will be the harp to sing our song?

And that "Who?" was pensively echoed by the reader, who looked for the name under the poem: it was signed Ch. N. Bialik.

For it was Bialik who became the poet laureate of the Jewish renaissance, its most beloved name and most popular figure. However great and significant Bialik's achievements, the fame he enjoys extends far beyond his own deeds: it is nurtured by the forces produced by the whole epoch, but which the people, in an overflow of gratitude, has attached to his name. It is as if the folk-memory did not care to cherish its minor gods, and heaped all their conquests upon the single chosen one. Bialik himself has summed this up in an ironic Hebrew rhyme: *Al Bialik leth man d' palig* (there are no differences of opinion about Bialik).

This popular affection which made him a classic during his own lifetime, and in fact, even during his youthful years of growth, rose out of the instinctive feeling of the people that this poet is the authentic mouthpiece of the folk-spirit. They believed him still to have access to the buried ancient treasures of the nation and to draw sustenance from them. Unlike all the other poets of his time, Bialik at once took his place in the canon, though even some of the Biblical books in olden times had long struggles not to be relegated to the apocrypha. In Bialik the people have felt that something which pious faith calls divine inspiration. Alone among the whole generation of poets, they believed him to be the very domicile of the folk genius, so Jewish, so true to tradition, so "ritually pure" was the effect of his poetic art. Alcharisi said of Jehuda Halevi, "He came into the treasure-house of song and took all its choice vessels. When he went out, he closed the gate behind him." Bialik's adherents say that he reopened that gate, and found the way to the hidden golden fleece of Hebrew song.

In modern times such a direct enthrallment of the people is exceedingly rare. In late civilizations the artist writes not for the *people,* but for the *public,* an accidental group with nothing in common but its tastes. A people, however, is an organic unity wherein, if the poet have the warrant to invoke it, blood will answer the call of blood. Then comes that bright, golden resonance when the soul of the folk-unit and its individual poet ring in harmony. Such a happy concord of folk and poet resounds throughout Bialik's creations.

No wonder, for he grew wholly out of the folk-soil, drawing his characteristic inspiration from Jewish sources, free from alien influences to a degree quite unique in modern times. Later, self-taught, he appropriated much broad non-Jewish knowledge to himself, but by that time the contours of his soul were firmly drawn. The new culture could become no more than an outer stimulus, and could not begin to equal the wide scope of his knowledge in all fields of the Jewish legacy. Hence, his Hebrew style remained so idiomatically genuine, so true in root and in spirit, that he became the conscience of the Hebrew word and its supreme trustee. In this respect he towers above all contemporary and even above all earlier Jewish poets from the time Hebrew ceased to be spoken in the homeland. The Hebrew of the great Spaniards, with perhaps the sole exception of Gabirol or of Halevi, is eclipsed by the oppressive wealth of language in "The Dead of the Wilderness"; and one does not shrink—yes, one does shrink—from comparing it with the sacred force and fury of the prophets themselves. Translations of Bialik, of which there are a number in European languages, can give no adequate notion of his worth. For, however great his poetic value, the best of it lies in the language, and that is untranslatable.

II

Chaim Nachman Bialik was born in 1873 in Radi, Volhynia, and he owes his robust and almost unpoetic health to the fields and woods of his native village. His father, a learned, gentle sage, was obliged to lease an inn in order to maintain his family. The image of that father, bowed over his books in the dirty smoke of the hostelry, was graven deep in the poet's memory, as can be seen from one of his latest poems (published in 1929):

Behind barrels of liquor, over a book of yellow parchment,
I see the head of my father, the skull of a tormented martyr,
As if hewn away from its shoulders, floating in clouds of smoke,
The face drawn with pain, and eyes bloodshot. . . .
Drunkards shout round about, and sots wallow in their vomit,
Base visages and filthy talk,
The walls shrank back, the windows hid their faces.
But into my ear alone, the undefiled ear of a child,
Bubbled and flowed the silent murmur of pure lips,
A murmur of Torah and prayer and words of the living God.

It is not hard to understand why the father died early, during the poet's tender boyhood years. The whole burden of support then fell upon the mother, who battled desperately with bleak poverty. We read Bialik's description of the brave, unfortunate woman who wearily dragged herself about the market place the livelong day; and who, when she returned home, "crushed like an outcast dog," worked at her household tasks until late in the night. Yet, in the gray dawn, her lean figure was already bending over the rolling board, making bread for her children:

> My heart tells me and I know
> That into the dough dripped tears from her eyes.
> And when she gave a warm breakfast slice to her children,
> It was the dough of her baking, the bread of her tears
> That I swallowed, and her sigh entered into my bones.

So Bialik explains why so many sighs and tears tremble in his songs, as if in justification for having stood throughout his whole first decade (1891-1901) under the sign of tears: practically every poem he wrote during that period contains not only the mood of tears, but the word itself.

Life was no easier for him during the years of his wanderings, at the Yeshiba of Volozhin, where the nook where he stuck with stubborn diligence for two years is still pointed out with pride, or in Odessa, where he was attracted by Ahad Ha'am's circle. It was in Odessa that he published his first poems and prepared for his literary career. But soon, to his disappointment, he had to return to Zhitomir, to the deathbed of his grandfather who, after his father's death, had become his guardian. After his marriage our poet tormented himself with a variety of

unsuitable occupations in little Russian and Polish towns
—traded in lumber, taught small children, etc.—until the
publishing house established in Odessa in 1905 assured
him of a degree of economic independence. He remained
in Odessa for about two decades. In the spring of 1924
Bialik settled in Tel Aviv, where he became the center of
literary and cultural activity. He died in 1934, after a
surgical operation in Vienna.

Aside from the mournful poems of his first period,
which are a deeply moving utterance of his personal woe
and distress (and, as always with Bialik, the personal
typifies the folk-destiny), his best achievement of that time
is *Hamathmid,* or The Yeshiba Student (1895). The
poem is an eternal monument erected to that "unknown
soldier" to whom our unwarlike people owes its existence
despite all the severity of fate: This anonymous hero,
whose name during the long pilgrimage through the ages
was Legion, buried his youth and all his longings in the
assiduous sacred fervor with which he devoted himself to
the Talmud, day and night, year after year, deaf to all the
whispers of nature and the lure of his own young blood.
Hamathmid is autobiographical, but again most genuinely
typical. Its peculiar charm, aside from Bialik's usual
artistry of language, lies in the emotional conflict between
love and revolt, between enthusiasm and protest, which
this life and this kind of heroism inspire in him. A whole
people laments the deadening, desolating confinement of
the Ghetto, in which its sons pine away. Yet it realizes
that it has not gone to rack and ruin entirely as long as
it still has the power to inspire its youth with such zeal
and to such sacrifice.

Out of other poems of that period, too, there speaks Bialik's intense love for the Jewish home of study, "the potter's house where the nation's soul is shaped," which he vows to restore (*Upon the Threshold of the Beth Hamidrash,* 1894), and in which he sees the bulwark for our continued fidelity to type (*If Thy Soul Would Know,* 1898). After the Maskilic criticism of the Jewish institutions of learning, this struck a new and unusual note in Hebrew literature. Bialik, more than anyone else, effected the romantic return of his whole age to the beauties of Ghetto life. But romance is a flight from present duties; and Bialik, in spite of his nostalgia for the shadows of the past, was called to lead the vanguard of youth toward the morrow.

The struggle between attachment to the old and the urge of the new is depicted in his moving poem "Alone" (1902), where the Divine Presence grieves in the house of study for all those youths who, allured by the call of the new times, have forsaken it. It wants to shield him, the last of the youth, with its broken wing, but knows that he too will go away. And he does go away. After the drab and cheerless nineties, a period which the Russians called Non-Time because of its lack of all distinctiveness, and which was no less dreary and stagnant in Jewish life, came the political strikes in Russia, presaging the storms of the approaching revolutionary upheaval, to which in Jewish life Herzl's bold venture of statesmanship, and also the first triumphs of the *Bund,* a Jewish revolutionary labor movement, ran parallel. Then Bialik renounced the reign of *tears,* and his period of revolt began.

From his nature-poems a torrent of *Radiance* (1901)
breaks forth.   As if to compensate himself for all the
years of denial and renunciation of the joys of vision and
of all the other senses, he celebrates orgies of light with
a wealth of dazzling, blinding synonyms for light which
actually hurt the eye.   His most finished work of that
period is, however, his masterly epic fragment *The Dead
in the Wilderness* (1902).   Basing himself on a Talmudic legend, he describes in marble-hewn hexameters the
virility of Israel's desert tribes, who insisted on pushing on
to their new land against the interdict of God, and then
went down to defeat in a magnificent struggle with
heaven and earth.   Bialik sees them, a great array of silent
warriors, sleeping in the desert sands, and in their very
sleep inspiring fear and awe even in an eagle, a monstrous
serpent and a lion: "Affrighted before the splendor of
their repose and the glory of strength in slumber."   The
poet lets the storm awaken them, and the mighty giants
sing a hymn of revolt which breathes majestic power and
unyielding defiance.

Upon the tops of the cliffs, between the massed clouds,
We drank freedom at the source with all the eagles of heaven,
And who is lord over us?
Against the anger of the heavens and their wrath,
Behold, we go up
To the storm!

The Kishineff pogroms showed the poet how shameful
was the chasm between those heroic ancestors and their
degenerate descendants in the Ghetto.   Bialik's revolt
now loosed itself against his own generation in burning,
prophetic anger.   His most celebrated poem of that time,

which made history while it exhorted and educated the Jewish youth, is the *City of Slaughter*. That poem rings not with an accusation against heaven and the world-order, cruel in its cheerfulness and cynical with its sunrises, not against the dehumanized, murdering mob, but with a burning shame and indignation at his own people, the victims of the pogroms. How petty, mean and cowardly were the grandsons of the Maccabees as they crept away into holes: "They ran away like rats, they hid in cracks like bedbugs." And this same poet who in his youth had held it a virtue "rather than to be a beast among beasts, to choose to perish with the lambs," now lets God, humiliated by His Chosen People's crime of cowardice, lose Himself in rage when they dare to pray to Him: "Why do they supplicate Me? Let them raise their fist, let them shatter the heavens and My throne with their fist!"

With the *City of Slaughter* begins Bialik's third phase: Wrath, or, rather, Despair. He realizes that his priesthood of the Hebrew word has been profaned; that his words, born in pain and anger, have become trite, ineffective phrases, incapable of rousing to life, of inflaming to deeds. Break up your altar, O Prophet, break your hammer,

> For it is broken with much pounding
> In vain upon hearts of stone.
> Beat it into a spade, and dig us a grave! . . .
> Why should we fear Death,
> When its angel rides upon our shoulder,
> With his bridle upon our lips.
> With trumpetings of "Rebirth"
> And neighings of joy,
> We hop toward the grave!

He repents of all his years of self-denial and personal renunciation: "I sought your penny and lost my pound." Like Amos when driven forth from Bethel, he wishes to retire into seclusion.

> If my strength was consumed in vain, the guilt is not mine.
> It is your sin, and you must bear the blame. . . .
> I shall bind my tools to my girdle
> And as a hireling without wage for my day's labor,
> I shall go unfelt as I came. . . .
> And ye—ye are moth and rust,
> Tomorrow a storm shall carry you all away.

He sank into his last, unremitting phase of silence. When he did sometimes break forth, his soul lamented the unlived personal life foolishly and futilely smothered in sorrow and song for his people.

> A twig slipped down upon the hedge, and fell into slumber.
> Thus sleep I:
> The fruit dropped,—but what care I for my stock,
> For my bough?

What had really happened?

III

It has been said of Bialik that he too is the great poet of the Jewish past, of the Galuth. And that his silence proves how little the whole modern renaissance has inspired him to production. This is to be taken *cum grano salis.* Bialik's genuine enthusiasm for Pioneer Palestine is evident in many passages of his work, not only in his letter to the Jewish workers there: "The very dust will come back to life under your bare and sacred feet."

As a matter of fact Bialik at an early date displayed a

profound understanding and sympathy for the Chalutz endeavor—at the very dawn of the Zionist idea. I refer to his poem "In the Field," written in the year 1894. The bitterness and orphanhood of a people bereft of its soil, exiled from fields and meadows and alienated from the green urge of nature lament here in unforgettable verses. Even more bitterly is lamented the curse of estrangement from labor:

> Not my hands formed you, O ears of corn,
> Not my hands fostered your growth;
> Not I have spent my strength here,
> Not I will enjoy your harvest.

For the same reason, concludes Bialik, I must not, I cannot enjoy your beauty. This ban upon the beauties of the alien environment reminds us of the ancient lesson of the *Pirke Aboth,* originating in the fear lest the lure of foreign countries make the Jews forget the cradle of their race or their eternal Law: "He who walks by the way and studies, and then breaks off his study, saying 'How beautiful is this tree, how beautiful is this fallow ground'—Scripture holds it as though he were guilty of mortal sin." However, Bialik's objection is not to breaking off study in order to feast our eyes on alien nature, but is due to an inhibition that we ought not, or rather *cannot,* enjoy beauty not created by ourselves. Here we strike the most salient of Bialik's ideas: He does not take the obvious moralistic attitude that it is parasitical to enjoy æsthetic values created by others, but simply that it is *impossible* to do so sincerely. Only originality of creation entitles, enables one to enjoy the thing created.

This sounds like an anticipation of the ideas of

A. D. Gordon, the peasant-philosopher of Dagania, who demanded a return to Jewish manual labor in the name of Jewish culture, of the genuineness of Jewish culture. When Bialik wrote those verses, wherein he again comes into conformity with Jewish tradition, even though it be for other reasons, the younger talents among his contemporaries revolted against the olden ban upon nature. Micah Joseph Berditchewski reversed the lesson of the Fathers, saying: "He who walks by the way and *does not break* off his studies and *does not* say, How beautiful is this tree, how beautiful is this fallow ground, sins against himself." Bialik, however, reverts to the ancient text, and in spite of his obedience to tradition, is freer and more modern than Berditchewski, for in his ethical enhancement of the old doctrine, in his profound understanding of the national, he rises to the supernational, to the universal.

Bialik has written most beautiful words in glorification of manual labor which the Hebrew renaissance has exalted to an ideal. It was in his years of silence that he composed his justly famed psalm of labor, finding eternal words for the noble restraint and silent grandeur of the worker.

Let my portion be with you, meek of the earth, dumb of soul,
Weavers of life in seclusion, humble in thought and deed,
Secret dreamers, who lessen words and increase glory,
Nobles who know not your caste, lords of the spirit unknowing,
Masters of the art of fair silence, priests of divine stillness . . .
You who pass by, sowing about yourselves, without effort and intent,
The faith and purity that emanate from your very being,
As emanate the blue from the skies and the shadows from the green woods . . .

THE MOUTHPIECE OF THE FOLK

You have no place in the ranks of seers, nor a claim in houses
    of art. . . .

But day by day—

The beauty of your life pours forth into the world even like a
    sealed fountain,
Into the heart of a river, to quicken it, without its knowing—
By the living God, not a quiver of your eyelids shall be in vain,
Not the least tremor of your soul shall fall to earth!

In the light of this magnificent and yet so modest dignity of labor, the pursuit of the poet seems to Bialik vain
and shallow. Compared with the anonymous munificence
of the laborer who lavishes himself self-effacingly on his
work, what matters the poet's anxiety lest some trivial
experience of his be lost, what matters his concern to
preserve his individuality as the highest good? Such
concern about "originality" seems hollow to him; something to be ashamed of before the calm greatness, the
self-forgetfulness of the common worker.

Bialik seems also to mistrust the instrument of the poet.
He sees the inadequacy of the human word. He who
has a magic power over words is disgusted with the lie
inherent in words. The best in life is not made clear with
words. Words profane. And he warns against words:
Cave verbum!

My language, O Lord, is polluted and unclean to its roots,
There is no phrase in it which filthy lips have not abused,
No word which has not been dragged to the house of shame.
The pure doves which I sent of a morning to heaven,
Returned to me toward evening as ravens reared on dunghills . . .
Where is the seraph to cleanse my mouth with his live coal? . . .
Rather shall I go to the children who innocently play in the gates.

I shall mingle in their crowds, I shall learn their talk and
  chatter—
And I shall become clean with the breath of their mouth, and in
  their chastity I shall wash my lips.

And Bialik actually did go to the children, and for years
did sing children's songs. The writing of these songs
became a matter of doctrine with him: he thought that
the restoration of the Jewish people must begin at the
very bottom, with the Jewish child; and for this child
Bialik wrote poems and books.

When we behold these superb manifestations of Bialik's
talent, in spite of ourselves the question sometimes arises:
Is it not a pity that such excellence was spent on books for
children? But Bialik believed that only the best should be
incorporated into children's books; for the very best is just
good enough for children.

To be sure, other unsuitable tasks also were imposed
upon Bialik. And he accepted the burden.

> I am neither poet nor prophet,
> I am but a hewer of wood.

For years Bialik hewed in the forests of Jewish literature. He toiled to collect the scattered remains of the
Jewish past, the rabbinic lore of *Aggada* and *Midrash,*
and the poetry of the Middle Ages. He spent years in
assembling the *disjecta membra* of the ancient post-
biblical legends. He engaged in interpreting anew both
the Bible and the *Mishnah* for the children of Israel.
After these tasks, he devoted more years to the recovery
of medieval poetry of Spain, searching diligently for long-
lost poems of such classics as Solomon Ibn Gabirol and
Moses Ibn Ezra.

THE MOUTHPIECE OF THE FOLK

Thus for years Bialik was doing every imaginable variety of useful work. To the exclusion, however, of that which he alone could do, and in which no one could substitute for him. The work peculiar to himself he did not do. He seemed to throttle the poet in him to become in turn a philologist, exegete, scholar, teacher, publisher and communal worker.

Why this ruthlessness toward his own artistic constitution?

IV

In Bialik's own lifetime, a web of legend began to gather around his sudden silence as a poet. At the height of his creative power, the much heralded poet laureate of the national renaissance abruptly stopped writing poetry. Years passed, and he remained silent, stubbornly silent. His silence rankled the people, it startled them like the bursting of taut strings of a musical instrument. Of anyone else it would have seemed natural to suspect that perhaps the harp was no longer fit. Not so with Bialik: the rare verses that found their way to the public bore witness to unabated power of inspiration. Endowed with such innate gifts of song, why should he spurn the poet's craft? Why waste himself on labors, desirable but dull, which could well be done by others, while in his own calling he had no rival in many a generation?

With careful reading, the foretokens of Bialik's later mood can be traced in his writings. Both in his poetry and prose one encounters hints of distrust and dispraise of poetry. An ancient people is struggling between life and death: what use can it have in art for art's sake?

Poetry for its own sake, as the bird sings, is a fit recreation for those who work with the sweat of their brow all the day long, who produce letters, sciences, arts, a many-sided civilization that creates and builds up. Such workers may sing. But poetry that is the product of idleness and boredom—who wants it?

Bialik, the master and interpreter of the Hebrew legend, challenged the modern cult of the Aggada with the untimely call: Back to the Halakha! Away from vague, intoxicating sentiments, and back to clear, imperative obligations! In one of his most finished essays, *Halakha and Aggada,* he writes:

Before our eyes rises a generation steeped in phrases and slogans that are trifles light as the breath of the mouth and as the wind of the lips. We call these Nationalism, Renaissance, Creation, Hebrew Thought—and all these things hang by the hair of a bit of love for a land, for a language, for a literature. What is such airy love worth?

Love? But where is the sense of duty? (Love—in Hebrew—*Chibba;* Duty—*Choba;* a play on the similar sounds of the two words). Aspirations, good will, an awakening of the spirit, an inner love—all these things are good and useful when they culminate in action, in hard, unremitting action.

You desire to build. "Make a sure covenant and subscribe it, and our princes, Levites and priests seal their seal unto it . . . and make *ordinances* for yourselves!" (Nehemiah x, 1 and 33). Is not that the way your fathers began to build?

The sublime visions of the Second Isaiah aroused the hearts of the people; but when the hour for building had struck, there were two prophets among the builders, Haggai and Zechariah, who ended the prophetic era and began that of the Halakha. Those who came after them—Ezra and his disciples—were no longer prophets; they were proponents

of the Halakha, of the rules of individual and social conduct.
Come and set up ordinances for us! . . . We are bending our necks: Where is the iron yoke?

Bialik truly bent his neck under the yoke of ordinances.
He felt that he had been born for the hour of reconstruction, and must follow in the path of Haggai, Zechariah and Ezra. He recognized that he had to apply himself to the realities and the necessities of our new life.
He performed the useful everyday work of the Halakha.
He gathered up the treasures of past Jewish generations;
he strangled his own talents in order to resuscitate the
ancient treasures of his people.

The young generation of Jews which is the nucleus of
the future Hebrew people must be reared on the noblest
and most genuine products of the Jewish spirit, and these
products must be prepared for it in suitable form. The
education of the new generation should be the task of the
most talented Jews. Bialik felt this responsibility. He
did crude, dirty "black work," as the coarse labors of the
unskilled workers in Palestine are called. He did work
for which he was not cut out, but of whose necessity no
one was so profoundly conscious as he; for in such work
are the foundations of the Jewish spirit, and hence also
the future of the Jewish people.

The meaning of his labors was not lost to his generation. They witnessed the rise of *Chalutzim,* sons and
daughters of their people who abandoned higher schools
of learning and age-long traditions of intellectual pursuits
for the swamps and wilderness which their heroic will-
to-sacrifice redeemed to new life. Bialik, too, in his own

way, seemed to have chosen the path of the *Chalutz*. In this spirit, at least, his contemporaries viewed Bialik's farewell to poetry; and perhaps so will posterity interpret the labors of his last decades—as a *Chalutz* offering, as a poet's sacrifice and pioneer contribution to Israel reborn.

CHAPTER XIII

THE BARD OF HEBREW PAGANISM

Every drop of color that runs from my brush upon my palette turns to streams of light and glory and melodies; and all the world glows with roses, roses, roses. . . .

TCHERNICHOVSKI.

It is singular (the poet himself may not remember it) that Saul Tchernichovski made his literary début in America.

His first poem was published in *Hapisgah,* a Hebrew weekly edited in Baltimore by W. Schur. On December 9, 1892, "In My Dream" (from *The Songs of Zion*) was printed in *Hapisgah* without vowel points—a procedure that reduced the poem to the level of prose writing in Hebrew; and was signed with the unknown name of the then seventeen-year-old Saul Tchernichovski. As the weekly was unobtainable in Russia, the poet may never have seen this first effort in print.

Very soon after there appeared a second poem, "My Ideal," in *Hasharon,* edited in Lemberg by Gershom Bader, who has since been active in America, and Menahem Mendel Malles. Publication was doubtless achieved with the aid of Joseph Klausner, now professor of Hebrew literature on Mount Scopus, who was attached to Tchernichovski with the bonds of a warm youthful friendship, and fought his battles enthusiastically in the world of Hebrew letters.

Tchernichovski considered both of these poems unworthy to be included in the first little volume which he published in his early twenties under the title of *Visions and Melodies.* The preface to this collection was written by Reuben Brainin, the veteran Hebrew critic. Mr. Brainin can never be praised enough for having recognized and whole-heartedly encouraged the young poet who was still stuttering awkwardly and appallingly mishandling the Hebrew.

Years of rapid progress and abundant production followed. There were the sunny, life-storming university years at Heidelberg (1899-1903) that produced the most beautiful and authentic love-songs written in Hebrew since the Song of Songs; the historical poem of *Baruch of Mayence,* where a Jew again dared to fling against the tormentors a curse weighted with the classical power and fury of the Biblical "Pour Out Thy Wrath upon the Heathen," so rare and repellent in these modern days of denied and thwarted primitive instincts; the lovely idyll, *Boiled Dumplings,* which, as the protest of youth against the enslavement of the schools, will always delight young souls, and win the mature by its masterful adaptation of the ancient idyll-form.

Then came the Lausanne years (1904-7) with their tenderer, pain-taught, and yet always life-affirming rhythms: their philosophic poems which are among the best of Hebrew thought lyrics; the delicious idyll of the naïve Velvele, who took the love of Zion literally and wanted to go on a pilgrimage to Zion—paying for his love with his life (*In the Heat of the Day*); a pained confession by the fate-tried poet, that he who takes ideals seriously is always thought a fool by the world.

After that came years of practicing as a physician in small Russian villages, daily witnessing misery and benighted ignorance; and yet, behind filth, whisky, humility, music and strange sorrow, discerning something unfathomable in the Russian soul. Then come subtle tones, words no longer, breathing music, flowing into music—full of bravely borne woe (*Laila, laila, lel elilim*). As an army physician, in the midst of all the horrible human suffering, he wrote poems of a noble, comforting humanity that belong among the most human documents of the World War. Then followed his classical, perfectly modeled cycles of sonnets—a masterpiece of Hebrew for all time.

In the years that followed there have come ever and again mature, sincere creations, the great idyll of *"Elka's Wedding," "Saul's Song of Love,"* which reads like the Canticles, *Simcha lav Davka,* and *Mayyim Shelanu* ("Waters that Have Stood Overnight"), a poem pervaded by the most delicate humor, and an exceedingly interesting and kindly document of contemporary Russia.*

Throughout all those years Tchernichovski has carried on a fertile activity in translations that is unique in its scope and universality. He has translated into Hebrew the Gilgamesh epos, the old Babylonian creation myths, the Egyptian sun poem by the heretic king Akhnaton, the Greek love songs attributed to Anacreon, Plato's philosophical dialogues, the idylls of Theocritos, the Finnish epic *Kalevala,* Molière's comedies, Longfellow's *Hiawatha* and *Evangeline,* poems by Burns, Shelley, Alfred de Musset, Goethe, Richard Dehmel. And, finally, there appeared Homer's two epics, the whole *Iliad,* and the whole *Odyssey,* molded into such ringing Hebrew hexameters as

*[Tchernichovski settled in Jerusalem in 1931, where he worked on a dictionary of Hebrew medical terms. He moved to Tel-aviv, where he served as school physician of the city. He died in 1943.]

only Tchernichovski can marshal, a work that ranks high as a monument in the life of our language and literature.

No Jewish poet has ever before united such widely differing worlds. It has therefore been rightly said that Tchernichovski's creative universality, which embraces the whole heritage of modern and ancient culture and deals with all problems of contemporary striving and thinking, exalts him far above all other Hebrew poets even though, in certain aspects of their talent, they may surpass him.

There has been no lack of recognition in Tchernichovski's life. He has never been overlooked; but neither has he been properly recognized. He became famous too early—not for his artistic worth, but as an exotic phenomenon: which is most dangerous for a true poet. It was not his inner merits, but his outward peculiarities, that long attracted his contemporaries; and this blocked the way to an understanding of his real values. Led astray by the estimate of his contemporaries, he mistook himself for a noteworthy exception in Jewish life. He was so much persuaded that at last he seemed to himself a "strange plant" in Jewish letters: "An alien am I to a sick people, to the house of pain" (referring to the Jewish people).

In very fact, Tchernichovski was an unusual, an altogether new phenomenon in Hebrew literature. Descended from sturdy South Russian village Jews, who bequeathed to him robust health and the tradition (quite foreign to Judaism) of physical heroism, and even of violent deeds; born in the quiet village of Mihailovka in the Crimea in 1875, he grew up broad-shouldered and sure of instinct in free, natural surroundings. He was taught Russian before he was taught Hebrew. He knew nothing of the Cheder and the Melamed with his whip; of the Six Hundred and Thirteen Commandments; of prohibitions and the fear of hell-fire. He never studied in the Bet Hamidrash or Yeshiba; never learned the Talmud. But he was excellently versed in secular classical and modern languages; trained not only as a physician, but with unusual thoroughness as a naturalist. How different is all this from the typical career of the Hebrew litterateur who, estranged from nature, cowered over his Talmud folios, and later grasped at profane knowledge in stray fragments, never able to conceal the traces of the auto-didact and his *Pilpul* youth.

What wonder, then, that the cadences of Tchernichovski's poems were different and quite unusual in Hebrew letters. Not from the "cricket, the singer of poverty," as Bialik once wrote of himself (and, as always, typically of all Hebrew poets), did Tchernichovski learn to sing. Not the moldy atmosphere of the Ghetto, but the open spaces of the Black Sea, of the Dnieper, the great river of South Russia, the broad steppes lent fresh, strong, primeval nature-accents and austere, compact force to his poems. Like a mischievous mountain brook, he poured himself down through the death and pain-stilled river bed of Galuth poetry—too wild and impetuous to be taken seriously, or to be understood. "I was still in my green youth, when a line of separation was drawn between me and my comrades"—so the poet saw himself an alien among his own. He sang of happiness and love and sun and roses; and his only care seemed to be that the language of his poems was unknown to the fair whose praises he sang. "Every drop of color that runs from my brush upon my palette turns to streams of light and glory and melodies; and all the world glows with roses, roses, roses. . . ." It is hardly to be wondered at that his squirrel-like joy of life was taken as a "sneer at the poor," and answered in that strain by J. L. Perez in his well-known letter, "To the man of roses from the man of thorns."

But it was no lack of sympathy with the tragic destinies of his people that resounded in Tchernichovski's symphonies of joy in life. It was also not—to quote the splenetic Schopenhauer—the "damned optimism" ("And God saw that it was good") of one who does not see the faults in Creation. Tchernichovski had deep insight into the evil of the world and the inadequacy of humankind. In one of his idylls, "The Broken Spoon," all the values of modern civilization are denied: Science, art, technical progress, national, social, religious ideals—all revert back to the human, the all-too-human, and are disprized. For all that, his songs breathe a mighty life-affirmation unique not only in the Hebrew but in contemporary literature.

It is his heritage from robust village folk and a virile breed that, as the poet himself realizes, begets his joy of life.

> The odors of the clod, of fertile, crumbly earth,
> The stifling heat wafted with the chaff dust from the granary,
> The ring of the ploughshare furrowing the field; the swish of the scythe in the corn

Had I not absorbed them into my soul, in freedom, in the
    thorp, while I was yet very young
Who had stood by me in the time of stress, in battle;
    when my heart was shrunk together
When I stood between the living and the dying?

This purely biological strength of nature is, however,
refined by the philosophic Eros: he is the thinker who
rises above the anthropocentric view of the world and,
in spite of all, affirms the World and Life. If for once
not man is seen as the center of the Universe, but the
powerful play of life-forces, which ever change and ever
renew themselves, mocking at what is transitory, one no
longer trembles before Nothingness. He is ready, when
the storm of life is lulled, and the tumult ceases, to yield
without fear to the end; for he will become, as the forms
and the days change, "one thread in the net of all the
forces of the Universe, weaving openly and knitting in
secret, the riddle of life that forever will not be solved."
The form may change, but the energy which once flamed
in man continues to leaven the Universe. To the thoughtful spirit of Tchernichovski all forms of life appear related: In man and the plant; in the lizard and the waves
of the stream; in the stone and the sunlight, there is the
same quickening flow of life—in all things the poet recognizes a living entity, a common origin for all that
exists. He hears the ancient speech (*Siach Kedumim*, the
title of one of his poems) of Nature reminding him, in
the rustling of the woods, in the play of the waves, that
she is the kin of man, and complaining that he has forgotten the common origin of all existence. The poet
experiences, as it were, a Platonic anamnesis: he redis-

covers in the elements of Nature his brethren from whom
man has estranged and separated himself for tens of
thousands of years. The whole world—cliff, forest,
mountain, river, man—is a "splinter of Chaos and its
fragments," a single destiny quickens them all, a cycle of
never-to-be-extinguished life. Whoever thus experiences
the oneness of all life-forms cannot complain of transitori-
ness. "The sea, the vineyards, the gardens will forever
remain," and their perennial joyousness banishes all grief.
In weak hours, when doubt and despondency steal upon
the soul, the poet turns to great, wild Nature, to the riv-
ers: "Then I am ashamed before the waves that strive
with the rocks; before the cliffs I am humbled that battle
boldly and hold up their heads to the sky." Deeply
stirred by the might of the Life-force, he forgets human
suffering. Hölderin's phrase has well been applied to
him: "He who has thought the deepest things will love
the most vital."

Tchernichovski's great affirmation of life has been
looked upon as un-Jewish, and he himself called a Greek.
For this view, he might have given reason in schematic
poems such as his "Before the Statue of Apollo." It
seems to me that he himself has been led astray by his
critics. He was made out to be a Greek on the basis of
that superficial division between Jewish spirituality and
the Greek love of the physical which has been popular
ever since Heine's abusive attack upon Boerne. "All
men," said Heine at that time, "are either Jews or Greeks:
either they are driven by ascetic, image-hating, spiritual-
izing impulses, or they are cheerful, taking pride in self-
development, realistic." That this is not only a caricature

and libel upon Judaism, but a misconception and a banal rendering of Hellenism, everyone knows since (and thanks to) Jacob Burckhardt and Friedrich Nietzsche.

When the poet speaks not of programs, but fashions a true creed unconsciously, he betrays, as in "Before the Statue of Apollo," that he is really not kneeling before the Greek sun-god, but before a symbol much more akin to his own and his forefather's blood: "I shall kneel down to Light and all precious things that corpses of men robbed from the hand of my Rock, *Shaddai,* God of the gods of the wastes, God of the gods of the conquerors of Canaan in storm. . . ." His close with *Shaddai* sounds far more genuine than his opening with Apollo.

Tchernichovski has also been called a Jew of the pre-Torah period. And here too he himself has given cause for such a view through a series of songs of Hebrew paganism. In his "Visions of False Prophets," he calls for a transvaluation of Jewish traditional values. The so-called "true" prophets falsified the sound life-instincts of the people; the tyranny of the Law broke down the natural joy in living. The poet sings in praise of the wrongly decried "false" prophets of life-affirmation. In contrast to Ezekiel [(viii, 14): "Then He brought me to the door of the gate of the Lord's house which was toward the north; and behold, there sat the women weeping for Tammuz"] who, in disgust, calls the Tammuz cult of the women an "abomination," Tchernichovski gives us the very charming "Death of Tammuz": With mystic dances at the head of the streets, in the footsteps of every secret and every wonder, he is seeking like the old pagans

Tammuz the bright, the living. For, with his death—
the death of the whole pagan world of wonder—the days
to come will be "days of cloud, eclipses of the soul,
autumn without end."

The Mishna relates (Sukka 5, 4) that on the Festival
of the Drawing of the Water, they used to sing in Israel:
"Our fathers were in this place with their backs toward
the Temple of the Lord and their faces toward the east,
and they worshiped the sun toward the east; but we turn
to JAH, and our eyes are toward JAH." But Tchernichovski leaves off the pious tag at the end, and uses the
heathen motto for his cycle *"To the Sun,"* finding worth
and excellence in the old idolatrous sun-cult.

> And I was unto my lord as a hyacinth and a mallow
> In whose world there is naught but his bright sun.

And it must be confessed that in this splendid cycle of
sonnets, old pagan mystery and modern scientific knowledge are paired together in a beauty of form and depth
of thought that belong to the best that has been sung in
the Hebrew tongue.

In the "Sonnets of a Pagan" there dreams a "pillar in
the fields of Judah and Moab": Once again are the idolatrous temples risen, and a celebrating multitude comes
to the stones and says: "We have been conquered by our
pagan fathers, a mighty people!"

After all the long millenia of sages and saints, Tannaim,
Amoraim and Saboraim, Geonim and Poskim, Kabbalists,
Chasidim and Mithnagdim, there resounds again in the
holy language a call to the old, vanquished paganism, a
call to pre-Torah Judaism. This had a fascinating ring,

and many an "intellectual" became enthusiastic. But it is unreal and affected romanticism.

For, here too, Tchernichovski's non-schematic, naïve and (therefore) authentic creativeness reveals a great and (in modern Hebrew poetry) unique love for traditional Judaism and its authentic life-forms.

No one in the new Hebrew literature has sung more tenderly or more lovingly of the Jewish rites and religious ceremonies and festivals. A reading of his earliest as of his latest poems bears this out: "The Sabbath Eve" (1893); "The Outgoing of the Sabbath" (1898); *Hakkafoth* (1901); *Berith Milah* (those were the Heidelberg years). Then, *Elka's Wedding* (1921); on Purim in *Simcha lav Davka* (1924); and later, *The Waters That Have Stood Overnight* on Pesach. Looking at degenerate post-war humanity, how genuine and profound he felt the holiness of the traditional customs of Israel to be— he, the alleged bard of Hebrew paganism.

It is the great poet who is captured by all that is creative in a people, who is unwilling to surrender anything of Jewish spiritual achievement, who is even not insensitive to the creations of the folk-spirit vanquished by history; it is this great love of Tchernichovski's that embraces all the Jewish generations that made him affirm Judaism in all its phenomena and all its aspects from the prehistoric Jewish idol worshiper to the rigidly pious village Jew of Eastern Europe.

Tchernichovski's development in later years seems to me so typical for the whole of modern Hebrew letters, that I choose to discuss it in the concluding chapter of the book.

CHAPTER XIV

TWO HERETICS

The best thing about religion is that it produces heretics.

HEBBEL.

HAD these lectures been planned in the Plutarchian manner of contrasting biographies, Berditchewski would necessarily have been paired with Ahad Ha'am. The two men exhibit every possible antithesis. While Ahad Ha'am from the very outset displayed poise and calm, refraining from appearance before the public until he had won his way through to inner clarity of thought and form, Berditchewski was a storm incarnate, never achieving balance, driven by contradictions, ever changing, unashamedly lusting for change and adventure. The contrast is plain even from their style. While Ahad Ha'am, who became the most distinguished Hebrew writer of his day, considered himself a mere sojourner in Hebrew literature, Berditchewski, the born writer, never learned the secret of an agreeable style. Ahad Ha'am was a model of finished form, Berditchewski all chaos and abyss; and not by accident does the word "abyss" occur so often in his work. Writing once of an author whom he knew personally, that "he had never stood over the abyss," he hesitated long over the words, because they seemed to him a most insulting disparagement of the man. To the friends who heard it, it was as if Dante were striding through the streets of Florence or Ravenna, crying out in contempt, "Behold, here are people who have never even been in hell!"

Where Ahad Ha'am raises the most subjective problem to an objective idea, to impersonal remoteness, for Berdit-

chewski every impersonal problem becomes his very own
concern, he thinks and lives it in terms of "I". For him
there is no far and near, no outer and inner. "Things
are not extrinsic, they all belong to us, and make their
claims upon our soul," he confesses autobiographically in
one of his early novels. More and more in his later years,
he attached value to an idea only in the ratio of its personal intensity: how genuine had been the spiritual compulsion of its author to think it, had he the personal right
to think it? He hated nothing more than disinterested
thinking, *sine ira et studio,* learned stuff without personal
necessity to know, without the personal hurt of knowledge. Out of his own experience, he knew that genuine
ideas are suffered into being.

If Ahad Ha'am did his utmost to banish all uncertainty
and to hold fast to the truths and principles won in his
quest, Berditchewski lauded the quest itself, the wealth
inhering in the problematical, the thought in the unde-
cided, the fountain of the thousand potentialities before
the one bucketful—the result—was drawn up. In reversal of the Talmudic saying, "As between 'certain' and
'doubtful,' choose 'certain,'" Berditchewski taught the
advantages of the *perhaps:*

> To my mind, the "certain" puts a stop to all thinking;
> with it, thought and knowledge can advance no further,
> whereas the "perhaps" is the very life of thinking, the
> inner force of all thought and meditation. Certainty is a
> weakening of the spirit, a ceasing further to question and
> to answer. Doubt stirs us to life, to a constant urge to
> make a reckoning of our world, to a never-stilled need;
> for, even when we arrive at a result, we say, *perhaps* the
> matter is otherwise. . . . Every certain bit of knowledge
> means only a single contact with an object, with only one

point in it, but not with the whole object, its whole essence.
That essence will be revealed to us through that very "perhaps," through the capacity to throw doubt upon what we think we know of it. Such doubt leads us to other doubts, and those doubts to still others, to questions and inquiries, until we penetrate into the soul of things. Only the "perhaps," the capacity for doubt, can redeem us from intellectual slavery.

The life-work of Ahad Ha'am, though developed merely in ephemeral articles, forms a rounded system. Berditchewski, on the contrary, despite his constant efforts to organize his sporadic utterances into an elaborate scheme of divisions and sub-divisions, lacked systematic unity. At bottom he may have disdained system as something necessarily implying narrowness and falsity. He trusted to his intellectual integrity to save his discoveries from mutual exclusion.

As in their habits of thought, so Ahad Ha'am and Berditchewski differed in their thought-content. While Ahad Ha'am was concerned not with the Jews, but with Judaism, Berditchewski battled for the rights of the individual Jew whom Judaism stifles, for the contemporary being cramped by the traditions of dead generations. While Ahad Ha'am paid high tribute to Moses, Berditchewski wrote a profound, revolutionary book which makes Joshua appear as the founder of the Israelitish religion, and Mount Gerizim, not Mount Sinai as its birthplace. We are even given a hint that the cunctative and aged Moses, if not actually murdered by the stormers of Canaan, whom he vainly tried to restrain, was at any rate left behind in the wilderness.

The contrasts between Ahad Ha'am and Berditchewski

could be spun out still further. For, at times, Berditchew-ski's teachings also originated out of direct reversals of the formulations of Ahad Ha'am. He himself confirmed this gratefully when applying to Ahad Ha'am a state-ment of Nietzche's concerning Paul Rée: Never in his life did he find a book which, despite his respect for its masterful train of thought, he had to contradict more violently, and which, just because it led him to contrary conclusions of his own, stimulated him greatly.

Ahad Ha'am, too, reluctant as he would have been to admit any stimulus from this source, and indignant as he was when Berditchewski's stormy challenges forced him to reply, nevertheless owes some of his finest conquests, his most valuable essays, to this strife. And though he would have resented it, posterity will read many of the heretical and disordered ideas of his opponent into his own calm and well-ordered system in order to strengthen it and to assure it of further effectiveness.

The life-stories of the two, also, are as opposite as can be imagined. Ahad Ha'am's life ran its course in an unperturbed regularity that would seem almost Philis-tine were nothing known of the noble, secret pathos of his inner life, while the trajectory of Berditchewski's life is a stormy, oft sharply broken curve. Only through his life-story can the struggles of this tragic personality be understood.

I

Micah Joseph Berditchewski, born in 1865, was the son of the pious Rabbi Moses Aaron of Dubowa, province of Kieff, himself a scion of an esteemed rabbinical family.

TWO HERETICS

This father could hardly have imagined that his first-born was to think the most radical and heretical thoughts in modern Hebrew literature, and was to make it the purpose of his life to challenge his people's ancient tables of the law. In later years, the heretic was to tell his friends, not without ancestral pride, that he belonged to the Chasidic aristocracy and traced his descent from Rabbi Shmelke of Nikolsburg.

Gentle lineage and bitter poverty are not mutually exclusive in the Ukraine. During the lifetime of his mother, an educated, kindly woman upon whose delicate spiritual beauty he apparently modeled all his female characters, the pressure of poverty was barely felt in the home. But she died in her twenty-eighth year, leaving Micah Joseph and two younger children. Following the rigid Jewish custom, the father shortly took a new wife, who brought with her children by her first husband, and soon gave birth to still more. From the many passages wherein Berditchewski repeatedly refers to the circumstances of his youth, a student of Freudian psychology might care to infer the reason for his later rebellion against all authority. For it was in those unhappy days that animosity against his father originated, and—in the image of his father—against God and all other authority.

> His father thou'd the new wife just as he had his mother, and nothing whatever was changed in the home. But in himself [the hero of the tale is none other than the author] everything was changed with the death of his mother, and thenceforth he could never quite speak to his father in friendliness. . . .

In another place he says again:

Then I imagined to myself that my father too had died, that I was freed from the yoke of the *Cheder,* and that I was learning to swing the hammer upon the heated iron at the blacksmith's, whither I used to steal away to watch him at his work. . . . And in my heart there rose the devastating thought to start a fire in the street, so that the upflaring flames would shoot against the skies. The Glory of God is in exile, and wears widow's weeds. . . .

It was then, also, that the question rose in his mind:

Why is there no mercy from the Heavenly Judge? When, in the funeral procession, the tin charity boxes jingled in tune to the litany, "Charity redeemeth from death," a presumptuous defiance against Heaven welled up within him. I knew that my mother had given much charity, and that there was no better or more pious woman in the whole world. Inquire not into the ways of God!

Doubt begot doubt until finally he made bold to turn everything topsy-turvy. "There is no justice under the sun. Hence it follows that there is none above the sun. So he said within his young soul."

Possibly the truth here is combined with much fiction, but that is common to all autobiographies. Nor does it matter if later perceptions are interpreted back into earlier days. For fiction, too, has its truth, and the self-portrait an author wishes to leave behind is not less valuable for a knowledge of him that the actual data of his life. I therefore follow the author in what follows, if only for the simple reason that no other sources are available.

The poverty in his father's house increased with the number of children. In that townlet the rabbi maintained himself by the sale of yeast. But when, instead of the liquid yeast sold by the rabbi's wife, dry yeast was introduced from the neighboring city with other novelties, the household was in extremities.

> Despite our troubles, my father did not let his wife persuade him to ban the use of the dry yeast, which might have been ritually unfit through the suspected use of milk. He said that it was better to sin in ignorance than knowingly, all the more so since the suspicion was not well-grounded, and it was not permissible for a teacher in Israel to issue bans in his own interest. And so the poverty in our home grew even worse.

For the sake of economy, the wife used to bake cheap, black, almost inedible bread for the children during the week, but at the midday meal on Friday, in honor of the approaching Sabbath, she would serve them with the white bread for which they waited so hungrily. One Friday, Micah Joseph, trembling with hunger and long expectation, greedily reached out for the white bread as soon as his father had pronounced the grace, but the pious rabbi restrained him: "I see that your mouth waters for the white bread, but every Jew must be able to subdue his instincts. Delay eating it for a few moments. It is Israel's duty to banish darkness with light, the evil desire with the good. So he spoke, and his eyes shone." With tears, very likely. His stepmother bestowed similar lessons upon him, but in a less friendly spirit. She was not bad, as he himself admits, but did the natural thing when she preferred her own children.

One cannot but be deeply moved by his recollection of one sultry summer evening when the children were deprived of their usual tea because there was no lump sugar in the house. And the granulated sugar might be used only for the father. But, when the wife left the room, the father secretly allowed his first-born to help himself to a glass of tea. "I was still swallowing the warm drink when she returned to the room. In a blaze of anger she seized the glass from my hand and poured out the contents upon the floor. I sprang up and cursed her. My father sat benumbed. I too was aghast at what I had done. Henceforth I was to eat alone. My brothers were kept away from me. I was ostracized."

At school, too, things did not take their ordinary course. At an early age he began to embarrass his teachers with unusual questions and even affrighted them with some that seemed heretical. His fancy correlated the Bible narratives with the pious local environment, and interpreted the patriarchs in the light of the usages and customs of the little town. "I imagined Moses a long-bearded man wrapped in a prayer-shawl all day long and laying on his phylacteries after the manner of Rabbenu Tam (a French rabbi of the twelfth century). But there was one thing I did not understand: How was Jacob allowed to kiss Rachel, and how were the chaste daughters of Israel allowed to go out and dance?" In a later narrative, Berditchewski has a pious mother ask similar questions: How could the godly Jacob marry two sisters during their common lifetime, and on top of that take unto himself two concubines? Or, how could the Lawgiver Moses marry the daughter of an idolatrous priest? For, there could hardly have been a rabbi in Midian—as there was in her little town—to perform the marriage ceremony and to recite the Seven Blessings. . . .

His teachers naturally disapproved of such questions, regarding them as blasphemous or merely silly, as, for

instance, when he once asked why God had not revealed
the Written and the Oral Law at the same time, anticipating in all innocence and in childish form the problem
that was to engage him all his life long: the difference
between the "teachings of the long exile upon alien soil,
and those of the hills and mountains of the homeland
yonder."

Berditchewski gives a delicious description of how the
Pentateuch—the only portion of the Bible which it was
permissible to teach—went by the calendar and the sea-
sons. In the winter, youthful imagination sojourned in
Egypt and saw the cruel serfdom of the Jews. "All summer long we were tormented forty years in the wilderness," and longingly awaited the entry of the victorious
tribes into the Promised Land. But, when the high festivals were over and gone, the Torah scrolls were rolled
back, and they began again from the beginning: From
Moses dying within sight of Jericho, there was a sudden
jump back to the Creation of the World. "Shem was
yet unborn and Abraham, who was to journey from his
own land to Canaan . . . God of our fathers, how long
is yet the way!"

The way from his present condition in the Jewish
townlet to the Promised Land seemed even longer to the
youth. Secretly he read the books of the prophets and
the kings—a world that seemed utterly different from
the Jewish life he knew. He read of the victories of
Joshua, who won the land by the sword, of Jephthah and
Samson, Saul and David, Solomon and Omri, of altars
and sacrifices upon every high hill. "What strength and
power and innocence of soul!" Pehaps he did not cry

out then as in later years, but the dim feeling may already have been there: "Life before the Scriptures—how beautiful, how pleasant, how exalted, how powerful! How strong, how goodly were thy tents, O Jacob!" Wholly unexpected and clumsy his teacher of those days found his sudden question about the geography of Palestine: What difference could it make where a certain place was situated? . . .

The boy was still more acutely impressed by the tales in the book *Josippon,* which he read with wild enthusiasm, and which, rousing him to the realities of his little Ghetto town, made him ask bitterly: "Why were there such men only in those days? Why only in those days could men fight, triumph, conquer? . . . I was like a man returned from a far journey." This book appealed to him so greatly that in later years he called himself and his family by the name of its legendary author: bin Gorion.

With his growing years came the first influences of the Haskalah, the writings of Isaac Baer Levinsohn, whom he revered all his life long, and whose portrait, beside Spinoza's, graced the walls of his study in later years. Finally came the overwhelming experience of Krochmal's "Guide":

> And there, in that small room beside the small window hung with a white curtain, I lie reading with awe, swallowing what I understand and feel, what I do not understand . . . I read and tremble with fear, with fear and yet with delight. Almost I see the lips of the aged man moving as he says to me: "Know and understand, that what we have called the spirit peculiar to each nation is called in the Law and the Prophets—in the language of early thought —the God of a nation. . . .

With such thoughts in his head, the pious rigidity of his parental home and the small town became doubly intolerable. Moreover, his poverty so oppressed him that he could not but welcome the thought of release from guardianship and from the pressure of need, even though the price thereof were marriage. So it happened that before he was seventeen, Micah Joseph appeared in a small town in Podolia, where a well-to-do Jew gladly gave him his daughter in marriage, with a dowry of six hundred roubles, and maintenance as long as the father-in-law lived. For the latter felt himself very fortunate to secure a sprig from a holy rabbinical family. The quiet melancholy of those days is wafted to us from Berditchewski's *Recollections of a Runaway*. The commercial atmosphere of the home disgusted the rabbi's son, and he found their naïve faith even more confining than the scholarly Judaism of his father. He loved his young wife, and felt sorry for her. She, in her piety, could not understand her husband's torments. "She kissed his hot forehead and pleaded: Don't think so much. . . ."

But worlds were at war in his soul. Heretical, evil thoughts surged within him. He read books of which his father-in-law disapproved, consorted with people in the town whose ritual laxity had brought them an ill name—he, the heir of a long rabbinical line. "Remember your holy ancestors, remember who you are, and who are the Maskilim with whom you consort," his father-in-law pleaded, exhorted, warned and threatened—in vain.

> One day he called to me in the presence of my wife: Do you see this innocent youth? Do you observe how he

is sunk in thought? My head be forfeit if one day he does not forsake his people and his home to go abroad and study at a university! At the word "university," a tremor of fear passed through the house. My mother-in-law was dumbstruck! My wife almost fainted, and I too was overcome.

His father-in-law's prediction was justified, though at twenty Berditchewski did not as yet flee to the alien West, but to the Yeshiba at Wolozhin. Whether the immediate cause of the break was his intercourse with the Chasidim of Rabbi Nachman of Bratzlav, as his biographer relates, or his Haskalah books, is immaterial. He himself relates that his father-in-law discovered him reading Nahum Sokolow's *The Eternal Hatred for the Eternal People,* a book which the older man thought could do nothing but awaken eternal hatred for its own people in a Jewish heart.

In Wolozhin the lonely heretic added his voice to the choir of the four hundred young men who sought to still their hunger in the Torah. There he sat—as Druyanov, a friend of those student years relates—wrapped in prayer shawl and crowned with phylacteries, poring diligently over the ancient folios until deep in the night. Here the Chasid experienced the beauty of Talmudism: he became a *Mithnagged*—one of the many changes he was destined to make. Despite all the young man's seeming piety, the head of the Yeshiba, Rabbi Naphtali Z. Berlin, did not approve of him, divining that he did not belong there. Berditchewski subsequently proved him right by publishing (1887) a series of letters on the inner life of the Yeshiba, revealing many of its secrets, as for instance, a secret group for the study of history, thus causing some of his former associates much unpleasantness.

Through the intervention of his father, Berditchewski was persuaded to give his wife a divorce, receiving in return therefor a sum of six hundred roubles, which he spent on books and on extensive correspondence with numerous scholars near and far. Soon of course he was penniless again. Now he had the choice either of a return to his father's home, where he would have to listen to his stepmother's lectures, or a second marriage. Thus he came to Bershad, where he courted the divorced daughter of a well-to-do trader, who set up the young couple in a shop for tinware and clay jars. The wife conducted all the business affairs, and Berditchewski carried on an even more extensive correspondence with scholars all over the world, occasionally also writing for the Hebrew press. Soon after he suggested to the publisher of *Ozar Hassifruth* that he add a scientific supplement to that Hebrew periodical which he, Berditchewski, was ready to finance. Thereupon, in 1888, there appeared the *Beth Hammidrash,* "dedicated to the Torah and the wisdom of Judaism, containing contributions Talmudic and historical," etc., most of which, Berditchewski, as editor, wrote himself "with the aid of the élite among our rabbis and authors." Here and there we find flashes of thought that foreshadow the later Berditchewski: "Upon those who faithfully occupy themselves with the wisdom of Israel and study it for its own sake rests the obligation to empty their minds of all preconceived notions." Or: "Man is entirely free to judge, to criticize, and to observe; and it is his right and duty to put everything to the test of scrutiny." But his father-in-law and his wife had no taste whatever for such radical ideas and, in particular, for his mad extravagance in using their hard-earned money for literary adventures. For the second time there was a divorce; and Berditchewski, with empty pockets and a trunkful of copies of his magazine, went wandering through the Ukraine. One year was spent in Odessa, where he was attracted to the *Chibbath Zion* movement. In 1890 he landed at Breslau, and at first intended to enter the rabbinical seminary there; but he was soon disgusted with the idea, and enrolled at the university (as his first father-in-law had foreseen), and also, for a time, studied at an art academy.

The evolution in his spirit caused by the contacts with the strange Western world and the abrupt change in his life, is revealed in his brochure *The Views of One on the Many* (1892). This is an immature, confused, ill-written pamphlet full of chaotic thoughts and leaps from one idea to another; full, too, of pretension and brazen charges. Had it been left to stand alone, it would suggest merely an addlepate whose arrogance went beyond all lengths. Such must have been the impression he made at that time. And it is not strange that his violent attacks upon the nationalist movement of those days and upon the personal integrity of its leaders called forth bitter hatred which vented itself in a flood of replies in the Hebrew periodicals. It was from that time that Berditchewski long had to wage a vain fight for reëntry into the Hebrew press.

One who takes the trouble to give this barely readable

pamphlet an attentive reading is struck by its similarities with his later thought-world. Here his ideas on the nation and the individual, history and literature, gradually take shape; and his gospel of individualism already strikes its note: "Man is an individual, a world existing for its own sake. He is surrounded by the group, and within it he perfects himself. But it is his individuality that is the chief thing, for it is his very self." Therefore he thought that the Jewish national movement of his day, being based on charity and not on personal interest, could not be successful. In this pamphlet, he reproaches the new Hebrew literature with ungenuineness and with lack of a solid foothold, playing up against it the truth and the folk-power of Chasidism, which he was later to apotheosize in Hebrew literature. Here again is a presage of his revaluation of Jewish history to which in later days he looked back happily, as when, for example, he corrects the slanderous picture drawn by the Pharisees of the zealots in the last Jewish war of independence, and praises them as heroes—this by one who later branded Rabbi Johanan ben Zaccai's visit to the Roman emperor as high treason, and pointed to his sly escape in a coffin as a symbol of the encoffinment of the free Jewish spirit that was then begun. There one also finds a profound personal admission, showing how sad at heart he was to deny where he would so gladly affirm. In spite of all his antagonism, "I desire with all my heart and soul that our long and blood-encrimsoned chain be continued down to the end of time, that we renew ourselves as in days of old. This is my desire; and the thought of its opposite, our non-being, fills my heart with fear and my eyes with tears." This ambivalence of attack and love, dissent and devotion, remains typical of him. The violence of his assault proves only how much he had at heart the things attacked.

A better insight into the state of his soul in those days can be had from his descriptions of his student days in a series of intensely personal sketches. He had left his old East European past for the strange alluring world of the West; but there, too, he lived on little bread and many books. Soon, he realized that in spite of his sudden break with the old, the hoped-for change in himself had not occurred.

> Little by little he saw that only his books, not the core of things had changed for him, that he was still straying in the wilderness. To what end was he heaping up knowledge and thoughts, which are but shadows, and not life itself? . . . His head was full, but his life was empty. He had neither a people, nor bonds with a people; neither parents nor the tenderness of parents; neither love nor intimacy. A stranger he was there and here, a stranger in the world and in life. He had thought himself a citizen of the whole world, but in truth he belonged nowhere. . . .

In lonely torment the young student sets down the words: "My head is an old folks' asylum. . . ."

He longs for the strange outer world, but shrinks from it. Or, rather, he divines that it must forever remain strange to him.

> He does not wish to give Hebrew lessons, because he no longer believes in the revival of the language. The rabbinical students in the city he hated with all his heart, as well as all the other "holy vessels" and men of professional piety. On the Sabbath he sees from his window the passers-by from the reform synagogue and draws the

curtain so as not to see human beings in their degradation. He no longer reads Hebrew books; he intentionally forgot his phylacteries and prayer books somewhere in order to be clear of all things Jewish. Nevertheless, the word "assimilationist" causes him acute pain, and his heart aches for the falsehood in such souls. Nothing remained to him of his people—and yet he was a *son* of that people. . . . Though his mind was emptied of the ancestral heritage, but his heart was still imprisoned in the graves of his fathers."

His inescapable folk-inheritance reveals itself even in his small personal habits, and this irritates him. Thus, on a Sabbath eve, he is in an odd mood:

This hour for him is still pervaded with religious emotions. He is never able to work then, and feels the end of the week within his soul. He bathes himself, changes his clothing, arranges his books, and falls into reverie. . . . Were he frank, he would admit that vestiges of his Judaism stir in his bosom, and that he would almost enjoy covering the table with a white cloth. But he does not admit this, and strives to subdue his soul. . . .

Obscure instincts draw him toward the strange world, toward the strange woman. He has treated this subject repeatedly, with a shivering soul that testifies to its personal implications. He did not need the outward, rather forced occurrence that made the hero of his story *Two Camps* run away from his beloved when he had unwittingly become unworthy of her. Much deeper and more compelling is the delicate little sketch "Without Her": "It is hard for me to overcome my strong love. But the ghosts of my ancestors of many generations come between us. Wherever I turn, in every nook of my soul, I hear the voice of Jacob, his sighs and his hopes, the grief in his hopes. . . ."

345

And so he remains "without her." He rages at the fate that makes him "the last" in the chain of the generations, unable to begin a new life. But in the very pangs of renunciation, there flashes upon him the consoling thought: "It is a misfortune for both of us."

In spiritual struggles such as these and in extremest poverty, he spent his university years in Breslau, Berlin and Bern, winning his Ph.D. in the latter city (1897) with a thesis on the relations betwen ethics and æsthetics. He then settled down in Breslau, marrying Rachel Ramberg, who earned a merited reputation with her German translations of her husband's legends *Der Born Judas*. The dental profession, which both wife and husband practiced, afforded him a certain degree of economic independence; and, when they moved to Berlin in 1911, he was able to give himself up entirely to his books and literary activities. The twenty volumes which he left behind in Hebrew alone, aside from some unpublished scientific works, form one of the richest yields of modern Hebrew letters, and prove not only how prolific, but also how very diligent was this—hater of the printed word.

During the Ukrainian massacres, among the many other victims of those terrible days, was Berditchewski's father, the aged rabbi of Dubowa, who was butchered by the bands of Petlura. The news of the tragedy, which was long withheld from him, shook him to the depths. Reading what his friends, Horodezky and Lachower, tell of the effect upon Berditchewski, one realizes the tragedy of these two men, father and son, who in all their lives never understood one another. Not long after, at the end of 1921, his heart gave out, having been weakened by years of privation and too strenuous labors. When he died, in his fifty-seventh year, his head was still full of plans for writing.

II

For many years Hebrew readers remembered Berditchewski from the days of the "Youth," (*Ze'irim*) a small, aggressive band of congenial Hebrew writers whom this solitary soul had grouped around himself in order to force his ideas into Hebrew literature. It was at the turn of the century, about 1900, that a whole series of Berditchewski's bold, controversial writings hailed down thick and fast, together with the devout, ecstatic *Book of the Chassidim*—one of those contradictions so typical of him. Thereafter, though seeming to stand to one side, he yet remained alive to all that was genuine in the Jewish renaissance. Hardly a problem in Jewish life and letters but had his vigorous personal comment which, whether it was violently attacked or lauded to the skies, was always stimulating, unusual, new. He had in a high degree the capacity to begin questioning at the very point where others found certainty. There was in his way of looking at things a theoretical innocence, a freedom from preconception, an independence of all traditional views which enabled him to see things differently, to discover, as it were, the world anew. Even his opponents had to admit: "I have never yet seen the thing from that angle!" Through long years of strenuous thought he had developed what Nietzsche calls the "daring of suspicion," a mistrust of old, soporific answers, a *de omnibus dubitandum*. His intellectual integrity never quailed before his own ideas: he did not ignore what could be brought against himself, and often spoke the most penetrating word in criticism of his own work. For he wanted truth, not opiates, even if it presupposed "the courage for the forbidden and a predestination to the labyrinth."

It is not by accident that Nietzchean references flow from my pen. Just as it was no accident that Berditchewski was so powerfully attracted by the great German breaker of tablets and transvaluator of values. There is a fatal affinity between them. Admitted that Berditchewski did take over thought-content from Nietzsche, what weighs even more is the kinship of type, their similar two-souled character. Both were of that rare breed whose being, like that of Proserpina, must belong to two realms: believing doubters, God-seeking blasphemers, slayers and proclaimers of God—brothers in destiny.

No wonder, then, that acquaintance with the German philosophy of the "dangerous Perhaps" was a momentous experience for Berditchewski: here he found things formulated that had surged darkly within his own soul, and *how* formulated! With a magic force of language whose abundance of simile borders on the visionary, whose witchery of sound vies with music. The thinker and the poet in Berditchewski must have been thrilled, intoxicated, desperate, for such verbal craftsmanship was denied him. To this contact I attribute Berditchewski's crop of writings of those years: a storm had passed over him, and unchained long-slumbering, unarticulated forces. Berditchewski himself gratefully testified to the stimulation he received from Nietzsche.

In outlining the train of thought in those writings of

Berditchewski's, it therefore seems advisable to begin with words of Nietzsche's which Berditchewski himself quotes partly, and which contains his teachings *in nuce*.

> The Jews are the most remarkable people in the history of the world because, when faced with the problem of Being or Not-Being, they preferred, with perfectly uncanny consciousness, *Being at any price*. That price was a radical falsification of all nature, all naturalness, all reality, the whole inner as well as the whole outer world. They cut themselves off from all the conditions under which a people had hitherto been able to live, had the *right to live;* out of themselves they created an antithesis to natural conditions, and unwholesomely reversed, in turn, religion, cults, morals, history into a *contradiction of their natural values.* We meet the same phenomenon once again in ineffably larger proportions, but nevertheless only as a copy: In comparison with the "people of saints," the Christian church has no claim whatever to originality. For that very reason the Jews are the most fateful people in the history of the world: through their influence they have made mankind false to such a degree that even today the Christian can feel anti-Jewish, not realizing that he himself is the last Jewish outgrowth.

Berditchewski wants to make this process of life-perversion retroactive. He wishes to leave behind the degenerated Judaism of later generations for the wholesome values of ancient Israel. Had not Nietzsche himself spoken in enthusiastic terms of the folk of the Bible:

> I do not love the New Testament. The Old Testament —that is quite another thing: all respect to the Old Testament! I find in it great men, an heroic landscape, something of that rarest thing on earth, the incomparable naïveté of the strong heart; still more, I find a people. In the New Testament, however, I find nothing but petty sectarianism, rococo of the soul, the air of the conventicle, not to mention an occasional breath of bucolic sweetish-

ness. And this continual thou-ing of a God of the most wretched taste!

Many similar passages occur in Nietzsche, as for instance:

> In the Jewish Old Testament, that book of divine right-eousness, there are men, things, and words of so great a style that Greek and Indian literature have nothing to place beside it. One stands fearfully and reverently before this colossal remnant of what man once was, and thinks sorrow-fully of Asia and its protruding peninsula Europe which would by all means wish to claim for itself, as against Asia, the "progress of humanity." . . . To place the New Testament (in which there is much of the simple, weakly, flat praying-brethren-and-petty-soul smell) with the Old in one book as a "Bible," as the "Book-in-itself"—this is perhaps the greatest single act of presumption and "sin against the holy spirit" that literary Europe has upon its conscience.

Berditchewski saw a similar decadence in later rabbinic Judaism, and wished to lead the new Jewish generation back to the grand style of unperverted values of the Bible. While others spoke of the Hebrew renaissance and the Hebrew language in general, Berditchewski showed that Hebrew was almost two different languages: that of the Bible, "with its powerful rhythm, and that of the Talmud, the language of wisdom. At bottom these two languages belong, so to speak, to two different peoples—the old *Israel* and the later *Judah*. The one is the language of the people which built an altar to the sword, the other the language of doctrine and devout books."

Himself the greatest bookworm in recent Jewish generations, Berditchewski attacked the tyranny of books most violently:

> Our world is nothing but books, our questions are written questions, our problems written problems. Our soul is but a scroll written within and without, but a collection of printer's type. . . . Life has withdrawn itself from us because of books . . . which have held our souls in bondage since days of old. We have thoughts upon thoughts . . . we have much knowledge, we are able to understand everything. But *live* we cannot, for we lack wholeness, innocence, simplicity. Even our emotions and desires are tinged with thought, crippled with purpose. We observe too much, we know too much.

Books have made us heirs, epigons, echoes of our forefathers. But Berditchewski proclaims the rights of the present as against the dead memories of the past. With Nietzsche he revolts against the immoderate cult of history, against the hypertrophy of historic memory, which makes us unfree, uncreative, imitative; we no longer shape our own rhythms, but copy the men and the deeds of the past, we live historic recollections. He quotes the profound saying of Pascal that "those peoples whom we call *old* were new and pure with youth, while we, the new peoples, are really *old.*" . . . Those ancient peoples lived in To-day and To-morrow, while we limp after Yesterday: "I believe in my fathers, in our fathers, believe that they were what they were, lived what they lived! But allow us, too, to live on our own account, to stand upon our own feet. Let us have hopes of creating, and do not make us mere guardians of the old inheritance." And he cries out to the new generation: "Forget! Free yourselves from the bonds of too much historical thinking, so that you may be what you are—and live your own lives!"

When Ahad Ha'am reproaches the new Hebrew litera-

ture with having at one bound overleaped all the generations that thought and wrote between the closing of the
Biblical canon and their own day, Berditchewski insists
that the greatness of the new literature consists in just that
bold leap. The four thousand years of Jewish culture
which Ahad Ha'am stresses are for Berditchewski a mere
abstraction, a mental sum of many single centuries and
generations each of which was as solid and as real as our
own century and generation; but the latter, just because
they are ours, have for us more meaning, more reality. It
is as though Berditchewski wishes to say: For each man
the world in which he lives is—to speak with Leibniz—
the best of all possible worlds, simply because he himself
lives in it.

Therefore he contended against Ahad Ha'am that Judaism has supplanted the Jews, that abstractions banish the
living reality. No general cohesive content, no fundamental principles of Judaism exist such as Ahad Ha'am sought
to define and to hold binding upon every Jewish individual. The people of Israel is a living, changing reality,
not a dogmatic and hide-bound world-conception. And
when Ahad Ha'am charged that Berditchewski's teachings were foreign and never could be reconciled with
Judaism, he asked: With which Judaism? Was there a
common and eternal Judaism for all time?

> We ask, Is this Judaism where Joab ben Zeruiah admon-
> ishes David that a man must be ashamed to love his enemies,
> or this of someone in the Oral Law that a man ought to be
> humble, soft as a reed even towards one that has humbled
> him? Tell us, please, which Judaism is authentic, that which
> speaks of living on bread with salt, or that which says, "it
> will be required of man to account for all that he saw with

his eyes and did *not* enjoy" (Jerusalem Talmud)? Is it the Judaism of Rabbi Johanan who says that moral perfection consists of self-mastery in the service of the *Shekhinah*, or that of his brother-in-law, Resh Lakish, who had been a robber and then won self-mastery under the wings of the *Shekhinah*, when he asks: What have I gained? I am called master now, and was called master then [in the days of his banditry]. Is Judaism the ascetic denial of desire and passion, or the doctrine of the early Chasidim: "The soul is part of God above, and everything within it is a part of Him—everything, without distinction. Hence, our deeds, our desires, our thoughts, our passions are all the will of God, Blessed be He, and it is our duty to obey that same divine will, as it were, without discrimination. If we restrain our passions and do not follow the inclinations of our heart, it is like a refusal to obey the will of God, Blessed be He. And by such refusal we banish the *Shekhinah* from our midst."

Judaism, like life, is a much richer and more complex phenomenon than any one-time scholarly formula: "we are the sons of our fathers, not their coffins."

In one of his finest essays, Ahad Ha'am analyzed the teachings of Nietzsche, and proved that their universally human core, when divested of what was incidental and national in them, was not irreconcilable with Judaism. It was necessary only to strip away their non-essential, Germanic particularities as, for instance, the cult of the "blond beast," of physical force (in Berditchewski's terminology, "the sword,") with which the spirit of Judaism can never agree. Contempt for the "power of the fist," for aggressive physical courage, is inborn and inbred in Jewish minds and hearts as the deepest legacy of the prophets. Through their ministry, reverence for things spiritual, for the power of the spirit, had become almost instinctive with the Jew. However, with the modification offered by Ahad Ha'am, Nietzsche's brave and creative moral philosophy, which never regards pleasure and pain as ultimate values, can well be adjusted to Judaism. When the superman is translated into the realm of the spirit, he will probably appear not much unlike the ideal Jewish type—the Zaddik or saint.

Against Ahad Ha'am it can be urged that neither Nietzsche nor Berditchewski ever seriously proclaimed the raw cult of force. Both must be considered apart from their occasional exaggerations of language, their needless vehemence of polemic. Berditchewski, in particular, was given to extreme and superlative expression. It might rightly be said of Ahad Ha'am that he stormed open doors. For, to whom did he give counsel to translate Nietzsche into spiritual Jewish terms. To the writer of the *Book of the Chasidim,* who glorified the spiritual greatness of the Chasidim and rendered homage to Rabbi Jose, the silent hermit. In point of fact, those booklets of Berditchewski's which show the influence of Nietzsche most strongly, reveal perceptions derived from genuinely Jewish sources; which should prove to us that Nietzsche was merely the stimulus to independent creation. Years before Berditchewski knew even the name of Nietzsche, he was advocating similar ideas of his own. I refer the reader to his early articles (1888-89) in *'Ibri Anokhi,* a Hebrew periodical, written before he went to Germany, which explain why he had finally to arrive at Nietzsche.

But also why he had to get away from Nietzsche. In the very first articles of his Nietzschean period, when he was affirming the natural life-instincts against life-denying ascetism, he quotes from Jewish sources and revives Chasidic ideas. Yet, even more, he admits at the same time in a significant passage how deeply Jewish and how un-Nietzschean his moral valuations are. "At times I would say to myself: What will remain of our ancient civilization after all its values are changed? What is eternal in us, what will guide us even if we become new men? And then I remember an explicit scripture command: 'Sanctify yourselves and be ye holy.'"

This is one of the fundamental teachings of traditional Judaism. An interpretation in the Sifra even bases upon this scripture all the religious duties of Judaism showing the way to such sanctification: through the fulfillment of the holy commandments. And here the great thinker of *Religion of Reason from the Sources of Judaism,* Herman Cohen, is in remarkable accord with Berditchewski the heretic. Still more, the herald of self-sufficient individualism understands that "before we can become holy human beings, we must become a holy nation,—a *nation!*" It is therefore not surprising that Berditchewski, just because he thought individualism through to its final implications, should have enriched the national idea. Unless the people is rehabilitated, the individual cannot unfold himself fully. Or, as Berditchewski phrases it, "without liberation (of the people), there can be no salvation (for the individual)."

Jewish life in the Diaspora seemed to him a continually recurring catastrophe of the spirit. We grieve, he said, because Moses threw down the tablets whereon the finger of God had written, shattering them at the foot of the mountain. How would it have been, however, if at the moment when Moses descended, the mountain had begun to quake under his feet, and the tablets had fallen and been shattered of themselves! "This is our lot, the lot of Israel in the Diaspora, the lot of his books, his thinkers and poets and all those in whose nostrils is the breath of the Lord. Our soul demands great things, but our body has no ground on which to stand." And when he heard spiritual "missions" spoken of, he pronounced the profoundest word that has been said in Zionism: "Give us first a stone whereon to lay our head—and then we shall *dream*."

Though he often opposed both political and cultural Zionism, both Herzl and Ahad Ha'am, he perhaps more than anyone else helped to train that youth who have taken Zionism seriously and realized it in their own persons. Berditchewski's individualism has at times been looked upon as hedonistic: the individual demands the rights which the collectivity has abridged. But his articles on Zionism show that he meant an heroic individualism. His ethics demand not something less of the individual, but something different, and in reality something more— more earnestness, wholeness, honesty! He pointed to the work of Cecil Rhodes, which was animated far less by altruistic motives than that of Montefiore, Baron de Hirsch, or Herzl.

> Yet how much more he accomplished than they! How much he achieved for the English people, and how much he created by his power—yet for the most part he labored only for himself. He put his whole self and all his millions into the undertaking: he created great things because he staked all his strength and all his wealth upon the place he meant to build up.

TWO HERETICS

And animadverting to political and cultural Zionism, he taught that the salvation of Israel would come not through diplomats or through prophets, but through men working for themselves, who would thereby be paving the way for the whole people. In certain moments of exaltation, the individual will, it is true, ignore his private interests and concern himself with the public welfare; but daily life tends to run its natural course. Leaders and movements should reckon with human nature, not fight against it. They should try to set the strivings of the individual within a general framework in such a way that what he does for his own good will redound also to the good of the community.

> This is not our misfortune,—that we have not many men who are ready to neglect their private interests for the good of the community, but that the life of the individual and his strivings in his own behalf do not, cannot accrue to the benefit of the whole. A people cannot live by abstract sacrifices, nor can it be restored by them. A people is the sum of individual men working for themselves in their own places, each in his own house and homestead. And all the wealth created for the needs of the household, of the individual and of the family constitutes the community, makes possible the existence of the community.

Zionism will become a reality only when it becomes a personal aim:

> Whatever the individual will not do for the sake of himself and his family and the next generation, the community will not do for him. For the community is merely the material and spiritual sum of the deeds and the strength of individuals. However we may envisage the redemption of the people, the *beginning* will be made by individuals, and will come only through individuals.

Berditchewski, while seeming to speak for the self-interested ego taught the highest form of national service: to give not bits of charity, but one's whole self—a postulate which is being proven and lived by the young Jewish pioneers who are now building up Palestine. His heresy gave birth to new believers.

III

Such was the fate of Berditchewski's scientific as well as of his publicistic work. In his scientific work, also, he searched the past not for pious, but for strong Jews. Or, as he put it, for the literary remains of ancient Israel, not of the later Judah. He complained that much in that great and free tradition had been confiscated by the makers of spiritual history in Judaism. "That the leaders of the people should have presumed wilfully to obliterate national treasures, the spiritual conquests of individuals, was frightful tyranny, and the greatest spiritual theft in the history of the nations." The aim of Berditchewski's scientific work was to make good this cultural loss as far as might be. Wherever he found heretical and heterodox ideas and traditions deviating from those of the Jewish church, he followed up their traces and tried to reconstitute what had been lost. He sought to free the old myths from the late censorship to which they had been subjected, and listened for archaic heathen echoes in the most innocent official traditions. His collection of legends is an attempt to reveal Judaism in what had been branded schismatic, in the banned, the apocryphal. And, however we may judge his license in the reconstruction of certain mutilated myths, the very effort to place a picture of the Judaism that was ousted beside official Judaism is in itself a scientific venture.

A similar purpose runs through his *Sinai and Gerizim,* a posthumous work full of the most radical Biblical criticism. Here again he seeks in rabbinic literature traces of suppressed old traditions that are older than the Bible itself, that is to say, that antedate the editing of the Biblical text. He wishes to reveal the undercurrent of Jewish paganness that still runs through the post-Biblical literature. The task is performed with much arbitrariness and with a vast scientific apparatus which makes the book difficult reading. The chapter on the sacrifice of Isaac might serve as an example of his method. He searches in late Jewish sources for a different version from that of the Genesis narrative. From the attempts of the rabbinic commentators to explain certain unevennesses in the accepted text, he infers a surmise on their part that something has been suppressed. The text of Genesis xxii. 19—"So Abraham returned unto his young men"—makes the rabbis ask in astonishment: Where was Isaac left? A question similar to the quaint traditions in the Tanaitic and Amoraic literature, which know of another end of Isaac than told in the Bible. For example, the Mekhilta explains Exodus xii. 12—"and when He seeth the blood" —by adding that He then sees the blood of the *sacrificed* Isaac. Or, when the origin of the custom of strewing ashes on the head is discussed in the Talmud, Rabbi Chanina offers the explanation: so that we may recall the *ashes* of Isaac. In such sayings Berditchewski sees a fund of archaisms, a residue of elder traditions, survivances from the time when the Genesis story had a form in which it was clear why Abraham went back alone.

In the same way, Berditchewski tries to discover remnants of ancient traditions in the rabbinic literature which set Joshua above Moses: A verse from Proverbs (xviii. 23)—"The poor useth entreaties; but the rich answereth impudently"—is explained to mean that the poor man is Moses, the rich Joshua. The Talmud relates that of the fifty gates of wisdom only forty-nine were opened to Moses; to Joshua, however, the fiftieth was opened as well. Therefore he was called the son of Nun (the letter *nun* in Hebrew having the numeric value of 50). Another legend relates that the messiah will spring only from the stock of Joshua. Berditchewski even credits the traveler Eldad ha-Dani who says of the inhabitants of the kingdom of the Ten Tribes that their whole tradition derives from Joshua, and that all their laws read: thus spake Joshua bin Nun, who heard it from the mouth of the Almighty. In this manner Berditchewski plows through the whole field of later Jewish literature seeking for pre-Torah traditions. Upon the basis of these and also of some new philological criteria for the analysis of sources of the Biblical text, he arrives at the thesis that the assembly of all-Israel before Joshua at Shechem was the birth-hour of the Israelitic religion; that Gerizim in Palestine and not Sinai in the desert is the holy mountain; that the twelve curses (Deut. xxvii. 15-26), the dodecalogue of Shechem, are older than the ten commandments; that the single, unhewn, uninscribed stone, the stone of the testimony which Joshua set up under the oak at Shechem (Joshua xxiv. 26) is earlier than the two hewn, inscribed stone tablets; and that, finally, the founder of the religion of Israel is to be seen not in Moses, but in Joshua.

Berditchewski's poetic boldness in interpreting the sources shall here be passed over without comment, since

it is not the scientific value of his discoveries that interests
us, but the personality of the writer, for a knowledge of
which the book offers many hints. When we see how
from his early youth he sought the center of gravity for
the Israelitic religion in Jeroboam's kingdom of the Ten
Tribes, we understand the prolonged diligence with which
through many decades he tried to prop up the dogmatic,
preconceived pet notions of his youth with scientific
reasons.

We know that from childhood he preferred the northern
tribes of Israel and grieved over the tradition that the
messiah of the tribe of Ephraim must die before the coming of the messiah of the house of David. He chose rather
to believe that "Ephraim is My dearest son, a child of
delights." When in his brochure, *The Views of One on
the Many,* he wishes to praise Rabbi Jacob Emden, no
more flattering comparison occurs to him than that of
Jeroboam ben Nebat. In another of his early novels, the
hero, when he takes a despairing farewell of his beloved,
has no better comment to make than that "now he has the
same feelings as the dying Moses when he saw Joshua
tender and forsaken. . . ." In this story, Joshua is still
the object of sympathy; in his posthumous work he finally
succeeded to place Moses in that rôle.

IV

In Berditchewski's artistic creation, also, similar tendencies can be found. Again in his novels he draws strong,
not pious Jews. In the Jewish life of his own day he also
seeks for survivals of ancient urges, mental and emotional
archaisms, heathen atavisms older and stronger than the

later ethical prohibitions. Early condemning sentimental love tales as untrue to the life of the Ghetto, he portrays with a skillful economy of words the dark soul-forces, the primeval wild passions that still run an underground course in the pious East European communities. A fascinating novel, *The Red Cow,* is prefaced with the following words (which apply equally well to the rest of his stories).

> I shall not deny that it is rather offensive. One moment, I said, I shall conceal it, and the next, Let it be written down. . . . A generation will arise after us that will not know its fathers nor the ways of their life in the exile, therefore let it know . . . what our life was . . . know that we were Jews, but also men of flesh and blood, with all that is implied therein. . . .

The story itself is about the revenge of some butchers upon the owner of a splendid red Dutch cow. One dark night they killed the beautiful animal in a cellar, the essence of the story being in the struggle—the wild, raw, desperate struggle—of the men with the raging animal. Primitive heathen passions flare up hotly:

> The animal was flayed, the men divided it into parts, and chopped off the head and the legs. Unable to wait, one of the butchers seized the fat liver and spread it over some hot coals. And when the blood dripped down into the fire, the men ate the liver unsalted, with a strong, greedy passion, licking their fingers covetously. . . . Like the priests of Baal they seemed in this hour, dividing a sacrifice before the altar. And this thing happened not in Bethel or Dan, but in the Jewish town of Dashia; not before the exile of the Ten Tribes, in the northern kingdom of Israel, but in the year 5645 of the creation of the world [i.e., 1885].

In another narrative, *Hakkaddish,* the head of the community is beside himself with wrath when he sees the local

Chasidim building themselves a house of worship. Set beside the existing synagogues, it seems to him like an idolatrous Bethel beside Jerusalem or Shiloh. "In olden days they used to shatter the images of strange gods in the name of the Lord!" One night he sets fire to this new Chasidic synagogue, and the whole street, including his own property, is reduced to ashes.

In his erotic stories, Berditchewski describes the primordial power of the sexual instincts that do not shrink even from incest. Here too he loves to make comparisons with Jewish-heathen antiquity. When he draws a picture of a self-willed, passionate old magnate in an East European community who likes to flirt occasionally with the daughter of his secretary, the simple scene suddenly evokes memories of the ancient days of his people: "A descendant of the conquerors of Canaan and perhaps of the tribe of Dan or of Gad or the half-tribe of Menasseh, sits upon a bench in a small room whose every corner breathes of cleanliness, and strokes the red hair of a blooming maiden in one of the lands of the exile." In order to suggest the irresistible charm of the heroine of this tale, he says— reminding us of Homer when he lets the old men of Troy approve of Helen: "Even the most pious in the community agreed in their hearts that she resembled Cozbi the daughter of Zur after whom lusted a prince of a father's house among the Simeonites." And when the old Jewish magnate does not shrink from sin, Berditchewski chooses to illustrate the situation with a peculiar comparison from the early history of Israel:

> When I was a boy studying the chronicles of the kings, I read that Adonijah, the son of Haggith, asked of the king's

mother that she give him Abishag, the concubine of David,
to wife. And when Solomon heard of the matter, he swore
that Adonijah had spoken against his own life. . . . Then
I had another vision, and the whole incident was changed
from end to end: Behold, Adonijah met Abishag the Shu-
manite in the fields of Salem, and she was the most fair
damsel throughout all the borders of Israel, and no man
had yet known her. Love for her flamed up in his heart,
and he went to his father saying, A virgin among the daughters of thy servants hath found favor in mine eyes. Take
her for my wife and bless me. When David saw that
Abishag was lovelier than his wives, he too desired her and
said, She shall be my portion and mine inheritance only.
And the son went out affrighted from the presence of his
father. Then Adonijah conspired against his father, for he
was jealous of the maiden, and his soul knew no peace.
And the people flocked to the king's son, and the revolt
spread. . . .

This willful interpretation of, or rather against, the
ancient record is true Berditchewski. With a downright
uncanny scent he loved to guess at the secret, unavowed,
personal motives, the human, all too human roots in the
achievements and personalities of yore. In this eagerness
to trace the *pudenda origo* of every action, he did not
shrink from cynicism, and at times even had the courage
of bad taste. This almost sickly degree of clairvoyance
explains not only the merits but the excrescences of the
born "trier of reins" and psychologist.

In his novels, Berditchewski shows a fascinating narrative skill that one would not have expected of the amorphous publicist. He describes the wild beauty of the passions with such concise simplicity, so succinctly, that it is
hard to believe they were written by the chaotic, thought-
tormented Berditchewski. He knew also how to portray

the curbed, "sanctified" instincts, the fine discipline of Jewish custom. The quiet renunciation of his women has been caught by no one else with such subtlety. One who reads his *Excommunicated after Death,* or *The Last Hand-Basin,* or *The Question,* will never forget the tender grace of those chaste women. With a masterly hand he depicted Gentile women also, not only the educated type (Hedwig in his *Two Camps,* who, however, was a half-Jewess), but also women of the vigorous, unspent village breed in whom, all unknown to themselves, innocence and demonic passions still slumber side by side, as in the story of *Summer and Winter.* Here, as in most of his best stories, fable and reality, legend and fact are curiously interwoven —this being one of the charms of his narrative art. Of one of his Jewish orphan girls, he says, "the maiden was as a star fallen from heaven to walk on earth"; and of the lovely Ukrainian village maid, he tells us that "the dogs did not bark at her, the cows followed her, and the cart-horses . . . even on the slopes of the mountain, obeyed her like brothers." . . . One feels here as if one were reading an ancient fable like that Egyptian tale —the oldest in the world—in the papyrus of d'Orbiney, where the very domestic animals love the innocent young brother and warn him of danger. His is a conscious, late-born art, yet there pervades it (to quote Dionys of Halicarnass) *chnous archaiotetos,* a breath of antiquity. When he seeks ancient heathen survivals, he is partisan, modern, sophisticated; but when, in creative unawareness, he fashions characters from contemporary life or the "recent past" (the title of one of his best collections of stories), he is an objective artist, intensely true to life, and yet peculiarly archaic in the naïveté of his story-telling. Another of the numerous contradictions in his life!

VI

The much fought-over name of Berditchewski is gradually becoming historic, and permits of dispassionate judgment. Already he has behind him the first phases of literary destiny: fanatical hatred and unqualified praise, obscurity and vogue. We are still too near him to determine the altitude of so curious and richly contradictory a figure, to exclude errors and delusions of perspective. But to our generation, those features in him which make him so akin and so dependent upon the inheritance he combated, become ever clearer.

He himself, in clear-eyed moments of introspection, recognized with fear how bound up he was with his ancestral heritage: "All my thoughts and meditations are nothing but hereditary burdens, echoes of my ancestors' thoughts. Even now, while I loosen the chains, I am merely a son of the generations I would overleap." He realized that his conflict with traditional Judaism drew sustenance from the best forces of that Judaism, that his pious fathers lived on in his very blasphemies. And there are passages and moments in his life when this "Woe's thee that thou'rt a grandson" is transformed into a happy, willing, thankful integration into the long chain of Jewish generations, when ancestral predestination is felt not as a disgrace, but as a distinction, not a stigma, but a crown.

Possibly he divined that his life work would be subject to the law of all revolution: that it only helps the best in the enduring order it fights against to further endurance.

So, too, his radical transvaluation became a fountain of youth for what is permanent in Judaism. And, like many a bringer of offensively new and unheard-of things, it was he who safeguarded and reintroduced the long-established and the long-known.

Berditchewski perhaps more than anyone else has revealed to the modern Jew all the beauties and unsurmised wealth of the old values. A hater of books, he dug in forgotten old books, awakening dead treasures to new life. He enriched and enhanced the image of Judaism in the eyes of the youth because he spanned all the Jewish generations, searched through every phase of the Jewish soul, embraced all ages and all lands, and even affirmed whatever rebellious spirits in Judaism had created. He had the right to say of himself: *nihil judaici a me alienum puto.*

> Not one chapter, not one record, not one generation, one age or current of an age, can give us the complete picture, but all the tribes and all the generations; all the movements in our world and all the winds that have blown through it, whether accepted or not; all of them, allow us to recognize some part of our people, and to penetrate into the mysteries of its soul. All of them testify in us,—both the individual and the group, those we hold innocent and those we hold guilty, the destroyers and the builders, those who walk in the ways of evil and those who walk in the ways of good.

The Talmudic saying "All Israel have a portion in the world to come; and even if he has sinned, he is still Israel," he divested of its other-worldly significance: everything conceived by Jewish blood and Jewish genius is Jewish, and has a claim to immortality in the grateful memory of Jewish posterity.

When he spoke of memory, he meant the power not only to look backward, but also forward, not only reverence for tradition, but responsibility for the future. For, where was this fullness of passions, virtues, renunciations, struggles, sufferings, triumphs of every sort, as he saw them in the age-long history of the Jews, to find an outlet, if not ultimately in great men and deeds, in a great Jewish future? He wanted to become wise in the ancient origins that he might the better search out the sources of the future; to unearth the past in its entirety in order, with its pious forces, to underarch the edifice of the future. Without this vision, this love of the future, the earnest passion and self-sacrificial effort which make up Berditchewski's life work would have been impossible.

Future generations, for whom the freedom for which he fought in his East European ghetto will, we hope, be a matter of course, will perhaps be attracted to him most through his tragically unescapable Jewishness: "With my hands I destroy, but from my feet I remove my shoes, that I may not touch our holy ground." So he wrote in the heat of the struggle, never concealing, despite all his partisanship, his reverence for the old teachings and forces of Judaism:

> You wash your hands before a meal. As the water is poured out from the jug upon your hand, it does indeed cleanse and refresh you . . . but the act in itself is trivial and immediately forgotten. But otherwise, quite otherwise, is it when you wash your hands by the commandment of God, the God of the generations that hallowed and served Him, that sacrificed themselves for the sake of His commandments. The souls of all the generations that lived and died to sanctify His Name come into some kind of touch with you when you raise the jug to pour water over your

hands. Intending to fulfill just one of the commandments, you have become one with the whole community, with many generations, with the living God.

Not without deep emotion will posterity read with what awe and reverence this heretic regarded that which he attacked: how he admitted and understood that the "sins against life" with which he taxed rabbinic Judaism derived from the noblest motives and were committed by "true saints"; that the humility which he disparaged breathed greatness of soul; that in self-imposed humiliation before God there is strength, magnificence.

> One may refute the *Shulchan 'Arukh,* but one may not deny greatness to Rabbi Joseph Caro and Rabbi Moses Isserles. One may criticize the Gaon of Vilna for his hatred of life, but one will bow before the giant. Even if you dare to doubt the existence of God, you will quail before the glory and the majesty of those who died and were slain for the consecration of His Name.

His preaching of the virtues of the sword, of physical power, falls flat beside those profound moments of reconsideration when his Jewish heritage tells him how much of the old slave habit still inheres in kneeling before force; and that, if degrees of reverence-worthiness were to be determined, we should have to measure how far force itself had been overcome by a something higher whose tool it has become. In moments like this, his word rings in consonance with the authentic mouthpieces of Israel. Then, his complaint, his reproach, his blasphemy even, becomes prayer.

Heine said of the book of Job: just as when a person suffers, he must weep out his heart, so he must doubt out his doubts; this poison of doubt could not have been left out of the Bible, the great medicine-chest of mankind. Fully aware of the distance which separates the whole of modern Hebrew letters from that divine Book, one may say that Berditchewski's is a like function within this new literature.

When Joseph Chaim Brenner was living in Lemberg, he had a room in the home of an assimilated Jewess, a widow with several children. The oldest, then attending the second grade of the Gymnasium, was a boy of twelve, naïve, and a bit simple-minded. But Brenner loved him for his gentle eyes. One day the boy came quietly into Brenner's room and asked him in Polish, his eyes full of curiosity, *"Panie* Brenner, who is the greatest Hebrew writer of our time?" Brenner quickly rose, went over to the table, dipped his pen into the ink, and wrote in Latin characters on a slip of paper the name of Berditchewski.

This judgment was characteristic of Brenner. Though he willingly acknowledged Berditchewski's spiritual and creative superiority to himself, he divined in him a kindred soul. He recognized that Berditchewski's was no merely theoretical, bookish questioning; that here a heart was thinking, a personal woe philosophizing. Even Berditchewski's chaotic style, which others regarded as a lack of form, attracted Brenner. He saw in it the hallmark of sincerity, though he himself to an even greater degree longed for the comfort of artistic form and never learned the secret of orderly creation.

Brenner had neither the depth nor the range of Berditchewski's ideas. He was always the one to be gratefully stimulated, the one who received from Berditchewski. He had one trait, however, which, while it does not belong to literature, does explain his influence upon Hebrew literature and, beyond that, upon the new Hebrew life: his deep hatred of the observer's attitude, of the *litterateur,* his early manifested will to render active service. Pythagoras once compared mankind with those who attend public festivals: some come to compete in the games, others to look on, and still others to traffic. Like the elder Cyrus, both men disliked those who come to the market place to deceive each other with false oaths. Both had for them the contempt of the creative human being who does not— like the merchant—ask of life, What can I get out of it, but rather what can I bring into it. But they differed in this, that Berditchewski, despite occasional attempts at action, remained an observer who at most called out encouragingly to those engaged in the life-struggle, but took no part in it himself, desiring indeed to influence life through his books, but only through his books. Brenner, whether he was less gifted as a writer or more of a man of will, could never ease himself through authorship alone: a residue in him always remained unsatisfied, asking for the immediacy of deeds, for a direct share in the games: "We must not stand outside of life as mere observers. We must fight, improve, exalt. A curse on the mere observer!" His writing was always dynamically charged with the presage of action, pervaded with a deadly earnestness, an exaggerated estimate of his own doings, an over-prizing of literary influence in general. The glaring incongruity between the self-importance of his writings and their slight literary value was for many years misinterpreted even by eminent men of Hebrew letters. They overlooked the genuineness of his pathos, the upright sense of personal responsibility behind each word, which, despite all outward seeming, had nothing in common with empty magniloquence. In Palestine he matured a somewhat simpler and more modest style, both in his publicistic writing and his artistic creation; but, with the exception of a few passages, simple calm of form was denied him all his life.

There is little to be said about the outward course of Brenner's life. He was born in 1881 in a small, wretched town, Novimlini, on the border between Little and Great Russia, in a meager, empty countryside which was, as it were, to strike the basic chord of his life, to bear the responsibility for the word that occurs oftener in his pages than any other: "emptiness." He tasted all the pains of poverty early in life, both in his parents' home and in his unhappy years of wandering through Yeshiboth, where he became a *Mithnagged,* or opponent of Chasidism. He made early contacts with the literature of the Haskalah, with Tolstoi's teachings of world-abandonment, with the "Bund," a Jewish socialist-revolutionary organization. His connection with the last-named led to his forced service in the Russian army. He suffered unspeakably under the severe discipline of the Czarist barracks, tried to desert during the Russian-Japanese war, was captured, and then finally rescued by a daring stroke on the part of friends in the "Bund," escaping across the border. In between came his first literary attempts. In London, where he finally landed, he published (beginning in 1906) a Hebrew periodical called *Hame'orer* (*The Awakener*) for two years, a venture that at once reveals to us Brenner's whole personality.

One must visualize the period in question. Those were

years of profound disillusionment in Russian Jewry, then still the main reservoir of Jewish forces. The attempts at revolution in 1905 brought, not deliverance, but a flood of pogroms throughout the country, and intensified reaction everywhere. Hebrew literature lay as if lamed, no periodical appeared in the language. *Hazefirah* in Warsaw, *Hazman* in Vilna lapsed; even *Hashiloach* suspended publication for a time. The young talents were seized with a bitter apathy. Hebrew seemed to them a lost cause. In despair, they went over to foreign language, or, at best, to the language of the folk, Yiddish, but worked even in the latter field without faith. Some even grasped at suicide, despairing because Jewish life offered no aim, no duty. Thus for example, the gifted young publicist, Ben Israel, of whom his friends tell that he decided upon suicide during those years, though he did not carry out his intention until several years later. In such desperate days, Brenner had the courage to publish a new Hebrew periodical in the distant West. The little issues of *The Awakener* made at first an almost ridiculous impression. Even Brenner's closest friends did not know what he was really aiming at. Did he not know, like all of them, that Hebrew was doomed? And yet the illegal sheet was greedily read in Russia. Through its pages blew an austere, forceful blast of youth: it actually *awakened* people. It is a great pity that Brenner did not live to see the twentieth anniversary of the first issue of *The Awakener,* for then he would have heard the Jewish labor movement in Palestine attribute its ancestry to the modest little green pamphlets, quite unimportant as literature, which he printed on the banks of the Thames.

Brenner undertook the task with the heroism of despair. Not without symbolic significance was the statement on the cover of his monthly that it was published by the *Massada* association. It was of course Brenner who organized this *Massada* and named it after the bare, rocky peak in the magnificent wild country west of the Dead Sea which the grim zealots of the Hebrew war for independence were able to hold several years after the destruction of the Temple in Jerusalem; when finally they had to give it up, they chose to kill each other rather than to bow down to the Romans. The name therefore implied a program: a last battle in defense of Hebrew. Brenner published *The Awakener* at the cost of unbounded self-sacrifice. He usually wrote almost half of every issue himself, himself set up the type (he earned his living as a compositor), managed all the business affairs, carried the parcels to the post office for mailing. Despite all his sacrifices of time and money, he was obliged after two years to let the periodical lapse, having no more money with which to buy paper or to pay for the use of printing machines. And yet he complained less of these financial handicaps than of the lack of suitable material which, if it were available, he would have managed to print in spite of everything. The writers to whom he turned, even intimate friends like the highly gifted novelist, Uri Nisan Gnesin, did not share his over-esteem for the thing he was doing; they lacked the creative illusion without which sacrifice is impossible; it did not seem to them that the "to be or not to be" of the Hebrew language depended upon *The Awakener*. And so it perished.

Brenner then went to Galicia, on his way thither seeking out Berditchewski at Breslau who at that time would receive no one else; and, in 1909, arrived in Palestine, where he tried himself out as laborer, teacher, writer, always unhappy at being nothing but a writer, and yet irrevocably doomed to write. In later years, he became the conscience of working Palestine; and, though he saw and rebuked "desertion and failure" in its ranks, his constructive will was felt behind his anger and doubt, and his truthfulness honored. He was murdered by an Arab hand at Jaffa during the disturbances of May, 1921, being then barely forty years old. As he lived in a lonely house outside the town, friends wanted to take him away while there was yet time, but he refused, not wishing to leave the family with whom he had been living for a time. They too fell victims to the bestial mob.

Brenner's was a desired martyrdom, not unsought by himself. He was too much a man of ethos to desert through suicide the post of duty that life had imposed upon him; and yet he was deeply, tragically at variance with life. It was as if from birth he had been condemned to a profound pessimism. There was in him something of the prophet of old who had to swallow a scroll "written within and without . . . lamentations and mourning and woe," which, despite all its bitterness, seemed palatable to him: "it was in my mouth as honey for sweetness." Even the cheerful Goethe reports that men seem to have a lust for ill, some dark nostalgia for the bliss of pain. And Michelangelo, himself a classic example of that strange and yet real aberration, summed up a whole world of pessimism in a despairing cry full of splendid injustice: "My passion is for melancholy . . . a thousand joys cannot balance a single pain." Brenner, though a man of incomparably lesser caliber, was still of the type which, as a result of suffering, achieves a kind of taste for pain. His narratives, which are nothing but fragments of a confession, leaves from his diary, a setting down of his own experiences, his own torments, his own quest, contain a series of characters molded in the image of their author. All of them, whether they are called Jeremiah Feuermann (*In Winter*), or Abramson (*Around the Point*), or Eliezer (*Evening and Morning*), Johanan Maharshak (*Beyond the Boundaries*), "Stranded" (*Here and There*), Saul Gamsu (*Between the Waters*), Ezekiel Hefez (*Desertion and Failure*), are none but Brenner himself. All these characters have a gloomy propensity for self-torment.

In *In Winter,* Feuermann-Brenner testifies:

> Cruel is my quest for my own sins. Were a prosecutor to see me throw myself upon a sofa sighing heavily, he would doubtless condemn me to death and prove beyond doubt that I had murdered a man or set a quiet village on fire, when, actually, I had done neither good nor evil. I sigh and torture myself like a murderer out of the depths of boredom and great stupidity. . . .

No, it was not due to "great stupidity." That again is self-slander. The cause lay rather in an over-alert intellect with a keen eye for the inadequacies in everything, in a peculiar delight in discovering shadows everywhere. It is again an autobiographical admission when he says of Uriel in *Around the Point:* "When he cast his eye upon a thing, it melted away at once and lost its value." In theory Brenner disapproved of such a destructive view of things, and yet he could not free himself from it. One

377

cannot freely choose his manner of seeing the world. Indeed, Brenner catches himself secretly enjoying this wallowing in pain: "I cover my face with my hands, and immediately feel something pleasant in the nagging, gnawing pain, something I clutch at and try to keep inside of me. . . . And I think: even my torments are nothing but deception, hypocrisy, a kind of boastfulness, as though this had somehow increased my value."

It is the same in his last, most mature work where, however, he speaks as one purified, reconciled to his fate:

> In the book of the leprous Job, it is written: "And he took himself a potsherd to scrape himself therewith." I am not Job. And I do not rage. I am not Job, nor do I sit in the ashes, but on the dungheap,—on the dungheap of my ugly torments. But I hold tightly to the potsherd. I never stop scraping, it seems I cannot do without a potsherd.

This inexplicable tendency to self-torture is based on a deep hatred of self. That unhappy, tragically riven Jew and philosopher, Otto Weininger, who committed suicide in very early manhood, coined the term *misautic* for this type of self-hating human being, to which he himself irrevocably belonged. Of the same order, in Western history, is the *moi haïssable* of Pascal.

Brenner suffered from such ineradicable self-hatred. In *In Winter,* the hero, in truest self-knowledge, declares: "I hate everything in myself, despise everything, feel shame and disgust with everything. All that is in me seems contemptible, forged, despicable, nauseating. My whole being arouses a sense of guilt and a feeling of loathing in me. I have no place. . . ."

It is in such people that the idea of inherited sin origi-

nated: a mystic sense of sin before they themselves had
had time to sin. The sheer fact of existence is held a sin.

Such a man is incapable of happiness, even when it
beckons to him. Having awakened love in the heart of
a gentle girl, "he thinks it his duty to degrade himself
in her eyes at every opportunity. For he is unworthy
of love, he is unfortunate, and brings misfortune upon all
who come into contact with him." Thus speaks not only
Hafez in *Desertion and Failure,* but Johanan in the earlier
Beyond the Boundaries, when he evades a maiden who
loves him:

> Why do you want me? See, I am merely a shard of a
> man. Three years ago I asked myself, why should I live?
> And I found no answer. And yet I lived, lived on the past,
> on the torments of the past and wavered between life and
> death. Were I to live one year more, I should again live on
> my present torments and my present perplexity of soul.
> Why do you want me?

Such men marry finally not for love, but from a sense
of duty, of pity.

What wonder that, with such insuperable self-hatred,
the thought of suicide should crop up. Yet he lives and
works, and even seems to believe. Does self-torture provide content enough and reason enough for clinging to
life?

These complex natures cannot be fathomed unless one
of their crassest contradictions be disclosed. Brenner says
of himself, "I drown in the mire of hatred and physical
disgust for life, for my life." And elsewhere, but even
more passionately, "I am a pessimist, a pessimist to the
roots, without any reservations! I curse existence!"

And yet that same Brenner cherishes an almost unbelievable *love for life,* for life in and for itself, which he finds a wonderful, awe-inspiring mystery.

> In truth, everything—life and all—is worth while. And he who understands that everything is worth while, even where there is no content whatever, knows how to prize every token, how to make "content" out of everything, to bless every smile that flashes before him, every blade of grass and every stone, all good and all evil. Even though evil be painful, it too is life. . . . It is happiness to wander in the paths of life, happiness to live and to cherish life, its least tremors, with all their endless bliss.

In the same book, this inconsolable heretic, so unaccustomed to prayer, prays in a short, deeply moving hymn to life:

> My Father, Father of life and light, may thou be blessed, selah! My Father, Father of orphans, be gracious unto me, let the sun's rays send me a gift. And I, an orphan of orphans, shall receive Thy gift with thanks, with love, with hope. I know how to prize Thy gift, Thy goodness, selah! My heart sings and shouts to Thee, O Father of Life, blessed art Thou, selah!

Looking closer, one sees that this high valuation of all that lives, this love for life, wells out of Brenner's tragic struggle to master his inborn pessimism. His love of life arose only after he had crucified his innate world-negation. Defiance of his own self, born out of his self-hate, tyrannizes over his natural inclination, and forces it to become an ethical imperative for world-affirmation. It is a form of asceticism that commands him to love life—*notwithstanding!* This heroic "notwithstanding" did not without cause become Brenner's watchword.

In his *Between the Waters* there is an unforgettable formulation of this: "Particularly at this time, when all is destroyed, it is possible, it is necessary to live!" It is as if only with increase of pain that easement comes, as if only great woe sets free. We are reminded of Nietzsche's saying that "one who suffers has not yet the right to pessimism!"

Therefore Brenner's heroes turn, when all is lost, to the small duties of life. Saul Gamsu, the hero of *Between the Waters,* when his world sinks from under him, goes to a little, malaria-stricken settlement with many graves, and makes a fair copy of the simple textbook he has written. *There* is the final exit from a blind alley. So, also, Brenner's career, especially in Palestine, is a service to the small duties of life. Long before, *The Awakener* had been that service. After all was lost, after the final collapse, then, just then, should come the small, modest, exacting task. So he worked in Palestine, out of his very denial of the world as a whole, drawing courage for the *cult of small things,* for his ardor for the humble labors involved in making a wilderness fruitful: plowing, sowing, threshing, raised by him to cosmic height.

> The superb, the perfect man is not he who is able to derive æsthetic pleasures from delicate food and charming household furnishings, from beautiful singing, music, or keen discussion, but he who produces goods and increases the wealth of life through labor. Perfection of soul is not to be achieved through philosophical meditation on the world and life, but through deeds, work, sharing in the creation of the assets of life.

He was certainly in the thrall of the ethos of labor, as it is practiced in Palestine and was preached there by A. D. Gordon. But he went further with a peculiar, almost malicious pleasure, exalting the modest deed. If

Ahad Ha'am loved to insist that a very ancient people which had produced its prophets, ought not to have the same aspirations as small peoples in their beginnings, Brenner pointed out that it was the duty of the new Jew to "learn the great art of being small"—to borrow a phrase from the great Danish author Herman Bang, himself the son of a small people which has never held itself in too high esteem, and yet has given to the world an Andersen and to the elect a Kierkegaard, Jacobsen, and Herman Bang himself—and also good eggs and butter, of which it is justly proud.

Only in such a connection is it possible to understand Brenner's angry words concerning the racial self-conceit of his people: "With keen and passionate pleasure I would blot out from the prayer book of the Jew of our day the 'Thou hast chosen us' in every shape and form!" There came from him even more vehement words of the same kind, which touched to the quick not only the national vanity, but also the proper self-esteem of the people, and often roused the public anger. Such words pained no one more than Brenner himself. They were his form of asceticism.

Indeed, his whole way of writing bespeaks much self-imposed asceticism. Despite everything, he was an artist in instinct and consciousness, but ashamed of the artist's joy in the happy word. He seemed to punish himself by the forced use of a negligent outer form in order not to appear affected. He shrank beyond everything from the reproach cast at Israel the Mad by Mendele's mare: "Fe, fe, *melitzah!*" ("Sss! Pretty words, pretty words!") In hellish fear of this reproach, he chose ascetically the trite, common word, the plebeian estate of the language, as it were. He did not mind repetition even "for the hundredth time" (the title of one of his articles). When a person is in pain he does not shriek according to the rules of art, or in musical notes. But he understood that this impossibility is just what the miracle of high art makes possible. Of such artistry he was incapable. More modest achievement in accord with his capacity was, however, forbidden him by his will to truth, his art-hating, ascetic morality.

It may be objected that Brenner's whole attitude is sickly. His convulsive will to defend life against pain and negation, the self-martyrdom of an ego that preferred to say No and that yet constrained itself to defiant Yes, a decision that he holds to by the very skin of his teeth, subduing his own inclination, can be deprecated as spiritual flagellation and a chapter in pathology.

The term "pathological" belongs to natural science, not to history. I have intentionally avoided the use of psychiatric terms in a literary connection. Civilization would be too stupid without the contribution of those who have ever been descried as abnormal by the healthy "norm," the compact majority of the uncreative. But aside from the fact that "the world's work is done by invalids," Brenner's "sickliness" is not the impotence of the victim, the collapse of the defeated, but a victory of the spirit, an heroic mastery of pain in the service of an idea. Does this not require a higher spiritual health, the very antithesis of disease? Sickness is a burden to society, "pathology" that is creative a benefit to society.

Moreover, he turned his ascetism against himself alone,

not begrudging to others the joys of all their instincts. He fought moral imperatives out of love and pity for humanity. The world has enough of suffering, let people have a little pleasure and freedom, preached this man who for himself had always rejected both. From himself he demanded everything, but his tragic aristocracy of mind (despite much that was plebeian in him) would not permit him to make his own duties common to all, common.

It is told of Brenner that in Palestine he often carried bundles of the labor publication of which he was editor, as in London he had carried bundles of *The Awakener*. An eye-witness relates that during the famous unification conference of the Palestinian workingmen at Haifa, he walked through the narrow, dusky lanes of that town laden with two large and heavy packages containing the latest issue of *Ha-adamah* (*The Soil*) which he edited, in order to distribute copies among the laborers who lived in the various little settlements of Galilee. It is characteristic that none of those with him thought or rather dared to relieve him of his burden or to share it. He shouldered it so simply and so naturally that any attempt to offer help would have seemed like false courtesy.

This single incident yields us a symbol. So Brenner all his life seemed to have carried the whole heavy burden of the Young Pioneer Palestine—rising above personal suffering through self-assumed responsibility and service to his people.

A posthumous mythos has gathered about his personality since his death, freeing it from the dross of the accidental and exalting it to a legendary greatness. Like a legend indeed is the pledge in the last article he wrote a few days before his death, in which he imposed—first upon himself, as usual—and then upon the pioneers of Palestine, the duty of raising the Arabs from their wretched estate. Strolling once in a vineyard near Jaffa, he noticed the inimical looks of a weakly, neglected Arab boy, employed by an *effendi* in work far too hard for his years, and wrote:

> Laboring orphan, young brother, peace unto you, loved one. Whether you be akin to me in blood or no, responsibility for you rests upon me. It is for me to brighten your eyes, to teach how men ought to deal with one another. Not politics, but contact of soul with soul throughout many days, throughout the generations. Not for any aim and not from any motive save the motive of a brother, friend, companion.

When, soon after writing these words, he was murdered by an Arab hand, Jewish Palestine accepted this pledge together with all the rest of the legacies of Brenner.

CHAPTER XV

TWO FANATICS

The hero is he who is immovably centred.

EMERSON.

THE two men here united under one title showed in their lives the most striking differences. But when they died in the same year (1922), the coincidence was felt to be symbolic: a something similar had been lost with both; in spite of all their contrasts they had had something great in common. Both had the rare power of being "immovably centred" in one and only one idea. Such exclusive concentration tends at times to narrow-mindedness, those who practice it are unlovable, of necessity intolerant in everyday life. This fanaticism has greatness, but also—like the stony wastes of southern Judæa—gloom. And yet it is their holy monomania that made these two men historic figures in Pioneer Palestine. Indeed, it was their life work that made the new Jewish Palestine possible at all.

I

In the well-known *Kusari,* the book written by Rabbi Jehuda Halevi "in defense of the slandered faith," the protagonist of Judaism speaks with great enthusiasm of the Promised Land. Domicile in it hallows one both in life and in death, God's spirit sojourns only there, only there is true worship possible. The direct, consistent Gentile mind of the king of Kusar, however, cannot grasp why, in view of all this, his interlocutor and the Jews in general do not emigrate thither instead of contenting themselves with bowings and prostrations, which seem to him either hypocrisy or unthinking custom. The rabbi has no reply ready save a stammering:

> You have shamed me, O king of Kusar! For, had we come toward the God of our fathers with a whole heart and a willing soul, we should have won from Him what our fathers in Egypt won. But when we pray "Lead us back to Thy tabernacle in Zion," and so on, it is mere chatter of starlings; we think not of what we say, even as you have said, O king of Kusar.

Eliezer ben Jehuda heard a similar reproach from another direct *goyish* mind which stimulated him to his first move toward the execution of his idea. Not that in reality he needed such stimulation. For he had the ability to come with a whole heart and a willing soul toward the God of the fathers, or, more exactly, the land and the language of the fathers; to submerge his entire self in an idea. This slightly built man, whose constitution was early sapped by a terrible disease, but whose nature was as if woven of threads of iron, could have been called an idea incarnate. For the will which animated him, which urged him on and sustained him, stands out strikingly in everything he did: there is something terrible in this strangely one-sided force.

Men live in a certain state of vagueness, of distractedness, changeability. Time as it passes robs us of ideas, the time that comes brings us new ones. We can neither hold fast to the first, nor escape the second. We go from the one to the other, driven now hither and now thither, and think much accomplished when we have been able to steer even for a while, when we know that on the whole we are not drifting. This man, however, cut through the foggy sea of life like a ship which can dispense with sails and favorable winds, and which storms can delay, but not divert from its destination. For he possessed in himself, in his idea, a power by which he drove directly forward, deviating not by a single degree from his charted course.

His father's name was Jehuda Perlman. He was born in the little town of Lushki, province of Vilna, in 1858, and seemed to owe his characteristic stubbornness to his Lithuanian environment. He received the usual Jewish education; but it is typical of the time that he was introduced to the Haskalah by his Talmud teacher, the head of the Yeshiba at Polotzk, Rabbi Joseph Bloker, who read the Jewish codices with him and also (in secret) a neo-Hebrew translation of *Robinson Crusoe*. In after years, Ben Jehuda confessed that he owed his unbounded love for Hebrew to this unusual man.

Though intended for the rabbinate, he was drawn to the newer currents of the day. From a backsliding Chasid (who later became his father-in-law) he learned that hastily snapped-up and self-taught Haskalah was not educative, but that, on the contrary, it ruined a man's mind and led to the unhappiness that comes from knowing one's self useless in practical life. Eliezer thereupon decided to study in an orderly manner, and entered the state secondary school at Dwinsk, where he was soon captured by the slogans of the Russian folk-socialism. In his autobiography, he confesses that under the influence of the positivist literature of the time, "I did not hesitate long, and vowed that I too would devote my whole life to the people, that is, to the Russian people. I would labor for the people, be afflicted and suffer for their sake, offer my whole future as a burnt offering upon the altar of their freedom, quite in the style of the Russian nihilists of those days." Yet Ben Jehuda remained attached to his Jewish heritage, thanks to an ineradicable passion, an insuperable love for the Hebrew tongue. His later career shows strikingly how powerful the magic spell of an ancient language can be.

He relates in his memoirs—and his biographers follow in his traces—that the Russian-Turkish war of 1877-78 created a spiritual revolution in him and helped him to master his Russian nihilism. It was then that the basic ideas of his nationalist-Hebrew view of life first flashed upon him. The small Balkan peoples had risen against the Turkish régime, and throughout Russia there resounded a call to the sacred duty of the largest Slavic state to help its little brothers to national independence. Ben Jehuda was swept away by these slogans of the Pan-Slavic movement, far more so than were his Russian friends. And one night (in this autobiography he loves to stage the most decisive hours of his life at midnight, the legendary hour of Jewish historic marvels), he suddenly understood the reason for his agitation: the destiny of the small peoples pointed the way for his own, "the rebirth of Israel and its language upon the home soil." According to his testimony, this vision of the night decided the course of his whole life. It was only later that he came under the influence of George Eliot's *Daniel Deronda* (published in 1876), which strengthened his resolve to go to Paris to study medicine, a profession which seemed best suited for establishing himself in Palestine.

Questions of priority are irrelevant in connection with the man who in any case was the *first* to live his idea consistently. Furthermore, we are apt not to understand that for which inner experience has not prepared us. So it is but natural that Ben Jehuda had an attentive ear for Deronda's Zionist fantasies because he himself, whether he knew it or not, bore them in his own soul.

In Paris, a sympathetic Russian noble, the correspondent of a leading Russian newspaper, advised him to proclaim his dreams about the rebirth of the Jewish people and its national language. His sound Gentile brain could not conceive, as has been said, how, when such ideas buzzed in a man's head, he could keep them to himself. After an unsuccessful attempt to place an article on the subject with *Hamaggid,* which, though pro-Zionist, shrank before so radical an idea, he published it in *Hashachar* in 1878 under the title of "An Important Problem," anticipating therein the whole ideology of the *Chibbath Zion* and the Zionist movements. He pointed to the collapse of the Napoleonic cosmopolitan conception of the state in Europe, in place of which national movements were everywhere growing up. Young, small peoples were achieving political independence. Was the Jewish people alone to be incapable of a similar escape from its misery? Were we to look on passively while the forces which had hitherto maintained us as a people—our religion and the hatred of the other peoples—could no longer stem our dissolution in the face of the currents of the new period? "If only we desire that the name of Israel be not blotted out, we are bound to make something that might serve as a center for our whole people, like the heart in an organism from which the blood shall stream into the arteries of the nation's body and infuse it with life. That something is settlement in Palestine." Even in his wording, he here anticipates Ahad Ha'am's later theory of a spiritual center for the Jewish people in Palestine. The future regenerator of spoken Hebrew also indicates here the motif of his later life work: "Why have some among our people declared that we are unfit for national life in that we speak no common language? And have not we Jews a language in which we can now write whatever we have in mind and which we can even speak if only we will it?" *If we will it*—here he strikes the Herzlian note—the renaissance of the spoken Hebrew tongue will be no fable. To this article he for the first time signed himself *Ben Jehuda,* which was thenceforth to be his proper name; and in later years he was to resent as an insult the use of his Diaspora name.

The idea that Hebrew might become the daily vernacular—as he had mentioned in his article—began to occupy him more and more. From discussions with G. A. Selikowitch, a well-known Jewish traveler, and with A. M. Luncz, of Jerusalem, an authority on Palestinian geography, he learned that Hebrew was still spoken by the Jews of the East and in the Sephardic pronunciation, which he thereupon adopted in speaking with his friends. Soon, too, he realized that the language lacked the necessary everyday words. The notes which he made on such words form the embryo of his life work, the great lexicon of the whole Hebrew language. It was then, also, that the first modern Hebrew word was coined: *millon,* dictionary.

Meantime, obstacles rose which might have prevented the realization of his dream. Owing to tuberculosis, of which he early showed traces, he was forced to give up his medical studies. Instead, he did something that would bring him to Palestine the sooner, and entered the teachers' seminary of the Alliance Israélite Universelle in Paris. By 1882, he was ready to go to Palestine, and traveled by way of Vienna, where he visited Smolenskin. In Vienna, he was met by his future wife, who had taught him Russian in their native land, and waited for him all the years between. She accepted his venturesome idea of living in Palestine, and was ready to go with him. While they were still on board ship, the gloomy fanatic told his young wife that on Palestinian soil he would speak no word to her but in Hebrew, though it was on that very trip that he began to teach her the language. His ruthlessness produced the miracle, and when Deborah gave birth to their first boy, the child from his first hour heard nothing but Hebrew from both parents. After thousands of years, he was the first Jewish child to be reared wholly in the ancestral language, and so set the precedent for the matter-of-course habit of the Palestinian life of to-day which, however, could not have been achieved without almost inhuman severity. Ben Jehuda relates of his wife in his autobiography that

she was weak and delicate in constitution, and became even more so owing to poverty and child-bearing. Nevertheless, she freely agreed not to hire a servant, so that the child would hear nothing but the holy tongue. We feared the walls of our own home, the spaces of our own room, lest they render back the sounds of a foreign language spoken by a servant, and their echoes reach the child's ears to spoil his Hebrew hearing, and make him unable to absorb the Hebrew sounds correctly. . . . In our exaggerated fearfulness, we wished to keep all foreign sounds far from his ears. And this gentle soul, who was appointed to be the first mother of the national rebirth that gave our people a Hebrew-speaking generation, lovingly shouldered the hardships of bringing up a child without the least help from a maid, though she was so very frail and delicate. She stood the hard test for a long time, doing all the household work as well as taking care of the child alone until the danger was past, and we were privileged to hear the first Hebrew sounds issue from the mouth of the child, to hear an infant babbling in Hebrew.

This ruthless tyranny of an idea, which is reminiscent of Ibsen's *Brand,* cost the poor woman her life. Unlike her husband, she was unable to overcome the tuberculosis she had contracted from him, and died in 1891.

It was not an easy task in those days to bring up a child in the Hebrew language alone. "Until his third year, the child refused to speak a word, and our neighbors attributed this to Hebrew." And not only from ignorant neighbors, but from friends enthusiastic for the rebirth of Hebrew did the parents have to withstand temptations without number. Even J. M. Pines, who was the first to league himself with Ben Jehuda in a covenant to speak only Hebrew with those who understood the language, tried to persuade him against restricting his son to Hebrew: the language was still undeveloped; the lack of playmates would hinder the child's spiritual growth, would make him an idiot. To this the reply of the unshakable fanatic was that it was worth while to sacrifice the talents of his son to the Hebrew language!

As time went on, he stubbornly forced those around him, with the same ruthlessness that he showed toward his own family, to speak only Hebrew with him. Untiringly, day after day, he insisted on this with an obstinacy that often seemed petty, discourteous, unmannerly. It was an unalterable principle with him, where Hebrew was concerned, "not to observe the laws of good manners or of gallantry toward women. In this respect, I conducted myself very rudely, and this rudeness has created much hatred and opposition against me in Palestine." He had no fear even of the terrible weapon of ridicule. If Henri Bergson is right in holding that certain comic effects depend upon automatic mechanisms whose reactions are calculable in advance, then Ben Jehuda's stereotyped, predictable automatic Hebrew responses were downright ridiculous to the observer. But he remained firm, and by his extreme fanaticism achieved the miracle: he proved that Hebrew could become the language of life and the home, of wife and children and all daily needs, an example which made the Hebrew Palestine possible. This could not, naturally, be the achievement of any one man, but Ben Jehuda's invincible concentration explains why legend, which always prefers a single name, made it the heroic accomplishment of one personality and will probably so keep it in the folk-memory for all time.

Our sympathy is awakened as we read how severe was the struggle the man had: with a lingering, fatal disease that was kept in check so long by sheer will power alone; with bitter material need for many years; with a corrupt Levantinian environment teeming with squabbles and intrigues, debased by the *Chalukkah* which he vainly fought in his journals, *Ha-zevi, Ha-or, Hashkafah.* Though these struggles undermined, they could not break his defiant spirit. The hectic, withered little man seemed to gain strength and courage just from struggle and opposition. With the old Roman Furius Antias he might have said of himself: *increscunt animi, virescit volnere virtus.*

After the death of his wife, Ben Jehudah's physician told his friends that he could hardly live six months longer, and forbade him to marry again. But the sick widower, who had two small children, wrote to the sister of his dead wife, then studying in Moscow, explaining just how matters stood, and not withholding from her the doctor's verdict. The half-assimilated Russian student agreed unhesitatingly, so overwhelming was the power of the idea which radiated from the consumptive. Hemda Ben Jehuda was soon to learn to speak and to write Hebrew, and to compose stories of literary merit in the language. She has earned for herself the sincerest gratitude of the devotees of Hebrew, for she cared for the children and the sick husband with self-effacing devotion, and herself provided for the needs of the family, so that Ben Jehuda might give himself over undisturbed to the great work of his life, the dictionary of ancient and modern Hebrew.

Only a man of enormous, stubborn will-power could have dared to enter single-handed upon a gigantic scientific undertaking such as is usually carried on through many years by a large scientific body. For decades he labored at it in cloistered seclusion, rummaging through the great libraries of Paris, Berlin, Parma, Florence, the Vatican, the British Museum, Oxford, New York and Washington, adding word to word in order to expand the passionately beloved language. It is not fair to measure by scientific standards alone a work which never aimed at mere science. Ben Jehuda did not compose his lexicon for the learned guild that swallows dust *ex professo* and that would not fail to point out errors and inaccuracies. He wanted to serve the budding life of a revived language. Hence he took an especial delight in searching out suitable terms to fit the more homely and common needs of the living language in all sorts of crafts and occupations: the needs of laborers, farmers, teamsters, porters; even those of the obscenities of coarse jokes. When he found no suitable terms in ancient literature, he unhesitatingly invented new ones. These artificially formed words were at times most arbitrary, forced, contrary to tradition; but he believed it his duty to fill the gaps until better and more natural words would spring from life itself. Some of his innovations, however, were happy; and, despite violent objections, enfranchised themselves in the language, being at times hardly felt as new coinages or foreign bodies. He even borrowed foreign roots from which he formed words in so Hebraic a mold that they were absorbed unconsciously. To cite one instance: his use of the Occidental root "brush" (*brosse, Buerste,* used also in the vulgar Arabic), from which he formed the Hebrew *mibresheth.* The less apt neologisms, which were not in harmony with the spirit of the Hebrew, soon died off. For a language is not made with hands; like a living organism it grows naturally, and grows best in the obscurity of the unconscious.

But Ben Jehuda had the fanatic's impatience. He wanted at any cost to hear Hebrew spoken, even at the risk of corruption, of barbarization. The mere sound of the language, not its inner purity, was his delight, his fetich. This fanatical haste had its dark sides, and was rightly fought against, for it is just the great cultural heritage of Hebrew that warrants its rebirth, that justifies sacrifices in its behalf. Debasement of the language would soon make the instrument itself valueless. But it would be unfair not to see deep and honest concern for the future of the language in these very strayings from the straight path.

In fairness, also, we shall ignore his other journalistic and communal activities, which often were not free from error, bias and inconsistency. His claim to greatness lies not in them, but in his unique will-power and passion for Hebrew. However, one error in his *Weltanschauung* shall be mentioned here, because it relates to the theme of this book, namely, his attitude toward the Jewish religion.

He himself relates how, when he first came to Palestine, he made it his duty to show outward respect for religious customs, though he had long cast off all religious bonds. He believed that in this way he would be able to win the religious elements in the country to the idea of the Hebrew renaissance. His inconsistency with his "enlightenment" in matters religious he felt would be balanced by the national unity which he would achieve by this means: "We need unity, complete and absolute unity! What is 'enlightenment' and all its benefits compared with the life of the nation!" And he tells how, for years, he imposed religious duties on himself:

> I observed the Sabbath faithfully, I laid on the phylacteries and prayed every day, even in private, in my own home; and so with all the religious customs. I said: These are the laws of our country. It is our duty to observe them even if we do not like them, even if we do not think them proper laws, until they are repealed or changed by legal

processes, just as the members of all other nations observe the laws of their countries even when they do not approve of them, so long as such laws have not been abolished by their governments. And not only this, I tried in every way to make my outward appearance conform to the ways of the Jewish community in Palestine. I grew a beard, left off my European clothing, wore a fez on my head instead of a European hat, and walked about the streets of Jerusalem, especially on Sabbaths and festivals, wrapped in a praying-shawl and wearing the ritual fringes. I conducted myself thus for many years until I was convinced that it was all for nothing.

In his bent toward extremes, Ben Jehuda became a non-religious Jew. He did not even hesitate to state that he, his wife, and his children belonged to no creed, and championed the idea that Judaism was to be built up on the purely mundane idea of folk, language, and homeland. Indeed, he saw a holy war against religion and tradition as a duty of the Hebrew renaissance. A very grave error on his part, balanced by the dark fanaticism of the rigidly pious, who excommunicated him repeatedly, refused to bury his wife and child, and even had him thrown into jail by slandering him to the Turkish government. Bitter strife, such as is possible only between brethren! He never divined, in the defiant obstinacy of the zealots, constructive forces from which his own life work was nurtured. Just as *they* could hardly have surmised that this heretic, through his unwearying service to the Hebrew word, unconsciously aroused the religious forces latent within it. For there is no such thing as creedless Hebrew. He who conjures up Hebrew at the same time involuntarily opens sluices for the obstructed springs of an ancient religious civilization. Though he may not welcome them, neither can he rid himself of the spirits he has called up.

So, too, against his own will and intention, will the life work of Ben Jehuda, who thought to command the destinies of the Hebrew language, succumb to the effaceable runes of religion within the language. Which will do his life work no harm, but rather give it deeper significance. Unwittingly, he has become more than the mere renewer of spoken Hebrew.

In 1924, when the wave of immigration to Palestine was at its height, the Palestinian press frequently contained protests against the affair of the swamps at Kabara. Owing to local politics, the government had originally proposed to forbid drainage at Kabara altogether, even though, after Huleh, its swamps were the largest and most dangerous in the country. A few malcontents (leaders in the Arab agitation) raised the cry that such drainage would deprive some Arab families of their livelihood from the cane that grew in the marshes. The government then felt itself obliged to prefer the alleged interests of a few to the good of the whole community, even though the amelioration would benefit thousands of families once the region had been made healthy and fit for settlement. Fortunately, the *Pica* (the Palestine Jewish Colonization Association), after compensating the few Arab families in question, succeeded in obtaining permission to proceed with the drainage; and the work began. Then, for a second time, for inner Jewish reasons, the Kabara swamps became a burning issue: the *Pica* officials employed Arab labor, and even imported "gyppos" from Egypt for the job. Only a few Jewish laborers were taken on, with the obvious intention of discharging even those few at the first opportunity. The *Pica* officials argued—ostensibly, and perhaps actually—in behalf of Baron de Rothschild that he did not wish to have Jews employed on the swamps because of the danger to health and life.

They argued, furthermore, since there was no unemployment in Palestine at that time, Jews could settle into other and safer occupations.

Whether this argumentation was wholly sincere, it was difficult to say, though the Baron was no doubt genuinely concerned for the welfare of the Jewish workers, and was reported to have said that all his money could not make compensation for a single Jewish life that the swamps might claim. But it may fairly be questioned whether the *Pica* officials did not prefer the non-Jewish labor for its cheapness. In any case, they did not expect protests from Jewish labor because, from the purely material viewpoint, the work was not worth their while.

But the organized Jewish workers of Palestine did protest, and their protest had a bitterness and vehemence that organized labor elsewhere displays only when it is deprived of employment, political rights, or other material advantages.

It was forunately true, they admitted, that economic necessity did not compel the Jews to work in mosquito and malaria-infested districts. Nevertheless, they claimed the *zekhut ha-kibbush,* the "privilege of conquest" (of the land by labor), and insisted on the opportunity to subdue the Kabara swamps, resenting the compassionate attitude of the *Pica* as a reflection upon their dignity as pioneers who had shouldered the task of redeeming their own land. They said: The drainage of these swamps is an historic achievement; and, in the making of Jewish history in Palestine, we workers have the right to stand in the vanguard. It is our privilege to drain the soil of Palestine; and we refuse to be deprived of that privilege

by guardians who graft foreign labor upon our colonization. One Jewish worker addressed the Baron to this
effect:

> When you come to redeem the soil of Kabara, and to
> found Jewish settlements upon it, you continue your many
> good works for the upbuilding of the land. And we, the
> organized Jewish workers of Palestine, wish to share in that
> work with you as partners. To you have been given the
> good will and the material means for the enterprise. And
> we bring to it will-power, patience, muscle, the ability to
> give reality to your intentions. We want to stand up to our
> necks in the swamps of Kabara, there to feel the travail of
> creation. For us no labor is too hard; of death we have no
> fear. To create and to upbuild is our task, it is our work
> that will hasten the *Geulah* (redemption). This our aim
> is also your desire.
>
> We have conquered the swamps of Nahalal and of Nouris,
> and now we are draining the fields of Gederah. In the
> swamps of Kabara, too, we must stand in the front ranks,
> and win. If Kabara demands human sacrifices from us, it
> shall have them. Even at that, we shall have far more
> courage and vigor than if others were to fall on our field of
> honor. Ours is the privilege of dying for Kabara, because
> we claim for ourselves the privilege of living upon it.

Had these young Jewish pioneers been asked who taught
them these heroic motives for their economic class struggles, whose image and example guided them in their mode
of action and thought; and had they been asked to name
but one name, their answer must have been: Aaron David
Gordon. For, though these views had cropped up anonymously and sporadically from the very beginning of the
new Jewish colonization in Palestine, no one preached and
practiced them with truer devotion, with more exclusive
zeal, no one thought them through with more persistent
thoroughness than this fanatical and yet so gentle-souled

apostle of the "religion of labor"—a term of which it has rightly been said, that the Jewish renaissance has uttered nothing more profound or more revolutionary.

A. D. Gordon laid the philosophic foundation for the change in the Jewish estimate of the worth of labor, an estimate to which modern Pioneer Palestine aims to give practical realization. The young pioneers, though reared on books and more accustomed to the pen than to the hoe, believe it their duty not to avoid, but rather to seek labor of the hardest and coarsest kind—'*Avodah Shechorah* ("black" labor), as they call it. By their whole way of life they seem to wish to refute the Diaspora notion that some kinds of work are fit for Jews, and that other kinds are not. What was it that a visiting Socialist writer from America said when he saw Jewish workers laying a road-bed for a railway? "No, no! That's no work for Jews! It's hard, one sweats over it! A Jew has brains, he was created for more important work. Leave this to the *goyim,* they were made for it!" This distinction between "Jewish" and *goyish* work seemed to young Pioneer Palestine a fruit of Golus-parasitism. They saw in the "compassion" of the *Pica,* an offense and a snare against the national and ethical aspects of the Jewish renaissance. In these notions of the "superior intelligence" of the Jews, of the tenderness of mind and body that permits them merely to supervise hard or dangerous work done by others, Young Palestine sees the Golus degeneration of the Jewish spirit, for which the one remedy is a return to the life of labor on the soil of Palestine. All the daring and boldness, all the labors and hardships with which thousands of the youth of Israel are paving a new way of life in Palestine with their bodies and souls form a mighty repudiation of the Jewish trait satirized by Mendele Mokher Sefarim in his epic of Jewish beggardom: where two Jews, wrapped in prayer-shawls and phylacteries, wait for the *goyim* to come and pull their wagon out of the mud, themselves helping along with shouts of "hu-ha!" . . . "The voice is the voice of Jacob, but the hands are the hands of Esau."

No one scourged this Golus philosophy more untiringly, through many years, than Gordon. He rejected as un-Jewish, because unworthy, the dictum that "if Israel performs the will of God, its work will be done for it by others." He insisted that we pull our own wagon out of the mud, however hard or dangerous the task. He would have nothing to do with the Golus attitude which says "Let Ivan work, let Johann work, let Mustapha work. For our part, we shall create culture, we shall produce national works of art, we shall enthrone absolute justice in the world." . . . Gordon held this to be parasitism upon the hard labor of others, the very antithesis of true culture.

He taught that without Hebrew labor there would be no Hebrew culture; that we must seek to do in Palestine, with our own hands, every manner of labor required in life, from the easiest, cleanest, most intellectualized, to the hardest, dirtiest, crudest. Then we shall feel within ourselves all that is felt by one who performs such labors, think his thoughts, experience his experiences. Then we shall achieve culture, for we shall have achieved life.

For Gordon, then, labor is not a curse upon one cast out from the paradise of idleness, an inescapable evil of civilization, but rather an ideal, a blessing upon him who has found favor in the eyes of the Lord. Labor, rather than Art, becomes the freest expression of the human being, becomes itself an artistic urge which, unable to ease itself completely in words, seeks a redeeming complement in manual activity. Labor to him means the zest of creation, nobleness, bliss. Labor is transformed into religion, is expanded into the cosmic.

The Hebrew word *'Avodah* means both work and worship, *laborare est orare,* in one word. And since Gordon *'Avodah Zarah* (work done not by one's self, but by others) has as repellent a connotation as idol-worship, its meaning in the ancient pious writings. The content of the phrase has been completely changed, but the phrase itself and the sentiment behind it have been resurrected by Pioneer Palestine.

Gordon thus describes the "blessed glow of labor":

> One works, simply works, at rough, hard tasks. Yet, at times, one feels that which cannot be better expressed than by saying that one works oneself organically into the work of nature herself, that one grows into her life and creation. Something seizes one, a something large as the world, wide as the heavens, deep as the lowest abyss; and it seems to a man suddenly that he too has taken root in the soil in which he digs, that he too is nourished by the rays of the sun, that he too, like the grasses and bushes and trees, is merged more deeply into nature, more greatly into the great world.

This sense of nearness to the cosmic is wholly new to the Jew of the Diaspora, just as the informing, religious passion for labor is rare, not only in Palestine, but in our whole era. The life of a man who rose from the close confines of the Ghetto, which has none but middlemen's pursuits, into this cosmic intimacy with nature, therefore has far more than individual significance.

Gordon's career (1856-1922) began when he was forty-eight, that is, at an age when other men usually have their achievements behind them. He had lived the simple and unnoteworthy life of a minor official in the forest-lands of Baron Ginsberg of Podolia, and then, at the threshold of the fifties, he left his wife, son, and daughter, and went to Palestine (1904), where he became an agricultural laborer. There, in a malaria-infested region, sunk in deepest poverty, he lived his own teaching that everyone, without exception, ought to work with his hands. At the same time, he sat through the nights writing his ponderous essays. When his comrades of Dagania watched him set down his great teachings on little slips of paper by the dim light of a lamp, they knew he was keeping a vigil— over the purity of the spirit of their pioneer enterprise. And now he lies buried in the eucalyptus grove at Dagania by the Jordan, his grave a shrine for Jewish Palestine.

His work consists of collected essays, letters, and speeches, all written on the spur of the moment; but he always tried to formulate them systematically, to give them a metaphysical underpinning. Labor in his eyes was an outlet for human energy, to be added to the sum of the energy that quickens the universe. So, labor releases us from our small, subjective orbit, and connects us with the great stream of universal life. Time and again he sets up these trains of thought in a clear and unified way, conscious (perhaps not without a pang) of his lack of ease and grace of presentation. He hated nothing more than rootlessness; therefore he believed that in writing, also, everything ought to be firmly anchored, thoroughly grounded, and tried too hard to present proofs. For he did not know that in prophetic proclamation, assertion matters more than proof. Nor did he practice the writer's craft for its own sake. When he visited the gifted Hebrew poet and essayist Jacob Fichman at Tel Aviv, the following discussion took place:

"You are a writer; and I do not, God forbid, hold your work in light esteem. But how is it possible for a man to be a writer only?"

"He who is not a 'writer only,' " jestingly replied Fichman, "is not a writer at all. It is not enough to be 'only a writer,' since the work is so very difficult." . . .

"It is so difficult," replied Gordon earnestly, "just because you are 'writers only.' Writing ought by no means to be a man's only function; it ought to be merely the result, the outcome of an actual task in life."

Gordon thought that for a writer to do a few hours' manual work a day was not enough, since that brought him no closer to life and to the miseries of mankind. The writer's product was genuine, he held, only when it was a by-product.

That division of labor, declared Gordon, which frees the more capable from manual work, is not suited to our people, for unlike others, we have no natural working class. The Jewish worker has certain intellectual capacities, and soon flees labor for lighter occupations. Thus we are a nation of traders, brokers, speculators, intellectual proletarians; we create no new values, we are mere middlemen for the values of others, we at best complete such products. In practical, as in the spiritual life, we are a parasite people. We have no ground under our feet. And we are parasites not merely in the economic sense, but also in spirit, in thought, in song, in literature, in the finer traits of character, in idealism, in high humane strivings. We are dragged along by every current in others' lives, carried by every wind that blows in their world. . . . We have forgotten the life-savor of a living people. . . .

Our salvation lies in a creative life upon our own soil. Only intimate intercourse with the mothers of being—Earth, Sun, Wind, Rain—can reawaken us to genuine life. Our historic claim to Palestine is not enough, it must be renewed through a creative union with its soil and its landscapes; and that can come only through labor, manual labor, which will give us the ultimate right to the ancient homeland of our race. The two destructions—of our land and of our soul—testify that each belongs to the other, and can be saved only by the other. The fact that the Arabs of Palestine could let the land lie waste for so many centuries is proof that they have no veritable relation to its soil. "They have created nothing upon that soil, nor have they in any way renewed themselves upon it."

The soil of Palestine can be won for the Jews not with money and still less with military force, but only by means of labor, of the creative values to be drawn from it. That is the "redemption of the soil." However, since we lack a natural working class, it is just the best elements among us, those who feel the misery of our people most keenly, who have the most unqualified duty to fulfill in the Jewish renaissance: labor on the soil. Only through their heroic example can Jewish life be thoroughly revolutionized, freed from unsound pursuits, made productive. For Gordon the issue lay not between what he termed the superficial socialist opposition between capital and labor, but in a deeper and more tragic conflict, a conflict wherein Jewry especially had sickened—between creativeness and parasitism.

> Not capital is the chief thing, for it is not power; the happiness of life is not in it, nor the savor of life. The chief thing is creation. And so it is also in relation to other nations and lands where our people are scattered. In the Diaspora, too, our people ought to labor. . . . It is the task of Zionism in the Diaspora to transform the Jews domiciled there into workers and producers. There, too, the chief thing is creation, and not wealth. Though we dwell among the nations, there is no mutual understanding between ourselves and them, nor the proper human relations. Through labor and creation we shall learn how to delve to the very depths of Nature in their land, and to understand the spirit of those peoples. Through creative labor, we shall learn to understand our own spirit also.
> Hence the demands which we have a right to make upon them. We do not require special rights from them,—only human rights, the rights they have deprived us of,—primarily the right to be a working, creative people. It is their moral duty to help us, to use their influence to secure our land for us, without, of course, prejudicing the rights of the inhabitants thereof. It is their duty to permit our people who live among them to do creative work, to till the soil and live by labor.

Palestine was to become a center of productive life, whence a healing influence would radiate to all parts of the Diaspora, which, following the example of the homeland, would become economically sound organisms, built up on productive labor. Productive labor was to restore our lost dignity among the nations, teach them to understand us again. Palestine, moreover, was to have a more than Jewish significance. There the *ethos* of labor and of a just social order was to establish a model common-wealth that would challenge all men to emulation.

> We were the first to proclaim that man was created in the image of God. We must now go farther and say, The nation must be created in the image of God. Not that we are better than others, but because what we have borne and suffered demands this. . . . By the price of our torments, which are unique in all the world, we have bought the right to be the first in this mode of creation; and in the very strength of our torments, we shall find the strength for such creation.

That people in whose wrongs humanity has been most outraged, ought, more than any other, to have the right, the capacity, the strength to restore humanity.

EPILOGUE

THE MAGIC OF AN ANCIENT LANGUAGE

Credunt homines rationem suam verbis imperare, sed fit etiam, ut verba vim suam super rationem retorquant.

BACO.

IN a mad war hymn entitled "By the Might of My Spirit," written by Saul Tchernichovski at seventeen, a young Jewish hero rants about avenging the ignominy and woe of his people:

My sword! Where is my sword, where is my avenging sword?
Give me my sword, that I may charge my enemies!
Where are my foes? I shall hew them down,
Destroy, consume, crush. . . .

But in the end he discovers that he has forgotten how to use his sword during the long exile, and can only bite at his chains in impotent wrath.

The warlike note struck by the young Tchernichovski did not go unnoticed by the youth of those days, who saw in Jewish martyrdom nothing but unworthy passivity, and expected salvation to come only through active heroism. In a Chanukkah poem (1892), he pictures the spirits of the Maccabees gazing with shame upon their degenerate heirs of the Ghetto who, for a morsel of bread, are obliged to commit petty sins, and who have forgotten the taste of freedom: "A people whose proud sword has mouldered away."

During his student years at Heidelberg, Tchernichovski sang of the august Bar Cochba whom weak generations, "downtrodden worms," had branded as a charlatan, humbling the "Son of a Star" to a "Son of Lies" (Bar Cosiba). A future generation of Jews, cleansed from the filth of the Ghetto, with eyes "undimmed by vain writings, by the falsehoods of misleading teachers" (i.e., the rabbinic heritage) would, the poet hoped, joyously exalt the name of Bar Cochba to high renown.

It was in Heidelberg also (1902) that he wrote his hate-filled poem *Baruch of Mayence,* which reeks with sanguinary curses and vengeance-mad passion, sounding a note that is incredibly fierce not only in Hebrew, but in the general literature of our times: "Cursed be thou, fiendish nation! Cursed be thy name forever and ever! May the malediction of the Most High lodge with thee to eternity!"

The hero of *Baruch of Mayence* is a man crazed by suffering: his wife has been murdered, and he has himself slain his two daughters so that they may not be brought up in Christian convents to hate the Jews. When, finally, he is forced to accept baptism, he sets fire to the convent, and the flames spread through the whole city. Baruch runs through the blazing streets, and upon his wife's grave, shouts the wish that both he and she may become vampires lusting for blood and delighting in torture:

Night after night we shall arise, we shall go up from the graves,
    we shall drink ourselves drunk:
Drop by drop, drop by drop, we shall suck the blood of these
    cruel ones,
We shall become drunken upon their screams, their shrieks of
    torment!

As he reads in the history of his people of the slaughter of whole Jewish communities, deep rage seizes the poet, not so much against the bestial enemies, as against his own forefathers for their cowardly submission. *Baruch of Mayence* rings with a pained, abusive indignation at passive suffering which the poet, having been reared in freedom, regards as beneath human dignity. There is in his attitude something of Lasalle's burning anger over the Damascus affair: "Oh, it is terrible to read about, terrible to listen to. One's nerves are numbed, one's whole heart is filled with rage. A people that endures this is terrible. It ought to take revenge; else it deserves such treatment. . . . Even the Christians wonder that our blood is so sluggish, that we do not rise up, do not prefer to die on the battlefield rather than on the torture rack. Were those greater persecutions against which the Swiss rose? Could any revolution have been more justifiable than one in which the Jews of Damascus would have risen up, set fire to the city on all sides, exploded the powder magazine, and slain themselves together with their tormentors? Cowardly folk, you deserve no better lot! The downtrodden worm turns, but you bow down still more! You do not know how to die, you do not know what just vengeance means, do not know how to bury your foes together with yourselves, rending them to pieces in the very death-struggle! You were born to be slaves!"

The artist in Tchernichovski preferred to unburden his anger in a narrative of the distant past, and this remoteness in time dulls the edge of his fervor; but the personal note, the direct hint to his own age speaks out undisguised. If I mistake not, Tchernichovski has deliberately altered, poetically "falsified" the historic events; and his deviation from the facts bespeaks his intention even more than his choice of the theme itself. The historic kernel of *Baruch of Mayence* seems to have been taken from the Jewish accounts of the massacres of the First Crusades.

There, Isaac ben David and Uri of Mayence, after forced
baptism, returned to that city, where the former slew his
two daughters and set fire to his home, perishing in the
flames with his companion in misery. Tchernichovski
makes Baruch set fire to the convent instead, and then
sends him rioting through the streets of the city, to which
the flames are spreading beyond control. Unlike Isaac ben
David, Baruch does not desire martyrdom for the sanctification of God, nor is he concerned for the purity of his
own and his daughters' souls; but he longs for revenge, for
bloody compensation from the hooligans who have shattered his domestic happiness. This criticism of the historic facts is even more eloquent of the poet's true purpose than is his untamed song of hate.

In his later songs, also, he strikes similar chords. While
studying at Lausanne, he implored God to send a storm
to rouse the "people that died in slavery," and with a
miracle shock into life the "heap of corpses" (his term
for the Jewish people). In all his Greek poems, of whatever date, he has none but the most contemptuous words
for the life of the Ghetto. In Greece there lived a proud,
godlike, victorious race of men; but among the Jews there
was nothing but book-dust, the corruption of the grave, a
"death agony enduring through generations," a hatred of
life. Even in the great figures of rabbinic Judaism he
sees merely the "guardians who have mummified us for
generations."

I have said in the first chapter on Tchernichovski that
because of this sharp dissent from the prevailing view of
inherited Jewish values, he has been called a "foreign
plant," a Greek, a pre-Torah Jew, a Hebrew pagan—

terms with which he himself has coquetted not without self-complacency. An attentive reading of his earlier poems teaches us better, but his book of *New Songs* in particular shows what a thoroughgoing change has taken place in Tchernichovski's work during the last decade. Many notes are heard in that book which we might have thought impossible in him, and which at first we are inclined to mistrust. But these notes repeat themselves over and over again, affording us an interesting glimpse into the poet's later development, and, in fact, into the very life of an ancient language.

To the souls of the murdered of the Ukraine, Tchernichovski dedicates a deeply felt, poignant poem called "This Be Our Revenge" (1920). Of the author of *Baruch of Mayence,* one expects that he alone will find the word that will strike future generations with horror, the word that will brand the frightful massacres of the Ukraine which, even in the bestial days of the World War, revealed the very lowest depths of human baseness.

One remembers that Tchernichovski, when asked after the Kishineff pogroms how he could keep silent, replied that he cared neither to plead like children when weaned from the mother's breast, nor to cry out like an impotent woman cursing in the pangs of her travail. For a man, like a wounded lion,

> Has a roar . . . that when it breaks forth
> The earth will shake
> And the pillars of the world tremble
> At his roar of revenge.

It was for such a "roar of revenge" that Tchernichovski was looked to. But it was not forthcoming. In "This

Be Our Revenge," occur lines of quite another kind, which, coming from him, echo unforgettably in our memory:

We shall not go up against you,
To cleave pregnant women with axes
As you do; nor shall we set fire
To your roofs over your heads, and with iron bars
We shall not shatter the skulls of babes!
Not until with your brute hand you have uprooted,
Not until with your contaminated palms you have erased altogether
The image of God stamped upon us,
The tokens of ancient nobility of spirit,
And of descent from princely generations,—
All we have gathered, all we have delivered into the hearts of men,
Little by little, in gleams and sparks,
Through hundreds of jubilees and hundreds of generations,
Which we have reared in asceticism and chastity
And the yoke of the Ten Commandments.

Let us hearken well: This bard of pagan joy in war, who had sung of the sword and vengeance and physical unrestraint, in these verses whose consummate artistry testifies to the genuineness of the poet's utterance, speaks of "ascetism," of "chastity," of the "yoke of the Ten Commandments"—matters in no wise akin to the scheme of a pagan world. . . .

As we turn the pages of this book of poems, similar notes ring out. In *Eli*, a poetic fragment pervaded with the most delicate humor, Tchernichovski tells about a quarrel between two brothers and their respective families in a village of his native Crimea. It is a delicious tale, laughter-provoking to the point of tears. The son of one of the brothers, Eli, is a Herculean young blacksmith.

Broad of bone and of shoulder, with a red bull-neck,
His legs were short, but his stride most firm.
When he set down his foot, it took fast hold of the ground . . .
Heaven's blessing was upon his sunburnt hand, it was like a pair
    of tongs.
When he grasped a horseshoe, it bent in his hand.
When in his smithy he took hold of a balky horse,
The horse would look at him with its beautiful eyes and—submit!

This massive young blacksmith once played a practical joke on his uncle's daughter, who was expecting a suitor who had been delayed on the way. Pretending to be this belated suitor, Eli very late one night aroused the family out of their sleep. They hastened in great confusion and embarrassment to deck themselves out to receive the visitor—only to find in the end, while they were still half-asleep and half-clad, that it was all a wild hoax.

With an amazing right-about-face, this frolicsome tale ends in the following grave, pregnant lines:

Thus there yet slumber forces and a remnant of the ancient might,
And the spirit of the Lord within them, the Jewish spark is
    asleep,
Like a precious stone hidden in a thick clod of earth,
Like a seed of rye concealed in the husk.
Until the great hour comes, when God shall call him,
Touch him with the finger of blessing and rouse within him
    hidden sorceries.
And he will bow his broad shoulder, load upon himself and carry
The great burden of holiness, all the suffering of the Holy Pres-
    ence,
Carry it from sea to sea, from generation to generation, Amen,
    selah!

Let us listen well. This bard of pagan joy in war holds physical strength not valuable in itself, but as a vessel for the spirit. He expects that the robust village Jewry, once awakened out of his historic lethargy in alien lands, will again take upon its broad shoulders not, indeed, pagan licentiousness, but rather the pious Jewish heritage of long generations: "the great burden of holiness, all the suffering of the Holy Presence!"

It is as if Tchernichovski found himself in agreement with that remarkable tale in the Talmud about the athletic Resh Lakish, whose extraordinary physical strength made Rabbi Johanan want to convert him to Judaism: "Thy strength fits thee for the Torah!"

Whence comes this change in Tchernichovski? How did he arrive at this peculiar consonance with the rabbinic teaching from which he believed himself so remote? How did he, the herald of the glorification of the physical, reach this strange unanimity with the Jewish emphasis upon the primacy of the spirit? he who, even in recent years, has at times disparaged Israel's whole achievement with the reproach that it is "a people of Tannaim."

There is a Jewish folk-song in which a simple tailor, with touching naïveté, makes bold to solve problems of high politics: "If I were the king of Prussia, I should simply propose to lay down arms: Let us go before *Din Torah!*" (arbitration by Jewish law). We may laugh over the song, but here is plain folk-speech in conformity with the legacy of Jewish prophetism. Here, but in a grotesque form, we have the sublime pathos of Holy Writ: "Not by might, nor by power, but by My spirit, saith the Lord of hosts,"—words that not even overmuch currency can make trite.

For many a year, when Tchernichovski heard this praise of the spirit, he inferred that here was physical impotence philosophizing a virtue of necessity. Never in those days could he free himself from the suspicion that the ethos formulated by Bialik for his people—"Rather than be a beast among beasts, I choose to perish with the lambs"—was an involuntary deficiency; that this lamblike meekness would turn into something else were it but possessed of the teeth and the claws of the beast. Now, however, a generation had risen in Jewry of which Tchernichovski himself was an example—a generation tested in the blood bath of the World War, which, in the Jewish legions in Palestine, in the self-defense corps of the Golus, and in the dangerous service of the Jewish watchmen of Pioneer Palestine, behaved not as martyrs, but as militant heroes. When, at last, the Jews had perhaps become capable of taking physical revenge for their wrongs, the poet of the sword song ("By the Might of My Spirit") and of the vengeance-crazed Baruch of Mayence, preaches "asceticism," "chastity," "the suffering of the Holy Presence"!

There is in this a remarkable inconsistency, hitherto unnoted and which even the poet himself seems not to feel. An explanation is therefore in place.

Those who have followed these pages will not be at a loss for this explanation. Tchernichovski's later work shows that the foreign influences have been dissipated, and that at last he has discovered his true core; that, after a long and hard struggle he has achieved the mastery over Hebrew which was long denied him, and so has become a true creator in that tongue. Having at last penetrated into the inner sanctuary of Hebrew, his mature work demonstrates how authentic the magic of an ancient language can be.

As in all genuine creation, he does not write alone, because the language, the genius of the race implicit in the language, writes along with him. This is so in every language. It is not the individual alone who writes: the generations that survive in the language have their word to say as well. In Hebrew there is a wonderful term for this—"the merits of the fathers"—the whole ancestry of the language is a cocreator. The poet says not altogether the thing *he* wants to say, but that which the language is able, that which the language is willing, to allow him to say. Great poets rightly say that their work is done not by a single but by a collective self. Strangely and yet definitely they somehow seem to themselves a plural.

There is nothing mysterious in this. No one nowadays is apt to deny the rôle of the medium, of the raw material in the plastic arts. We speak of justice to materials, of ethics in their use. If the identical idea be executed in plaster and in stone, the result is two different works of art; and an artist is censured when he ignores the peculiar qualities of materials, and insensitively executes in one medium an idea conceived in another. In every act of artistic creation, the result is determined not by one, but by at least two forces: the creative idea of the artist, plus the inherent qualities of the raw material. Every creative artist, indeed, will admit that it is just in his most successful piece of work, that from the refractory medium a something additional accrues which he did not intend.

What is a truism in the plastic arts still sounds improbable in literary art. Nevertheless, the same law holds good here as well. Tchernichovski himself was a striking example of true creation functioning under the persistent spell wielded by an ancient language. Even this freest of Hebrew poets, who in no way went through the usual development of Hebrew writers and who represented a new type of Jew, was irresistibly caught in the grip of the old language. He may have called himself ever so free, behaved as independently as he pleased, may have been critical, even disdainful of the whole heritage of transmitted Jewish values; but there is something in the Hebrew language to which, the more artist he was, the more he was subject. A something in the language guided him, drove him along a predetermined course, and made him—not without self-fear and astonishment— fatally similar and akin to the whole inheritance of Hebrew poetry. No matter how spontaneous and original he may have seemed to himself, how little to his own mind prefigured by the history of his people, he belonged to a distinct spiritual destiny just as much as the species of a fauna belong to a given continent. Writing in the ancient language, he was almost bound to decide and answer all questions in a foreseeable manner, as if branded in advance by the character of his heritage: So must you be; you cannot escape from yourself!

Poets who have discovered this ancestral predetermination in themselves usually have a conscious solidarity with the chain of all their generations backward and forward to infinity, and a reverence for the inescapably binding and preserving forces of tradition. They know themselves at

one with all the bygone and all the still unborn generations of their people.

Tchernichovski discovered in his soul the choked-up
approach to the old Jewish idol-worshipers and conquerors
of Canaan, and identified himself with the far-off future
sons of his kindred, to whom he sang proud, triumphant
songs instinct with the joy of the peaceful new conquest of Canaan. He long believed that a man is free
to choose single links in the chain of his generations, and
for many years did not know that one whose magic wand
has helped to restore any one of these links must necessarily have helped to restore them all, must have affirmed
the whole course of Jewish history, the Jewish destiny in
its totality. In his latest and artistically ripest work he
realized, with a sense of awe, that he, who wanted to be
an ancestor, was inevitably a descendant; that he was not
only a promise, but a fulfillment, or to quote Zarathustra:
not only the plow, but also the harvest. And he felt the
mournful happiness of one who is linked to an ancient
tradition.

During his travels, Tchernichovski once found himself
standing deep in thought in a tumbledown Jewish house
of worship in Theodosia, which insinuated itself into his
heart like a "chaste legend told by a grandmother." He
caressed with his eyes every mark left by the passage of
time on the walls, the ceiling, the worn floor. It was as
if he longed to embrace all the generations that for centuries had prayed there. A maternal voice seemed to
whisper to him:

THE MAGIC OF AN ANCIENT LANGUAGE

Peace unto thee, my son! *Hast thou too come back?*
During these hundreds of years I have seen many
Captives . . . men of renown . . . those who escaped bap-
   tism.
Some withered, others sprouted again, like grasses . . .
From the north and the west, they join altogether in "the Lord
   is One"!

"Hast thou, too, come back?" This may be said not
only to Tchernichovski, but to the whole of modern
Hebrew literature: Though it may seek distant, foreign
seas far from its fatherland and its spiritual inheritance,
though it may desire to break the old tablets and to herald
undiscovered coasts, it finds itself at the last—after encir-
cling the whole earth—back in its own harbor.

NOTES

FORENOTE

In the transliteration of Hebrew words I have tried both to reproduce phonetically the sounds of Hebrew and to follow the current customs of popular transcription. The letter *kaph* is reproduced by *k* or *kh* (*rāphè*), while *hêth* is rendered by *ch* (e.g. *chasid, chalutz*) and should be pronounced like the Spanish *j* or the German hard *ch*, as in *Macht, Sache*. Very rarely, in accepted names, *hêth* is represented by *h* (e.g. *Ahad Ha'am*). I have often disregarded the intensification of consonants by *Dageš forte,* particularly after the definite article, thus avoiding awkward doubling of letters.

Abbreviations used:

l.—line; lb.—line counted from the bottom of the page; p.—page; quot.—quoted or quotation.

JQR—Jewish Quarterly Review.

MGWJ—Monatsschrift für Geschichte und Wissenschaft des Judentums.

REJ—Revue des Études Juives.

ZAT—Zeitschrift für Alttestamentliche Wissenschaft.

ZfHB—Zeitschrift für hebräische Bibliographie.

GENERAL BIBLIOGRAPHY

The first attempt at a summary of modern Hebrew letters was done in Russian by Dr. Joseph Klausner, foremost Hebrew critic and literary historian, who now occupies the chair of modern Hebrew language and literature at the Hebrew University on Mount Scopus, Jerusalem. His Novo-yevreyskaya Literatura, Warsaw 1900 (2d ed. Odessa 1912) appeared in revised form in Hebrew: Toledoth hassifruth ha'ibrith hachadasha, Jerusalem 1920 (transl. into German by Hans Kohn, Geschichte der Hebräischen Literatur, Berlin 1921). Prof. Klausner's collected essays on leading Hebrew writers: Yotzerim ubhonim, Tel-aviv 1925-1930 (3 vols.) are especially recommended. Nahum Slousch, La renaissance de la littérature hébraïque (1743-1885), Paris 1902 (transl. into English by Henrietta Szold, The Renascence of Hebrew Literature, Philadelphia 1909) appeared, with additions, in Hebrew: Koroth hassifruth ha'ibrith hachadasha, Warsaw 1905. Slousch' second book treats of modern Hebrew poetry: La poésie lyrique hébraïque contemporaine (1882-1910), Paris 1911. Other books, planned mostly for school use, are: Dr. M. Rabensohn, Safruthenu hachadasha, Vilna 1913; S. L. Zitron, Yotzere hassifruth ha'ibrith hachadasha, Warsaw 1922-1924 (2 vols.); A. Urinovsky, She'urim betholedoth hassifruth ha'ibrith hachadasha, Warsaw 1923-1927 (2 vols.) and the latest and most thorough book by F. Lachower, Toledoth hassifruth ha'ibrith hachadasha, Tel-aviv 1927-1929, of which however only two parts, covering the period of the Haskalah until ca. 1880, have thus far appeared. [Since the appearance of the first edition of this book, there was published a detailed history of modern Hebrew literature in the century from Mendelssohn to Mendele (ca. 1750-1850) by Joseph Klausner (d. 1958): Historiah shel ha-sifruth ha-ibrith ha-chadasha, 2nd ed., Jerusalem 1952, in 6 vols. F. Lachower (d. 1947) completed his survey of modern Hebrew letters until his own days: Toledoth ha-sifruth ha-ibrith ha-chadasha, vol. 3, Tel-aviv 1932; vol. 4, 1948. Israel Zinberg wrote in Yiddish a history of Jewish literature, now available also in Hebrew: Toledoth sifruth Israel, Tel-aviv 1960, vols. 5 and 6. See also Barukh Kurzweil, Sifruthenu ha-chadasha—hemshekh o mahpekha, Jerusalem, Tel-aviv 1959.]

Among the English books are: Dr. J. L. Landau, Short Lectures on Modern Hebrew Literature from M. H. Luzatto to S. D. Luzatto, Johannesburg 1913; Abr. Sol. Waldstein, The Evolution of Modern Hebrew Literature (1850-1912), Columbia University Oriental Studies v. IX. New York 1916; Dr. Joshua Bloch, Modern Hebrew Literature (in: The Columbia Course in Literature, New York 1928, v. I. p. 195-218), a concise and instructive survey with good selections. The Jewish Anthology, edited by Edmond Fleg, translated by Maurice Samuel, New York 1925, also contains a number of excellent translations from modern Hebrew letters. [In addition, the following books were recently published: Simon Halkin, Modern Hebrew Literature, Trends and Values, New York 1950. Meyer Waxman, A History of Jewish Literature from the Close of the Bible to our own Day, New York 1936, vols. 4 and 5.]

The general books on the history of the Jewish people are still indispensable for the student of modern Hebrew literature: in fact, H. Graetz' evaluations (in v. XI. of his Geschichte der Juden, 2d ed. by M. Brann, Leipsic 1900) survive in almost all the extant manuals of Hebrew literature. Another book of similar influence is Franz Delitzsch, Zur Geschichte der juedischen Poesie vom Abschluss der hlg. Schriften des Alten Bundes bis auf die neueste Zeit, Leipsic 1836, a classical appraisal, by a great Christian scholar, which no student of Hebrew letters should leave unread.

Other books on modern Jewish history are: Martin Philippson, Neueste Geschichte des juedischen Volkes, Frankfort a. M. 1907-1911 (3 vols.) ; Simon Dubnow, Dibhre yeme Israel bedoroth haachronim, Berlin 1923-1924 (3 vols.) or in German transl. Die neueste Geschichte des juedischen Volkes, Berlin 1920-1923 (3 vols.), now forming v. XIII-XI of his Weltgeschichte des juedischen Volkes. Dubnow's History of the Jews in Russia and Poland appeared in English transl. by Prof. Israel Friedlaender, Philadelphia 1916-1920 (3 vols.) ; Max Raisin, History of the Jews in Modern Times, New York 1919; Max L.

GENERAL BIBLIOGRAPHY

Margolis & Alexander Marx, A History of the Jewish People, Philadelphia 1927; A. L. Sachar, A History of the Jews, New York 1930.

Bibliographic reference works on modern Hebrew literature are: William Zeitlin, Bibliotheca Hebraica Post-Mendelssohniana, 2d ed. Leipsic 1891-1895 and the catalogue of the Hebrew University Library: Hassifruth hayyafah be'ibrith (1729-1926), Jerusalem 1927. Cf. additions by Abraham Ya'ari in the bibliographic quarterly of the Hebrew University Library: Kiryath Sefer v. VI, no. 1 and 2. A useful bibliography of Hebrew periodicals of Vienna is Wachstein-Taglicht-Kristianpoller, Die hebräische Publizistik in Wien, Vienna 1930.

[For historical background of the era of Emancipation and of Nationalism one can now consult Salo W. Baron, A Social and Religious History of the Jews, New York 1937, vol. II, p. 165 ff. and 262 ff. See also his: The Modern Age, in: Great Ages and Ideas of the Jewish People, ed. by Leo W. Schwarz, New York 1956, p. 315 ff.]

NOTES

I. THE MIRACLE OF HEBREW REBORN

On modern Hebrew cf. Prof. J. Klausner, 'Ibhrith 'atikah ve'ibhrith chadashah, in Leshonenu v. II (Tel-aviv 1929) p. 1-21, where also Klausner's previous essays on the same subject are listed; E. M. Lipschütz, Vom lebendigen Hebräisch, in: Der Jude v. III (1919) p. 228-239 and 277-291, comp. also ib. v. IV (1920), p. 48-61; Dr. Leo Metmann, Die Hebräische Sprache, ihre Geschichte und lexikalische Entwickelung seit Abschluss des Kanons und ihr grammatischer Bau in der Gegenwart, Jerusalem (19..?) p. 73 et seq.; Leon Simon, The Renascence of Hebraism in Palestine (in his: Studies in Jewish Nationalism, London 1920, p. 129-147). [Also the following recent books: Joseph Klausner, Ha-ibrith ha-chadashah ub'ayoteha, Tel-aviv 1957; Wm. Chomsky, Hebrew: The Eternal Language, Philadelphia 1957.]

Page

4 E. Renan, History of the People of Israel, London 1888, v. I, p. 86.

9 part II, l. 1 and following, cf. Jacob Rabinovitch in Hedim v. III (Tel-aviv 1924), no. 4, p. 21.

14 l. 11, Kethabhe Moshe Smilansky, Jerusalem-Berlin 1924, v. II, p. 7-126.

II. A MESSIAH

28 Rom und Jerusalem, 2d ed. Leipsic 1899, p. 2.

32 l. 3. Shulchan 'Arukh, Orach Chayyim 307: 16. On Immanuel cf. A. Geiger in Jüd. Zeitschr. f. Wissensch. u. Leben v. V, p. 286-292; L. Modona, Vita ed opere di Immanuele Romano, Florence 1904, and S. Tchernichovski's Hebrew monograph, Berlin 1925.

l. 11. Fr. Delitzsch, Zur Geschichte der jüd. Poesie p. 54.

33 l. 2. Friedman's edition, publ by 'Ayanoth, Berlin 1922.

lb. 4. All three dramas have appeared with an excellent introduction by Dr. S. Ginsburg under the title Sefer ha-machazoth, publ. by Devir, Tel-aviv. Layescharim Tehillah has been transl. into Engl. by Herbert S. Goldstein and Rebecca Fishel, New York 1915.

NOTES

34   l. 14: Greek and French—so M. S. Ghirondi in his biography of Luz. in Kerem Chemed v. II, p. 55.   l. 15: sixteenth year—cf. however Brann's footnote in Graetz' History v. X, p. 334.

35   l. 8. The kabbalistic circle of L's friends was called Mebhakshe Adonai (in Almanzi time Metibhe Za'ad) cf. Almanzi's biography of L. in Kerem Chemed v. III, p. 114. On the constitution of the Zohar-Society cf. A. S. Isaacs, A Modern Hebrew Poet, life and writings of M. Ch. L., New York 1878, p. 46-53.
    l. 9. Migdal 'Oz was published only in 1837 by Franz Delitzsch and M. H. Letteris. On Guarini and Luzatto cf. Prof. Fleischer's review in E. G. Gersdorf's Repertorium der gesammten deutschen Literatur, Leipsic 1839, v. XIX. p. 140-145; Abr. Geiger in Wissensch. Zeitschr. f. jüd. Theologie v. IV (1839) p. 250-257; Israel Abrahams, By-paths in Hebraic Bookland, 1920, p. 122-128; Dr. Isaac Landman, M. H. Luzatto, in honor of his bi-centenary (Year Book of the Central Conference of Amer. Rabbis v. XVII (1907) p. 187-203) and Shalom Spiegel in Shebhile hachinukh v. IV (New York 1929) no. 9.
    lb. 5, The Hebrew critic F. Lachower (in Kethubhim, a periodical, Tel-aviv v. I, no. 19, and in his book on modern Hebrew literature v. I, p. 22 and 143) who has proved the allegoric interpretation of Migdal 'Oz from L's preface to the book, wants to assign the drama to a later date, and sees in it traces of the subsequent persecution of L. It should not be difficult to determine the exact time, since the drama was written for the occasion of the wedding of Benjamin Bassan (1703-1790) which could be traced.

36   Ghirondi l. c. p. 56. Almanzi l. c. p. 136.

37   on David Reubeni cf. Shalom Spiegel in The New Palestine for March 9, 1928: A Pseudo-Messiah Rehabilitated.

38   l. 18. Almanzi l. c. p. 137-138; also Abr. Kahana, Moshe Ch. Luzatto, Warsaw 1898, p. 26.   l. 21.—so Luz. writes in his Treatise on Redemption, Warsaw 1891, p. 6.   l. 24. cf. the comments on him in S. D. Luzatto's autobiography (German ed. by Dr. M. Gruenwald, Padua 1882, p. 19): "The good taste and the common sense, which M. Ch. L. showed both in the book on rhetoric, and in his later writings, as well as his integrity, the deep moral sense which all his works breathe, prevent me from regarding him as a fanatic, a fool, or a deceiver, as so many believed." I do not know where Dr. S. Bernfeld (Kämpfende Geister in Judentum, Berlin 1907, p. 31) has found a quite different estimate of Luz.

39   l. 2. the text of the anathema is given by Almanzi l. c. p. 150, note 73.   quot. from Almanzi l. c. p. 142-3 and Treatise on Redemption p. 22.   Emden, Torath ha-kenaoth p. 54 b.

40   l. 8. Almanzi p. 126. Abr. Kahana l. c. p. 69, suggests that L. hurried to Palestine, when he learned that the esteemed Kabbalist, Chaim ben Moshe ibn 'Attar had died in Jerusalem in July 1743.

HEBREW REBORN

According to ibn 'Attar the name of the Messiah was to be Chaim—which could not leave our M. Chaim L. indifferent.
l. 13. tomb of Akiba—cf. the death announcement by the rabbis of Tiberias, quoted by Ghirondi p. 61.

41 l. 5. The psalms appear to have been lost; we know only of two examples given in the Bikkure ha'ittim 1825, p. 56 by Reggio, and 1826 p. 99 by Absalom of Padua. And the seven songs in the booklet Chanukkath ha'aron, Venice 1729. Luzatto's poems were edited by S. Ginsburg and B. Klar: Sefer ha-shirim, Jerusalem 1945. l. 10 oust the Davidic psalter—cf. the anathema of the Venetian rabbis (Almanzi p. 156); David Kaufmann in REJ v. XXIII, p. 264; F. Rothstein, Nezir Elohim p. 39. See also Ahron Marcus, M. Ch. Luzatto, in Krakauer Jüdische Zeitung v. II. (1899). l. 15. quot. Ghirondi p. 66.
l. 19. stanzas for Passover, printed with the Treatise on Redemption, Warsaw 1891.

42 [A full bibliography of the Works of M. Ch. Luzatto was published by Naftali ben Menahem, Jerusalem 1951.]

43 Moses ibn Esra in his rhetoric, Hebrew edition by B. Halper, Leipsic 1924, p. 82. lb. 2. quot. from the Treatise on Redemption p. 12.

44 Being-in-Exile: Even in free Italy, at the height of the Renaissance period, the Jews considered themselves temporary sojourners, merely tolerated foreigners, and so indeed they actually were according to legal theory, since their rights in most Italian cities were based upon temporary condottas, which had to be renewed every ten years or so—cf. Prof. Salo Baron, Azariah de Rossi's Attitude to Life (in I. Abrahams Memorial Volume, edited by George Alexander Kohut, New York 1927, p. 35-36). With the growth of the Catholic Counterreformation the policy toward the Jews changed to one of open antagonism which, of course, could not but intensify the old messianic hopes of the Jews.

45 l. 10. see Franz Rosenzweig, Sechzig Hymnen und Gedichte des Jehuda Halevi, Konstanz 1925, p. 115, who thus excellently explains the peculiarities of the Hebrew Musivic style.
l. 17. quot. Meor 'Enayim, ed. Cassel p. 264.

III. A HUNCHBACKED PHILOSOPHER

48. Ludwig Lewisohn, Mid-Channel, an American Chronicle, New York 1929, p. 26.

49 Koheleth Musar (The Moral Preacher): the publication ceased with the second number, cf. M. Kayserling, Moses Mendelssohn, sein Leben und seine Werke, Leipsic 1862, p. 99; Hameassef 1785, p. 90 et seq., 93 and 103; S. Bernfeld, Juden und Judentum in 19. Jahrh. Berlin 1898. p. 36 et seq.

50 Abr. Posner—see Graetz v. XI, p. 5.

51 l. 2. cf. e.g. the Gedenkbuch für Moses Mendelssohn, published in Berlin 1929 by the Verband der Vereine fur jüdische

NOTES

Geschichte und Literatur, p. 8. Comp. with it the "non-Germanic appreciation" (Cecil Roth in S. A. J. Review v. VIII (1929) no. 37) of S. D. Luzatto in Jost's Israelitsche Annalen, 1840, p. 319-320. See also Abr. Geiger, Nachgelassene Schriften v. II, p. 236. A dispassionate evaluation of Mendelssohn has been written by Dr. S. Bernfeld, Dor Tahpukhoth, Warsaw 1897, who avoids both the exaggeration of Mendelssohn's uncritical admirers and the unjust vehemence of Smolenskin. The essay on Mend. by S. Rawidowicz in Hatekufah v. XXV, p. 498 et seq., XXVI, p. 547 et seq., merits attention. l. 21. Rudolf Eucken, Lebensanschauungen der grossen Denker p. 387.

54   On the Haskalah cf. Jacob S. Raisin, The Haskalah movement in Russia, Philadelphia 1913; Josef Meisl, Haskalah, Geschichte der Aufklärungsbewegung unter den Juden in Russland, Berlin 1919 (cf. also Meisl's Geschichte der Juden in Polen und Russland, v. III. Berlin 1925); Prof. J. Klausner, Shalosh tekufoth besifruth ha-haskalah ha'ibrith (inauguration lecture at the Hebrew University, Jerusalem 1926); Moses Kleinman, Demuyoth ve-Komoth, Paris, 1928, p. 13-28; Benzion Katz in the quarterly Hazeman (Petrograd 1903) p. 76-105, II, 1-33, III, 1 et seq.; M. G. Margulis, Dor ha-haskalah be-Russia, Vilna 1910; Reuben Fahn, Tekufath ha-haskalah be-Vienna, Vienna 1919; M. Weissberg, Die neuhebräische Aufklärungsliteratur in Galizien, Leipsic-Vienna 1898; Samuel Rosenfeld, Di Haskaloh Bawegung ba Jiden, Warsaw 1920.   lb. 2. cf. Dr. Ismar Freund, Die Emanzipation der Juden in Preussen, Berlin 1912 (2 vols.)

55   quot. from Kayserling l. c. p. 285. That the rabbis of Prague (Ezechiel Landau), Hamburg (Raphael Cohen), Fürth (Hirsch Janow), Frankfort a. M. (Pinchas Levi Hurwitz), all of them rather significant personalities, placed the ban upon Mendelssohn's translation, is now disputed—comp. L. Lewin, Aus dem jüdischen Kulturkampfe, Jahrbuch der jüd. liter. Gesellschaft, Frankfort a. M. 1918, p. 165-197, esp. p. 174, note 2. In Posen and Lissa Mendelssohn's translation is said to have been burnt. Rabbi Moses Sofer of Pressburg in his will (1839) forbade his descendants to read it. See also W. Jawitz, Migdal ha-me'ah, in Keneseth Israel, Warsaw 1886, v. I, p. 96 et seq.

56   quot. from Graetz l. c. p. 45.   Abr. Geiger, Jüdische Zeitschriften (in Wissenschaftliche Zeitschr. für jüd. Theologie, Stuttgart 1839, v. IV, p. 287). On the Meassefim cf. Israel Davidson, The Genesis of Hebrew Periodical Literature (repr. from The Jewish Comment in Baltimore, Febr. 16 and 23, 1900); J. Chotzner, Modern Hebrew Journalism (in his: Hebrew Humour and other Essays, London 1905, p. 174-180); Landau, Short Lectures, etc., p. 65-75; I. L. Kantor, Dor ha-meassefim (in the supplement of the Mefitze haskalah to Ha'asif, Warsaw 1886, p. 1-34) which is however based entirely on Graetz; J. Lin, Die hebräische Presse, Werdegang und Entwickelungstendenzen, Berlin 1928.

441

HEBREW REBORN

57 the quot. on Yiddish cf. Graetz p. 12.   Herder, Vom Geiste
   der ebraeischen Poesie, Dessau 1782.   Loewe's pun in
   Hameassef VII, 119: She'elunu, ha-meassef im ye'asef o yosef?
   Heshibhothim, lo yechedal kothebh ki im tam koseph.

58 Wessely's Mosaid: the suggestion for the theme may have come
   from Herder who wonders, how it is that no epic has yet been
   written on Moses, and who outlines a plan for such an epic—
   cf., W. A. Meisel, Leben und Wirken N. H. Wesselys, Breslau
   1841, p. 159-160; Landau l. c. p. 58 et seq. and Lachower v. I,
   p. 72. The miraculous conception of the poem, inspired by a
   dream of one of Wessely's disciples, is told in the review of the
   book in Hameassef 1790, p. 219 and Meisl, l. c. 165-166. On
   Wessely comp. the bio- and bibliographical essay of Zechariah
   Fishman in Ma'anith, Jerusalem 1926, p. 17-20; D. Friedrichs-
   feld, Zekher Zaddik, Amsterdam 1809; Meisl, l. c.   ` lb. 2.
   quot. from Franz Delitzsch, Zur Geschichte etc. p. 105.

60 Jehuda Halevi's Divan, ed. S. D. Luzatto, no. 58, p. 21b.

61 Heinrich v. Treitschke, Ein Wort über unser Judentum (repr.
   from Preussische Jahrbücher v. XLIV and XLV) 3rd ed. Berlin
   1880, p. 10.

63 J. L. Gordon, Hakitza 'ami (in his Collected Poems, Warsaw
   1905, v. I, p. 45); cf. also Ahad Ha'am, Al Parashath derakhim
   v. I, p. 85 et seq.—Mendelssohn's confession: "Was weiss ich
   von Geschichte! Was nur den Namen von Geschichte hat,
   Staatsgeschichte, Gelehrtengeschichte, hat mir niemals in den
   Kopf wollen." cf. Graetz p. 13.

64 Ahad Ha'am I, p. 89.

65 quot. from Mendelssohn's Jerusalem, Vienna 1838, p. 256 and 287.

66 Napoleon's statement cf. Martin Philippson, Neueste Geschichte
   des jüd. Volkes, Leipsic 1907, v. I, p. 13.

67 Bendavid on messianism—cf. S. Bernfeld, Juden und Judentum in
   19. Jahrh. Berlin 1898, p. 75.   lb. 2. cf. Ludwig Geiger,
   Die deutsche Literatur und die Juden, Berlin 1910, p. 101 et seq.

68 quot. from a letter of E. Gans to Wohlwill—cf. Adolf Strodtmann,
   H. Heine's Leben und Werke, Berlin 1873, p. 313-314.

69 Riesser, uber die Stellung der Bekenner des mosaischen Glaubens
   in Deutschland, Altona 1831, p. 35. Comp. Dr. Julius Höxter,
   Quellenbuch zur jüd. Geschichte und Literatur, v. V. (Frankfort a. M. 1930) p. 25 et seq.   l. 10. Graetz p. 156
   and 403; comp. however the 2d ed. p. 579-580, note 7; also
   A. Menes in Historische Shriften of the Yiddish Wissen-
   shaftlicher Institut, Warsaw 1929, v. I, p. 375-404.

70 Moses Hess, Rom and Jerusalem, 2d ed. Leipsic 1899, p. 22.

71 ib. p. 14. Similarly also Mendelssohn—cf. Hans Kohn in the
   Menorah Journal v. XVIII (1930) p. 409.

72 Delitzsch l. c. p. 94-95. For an answer of assimilatory Jewish
   Reform to Delitzsch see Abr. Geiger in Wissensch. Zeitschr.
   fur jüd. Theologie v. III (1837) p. 382 et seq.
   An original reversal of the current views on "Ghetto and

NOTES

Emancipation" is to be found in Prof. Salo Baron's illuminating essay in The Menorah Journal, June 1928.

IV. A PHILOLOGIST

74 Otzar Nechmad v. IX (1863) p. 131.

76 The modern educational reform of Wessely—cf. Luz's autobiography in Hammaggid II (1858) p. 66; Landau, Short Lectures p. 52-64; Meisl, Haskalah p. 17 et seq. and now Isaac Rivkind on Wessely and Morpurgo (Studies in Jewish Bibliography in memory of A. S. Freidus, ed. by Dr. George Alexander Kohut, New York 1929, p. 138-159).

77 on S. Löwisohn—cf. Landau l. c. p. 99-111; Jacob Rabinovitch in Hapo'el Hatza'ir v. XIII, no. 13; Jacob Fichman in Hedim v. I, p. 12-16; Reuben Fahn, S. Löwisohn, ziyyur tarbuthi, Lemberg 1922, and in his Tekufath ha-haskalah be-Vienna, Vienna-Berlin 1919 p. 53-57; also S. D. Luzzatto's Hebrew letters no. 22 and 26.

79 Ghazzali—cf. Dr. J. Oberman, Der philosophische und religiöse Subjektivismus Ghazālīs, ein Beitrag zum Problem der Religion, Vienna-Leipsic 1921. on S. D. Luzzatto—cf. his autobiography in Hammaggid, which ran serially, though with frequent interruptions, from v. II (1858) no. 17 to v. VIII (1864) p. 45. Most instructive is Luz's extensive correspondence contained in Iggeroth Shadal, Przemysl 1882—Cracow 1894 and the Epistalario, Padua 1890. His son Dr. Isaia Luzzatto compiled a Catalogo Ragionato degli Scritti Sparsi di S. D. L. Padua 1881. S. D. Luzzatto, ein Gedenkbuch zum 100. Geburtstage, published by the Verband der Vereine für juedische Geschichte und Literatur in Deutschland (Berlin 1900) contains Luz's life-story and the bibliography of his writings by Dr. S. Bernfeld (whose Dor Chakham, Warsaw 1896, may also be recommended); a historical sketch of the Luz. family by M. Brann; and essays on his philosophy of religion by Ph. Bloch; on exegesis by A. Berliner, on literary researches by M. Kayserling and on his personality by W. Bacher. Cf. also Abr. Geiger in Jued. Zeitschr. für Wiss. und Leben IV (1866) p. 1-22; Ismar Elbogen, Commemorazione di S. D. L., Florence 1901; Abr. Kahana's biography in Hashiloach v. III p. 58-68, 337-343; v. IV, 58-64, 153-159; Prof. Joseph Klausner, Yahduth we'enoshiyuth, Warsaw 1910, p. 42-93; J. L. Landau l. c. p. 144-171; J. N. Simchoni in Hatzefirah 1917; H. W. Saville: Shadal and the Emancipation, in The Jewish Institute Quarterly v. IV (1928) no. 4; J. Chotzner l. c. p. 154-159.

80 The commentary of Ezechia Luzzatto—Hammaggid v. III (1859) p. 2. on Reggio—cf. Landau l. c. p. 132-144.

81 Delitzsch l. c. p. 94. Jaucourt's article—cf. Luz's Autobiographie ins Deutsche übertragen von M. Gruenwald, Padua 1882, p. 79.

Page

82 Luz's reply to Zunz—cf. Gedenkbuch p. 91. on the science of Judaism—cf. Iggaroth VII, 979; IX, 1367.

83 l. 19. It is told—Graetz v. XI, 501 and A. Berliner, in Gekendbuch p. 79.

84 The letter to Jost in Epistolario p. 392. on Ibn Esra and Rashi cf. Luzzatto's Mechkere ha-yahduth Warsaw 1913. v. II p. 193 et seq. Iggaroth VII, 1031.

85 on Maimonides: Mechkere ha-yahduth p. 159-185. Krochmal's sharp, yet admirable reply in Kerem Chemed v. IV. p. 260-274; cf. also Zebi Hirsch Chayes: Tif'ereth le-Moshe and Darkhe Moshe (in his 'Atereth Zebi, Zolkiew 1841).

86 l. 5. cf. Otzar Nechmad IV (1863) p. 117 et seq.

87 against Spinoza—Mechkere ha-yahduth v. II, p. 198 et seq. 202, 206-207. Böckh—quot. by Ph. Bloch in Gedenkbuch.

88 Atticisme et Judaisme—Otzar Nechmad IV, 131-132.

90 Capsarii—in L's Briefwechsel über religiöse Zustände (Jost's Israelitische Annalen 1839, p. 235-236.) A. U. Kovner on Luz. cf. Zeror Perachim, Odessa 1868, p. 111-119.

91 lb. 5. quot. from Ludwig Lewisohn's Mid-Channel (p. 306), the latest—and very beautiful—attempt at a similar philosophy of the two approaches to life, arrived at independently of Luzatto, from a kindred Jewish inheritance.

V. A GALICIAN SOCRATES

94 Emunoth we-de'oth, preface (ed. Cracow 1880, p. 14).

95 quot. from Schechter, Studies in Judaism, Philadelphia 1896, v. I, p. 57. Graetz v. XI (1870) p. 494. On Galicia cf. Weissberg, Die Neuhebräische Aufklärungsliteratur in Galizien, Leipsic-Vienna 1898, and idem, in MGWJ v. LVII (1913) p. 513-526, 735-749; LXXI (1927) p. 54-62, 100-109, 371-387; LXXII (1928) p. 71-88, 184-201.

96 l. 1. Wessely, Dibhre shalom we'emeth, Berlin 1782. Cf. L. Lewin in Jahrb. der jüd. liter. Gesellschaft 1918, p. 165 et seq. and Max Raisin, The reform-movement as reflected in the neo-hebraic literature (Year Book of the Central Conference of Amer. Rabbis v. XVI. (1906) p. 273-295. esp. p. 277 and 286 et seq.
l. 19. cf. Meir Letteris' Life of Krochmal, in the supplement to the reprint of Hameassef 1784 (Vienna 1862) p. 96-97, and in the preface of the second edition of More nebukhe ha-zeman, Lemberg 1863, p. 13. On Lefin see Dr. M. N. Gelber, Mendel Satanower, der Verbreiter der Haskalah in Polen and Galizien (in Mitteilungen zur jüd. Volkskunde XVII, no. 2); Weissberg MGWJ LXXI, p. 54-62; on his place in the history of the new Hebrew prose see Prof. J. Klausner in Madda 'e ha-yahduth, Hebrew University Press, Jerusalem v. I, p. 163-178. On Ben Ze'eb see J. L. Landau, Short Lectures on Modern Hebrew Lit. p. 86-99; Fahn l. c. p. 38-46; lb. 1. quot. Kerem Chemed, Prague 1839, v. IV, p. 271.

NOTES

Page

97 l. 4. before fourteen—Weissberg in MGWJ v. LXXI, p. 372; Letteris l. c. p. 97; Zunz, Gesammelte Schriften, Berlin 1876, v. II, p. 151.   quot. from Rapoport's letter (no. 3) in Kerem Chemed, Prague 1841, v. VI, p. 45.

98 l. 10. Arabic and Syriac—see ib. p. 47.

99 lb. 3. quot. Letteris l. c. p. 110.

101 quot. from Zunz l. c. p. 156-157 and ib. p. 158.

102 Levinsohn on Krochmal—see S. J. Hurwitz, Ziyyun lenefesh Krochmal, Warsaw 1887, p. 61. Rapoport's indebtedness to Krochmal is often pointed out, cf. especially Isaac Hirsh Weiss, Dor dor wedorshaw, 4th ed. Vilna 1904, v. II, p. 181, note 1, and Zikhronothai by the same author, Warsaw 1895, p. 123. Comp. however the replies of Abr. Epstein, Dibhre Bikkoreth, Cracow 1896 and of Nehemiah Samuel Leibovitch in Ner ha-ma 'aravi, New York 1895, no. 10, p. 13. J. L. Landau (in his N. Krochmal, ein Hegelianer, Berlin 1904, p. 6) believes that Krochmal's ideas are to be found even in Rabbi Zebi Hirsh Chayes. But it seems that this significant personality whose place in modern Hebrew letters has not yet been adequately recognized, is the one independent mind in Kr's circle. While he may have learned from him in many respects, in the field of Talmudic research he was the superior. On Chayes cf. Prof. Louis Ginzberg, Jewish Encyclopedia v. III, p. 660 and the bibliography listed there; on the relations between Kr. and Chayes see S. Rawidowicz in Ha'olam 1927, no. 18, p. 359.

103 l. 3. Krochmal's Works, Berlin ('Ayanoth publishers) 1924, p. 6. This edition by Dr. S. Rawidowicz, with a thorough and conscientious introduction of 255 pages, will be quoted here. Through this monograph and a series of essays on Krochmal (in Ha'olam 1926, no. 31-33; 1927, no. 6, 7, 9, 10, 13, 17, 18; in Hatoren 1924, v. XI. p. 155-174; in Hashiloach v. XLII (1924) p. 167-182, 252-266 and v. XLV (1926) p. 32-44) Dr. Rawidowicz has earned the gratitude of every student of Krochmal.   lb. 9. perpetual student: Zunz l. c. p. 155.   lb. 4. quot. from Lefin's letter (no. 19) in Kerem Chemed, Vienna 1833, v. I, p. 74.

104 quot. from a letter to Luzatto, in Letteris' collection of letters Mikhtebhe bene Kedem, Vienna 1866, p. 66.

105 quot. from Krochmal, in Kerem Chemed, v. I, p. 92, letter no. 25; and Mikhtebhe bene Kedem p. 66.

106 quot. Krochmal's Works p. 143-144.

107 Gates of Pure Belief—cf. Zunz' foreword to K's first edition, Lemberg 1851, p. 5; Letteris, repr. Hameassef p. 110; Lachower in Hayyom, Warsaw 1925, no. 56 et seq. and in his book v. II, p. 28 and 300.   II part, l. 4. quot. from a letter K's to his son Abraham, published by Dr. J. L. Landau in Festschrift Adolf Schwarz, Berlin-Vienna 1917, Hebrew section p. 49.

108 lb. 3. Krochmal's Works p. 5.

NOTES

New York 1907 p. 60-77. On Megalle Temirin cf. Davidson l. c. p. 61-71; N. Gordon in Hebrew Union College Annual, Cincinnati 1904, p. 235-245. Mistaken by Chasidim as one of their own books—according to S. L. Rapoport in Kerem Chemed IV, p. 45. See also Lachower l. c. II. p. 14. Perl's biography: Baer Goldenberg, Ohel Joseph, Lemberg 1866; Busch Jahrbuch 1846, p. 209-232; Kerem Chemed V, 163; Weissberg in MGWJ, v. 72 (1928) p. 82-88.

127 'Emek Repha'im cf. Davidson p. 74 and 230.

128 Graetz on Erter p. 492. The biography of Erter by M. H. Letteris in the first ed. of Hatzofeh Lebeth Israel (Vienna 1858); R. Brainin's introduction to the ed. Warsaw 1908; S. D. Luzatto in Mikhtebhe ben Kedem, Vienna 1866, p. 110; J. Chotzner, Hebrew Humour p. 127-139, and in his Hebrew Satire, London 1911, p. 29 et seq.; Weissberg in MGWJ, v. 72 (1928) p. 184-192 ("der Jesaja der Haskala").

129 l. 4. furious satire: Mozene mishkal 1823.   lb. 4. quot. from Gilgul nefesh 1845.

130 Mapu intended to attack Chasidism in Choze chezyonoth (fragments printed with v. V. of 'Ayit Zabu'a) cf. Lachower II, 140 and 154.

131 Rom und Jerusalem 2d ed. Leipsic 1899, Note 5. p. 177-178.

132 Ch. S. Slonimsky, Hammelitz v. VIII, no. 37. comp. also nos. 42-45, 47; J. L. Gordon, Iggeroth Yalag II, 277.   Zweifel's Shalom 'al Israel, Zitomir 1868-1873 (4 vols.—v. III, 2 appeared in Vilna 1873).   lb. 3. all three manifestations of God—ibid. I, 22.

133 l. 6. religious and scientific—cf. I, 13, et seq. l. 18.   half of the Jewish masses, cf. Dubnow, in He'athid III, p. 73-74. On Zweifel cf. S. J. Hurwitz in Hammaggid v. XXXII (1888) no. 41, 43-45; Otzar hassifruth IV. 273-276; Ha'asif V, 214; Paperna in Sefer ha-Shanah I. (1900) p. 63-70; S. A. Horodezky. l. c. v. IV (1922) p. 126 et seq.; Berditchewski: Bi-sede Sefer I (Leipsic 1921) p. 29.

134 Simon Dubnow's first study on Chasidism appeared in the Russian periodical Woschod 1888, no. 5 et seq. All his works on Chasidism are listed by Gerhard Scholem, Bibliographia Kabbalistica, Leipsic 1927, p. 38-39, which contains also a remarkably thorough bibliography of all works on Chasidism. Zeitlin's Bibliotheca boasts of its "gaenzliches Ausscheiden des albernen Schrifttums des Chassidismus" (p. IV).   S. A. Horodezky's essays are now collected in 4 vols. Hachasiduth wehachasidim, Tel-aviv 1922. Some of them have appeared in English transl. by Maria Horodezky-Magasanik: Leaders of Hassidism, with a foreword by the Haham Dr. M. Gaster, London 1928. Comp. Prof. Chaim Tchernowitz in Haschiloach XIX (1908) 165-173, 346-356 and in 'Eyn Hakore I (1923) p. 33-48.   J. L. Peretz's first Chasidic attempt appeared in Hachetz, Warsaw (1894) p. 35-42.   Berditchewski's writings on Chasidism begin 1888

HEBREW REBORN

Page

in Ha'asif p. 65-73, all of them listed by Scholem l. c. p. 19-20. Berd's Sefer Chasidim with an introduction on "the soul of Chasidim" appeared in Warsaw 1900. Steinberg's chasidic stories in Kol kethabhe Jehuda Steinberg, Cracow 1913, vol. IV. p. 1-166. S. J. Agnon—cf. E. M. Lipschütz in Hashiloach v. XLV (1926) p. 239-247; D. A. Friedman, Hashiloach XLII, 80. et seq.; Zak in Miklat v. V, p. 133 et seq.; M. J. bin Gorion, Bisede Sefer III, 97-97; F. M. Kaufman, Vier Essays uber ostjüdisde Dichtung 1919. Martin Buber: Die chassidischen Bücher, Hellerau 1928, which contains a revised edition of Die Geschichten des Rabbi Nachman, Frankfort a. M. 1906; Die Legende des Baal Schem (1907), Mein Weg zum Chassidismus (1918), Der grosse Maggid (1921), Das verborgene Licht (1924). Not included in Die chassidischen Bücher is Des Baal Shem Tow Unterweisung im Umgang mit Gott, Hellerau 1927. On Buber cf. Hans Kohn, Martin Buber, sein Werk und seine Zeit. Hellerau 1930 and Ludwig Lewisohn in The Menorah Journal XII (1926) p. 65-70. I thankfully acknowledge my indebtedness to Buber's presentation of Chasidism, especially to his illuminating researches on its literary aspects.

136 On Kabbala: Adolphe Franck, La Kabbale ou la philosophie religieuse des Hébreux. 3d ed. Paris 1892. (transl. into German by Adolf Jellinek, Leipsic 1844, into English by Dr. I. Sossnitz, New York 1926); Ph. Bloch, Geschichte der Entwicklung der Kabbala, Trier 1894; C. D. Ginsburg, The Kabbalah, its doctrines, development and literature 1865; J. Abelson, Jewish mysticism, London 1913; Bernhard Pick, The Cabbala, its influence on Judaism and Christianity, Chicago-London 1913; Julius H. Greenstone; The Messiah Idea in Jewish History, Philadelphia 1906, p. 156 et seq. and 237 et seq. For a complete bibliography cf. Scholem l. c. l. 18. the content of the Kabbala which determined Chasidism—I follow Buber, especially his introduction to Der grosse Maggid p. XVII et seq. See also Paul Levertoff: Die religiöse Denkweise der Chassidim, Leipsic 1918. p. 7 et seq.; Schechter, Studies in Judaism v. II (Philadelphia 1908) p. 258 et seq. [The best introduction to the world of kabbalism is: Major Trends of Jewish Mysticism, by G. G. Scholem, 3rd edition, New York 1954, and in paperback, 1961.]

137 like the snail cf. Shivche Habesht ed. Horodezky, Berlin 1922, p. 25.

139 comp. S. A. Horodezky, Torath ha-kabbalah shel Rabbi M. Cordovero, Berlin 1924, p. 93 et seq.

141 On Lurya see Philipp Bloch, Die Kabbalah auf ihrem Höhepunkt und ihre Meister, Pressburg 1905, p. 13 et seq. Anger expiated with 151 fasts cf. Jacob Chaim Zemach, Nagid umetzaveh, Amsterdam 1712, 2d part, p. 15b. Dubnow's number in his Mabho Letholedoth hachasiduth, in He'athid III (1911) p. 98. seems to be a misprint.

NOTES

Page

142 Salomon Maimon, Lebensgeschichte, 2d ed. Munich 1911, p. 151 et seq. 185 et seq. gives a graphic account of Kabbala and Chasidism. See J. C. Murray, Salomon Maimon, an autobiography. Boston 1888, p. 163 et seq.

143 On Jacob Frank see Graetz' monograph (Breslau 1866); A Kraushaar, Frank i Frankiści Polscy, Cracow 1895; Meyer Balaban in He'athid V (1913) p. 132-150; Abr. Jacob Brawer in Hashiloach v. 33 (1917) and 38 (1921); Teodor Jeske-Choiński, Neofici Polscy, Warsaw 1904, p. 46-107; J. Meisel, Geschichte der Juden in Polen und Russland, v. II. p. 161 et seq. (Berlin 1922).

144 Letters of Ba'al Shem—cf. Reshumoth II, (Tel-aviv 1922) p. 386; Horodezky v. IV, p. 138; Dubnow in Kiryath Sefer II, 204-211 (Jerusalem 1925). The quoted letter—Shivche Habesht ed. Horodezky p. 30 and in the very handy anthology of Chasidic literature by Abraham Kahana, Sefer hachasiduth, 2d ed. Warsaw 1922, p. 72.   hamtakath ha-dinim see Horodezky I, 32.

145 Enoch—Des Baal Schem Tow Unterweisung p. 23.

146 Sussya—Die chassidischen Bücher p. 577.   repentance—Des Baal Schem Tow Unterweisung p. 34.   Moshe Leb—Die chassid. Bücher p. 609.   See Chajim Bloch, Die Gemeinde der Chassidim, Berlin-Vienna 1920; Ch. Bogratschoff, Entstehung, Entwickelung und Prinzipien des Chassidismus, Berlin 1908.

147 Shmelke—Der grosse Maggid p. 32-33.   Moshe Leb—ib. p. 150.

148 l. 7. Kahana l. c. p. 46. The tale of the ignorant peasant boy ib. p. 49; of the orphan: Die Legende des Baal Schem p. 102 et seq.   On Kawwana: the struggle for inwardness in Judaism—see H. G. Enelow (in: Studies in Jewish Literature in honor of Kaufmann Kohler, Berlin 1913. p. 82-107).

149 Torath Rabbi Nachman mi-Bratzlav (compiled by Horodezky) Berlin 1923, p. 103.

150 the letter of Ba'al Shem to Rabbi Gerson of Kutov cf. Kahana l. c. p. 73 et seq.

151 on Rabbi Nachman's pilgrimage to Palestine cf. Shivche Haran, ed. Lemberg 1901, p. 7b et seq. and Judah L. Fishman in Hator II (1921) no. 5-6.   on the attitude of Chasidism toward Palestine: Horodezky IV, 57-63; Dubnow in Pardes II (1894) 201-214; Asher ben Israel in Sefer Zikharon, in honor of A. S. Rabinowitz, Tel-aviv 1924. p. 102-105.   lb. 2. Schechter l. c. p. 3.

152 Buber, Der grosse Maggid p. LX.

153 l. 10. not a single word—Kahana p. 67-68 and Zweifel l. c. I, 50. On Jacob Joseph: Horodezky I (2d ed. 1927) p. 103-132.

154 on Rabbi Dov: ib. p. 75-102. That he wanted his Torah to be written down—see the preface of Rabbi Solomon of Lutzk to Maggid debharaw le-Ya'akobh, Koretz 1784. On Menachem Mendel: Horodezky II, 13-35.

155 on Shneur Zalman: Kahana l. c. 197-242. Graetz' estimate of Tanya deserves to be quoted (XI, 605): "nicht so bloedsinnig wie die uebrige chassidaeische Literatur."   l. 12. see Horo-

dezky, preface to his edition of Shivche Habesht, Berlin 1922.

156 l. 15. Buber, Der grosse Maggid p. LI. On Rabbi Barukh see Horodezky III, 12-17. On Israel of Ruzyn ib. 99-123 and IV, 154 et seq.

157 The tale of Ba'al Shem see Kahana p. 43-45, and what a true poet made of it: Buber, Legende des Baal Shem p. 134 et seq.

158 On Nachman see Horodezky III, 18-81 and IV, 89 et seq.; Buber, preface to Die Geschichten des R. Nachman; Rawidowicz-Horodezky: Sippure ma'asiyoth le-Rabbi Nachman, Berlin 1922; S. Z. Setzer l. c.; bibliography by Dr. G. Sholem, Kuntres ele shemoth sifre Moharan mi-Bratzlav, Jerusalem 1928.

VII. A SAINT AND A SATIRIST

162 Z. Shnëur, Chezyonoth, Berlin 1923, p. 268. On Schneur see Prof. J. Klausner, Yotzerim ubhonim III, 76-111; D. A. Friedman in Keneseth, Tel-aviv 1929, p. 361-378; Lachower in Hatekufah VI, 444-454; Moses Kleinman ib. XXV, 568 et seq.; Jacob Rabinovitch in Hedim 1924, no. 11-12; Feitelson in Hashiloach v. XVII, 82-92; I. Wassilevsky, Hebrew Poetry of To-day, Manchester 1918; transl. by Maurice Samuel in The Menorah Journal XI (1923) and The Jewish Anthology.

163 l. 7. Samuel Joseph Fuenn, Kiryah Ne'emanah, Vilna 1860.
The Gaon issued his first ban against the Chasidim on April 11, 1772. In the same year, on November 15th, the great Maggid, Rabbi Dov died. Another decree of excommunication against the Chasidim was pronounced by the Gaon on the night following the Day of Atonement, 1796. On the eve of the next Day of Atonement the Gaon became very ill, dying a few days later, Oct. 17, 1797. Folk-legend has not failed, of course, to utilize this coincidence. On the Gaon and Chasidism cf. Katz in Hazeman I (1903) no. 2, p. 11 et seq. On the Gaon see J. H. Levin, 'Aliyyoth Eliyahu, Vilna 1856; S. J. Jatzkan, Rabbenu Eliyahu mi-Vilna, Warsaw 1900; Schechter, Studies in Judaism, Philadelphia 1896; v. I, p. 73 et seq.; Prof. Louis Ginzberg, address at the 200th anniversary of the Gaon's birth, New York 1920 (repr. in his Students, Scholars and Saints, Philadelphia 1928, p. 125-144).

164 Ib. 2. Louis Ginzberg l. c. p. 21.

166 On the educational views of the Gaon and of Chaim Volozhin see Dr. S. I. Tcharno in Shebhile hachinukh v. IV (1928) no. 4-6; Jacob S. Raisin, The Haskalah etc.; Jatzkan l. c. p. 100 et seq.; Horowitz, Derekh 'Etz Chayyim, Cracow 1895; Schmuckler, Toledoth Rabbi Chaim mi-Volozhin, Vilna 1909.

167 l. 4. I learn that Mr. Isaac Rivkind, himself a graduate of Volozhin, is preparing a monograph on the Yeshiba. Comp. his article in Reshumoth V, 362-376, and his pamphlet on Hanatzibh veyichuso le-Chibbath Zion, Lodz 1919.   l. 11. Smolenskin, 'Eth lata'ath (ed. Jerusalem 1925, v. II, p. 78).   l. 15. I. H.

NOTES

Weiss, Zikhronothai, Warsaw 1895, p. 123-6 and Mimizrach umima'arabh I, 10. Comp. also Louis Ginzberg's essay on Weiss, in: Students, Scholars and Saints, p. 234, and the opposite view of N. S. Leibovitch in Ner hama'arabhi 1895, no. 10, p. 16. II. part. On I. B. Levinsohn see D. B. Nathansohn, Sefer ha-zikhronoth, 2d ed. Warsaw 1878; D. M. Hermalin, monograph in Yiddish, New York 1904; S. Zinberg in Russian, Petrograd 1910; Moses Kleinman, Demuyoth we-Komoth p. 48 et seq. Ib. 2. Kovner, Zeror Perachim, Odessa 1868, p. 124-129. Berditchewski, Michutz la-techum, Leipsic 1923, p. 47. Comp. also F. Lachower in Hatekufah XVI, 428.

168 quot. from Yalkut Ribal, Warsaw 1878.

170 quot. Kleinman l. c. p. 51 and Te'udah be-Israel, 4th ed. Warsaw 1901, p. 165 et seq.

171 Pliny and Aristotle ib. p. 167. The ukase of 1866, see Dubnow, Die neueste Geschichte des jüd. Volkes, Berlin 1920, v. II, p. 421, note 1.

172 Perl, Bochen Zaddik, Prague 1838; Chayes, 'Atereth Zebi, Zolkiew 1841 (first Derush). Abr. Baer Lebensohn (= Adam): autobiography in his Be'urim chadashim, Vilna 1858; cf. also R. Brainin in Ha'eshkol I (1898) 29-43; Ha'edre'i in Hashiloach III, 42-48; S. L. Zitron, Yotzere hassifruth I, 5-34; Slousch, La poésie etc. p. 17-35. M. J. Lebensohn (= Michal): Z. Fishman in Hadoar v. II, no. 101-102; Prof. J. Klausner, Yotzerim ubhonim I, 124-142; Jacob Fichman's introduction to the collected writings of Michal, Berlin 1924; Zitron l. c. I, 83-113; Slousch, La poésie p. 36-61.

173 Judah Klaczko, Haduda'im, Leipsic 1842. He became one of the foremost representatives of Polish conservatism and a famous writer in Polish, French and German. His treatises on Dante and Rome et la Renaissance (Julius II), Paris 1902 (2d ed.) are especially praised. Cf. Count Stanislaw Tarnowski, Julian Klaczko, Cracow 1919 (2 vols.) and in Oesterreichische Rundschau v. X (Bruenn 1906) no. 1, p. 12-20; Henri Welschinger, Notice sur la vieu et les travaux de M. Julian Klaczko (Institute de France. Acad. d. sci. mor. et polit. Séances et travaux, n. s. v. 69, Paris 1908, p. 389-437) and in Rev. d. deux monde. per. 5, v. 42 (1907) p. 589-621. Salkinson: cf. Israel Abrahams, By-paths in Hebraic Bookland, Philadelphia 1920. p. 303-310 (on his transl. of Othello); Beth Otzar hassifruth I, 31 et seq. (2d part); Reuben Brainin in Ha-modi'a lachodashim v. I (New York 1901) p. 132-134; Silberbusch in Hashiloach v. XLIII (1925) p. 553-561; Fichman in Hatekufah XIX, 415 et seq.

174 l. 2. Kleinman l. c. p. 45. On J. L. Gordon see Z. Fishman in 'Eyn ha-Kore no. 2, p. 135-156 (bio- and bibliography); Abr. B. Rhine, Leon Gordon, an appreciation, Philadelphia 1910; Dr. Joshua Bloch in Jewish Forum v. II (1919) p. 975-984; I. J. Weisberg, Yalag we-tholedothaw, Kiev 1892; Weisberg

Page

published also Iggeroth Yalag (2 vols. Warsaw 1895) ; Gordon's autobiography in Iggeroth Yalag v. I, 81-83 and in Reshumoth I (1918) p. 69-96 and ib. V (1927) p. 61-85, now repr. in Kathabhe J. L. Gordon, v. I (Tel-aviv 1928) ; Reuben Brainin, Zikhronoth umachashaboth, in Hashiloach I, 62-68, 244-254, 421-433. The passage I quote ib. p. 68; I. Ch. Rawnitzki, Gordon 'al pi iggerothaw, in his Dor we-soferaw, Tel-aviv 1927; Mordekhai ben Hillel Hacohen, Me'erebh 'ad 'arebh, Vilna 1913, I, 153-167; Lilienblum, Collected Works, Odessa 1912, v. III, 26-78, to which D. Frishman replied in Ha'asif II (1886) p. 469-495, repr. Collected Works V, 97-138; J. Ch. Brenner, Collected Works v. VII; Dr. S. Bernfeld in Hashiloach XXVII, 167-177; Jacob Fichman, Babhu'oth, Odessa 1919, p. 91-138; Saul Tchernichovski (pseudon. Ben Gutman) in Hashiloach XIII, 244-251; S. L. Zitron l. c. II, 3-113; Moses Kleinman l. c. p. 66-77 and Prof. J. Klausner, Yotzerim ubhonim I, 143-170.

176 quot. from Kol Shire Yalag v. I. p. 43 et seq.

177 quot. ib. p. 45 et seq.   Between the Lion's Jaws: ib. III, 175 et seq.

178 quot. ib. III, 164. The notes ib. p. 205.

180 Theodor Mommsen, The History of Rome (transl. by William P. Dickson) New York 1906, v. II, p. 175 et seq.

181 quot. from Kol Shire Yalag v. IV, p. 3. The two poems retold by J. Chotzner, Hebrew Satire, p. 43 and 55 et seq. Ahad Ha'am, Al Parashath Derakhim v. I, 95; Brainin l. c. p. 254.

182 Kleinman l. c. p. 76.   quot. from Kol Shire Yalag v. IV, p. 5.

183 Smolenskin, 'Am 'olam (in Ma'amarim, Jerusalem 1925, v. I, p. 154-158, note).

184 quot. from Chayes, Daarkhe ha-hora'ah, Zolkiew 1842, p. 7 b.— quoted by Dr. Boaz Cohen in the very thoughtful and instructive introduction to his Kuntres ha-teshubhoth, in Hazofeh v. XIV (Budapest 1930) p. 145.

185 quot. from Kol Shire Yalag v. IV, p. 107.

186 quot. ib. p. 103-104. The letter in Iggeroth Yalag, no. 472.

187 quot. Kol Shire Yalag v. IV, p. 119.   Turgeniev—see Jacob S. Raisin, The Haskalah Movement in Russia, Philadelphia 1913, p. 259-260.

VIII. AN APOSTLE AND AN APOSTATE

198 On Kovner see Leonid Grossmann, Die Beichte eines Juden in Briefen on Dostojewski, Munich 1927; S. Eisenstadt, in: Der Jude, vol. VI (1921), p. 241 ff., Hashiloach XLIV (1925) p. 347-361; comp. also Hadoar v. VIII (1929) no. 31 and Mozenayim I (Tel-aviv 1929) no. 12 et seq.   Kovner on Luzatto in Cheker Davar, Warsaw 1865, and especially in Zeror Perachim, Odessa 1868, p. 111-119.   The quot. from Zeror Perachim p. 119.—holiness of a language ib. p. 94-97.

NOTES

lb. 1 quot. ib. p. 76-77. [On Kovner's baptism see the memoirs of the Moscow chief rabbi, Jacob Maze, Zikhronoth, vol. III, Tel-aviv 1936, p. 169 ff.]

199   on Lilienblum see Ahad Ha'am, v. IV. p. 182-188; Berditchewski, Bi-Sede Sefer II, p. 20-26; comp. also his Reshuth ha-yachid, Cracow 1892, p. 33 and Nemushoth, Warsaw 1900, p. 59 (on Chatoth Ne'urim); Prof. Joseph Klausner, introduction to Lil's Collected Works (Cracow-Odessa 1910-1913) and in Yotzerim ubhonim I, 80-123; F. Lachower, Mechkarim venisyonoth, Warsaw 1925, p. 79-94; Kleinman l. c. p. 105-110; Zitron l. c. II, 114-157; Tchernichovski in Ha'olam 1928, no. 44; Druyanov in Reshumoth II, 390-405. Of English essays: Leon Simon, M. L. Lilienblum, Cambridge 1912 (Cambridge Jewish Publications no. 3); S. Rosenfeld in Reflex III (Chicago 1928) p. 31-39.

202   on Lieberman cf. Dr. Michel Berkowicz' introduction to Lieberman's writings, Tel-aviv 1928; David Isaiah Silberbusch in Hashiloach XLIII (1925) p. 553-561 and XLIV (1925) p. 269-272; Brainin in Hatoren v. IV (1917) no. 15 et seq.   lb. 2. Hebrew soon to be discarded—see Eliezer Ben Jehuda in Hatoren IV (1917) no. 41, p. 8.

203   On Lil. and socialism cf. Zitron l. c. and in Hatzefirah, Warsaw 1919, no. 24 and 25 (June 12 and 19). Comp. also Dr. M. Berkowicz ib. no. 30, 31, 40, 41, 43, 50, 51 (July 24-Dec. 18, 1919); M. Wintchewski in Lu'ach Achi'ebher II, 292-300.

207   Kleinman l. c. p. 27-28 and 15.   lb. 3. prank of history—see chapter I, p. 20 and 23.

IX. HOMECOMING TO ZION

212   Herzl's address at the second Zionist Congress.

213   Bahr in Zeitgenossen über Herzl, herausg. von Dr. T. Nussenblatt, Bruenn 1929, p. 21, and in The Herzl Memorial Book, edited by Meyer W. Weisgal, New York 1929, p. 67-68.   On Herzl see Jacob De Haas, Theodor Herzl, a biographical study. Chicago-New York 1927; A. Friedmann, Das Leben Th. Herzl's, Berlin 1914; Leon Kellner, Th. Herzl's Lehrjahre, Vienna 1920.

214   Comp. Dubnow, Die neueste Geschichte des jüd. Volkes v. III (1923) § 117, p. 112 et seq.

216   Judeophobia—Pinsker, Autoemanzipation, 2d ed. Bruenn 1903, p. 9.   The quot. ib. p. 14.

217   quot. ib. p. 17.   On Choveve Zion see A. Druyanov, Kethabhim Letholedoth Chibbath Zion veyishubh Erez Israel, Odessa 1919—Tel-aviv 1925 (2 vols.); S. L. Zitron, Toledoth Chibbath Zion, Odessa 1914.   lb. 3. twenty-two colonies—see Leon Kellner, Was Herzl vorfand (in Heimkehr, Czernowitz 1912 p. 97).

218   Nahum Sokolow, History of Zionism (1600-1918) 2 vols. London 1919; Adolf Boehm, Die Zionistische Bewegung, Berlin 1920; Richard J. H. Gottheil, Zionism, Philadelphia 1914; Horace M.

HEBREW REBORN

Page

Kallen, Zionism and World Politics, Garden City, 1921; Leonard
Stein, Zionism, New York 1925; Jessie Sampter, Guide to Zion-
ism, New York 1920; J. Stoyanovsky, The Mandate for Palestine,
London 1928; J. H. Holmes, Palestine, Today and Tomorrow,
New York 1929; Maurice Samuel, What Happened in Palestine,
Boston 1929. The Hebrew literature see W. Zeitlin, Bibliotheca
Sionistica in ZfHB v. xii, p. 52 et seq.

221 cf. Theodor Zlocisti, Moses Hess, der Vorkämpfer des Sozialismus
und Zionismus 1812-1875, Berlin 1921 (2d ed.). The quotations
from Rom und Jerusalem, 2d ed. Leipsic 1899, p. xiii-xiv; p. 22;
p. 25, note; p. 24.

222 ib. p. 24.   sabbath of mankind ib. p. 5.   lb. 5. quot. ib.
p. 48.

223 Comp. Moses Hess, Jüdische Schriften, herausg. von Th. Zlocisti,
Berlin 1905.   On Smolenskin: bibliography by Z. Fishman in
Hadoar v. III, 215-219; biography by Reuben Brainin, Vilna
1901 (cf. its review by Mordekhai ben Hillel Hacohen, Me'erebh
'ad 'arebh I, 230-244, see also ib. p. 186-229); Prof. J. Klausner,
Yotzerim ubhonim I, 198-221; A. Kleinman l. c. p. 88-104;
M. M. Feitelsohn in Hashiloach XII (1903) p. 26 et seq.
p. 127 et seq.; Brainin ib. III (on S's fiction); M. Ben 'Ami,
memoirs ib. v. XLIV (1925) p. 447-458; A. S. Waldstein, The
Evolution of Modern Hebrew Literature p. 57 et seq.; Jacob
Hodess, P. Smolenskin (Zionist Thinkers and Leaders) London
1927; L. Rosenblatt, P. Smol., einige Grundzüge seiner Zeit,
seine Lebens und seiner Wirksamkeit, Berlin 1916; Solomon
Schiller in Die Welt, v. V (1901).

230 the condensed story of Kebhurath Chamor in J. Chotzner, Hebrew
Satire, p. 57 et seq.

233 quot. from P. Smolenskin, Ma'amarim, Jerusalem 1925, v. II, p. 35;
p. 73; p. 78.

234 ib. p. 14.

235 ib. p. 145; p. 145 and 90.—lb. 5. one of them: Eliezer Ben
Jehuda in Hatoren v. IV (1917) no. 41, p. 8.

236 Ma'amarim v. II, p. 75.

238 quot. from Ma'amarim v. I, p. 17 and ib. v. II, p. 145.

239 Results of biblical criticism: see ib. II, p. 21, note.

240 The letter to Brandstaetter in Me'ah mikhtabhim, edited by R.
Brainin, Vilna 1901, no. 78.   quot. from Ma'amarim I,
p. 144.

X. THE NEW NOVEL

244 Chagiga 9b.

245 On Mapu: biography by R. Brainin, Piotrkow 1900; Prof. J.
Klausner, Yotzerim ubhonim I, 171-197; M. Kleinman l. c. p.
55-65; Fichman in Hatekufah III, 649-675 and in Babhu'oth,
Odessa 1919; Lachower, Mechkarim venisyonoth p. 44-54; Zitron l. c. I, 35-82; Pauline Wengeroff, Memoiren einer Gross-

NOTES

mutter, Bilder aus der Kulturgeshichte der Juden Russlands im 19. Jahrh, Berlin 1908.   quot. from Prof. Klausner in Madda'e hayahduth I, p. 11.

246   See Martin Buber, Die jüdische Bewegung, Berlin 1916, p. 131 et seq.

247   l. 5.   Kol Kethabhe Mendele v. IV, 69 et seq.

248   quot. ib. p. 33.

249   on the Talmud in Sefer Zikkaron, Warsaw 1889, p. 117 (repr. in v. VII of Mendele's Collected Works).   on Shlomele: vol. II. (Odessa 1911) p. 198.

251   The oriental flora and fauna: Kol Kethabhe Mendele v. IV, p. 45.   On Mendele: see v. VII of his Collected Works, 3rd ed. Berlin 1922, which contains a number of essays on Mendele by leading Hebrew writers and critics: Bialik, Frishman, Brainin, Fichman, Rawnitzki, A. Lubetzki, etc.; Prof. J. Klausner's five essays on Mendele are now collected in Yotzerim ubhonim II, 62-124; A. Druyanov in Mashu'oth I (Odessa 1919) p. 551-580; Moses Kleinman l. c. p. 111-140; D. A. Friedman, in Hatekufah II, 585-606 and ib. III, 676-700; Ben 'Ami's very valuable memoirs in Hatekufah XXIV, 461-486; Lachower, Mechkarim wenisyonoth, p. 55-78; Shalom Streit, Ba'aloth hashachar, Tel-aviv 1927, p. 107 et seq.; Menachem Ribalow, Sefer ha-massoth, New York 1928, p. 35-55; Zevi Sharfstein, Mendele Mokher Sefarim, Przemysl 1925; S. Niger, Wegen yiddishe Shreiber, Warsaw 1912; Fritz M. Kaufmann, Vier Essays uber ost-jüdische Dichtung und Kultur, 1919; Charles A. Madison, Mendele, the foremost of Ghetto satirists, in Poet Lore, a magazine of letters, Boston 1922, vol. XXXIII, p. 255-267.

256   Mendele's autobiography in Sefer Zikkaron, Warsaw 1889, p. 117-126; the quot. on Yiddish, p. 123. Comp. also the autobiograph-ical letter of Mendele, published by Isaac Rivkind in Reshumoth v. V, p. 416-418.   l. 3 it has been suggested: Prof. Klausner l. c. II, p. 100.   l. 8. thus S. Niger in his splendid treatise on Mendele l. c. p. 31 et seq.   on Mendele's style see Rawnitzki in Ha'omer I (1907) 23-31, repr. vol. VII. Kol Kethabhe Mendele p. 167-175. Comp. however Prof. Klausner in Madda'e hayahduth I, 163 et seq.

257   quot. from vol. II (Odessa 1911) p. 179.

259   quot. from vol. III (Berlin 1922) p. 12 and p. 56.

261   quot. from Sefer Kabtzanim, Cracow 1909, p. 68-69. Comp. Madison l. c.   The three typical sins of the Ghetto: Klausner l. c. II, 83.

262   quot. Kol Kethabhe Mendele v. III, p. 100.

263   quot. ib. p. 118.

264   quot. ib. p. 151.

265   quot. from v. II (Odessa 1911) p. 180-181.

266   Even an informer: see Niger l. c.   David Frishman, introduc-tion to Kol Kethabhe Mendele v. II, p. XXII (Odessa 1911). Frishman's bio- and bibliography in 'Eyn ha-Kore no. 1, p. 83-96.

HEBREW REBORN

NOTES

Page

Ahad-Ha'am issue of Hashiloach XXX (1914) p. 193-308; Dr.
Joshua Thon, Kathabhim, Warsaw 1921 p. 115-125, also 31-37;
Moses Kleinman, Demuyoth we-Komoth p. 228-248; S. B.
Maximon, Gewilim, New York 1925, p. 7-12, also 216-232;
Dr. S. Bernstein, Bachazon ha-doroth, New York 1928, p. 107-
111; M. Ribalow, Sefer ha-massoth p. 56-65 (on A. as editor);
Fichman in Keneseth (Odessa), 275-284; Berditchewski in
He'athid I, 140-164; on Ahad Ha'am and A. D. Gordon see
Jacob Rabinovitch in Hedim I (1922) p. 4-8. [See now Leon
Simon, Ahad Ha-am, Essays, Letters, Memoirs, Oxford 1946
(East and West Library); also his biography: Ahad Ha-am,
Philadelphia 1960. In Hebrew: Aryeh Simon and Yosef E.
Heller, Ahad Ha-am, ha-ish, po'olo ve-toratho, Jerusalem 1955.]

XII. THE MOUTHPIECE OF THE FOLK

295 Pardes, Odessa 1892, p. 219-220. two of Gordon's poems—
  ib. p. 104-106 (Sod ha'ibhur, bristled with bad puns) and p. 166-
  167 (Ha-bath ha-shobhebha).

296 l. 8. my introduction follows J. Ch. Brenner in Be-Sha'ah Zo II
  (Jaffa 1916) p. 8-25. In this almanach a number of essays on
  Bialik will be found of which A. M. Lipschütz' study in Bialik's
  language merits especial attention (ib. p. 59-69). Cf. also Jacob
  Rabinovitch ib. p. 26-53 and in Hedim no. 6, p. 3-5. [See also
  Abraham Avrunin, Mehkarim bi-leshon Bialik ve-Yelag (J. L.
  Gordon), Tel-aviv 1953.]

297 l. 4. Iudae Harizii Macamae (ed. P. de Lagarde) Hannower
  1924, p. 23. l. 8. M. Ehrenpreis in Hatekufah v. XVII,
  p. 428.

298 The New Palestine has published Bialik's Selected Poems master-
  fully translated from the Hebrew by Maurice Samuel, New York
  1926. Comp. also Ch. N. Bialik, Poems, from the Hebrew edited
  by L. V. Snowman, London 1924. [See now Complete Poetic
  Works of H. N. Bialik, ed. with an introduction by Israel Efros,
  New York 1948, vol. 1.] quot. Muzar haya orach chayyai (in
  Keneseth, Tel-aviv 1929, p. 200).

299 quot. Kethabhe Ch. N. Bialik umibhchar targumav, Berlin 1923,
  vol. I, p. 124.

302 quot. ib. p. 316.

303 The quotations ib. p. 328 and p. 186.

304 quot. ib. p. 221 and p. 231.

305 quot. ib. p. 42.

306 Berditchewski, Nemushoth, Warsaw 1900, p. 23. quot. Kethabhe Bialik v. I, p. 232-233.

307 quot. ib. p. 246-247.

308 Cf. Bialik, Dibhre sifruth va-omanuth liketanim, in 'Eyn ha-Kore
  (Berlin 1923) no. 1, p. 167. The quot. Kethabhe Bialik v. I,
  p. 248.

HEBREW REBORN

"One of my ancestors fled from Volhynia in the days of Gonta and
of Zelezniak. His family he saved, but he himself almost fell into

NOTES

the hands of the Haidamacks. A farmer took pity upon him, and
hid him under a heap of straw. The pursuing Haidamacks
searched for him over the whole farm. They suspected that he
might be under the heap of straw, and prodded it with a spear.
The spear wounded him in the foot, but he did not cry out.
The blood was soaked up in the straw, and was not visible.
The farmer cured my ancestor, and then sent him away. . . ."
"In the year 1848, my grandmother's brother went in the army
of Nicholas to Hungary. He was taken prisoner with a sergeant
who was a comrade of his. Both of them were dragged to the
gallows. One of the Jewish rebels recognized him as a fellow-
Jew, and rescued both him and his comrade. They did not
believe that miracles could happen twice—and fled. They hid
on the roof of a deserted house. In the night they found another
man there. They arose and killed him. . . ."
"He also took part in the Caucasian war, and was shut up in a
city whose name I have forgotten when it was besieged by the
Circassians. My relative ate his horse, for the famine was sore,
until he was rescued. . . . In his old age he almost became a
follower of Tolstoi. . . ."

319 lb. 6. quot. Shirim p. 120.
320 Kethabhe J. L. Peretz v. X, p. 22 et seq. (Tel-aviv 1923).
quot. from the cycle of sonnets: To the Sun (La-shemesh) no. 6,
in T's Shirim chadashim, Leipsic 1924, p. 38.
321 l. 16. quot. Shirim p. 16.   Si'ach Kedumim ib. p. 22-24.
322 l. 12. ib. p. 8.   Hölderlin—Klausner, l. c. 211.   Before the
Statue of Apollo—transl. by Maurice Samuel in The Menorah
Journal v. IX (1923) p. 20. et seq. and in his Jewish Anthology
p. 326.
323 on false prophets, Shirim p. 115-121.   Death of Tammuz,
ib. p. 292-294.
324 quot. from To the Sun (Shirim chadashim p. 33 and 47).
Sonnets of a Pagan, ib. p. 21.   lb. 5. see D. A. Friedman
in Hatekufah IV, 623-661; my reference to p. 638. Other
literature on Tchernichovski: Hillel Bavli in Hadoar IV, no.
15, 22 & 23; M. Ribalow, Sefer ha-massoth p. 97-104; Dr.
S. Ginsburg in Miklat I, (1919) 25-36; Abr. Goldberg, Sifruth
va-omanuth; J. A. Lapidoth in Hatekufah III, 613-628; Joshua
Friedman ib. 629-639; N. Grünblatt ib. 640-648; the Tchernichovski—issue of Hashiloach XXXV (1918) no. 2; of Hadoar
IV; S. Zemach in Mashu'oth (Odessa 1919) p. 581-597; Jacob
Rabinovitch in Ha'adamah I, (1920) p. 160 et seq. 271 et seq.;
J. Ch. Brenner on the idea of labor in T's poetry, in the almanach
Achduth ha'abhodah, Jaffa 1919; Slousch, La poésie lyrique
p. 209-246; L. Snowman, Tchernichowsky and His Poetry, Lon-
don 1929 (translations); A. S. Orlans, in Avukah Annual v. II
(New York 1929) 26-29; I. Wassilevsky, Hebrew Poetry of
to-day, Manchester 1918.

XIV. TWO HERETICS

329   lb. 4. I quote Lachower in Hatekufah XIV-XV, p. 610.

330   lb. 6. one of his early novels: 'Urba perach, Warsaw 1900, repr. in Michutz la-techum, Leipsic 1923, p. 147-8.   Quot. on the philosophy of the perhaps: 'Al Em ha-Derekh, Warsaw 1900 p. 56-57.

331   Micha Joseph bin Gorion: Sinai und Garizim. Über den Ursprung der israelitischen Religion. Forschungen zum Hexateuch auf Grund rabbinischer Quellen. Berlin 1925-26.

332   l. 5. 'Arakhin, Warsaw 1900, p. 25-26.   Berditchewski's life-story and bibliography: Z. Fishman in the weekly Ha-yishubh I, no. 6. (Tel-aviv, Nov. 13, 1924) et seq. Literary appreciation: F. Lachower in Nethibhoth, Warsaw 1913, p. 138-161, in Hatekufah XIV-XV, 607-616; XVI, 426-432; XVIII, 432-438 and in Mozenayim I (1929) no. 31. In Hatekufah v. XIII essays by Prof. Chaim Tchernowitz (p. 424-5, see also his article in Ziyyunim in memory of J. N. Simchoni, Berlin 1929, p. 194-196), Jacob Rabinovitch p. 426-445, S. B. Maximon p. 446-452 (reprinted in Gewilim p. 54-64), Shalom Streit p. 453-457 and S. A. Horodezky p. 458-475 (the last article quotes unpublished letters of B. and is biographically of interest). Prof. Klausner compared B. to the ancient Sophists in Hashiloach v. XIX (1908) p. 305. On B's fiction A. A. Kabak ib. XXIX (1913) p. 75-84. —Of German essays on Berditschewski: Dr. D. Neumark, Die juedische Moderne (in Allgemeine Zeitung des Judenthums, Berlin, Nov. 9, 1900, vol. LXIV, no. 45, p. 536-538); Hugo Bergmann, Jawne und Jerusalem, Berlin 1919, p. 34-42; Moritz Heimann, Nachgelassene Schiften, Berlin 1926, p. 127-137; Baruch Krupnik in Der Jude III (1918) no. 6; Alexander Chaschin ib. v. VIII (1924) p. 405-411.—In English: see Joseph Reider, Negative Tendencies in Modern Hebrew Literature, in: Hebrew Union College Jubilee Volume, Cincinnati 1925, p. 451-453, 472-473. [See now Yeshurun Keshet (Koplewitz), Mikhah Yoseph Berditchewski, Jerusalem 1959.]

333   descent from Rabbi Shmelke: Horodezky in Hatekufah XIII, p. 469.   Following the rigid Jewish custom: cf. Michutz la-techum p. 44.   The quot. from Machanayim (1899) repr. Michutz la-techum p. 83.

334   l. 1. quot. Beyn ha-Pattish veha-saddan (repr. ib. p. 43).
l. 10. Meora'oth uma'asim, Leipsic 1923, p. 18.   There is no justice: Machanayim l. c.

335   l. 3. quot. Michutz la-techum p. 16.   To banish darkness with light, quot. ib. p. 17.

336   l. 2. ib. p. 17.   I imagined Moses: 'Al Em ha-Derekh p. 47. a later narrative: "Isaiah" (in Beyn ha-Chomoth, Leipsic 1923, p. 110).

337   l. 2-7. see Michutz la-techum p. 14 (Shebikhethabh veshebe'al peh) and p. 120 ('Urbha perach).   On the Pentateuch: Meora'oth uma'asim p. 38 (Ha-yetzi'ah).   lb. 2. ib. 39.

NOTES

338   l. 2. quot. 'Arakhin p. 59.   Question about geography: Ha-berichah (in Meora'oth uma'asim p. 51).   On Josippon: Bederekh rechokah (in Michutz la-techum p. 23).   on Levinsohn: Beyn ha-Pattish veha-saddan (ib. p. 47). Portraits in B's study—see Lachower in Hatekufah XVI, 428.   quot. on Krochmal: Michutz la-techum p. 24.

339   Me'ebher la-nahar (ib. p. 29-42). The quot. p. 31, 41, and 39.

340   his biographer: Z. Fishman l. c.   Druyanov in the daily Ha'aretz (Jerusalem Dec. 25, 1921), where also Hugo Bergmann's address at the Berd. memorial meeting in Jerusalem is summarized. Remniscences on B. in his childhood-years in Dubowa: Zevi Kasdai in Reshumoth v. IV (1925) p. 222 et seq. B's letters on the Yeshiba: Toledoth Yeshibath 'Etz Chayyim in Ha'asif III, 231-242; 'Olam ha'atziluth in Hakerem (1888) p. 63-77 and in Hamelitz 1888, no. 12, 19, 30, 52, 56 and 59. I owe most of these references to Mr. Isaac Rivkind, who kindly brought to my knowledge many an unknown source of information.

341   Writing for the Hebrew press: see 'Ibhri Anokhi v. XXV (Brody 1888) p. 36, 44, 92-93, 99-100, 113-114; v. XXVI no. 2 (Oct. 9, 1889, p. 18) where he complains of his domestic troubles with an amazing lack of reticence; ib. p. 39, 52, etc.

342   Second divorce: comp. his Gereshayim, sippur ma'aseh shehayah, in Ha'ibhri, Apr. 4, 1890, p. 212 et seq.   Reshuth ha-yachid be'ad ha-rabbim, Cracow 1892 (the German title being: Die Ansichten eines Einzelnen über das Allgemeine von M. J. Berditschewski, stud. phil.).

343   l. 5. ib. p. 29.   l. 10. personal interest p. 21.   l. 14. folk-power of Chasidism p. 37.   On the Zealots and ben Zaccai p. 3 and Nemushoth, Warsaw 1900, p. 35.   lb. 5. quot. Reshuth ha-yachid p. 39.

344   l. 9. little bread and many books: Machanayim l. c. p. 80, also 75.   The quot. from Menachem l. c. 69; similarly 'Urbha perach ib. p. 115.   Old folks' asylum, ib. 51 (Beyn ha-Pattish, etc.).   lb. 6. quot. Machanayim p. 76.

345   On Sabbath quot. ib. p. 105.   lb. 5. Bil'adeha l. c. 64.

346   l. 5. 'Urbha perach l. c. 143.   Der Born Judas, Legenden, Märchen und Erzählungen, gesammelt von M. J. bin Gorion, übertr. von Rahel Ramberg, Leipsic 1919-24, 6 vols. Die Sagen der Juden gesammelt und bearbeitet von M. J. bin Gorion, verdeutscht von R. Ramberg 5 vols., Frankfort a. M. (reviewed in Ha-goren X, 159-166).   the Ukrainian massacres: see Rahel Feigenberg, A Pinkes fun a toter Stadt (Churban Dubowa) Warsaw 1926, where the picture of B's martyred father is reproduced.   Horodezky l. c., also Lachower in Mozenayim I, no. 31 (Tel-aviv, Nov. 15, 1929).

347   Youths: Ze'irim, including among others Dr. Osias Thon and Marcus Ehrenpreis. Comp. the latter's talks with Berditchewski in Der Jude VI (1921) p. 574-580.   lb. 6. opponents had to admit: Neumark l. c. p. 537.

461

HEBREW REBORN

NOTES

Page

365   cf. Nidduyah shel methah, in Romanim Ketzarim, Leipsic 1923, p. 134-142; Zilele 'erebh—ib. p. 171-181; Ha-kiyyor haacharon —ib. p. 193-200; Ha-she'elah in Meora'oth uma'asim p. 139-141.   as a star, Nidduyah shel methah l. c. p. 136.   the dogs did not bark, Kayitz wachoref—ib. p. 112.   legend and reality interwoven: see Lachower in Nethibhoth l. c.

366   The quot. from Nemushoth p. 7.

367   quot. Bachomer ubharuach p. 11.

368   With my hands I destroy: 'Arakhin p. 95, and similarly ib. p. 50; Nemushoth p. 96; 'Al ha-Perek p. 15; Din udebharim, concluding chapter.   On washing hands—quot. from Din udebharim p. 63-64.

369   quot. ib. p. 64.

Chapter XIV, Part 2

371   l. 1. see B. Felix (Asher Barash) in Hedim I, no. 1 (Tel-aviv 1922).

372   lb. 3. comp. e.g. Bialik's adverse criticism of Hame'orer: Kethabhe Bialik II (1923) p. 322-323; see also Rabbi Binjamin in Hashiloach XLV (1926), p. 54.

373   I. Ja'ari-Poleskin: Me-chayye J. Ch. Brenner, Tel-aviv 1922; Alexander S. Rabinowitz, J. Ch. Brenner, Tel-aviv 1922; D. A. Friedman, J. Ch. Brenner, Berlin 1923; Jacob Rabinovitch in Hedim I, no. 10, p. 51 et seq. and Hatekufah v. X, p. 463 et seq.; M. J. bin Gorion (Berditchewski) ib. p. 471 et seq.; Lachover ib. p. 482, et seq.; G. Shofman ib. p. 487; Jacob Fichman in Ma'abaroth III (1921) 374-380 and Hatekufah v. XII, 454-468; Hillel Zeitlin ib. v. XIV-XV p. 617 et seq.; A. Beilin ib. p. 646 et seq.; B. A. ib. v. XX, 525-528; S. Zemach, in Hashiloach v. XXVIII (1913) p. 463-473; Mordecai ben Hillel Hacohen ib. XXXIX, 357-364; D. Kimchi ib. p. 79-85; A. M. Lipschütz in Ma'abaroth III, p. 372-374; N. Bystritzki, ib. 366 et seq.; Rabbi Binjamin in Hashiloach XLV (1926) p. 45-61; Jacob Koplewicz in Ha'olam XIV (1926) no. 27-29; Simon Bychowski in Hadoar v. VI (1926) no. 17, comp. also 'Eyn ha Kore, no. 2, p. 157; Ch. Gomelski in Revue hébraïque, Paris 1914, vol. I, p. 105-144; Joseph Reider, Negative Tendencies in Modern Hebrew Literature (in Hebrew Union College Jubilee Volume, Cincinnati 1925, p. 461-64).

374   The Hame'orer appeared from January 1906-Sept. 1907.   Some even grasped at suicide: e.g. Ben Israel, (Israel Loeb Popes). His life-story is told by his brother N. Popes in Me'eth le'eth, Vilna 1918, no. 2-3, p. 43-47; the comment of Berditchewski upon his death in Horodezky's essay, Hatekufah XIII, p. 462; see also Nethibhoth, Warsaw 1913, p. 312-313.   The labor Daily Davar devoted an entire issue of its literary supplement to the commemoration of the 20th anniversary of the Hame'orer (Tel-aviv 1926).

XV. TWO FANATICS

NOTES

now Robert St. John, Tongue of the Prophets, New York 1952.]

391 Ib. 5. Hatoren IV, no. 41, p. 8.

392 ib. p. 9.

393 She'elah nikhbadah, in Hashachar v. IX, p. 359-366. their first boy: Ithamar ben Avi, editor of Doar Hayyom, a Palestinian Hebrew daily.

395 The quot. from Hatoren V, no. 37, p. 10.

396 died in 1891: according to Persky (l. c. p. 68) Deborah ben Jehuda died in 5643 (1882/1883) which is, however, clearly a mistake, since Ithamar ben Avi mentions her as alive in his sixth year, and reports that she lived in Palestine for 9 years (ib. p. 37). The correct date, I suppose, is that stated by Klausner: Elul, 22, 5651 (l. c. p. 229). not an easy task: comp. Jehuda's articie on the first four families who introduced Hebrew into their homes, in Luach achi'ebher v. I (1918) p. 21-27: Arba'harishonoth. until his third year: comp. Ithamar ben Avi, in Sefer Zikkaron p. 33. an idiot: comp. Dr. Israel Shapira ib. p. 8 and Klausner, Yotzerim ubhonim I, 227.

397 l. 3. Hatoren IV, no. 39, p. 8.

398 Thesaurus totius Hebraitatis et veteris et recentioris, Berlin— Schoeneberg; see B. W. Bacher, in Hatzofeh me'eretz Hagar I (1911) p. 46-57; II 11-15, 139-144.

400 quot. Hatoren, V. no. 15, p. 10.

401 He stated to belong to no creed: Klausner l. c. I, p. 238.

Chapter XV, Part 2

405 See Ha-po'el hatza'ir, Tel-aviv, November 13, 1924 (v. XVIII, no. 6, p. 15): A. Ben Barak, Be-bhizzoth Kabara; cf. also ib. the editorial of J. S. (J. Laufbahn).

407 Mendele, Sefer hakabtzanim (v. I, Cracow 1909) p. 5. l. 11-12. Gordon's essay "On Labor," translated into English by Chaim Arlosoroff, in Avukah Annual 1930 p. 125-132; the quot. p. 127. l. 16. ib. p. 128.

408 A biographical sketch of A. D. Gordon by Joseph Aronowitch in the first vol. of Kethabhe A. D. Gordon Tel-aviv 1925-1928 (5 vols.); I. Ja'ari-Poleskin, Cholemim welochamim, Jaffa 1922, p. 336-348; Jacob Fichman in Hatekufah XVIII, 483-486 and XVIII, 447-451; S. Rawidowicz ib. XXIV, 440-458; Jacob Rabinovitch, in Hedim I (1922) p. 4-8; S. Streit ib. III (1924) no. 3, p. 23-27; Abr. Levinsohn, A. D. Gordon (Yiddish leaflet) Warsaw 1924; Hans Kohn, Salvation through labor, in Avuka-Annual, New York 1930, p. 61-66. The articles of Fichman and Rawidowicz in German translation in Der Jude VII, p. 517 et seq. and Jüd. Almanach auf das Jahr 5690, Prague 1929. Some of Gordon's essays appeared in German translation: Erlösung durch Arbeit, Berlin 1930. The quot. from Gordon vol. II, p. 231 f.

Page

409   keeping vigil: see Fichman l. c.

410   ib.   On Jacob Fichman see S. Zemach in 'Eyn ha-Kore, no. 1,
      p. 21-34.

411   l. 1. Kethabhe A. D. Gordon v. II (1926) p. 36.

412   ib. p. 38.

413   ib. p. 36.

EPILOGUE: THE MAGIC OF AN ANCIENT LANGUAGE

419   l. 1. war hymn: Tchernichovski, Shirim (4th ed.) Berlin 1922,
      p. 133-4.   The Chanukkah poem: ib. p. 139-141.
      on Bar Cochba: ib. 154-158.

420   Baruch: ib. 185-198.   quot. p. 191 and 193.

421   F. Lassalle's Tagebuecher, May 21, 1840, ed. Paul Lindau, Breslau
      1891, p. 81, 160 f.

422   l. 1. Quellen zur Geschichte der Juden in Deutschland II, p.
      11-12, 40.   heap of corpses: Shirim p. 29.   death-agony:
      ib. p. 113.   lb. 6 ib. p. 157.

423   New Songs: Tchernichovski, Shirim chadashim, Leipsic 1924.
      lb. 6. quot. Shirim p. 285.

424   Shirim chadashim p. 69-70.

425   ib. p. 183-184 and 186.

426   l. 7. Tchernichovski based upon this talmudic tale his poem
      Shelosha ketharim, (vol. III of his Collected Works, Berlin
      1929, p. 16-21).

427   Kethabhe Ch. N. Bialik I (Berlin 1923) p. 37.

431   Shirim chadashim p. 61.

GLOSSARY

Aggada literally: tale; the literature of Jewish legends, folklore and homiletic interpretation of the Scriptures.

'Am ha'aretz literally: land-folk; used in rabbinic Hebrew in the sense of ignoramus, a rude and untutored person.

Amora'im literally: speakers or interpreters; the talmudic authorities who lived after the completion of the *Mishnah* (ca 220-500 A.C.).

Batlan literally: idler; men of leisure who, unoccupied by other business, can regularly attend the services of the synagogue—for which they receive at times some compensation from the congregation. *Batlanuth* (literally: quality or state of being a *batlan*) suggests unworldliness or indolence.

Beth ha-midrash literally: the house of study, but serving also as a place of worship.

Chalutz pioneer.

Cheder literally: room or school-house; the Jewish elementary school. Its teacher is called *melammed*.

Chibbath Zion literally: love of Zion; the first organized form of Zionism (see p. 214 et seq.). Its adherents are called *Choveve Zion* i.e. lovers of Zion.

Chutzpah audacity, brazenness.

Dayyanim literally: judges; members of the rabbinic courts.

Derash A fanciful interpretation of Scripture.

Epikores epicure, irreverent of authority and tradition, heretic.

Gabba'im literally: collectors; officers of a synagogue.

Ge'onim literally: (their) Eminences; the leaders of Babylonian and Palestinian academies after the sixth century. In later times the title *ga'on* was also given to great rabbis distinguished for their learning.

467

GLOSSARY

Goy literally: nation; belonging to the nations at large, as distinguished from the Jews; gentile.

Halakha literally: rule of conduct; the *legal* interpretation of the Scriptures as opposite to the homiletic or *aggadic* exegesis; the legal portion of Jewish tradition.

Haskalah literally: enlightenment; the literary movement for Jewish enlightenment (see p. 54 et seq.).

Kaddish or, more specifically, *kaddish yathom:* a prayer for mourners.

Kibbutz galiyoth literally: the reunion of the exiled; the messianic ingathering of the dispersed Jews in Zion.

Kosher literally: fit, proper; ritually pure.

Maggid literally: teller; a sort of itinerant preacher.

Maskil literally: enlightener, adherent of the *Haskalah;* a Jew versed in secular sciences.

Matzah unleavened bread, served on Passover.

Mekhilta literally: compendium or rule (of Scriptural interpretation); the oldest rabbinic commentary on Exodus.

Melitzah literally: (poetic) utterance; artificiality of style. *Melitze bichel,* in Yiddish: a booklet of poetry (contemptuously).

Midrash Scriptural exegesis; the literature of homilies.

Mishnah literally: instruction or repetition; a collection of traditional laws, edited about 220 A.C. by Rabbi Jehuda ha-Nasi. It serves as the basic text for the discussion of the *Gemara* (teaching or complement) both forming the *Talmud* (study).

Mithnagged opponent (of Chasidism).

Pilpul a method of talmudic study, distinguished for its sharp and subtle dialectics, often very intricate and clever, by which the dry subject matter of the law is, as it were, spiced and seasoned: the Hebrew *pilpul* (literally: discussion) being akin to *pilpel* which means pepper or seasoning.

Posekim literally: those who decide, deciders; rabbinic codifiers who record, without discussion of reasons, merely the final "decisions" of the law.

468

GLOSSARY

Sabora'im	literally: explainers or meditators (upon the words of elder authorities), a school of Babylonian scholars in the sixth century who completed the Talmud.
Seder Zera'im	literally: order of seeds; the first of the six "orders" (i.e. parts) of the *Mishnah*, treating of farming and arboriculture.
She-hecheyanu	literally: Who has kept us alive; a benediction on joyous occasions.
Shekhinah	literally: indwelling; the Glory of God "dwelling within" the universe (see p. 137 et seq.).
Shulchan 'Arukh	literally: a table prepared; the most popular code of Jewish law, compiled by Joseph Caro in 1555.
Sifra	literally: the book; the oldest rabbinic commentary on Leviticus.
Talmid Chakham	or the more correct form: *talmid chakhamim*, "the disciple of the wise;" a learned and well-bred Jew, the Jewish gentleman.
Tanna'im	literally: teachers or repeaters; the scholars of the *Mishnah* and coëval writings (e.g. *Mekhilta*, *Sifra*, etc.).
Yeshiba	literally: session (of scholars); a talmudic college.
Zaddik	literally: righteous; the leader and rabbi of Chasidim.
Zohar	book of "splendor," a classic of the *Kabbala* (literally: tradition), the occult lore of the Jews.

INDEX

471

INDEX

INDEX

INDEX

Tchernowitz, Chaim, 447, 460
—— Samuel, 456
Theocritos, 317
Thon, Osias, 457, 461
Tissot, 96
Tolstoi, 196, 373, 459
Treitschke, Heinrich v., 61, 442
Turgeniev, 187, 452

Urinovsky, A., 435

Vasari, 29
Virgil, 8
Vital, Chaim, 141
Volozhin, Chaim, 166, 450
Voltaire, 49, 65, 200, 219

Wachstein, B., 437
Waldstein, A. S., 435, 454
Wassilevsky, I., 450, 458, 459
Weininger, O., 378
Weisberg, I. J., 451
Weisgal, Meyer W., 453, 456
Weiss, I. H., 116, 167, 445, 446, 451
Weissberg, Max, 441, 444, 445, 447

Weizmann, Chaim, 272
Welschinger, Henri, 451
Wengeroff, Pauline, 454
Wessely, N. H., 58, 76, 80, 96, 121, 122, 442, 443, 444
Wintchewski, M., 202, 453
Wohlwill, 442
Wolff, 65

Ya'ari, Abraham, 437
Young, 58

Zacuto, Mose, 32, 36
Zak, M. A., 448
Zangwill, 181
Zebi, *see* Sabbetai
Zecheriah, 311
Zederbaum, A., 225
Zeitlin, Hillel, 463
—— William, 437, 447, 452
Zelezniak, 458
Zemach, Jacob, 448
—— S., 458, 459, 463, 466
Zinberg, S., 451
Zitron, S. L., 435, 452, 453
Zlocisti, Theodor, 454
Zunz, L., 82, 98, 107, 111, 118, 205, 441, 445, 446
Zweifel, E. Z., 131-134, 447